STRAND PRICE
HAMILTON, TH EN AND MANNERS IN
5/08/10
STRAND BOOK STORE
H

W9-DDG-905

REG PRICE
5 02
STRAND PRICE
$2.00

Reprints of Economic Classics

MEN AND MANNERS IN AMERICA

[THOMAS HAMILTON]

MEN AND MANNERS

IN AMERICA

[1833]

With additions from the edition of 1843

Two Volumes in One

VOLUME I

REPRINTS OF ECONOMIC CLASSICS

AUGUSTUS M. KELLEY · PUBLISHERS
NEW YORK 1968

First Edition, 1833
(Edinburgh: William Blackwood;
London: T. Cadell, *Strand*, 1833)

Reprinted 1968 by
AUGUSTUS M. KELLEY · PUBLISHERS
New York New York 10010

Library of Congress Catalogue Card Number
68-24821

PRINTED IN THE UNITED STATES OF AMERICA
by SENTRY PRESS, NEW YORK, N. Y. 10019

LETTERS.

To Sir William Hamilton, Bart.

Ship New York, at Sea, about 100 miles from New York, 12th November 1830.

My dear Brother—I think you will be glad to hear of my having got safely to New York, which, by God's blessing, we shall do to-morrow, after a fine passage of thirty days. We are now running directly down on the American coast, with a fine easterly wind; but, as I hear the packet sails for England the day after our arrival, I think it better to write now, as I shall be very busy on landing. Though the first three weeks of our passage was very stormy, I have stood it very well on the whole; but all my limbs feel terribly cramped for want of exercise, and my fingers, as you may perceive, almost refuse their office. Poor Alexander is a much worse sailor than myself, and told me, after we had been tossed about for a day or two, that he had a very great regard for me, but that, if he had known what he was to endure, no power would have ever brought him across the Atlantic. There are twenty-six passengers on board; about seventeen or eighteen of whom are Americans, five, Scotchmen. All has been harmony, however, on board, and the Americans have been most civil and profuse in their offers of service. . . . . . .

19th November, New York.

My dear William—Notwithstanding the anticipations of arrival which I expressed in the preceding part of this letter, we did not get in till yesterday. We had on the evening of the day I wrote a violent gale of wind, which made it necessary to stand off from the coast; and when we at length approached it, it was veiled from us by fogs so dense as to render it impossible to do any thing but keep our ground till these should disperse. After four days this was the case. The mist suddenly rolled upward like a curtain, and we saw the shore of America outstretched before us. The bay of New York is *beautiful*. The city very good. The people are most civil, and I am already quite overwhelmed by visits and invitations. All this, though in some respects gratifying, is unpleasant. Nature never meant me for the part I am now compelled to play—that of a *lion*. I shall be here about eight days, and then go on to Boston, where I certainly shall not remain above a week.

God bless you, my dear William! I have nothing to add to the requests contained in the preceding part of this letter. Again, kind love to Janet,

And believe me ever
Your affectionate Brother,
T. Hamilton.

To Lady Hamilton.

Philadelphia, 24th January 1831.

My dear Janet—I wrote William from New York on my arrival, and I have been somewhat disappointed at not having heard from Scotland during all the time that has elapsed since. . . . . I will now tell you all about my own movements. Whatever I am at home,

I assure you I am a very considerable person here; and the kindness and attentions I receive from all the better order of Americans is far beyond any thing I ever expected. 'Cyril Thornton' here is much *better known* than at home, having passed through four editions; and there is now an edition of the 'Annals' printing in this city, public curiosity, I presume, having been excited by the presence of the author. After three weeks spent at New York on my first arrival, I went northward to Boston, by Providence, where I spent a day. At Boston my reception was equally flattering. Every body was anxious to oblige; and I passed a fortnight there very pleasantly indeed. Tell William I met an old friend of his, Mr Ticknor, now professor at Cambridge, who was most kind and assiduous in his attentions. He is very rich, and has one of the best libraries in the United States. Mr Everett was gone to Washington, having cut the church and professorship, and become a member of Congress. I shall see him at Washington. Cogswell has left Boston, and keeps an academy somewhere in the interior. Everett's brother, lately ambassador in Spain, and now editor of the *N. A. Review*, I met and became acquainted with. Well, I quitted Boston in the midst of a snow-storm, and set out, on my return to New York, by a different route. The second day the snow was so deep that we were obliged to exchange our coach for a *sleigh*, which is a much more pleasant mode of travelling when the snow is deep and has not drifted. Three days' hard journey brought us back to New York. It was unpleasant travelling, for the thermometer stood fifteen degrees below zero; an intensity of cold to which we have no parallel in Scotland. Well, at New York I again remained ten days, and experienced no diminution of former kindness, though the gloss of my novelty must have been worn off. I then came on here, over the most execrable roads I ever saw. Philadelphia I do not like so much as Boston or

New York; yet I have no reason to complain, and do not. But, in truth, I was a little spoiled before I came here. The manners of the people here are not pleasant. There is a Quaker coldness about them, and less of that heartiness and cordiality with which I have hitherto been so much pleased. It was to this place that the great strength of my introductions lay—nearly all those from Walter Stirling; yet, though the people are kind, I am by no means *devoured* here, and am sometimes allowed to take "my pleasure in mine inn," which I was not suffered to do elsewhere. I have been here nearly three weeks, and have been for a week past anxious to be off to Baltimore and Washington; but the roads are obstructed with an enormous fall of snow, which has drifted into impenetrable masses, and it is again snowing to-night as heavily as I ever saw it; so, when I may get off I do not know. This is annoying; for, as Congress is sitting, Washington is the great centre of attraction to me, and more time spent here is *time lost*. Early in February I *must* be off for New Orleans, to get there before the unhealthy season; and I must spend a week at Baltimore, and a fortnight at least at Washington. In point of health I have had no reason to complain; having been free from all ailments, save one attack of ague which I have had here. However, as there has been no return, I must not grumble. By the by, I was astonished to see the changes of ministry that have taken place at home. The ignorance of the people here with regard to England is extreme. They all calculate on a *revolution*, and expect accounts of it by every packet. The nonsense one is obliged to listen to, with regard to their own country, is one of the annoyances of an English traveller in America. Tell William I was rather annoyed than otherwise at the review of 'Cyril Thornton' in the *Edinburgh*. If the man meant to cut up, he should have hit harder; if he meant to elicit thanks from me, he should have praised better. There is only *one* of his criticisms, I think, well founded. In all the others I adhere deliberately to my own taste and judgment in preference to his. I am already sadly tired of this life, though my troubles and difficulties have not yet begun. The view I take of the American constitution is *most unfavourable*. I shall come home more of a Tory than I went out. In writing of the Americans—should I ever do so—I see I shall be hampered terribly by my sense of their kindness. Captain Hall is here the object of general detestation; I shall most likely be so too. The most educated class of Americans are very good; the less so, detestable and disgusting. Then their habits—tobacco-chewing, and eternal spitting! They must be cut up. Alexander makes a tolerable servant, though now somewhat too familiar with his master. The people here tell him all his countrymen are slaves; and the idiot came to me to ask if this were so or not. I told him it was a lie, and that it was a duty he owed to his king and country to kick the first man that told him so. I have not heard whether he has given any *a posteriori* proofs of his loyalty and patriotism. Now, God bless you all! Write to me, my dear Janet, and let William write as often as you and he feel inclined. It cannot be too often for me. Ever your affectionate brother,

T. HAMILTON.

To DUGALD BANNATYNE, Esq.

WASHINGTON, 15*th Feb.* 1831.

MY DEAR UNCLE—I am going to bore you with a long letter, less from any expectation that you will receive any pleasure from it, than from the gratification it affords me to write it—which is selfish enough. But, at the same time, I do hope and believe you feel some interest about me; and therefore trust that the following detail of facts and opinions, formed and occurring during my journey, may not be wholly without interest to you.

I arrived in the U. S. about the middle of November, after a very tolerable passage. My reception every where in this country has not only been most cordial, but most flattering. My books I found were well known on this side the Atlantic, and 'Cyril Thornton' had passed through no less than four editions; so I am a bit of a *lion*, and the object of much more notice than is desirable to one who would rather look on the world around him from a corner, than be, as I fear I am here, the observed of all observers. Some advantage, however, I have derived even from this unpleasant notoriety. My society has been courted by the greatest men America can boast, and I have, in consequence, moved in a circle to which, without some literary celebrity, I should have found it very difficult, if not impossible, to have obtained access. But of this enough. My motions have been as follows :—

I first arrived at New York; after a stay of three weeks I went on to Boston; a fortnight passed there very pleasantly. I then returned to New York, where I again spent ten days; from thence I proceeded southward to Philadelphia, to which I devoted three weeks. One week was enough for Baltimore; and I have now been just a fortnight in Washington. Mr Vaughan, our minister, has been most kind and attentive, and whenever I have no engagement I dine with him. He has done every thing in his power for me, and is one of the most delightful companions I know. Two days ago I was presented to the President. I was prepared for a good deal of form, but there was none. I was introduced precisely as I should be to any private individual; and, after shaking hands, sat chatting with him, *alone*, for more than half an hour. The impression I made, I hope, was not unfavourable, for I dine with him to-morrow—an honour not frequently accorded to my countrymen. Perhaps you would like to know about him. He is, then, a very decent-looking old gentleman, something like a country minister in Scotland, and kind, though somewhat vulgar, in manner. He chews tobacco, and kept rolling an enormous *quid* about in his mouth, and squirting his saliva on the carpet, which, round his chair, was really covered with a fluid of the most disgusting description. We talked of the revolution in Poland, and the state of France; and the old gentleman's ideas, I confess, did not strike me as very luminous, or evincing any great extent of political knowledge. He makes sad mistakes, too, in grammar, and asked me about my *servitude* in the army, This rather foolishly touched my pride, and I even felt half inclined to reply that an English officer, though he may see *service*, can never know *servitude*. Indeed, the general has a good deal of the Malaprop blood in his veins; but what puzzled me most was to conceive, that a person so very mild and pleasant, and even *benevolent* in manner, could be the savage and ferocious duellist who, on several occasions, killed his antagonist as he would a dog. The house was dirty, and gave you the impression of a large, ill-furnished, and ill-kept hotel. His servants, with the exception of an Irish footman, are ALL SLAVES! From Mr Van Buren, the Secretary of State, I have received great attention, and have dined twice with him. He is certainly a *clever* man, and I can easily believe that the charge made against him here, of having too much *political cunning*, is true. If not, my penetration is at fault. Eaton, the Secretary for the War Department, is a very inferior person. Nothing brought him into office but his being the personal friend of Jackson. He certainly, whatever his other accomplishments may be, cannot write English. The Vice-President, Mr Calhoun, is unquestionably a man of considerable talent, and as unquestionably a very pleasant one in society. Through his favour, I am admitted into the body of the house whenever I go to the senate. Jackson and he are at daggers-drawing; and he will oppose Clay and Van Buren for the next presidency, though, I believe, without much chance of success. Jackson's re-election is considered certain by all south of New York. But the most delightful person I know is Mr Edward Livingston, Senator for Louisiana. He has just succeeded in drawing up a new criminal code for that State. No one, I should imagine, is better qualified for such a task. I spend some part of nearly every day with him, and shall always be proud to call him friend. He wants me to write a story illustrative of the evils of *punishment by death,* to which, as a philanthropist, he is strenuously opposed. Mr Webster of Boston is, however, the *great man* of the day. I know him intimately, but have not yet heard him speak on any occasion fitted to draw out his powers. The impression he has made by his speeches of last session is very great throughout the Union. I never saw a countenance on which great talent and acuteness were more legibly imprinted. His eye is one of peculiar power. He and Livingston are the *only two* Americans I have yet met who understand our constitution, not only in its prominent features but in its *under workings,* or who understand English feelings with regard to it. What strikes an Englishman in my situation as most strange, is the entire freedom of intercourse to which he is admitted with such individuals as those I have described. They have none of the *official reserve* to which at home we are accustomed, and even seem to *court* occasions of talking politics with you. The best-informed Americans even speak to me with greater freedom than they would do to their own countrymen; and thus I have had the best and surest channels of information open to me in every city I have yet visited. It may seem strange, but so it is, that in this *free* country a large body, and these the best-informed and most intellectual of the people, *dare not* publicly avow their political principles. The Federalist party, you know, is annihilated. I had the curiosity to ask some of its most enlightened supporters whether the opinions they formerly advocated were really changed, and, if not, why they did not publicly assert them. The answer was, "Our opinions are unchanged; but such is the state of things here, that were it even suspected by the people that we entertained them, we should be *proscribed men*—men excluded utterly from public life, and every object of honourable ambition, and liable in a thousand ways to petty but galling persecution. Such is the state of things in this country, that we *dare* not state our honest convictions to the world." "Good God!" I could not help exclaiming, "can it be possible that in this country of free institutions, in *republican* America, a despotism so degrading can exist? In England every man is free to form his own opinions, and free to express them. A man is not branded there because the opinions he entertains are not the opinions of the mob. In one Parliament you will find every shade of political opinion, from the highest Toryism to the most lightly veiled republicanism; and each has its champions and apostles, who support their views openly and manfully." It is not so here. No man can even enter public life without first truckling to the mob, and too often paltering with his conscience. He must profess—often falsely profess—to entertain all the prejudices of the ignorant men by whom he is elected. He goes to Congress with a halter round his neck. Let him dare to differ from them by one hair's-breadth, and he is kicked out, and his hopes blighted for ever. *Every* man in Congress *must* and *does* profess himself a *democrat*, though he may be at heart a monarchist. In short, he must lie in his throat; and the result is, that there is a regularly understood system of deception, which I cannot bring myself either to tolerate or admire. No man of high principles and honourable pride can enter public life in this country. The whole members of Congress (the exceptions are very few) are attorneys, many of them low, ignorant, and contemptible pettifoggers. I declare most solemnly, that I have never yet met with any man in this country whose opinions could carry with them any weight, who was not decidedly of opinion that the system of government here is in many respects a *decided failure*. It is a mistake to call it a *free government*. It is a *despotism* of the most degrading kind—the *despotism* of a *mob*. It is most unfavourable to the *development of mind*. Men here are judged of by a *lower standard* than in England; and this standard, both in regard to knowledge and manners, is becoming lower every generation. The crop of young men now coming forward is decidedly more vulgar and more ignorant than the preceding; and what, in God's name! shall we say or think of institutions which cause men to retrograde in the scale of civilization? In England every generation, taken in the mass, is better educated than its predecessor. A young man coming into Parliament *now*, comes armed with a mass of knowledge of which his father knew nothing; and thus our standard is progressively becoming higher, while that of America is sinking. But it is the fashion to call the American people *a sensible people*. I wish those who think them so could only spend a fortnight at Washington, and listen to the empty, frothy, and interminable speeches which are daily uttered in the Capitol. A man in our Parliament generally speaks because he has *something to say;* and, if he has not, the House will not listen to him. A far different rule, however, prevails among this *sensible people*. The demand here is not for *thoughts* but *words;* and I must say the market is well supplied. It is impossible to visit the Senate and House of Representatives, (less, however, the *former* than the *latter*,) and to bridle one's contempt for these legislative bodies. It is astonishing to see how little wisdom is required to govern America. Then the universal attempt at *eloquence*, or rather the profusion of tawdry and unmeaning suftian which here passes for eloquence! And, after having listened for several hours to a poor idiot vapouring forth his long string of little nothings—the *accouchement* of a mind never impregnated—to hear the silly effusion lauded as a masterpiece of eloquence, and to be asked whether our Parliament can produce any thing to equal it! It cannot indeed. But all the better informed men here speak with contempt of their legislative bodies, and their mode of doing business; and most surely not without reason. I only wish every Radical in England could be condemned to spend a year in America; and if he is not, in less than that time, utterly cured, he may be set down as hopeless. You see, my dear uncle, I am not now so strong a Whig as when I left England. I do confess, I regard the spirit now abroad in that country with great alarm; and entertaining the conscientious convictions I now do, I shall endeavour at least, on my return, to open the eyes of my countrymen to the real state of things in this country, and draw their most serious attention to the result of an experiment made here under the *most favourable* circumstances. Mr ——— * said to me the other day, in talking about England, "Depend upon it, if ever you introduce Universal Suffrage and Voting by Ballot into your elections, you do, *ipso facto*, introduce *revolution*. You may make something better; of that I do not speak. I only say it will be *different*; and that the constitution of which you boast so much, and which the world has admired for centuries, *will be gone*." In this I most cordially agree. Altering one part of the constitution is like altering one part of the works of a watch. Every other part of the machin-

* The name is given in the original.

ery must be altered and adapted to the change. "Situated as your country is," Mr ——— went on to say, "with the great majority of your population without property of any sort, I can only say, that if you place the power in their hands—as you certainly will, whenever, by the introduction of ballot, you annihilate the influence of property—they must be great fools, and act in opposition to all the received principles of human nature, if they do not proceed to a division of property." You have no idea how these men here laugh when they hear of you quoting the state of things here as an example for England. The safety in this country, and the *only safety*, consists in the fact, that the great majority of the population are *possessed of property*, and that it is therefore their interest to keep things as they are. But as population becomes more dense in the Atlantic States, and the scope for advantageous migration narrowed; and when this country shall succeed in having, what they are now attempting to have, a large manufacturing population without any property but the labour of their hands, THEN will come the struggle, *then* will be the trial of this democratic constitution of which people talk so much. If the mass of the people here were situated as the mass of the English people are, a division of property would take place TO-MORROW. But how do things stand here even NOW? Why, New York is the only spot where any thing like a redundant population is to be found; and there, *even now*, there is an organized body of the people who proclaim themselves the advocates of an *Agrarian law*. Of course this body will increase; all the needy and profligate men in the country will join it, and, like an avalanche, it will gain strength as it rolls onward in its course. I myself saw large placards stuck upon the walls, stating the demands of the *workies*, as they call themselves, in opposition to the richer classes. One of these demands was "EQUAL *and universal education*;" or, in other words, demanding that the richer classes should be reduced in point of knowledge to the level of the labouring class. But was not this to be expected? The mob hate an *aristocracy* of *any* kind—an aristocracy of knowledge or virtue, as much as an aristocracy of rank or wealth. The man who labours with his hands cannot be raised to an equality of knowledge with those who have greater wealth and time to bestow on its acquisition. It is therefore the object of the *workies* to reduce the knowledge of the rich to the level of that of the poor. Such is the state of things here. Is there any thing so enviable in it that we should imitate it? Are we prepared to retrograde in the scale of civilization? I trust in God not. I trust in God that the reform in Parliament, which is now *inevitable*, will be confined to the rectifying acknowledged abuses, and leave the great principles and landmarks of our constitution untouched. But *I fear* otherwise. What a bore you must think me, my dear uncle; but I like to state my opinions to you, for you will tell me when you think me wrong. God knows, I did not come out here prejudiced against this people or their institutions. I had always been a Whig; and if, as my views have become more extended and matured, I change my opinions, I cannot help it. *The people* I shall always like. Their kindness I never can forget; but as for their government——

I shall remain here about a week longer, and then go southward to New Orleans, and return by the Mississippi and Ohio. I then shall run down to Montreal and Quebec, and thence return to New York, to embark for England probably in October. Such are my plans. It is now more than time to speak of *you;* yet, what at this distance can I say but that I do most sincerely trust that you are all well? The winter here has been most severe; frost for the last six weeks; and the ground, during all that period, some feet deep in snow. Pray, remember me very kindly to my aunt and cousins. I have enjoyed perfect health since my arrival in the U. S.; but am subject to occasional depression of spirits, which are very distressing. But this is nothing. Now farewell, my dear uncle; if it please God that I return home from my travels, I shall trust to find you all well at Birkenshaw; better than I wish, you cannot be. I have not received one letter from Scotland since I left it. Believe me,

My Dear Uncle,
Your affectionate Nephew,
T. Hamilton.

To Sir William Hamilton, Bart.

New Orleans, 18th March 1831.

My dear William—I do not know how often I have written to you and Janet since my arrival in this country; but I know that I have not received one scrap of writing from Scotland since I left it, now five months ago. Indeed, the only letter I have received at all has been one from Lady Lucy. I suppose, however, that you or Janet have written, and that I shall receive the letter somewhere. If it was addressed New York, it will certainly reach me. I do not say any thing about all the changes of ministry, &c., which have taken place since I left home, though these are most interesting; because any thing I could say at this distance would be mere fudge. I trust in God, however, all will turn out for the best; but I see and have seen so much of the curse of democracy in this country, that, I confess, I do fear reform may be carried too far. But I will let you know about myself and my movements. I think I last wrote you from Philadelphia. My next resting-place was Baltimore, and from thence I went on to Washington. Of course, that was the chief seat of interest to a stranger. Vaughan, our minister, was most kind, and procured me instant admission to the diplomatic circle; of course, the best in the place. Besides, however, I was armed with letters from my friends in Boston, New York, &c., to *all* the prominent men in Congress; and I must say, nothing could be more kind than they all were. I was presented to the President, General Jackson, about whom, I dare say, you recollect Matthews's song. There was little or no form. He bid me take a chair beside him, and I sat above half an hour chatting with the old gentleman very comfortably. He makes sad havoc of the king's English, asked whether I had seen much "*servitude*," &c. &c. He told me he was always at home of an evening, and would be glad to see me when I chose to drop in. I received, the day following, an invitation to dinner, which, being engaged unfortunately to Mr Van Buren, the Secretary of State, I could not accept. I did, however, call one evening. The President was gone up stairs with a headache. I sent up my card with my respects, and he came down. The conversation for the first quarter of an hour was about the state of his bowels, the failure of calomel, the success of salts, &c. &c. We then got on European politics, on which all he said was common-place enough. He then talked of American politics, and some debates which had recently taken place in the Senate. In these matters he spoke quite in the tone of a partizan, abused some senators, approved of the line taken by others, and, in short, spoke his opinions, I am quite sure, without reservation or concealment of any kind. Indeed, nothing is more striking to an European than the utter absence, in this country, of *official reserve*, and the openness with which the Transatlantic statesmen speak of politics. Instead of avoiding the subject with you, they *court it*. Before I left Washington, there was a levee at the President's. Of course, I went there. Such a crew! The very labourers on the Canal were there. The refreshments were lemonade and *whisky punch*, which last the servants were actually obliged to *defend with bludgeons* from the attacks of a great part of the company. *This is fact.* Van Buren, the Secretary of State, is a man of another kidney. He is certainly clever, and has more tact than is usual among his countrymen. He has the character of being cunning, and this I should think probable; but he is pleasant, and certainly was peculiarly civil to myself. Calhoun, the Vice-President, is also a clever man, but somewhat coarse in manner. He and Jackson and Van Buren are at daggers-drawing. Van Buren and he are both manœuvring to succeed Jackson, after he has served another four years. Edward Livingston, senator for Louisiana, is the person I liked most. With him I was very intimate. He has drawn up a criminal code for Louisiana, a work of immense labour. His house was burned some years ago, when his task was nearly completed, and all his papers destroyed. With singular energy of character, he commenced working again immediately, and completed his task about a year ago. There is a great deal of benevolence about him, united to talents of the highest order, and an uncommon degree of enthusiasm. Mr Webster, however, is the great man of the Union at present. He certainly is a man of great mental power. There is no orator in Congress who can stand against him. But I will not bore you more with people about whom, perhaps, you care very little. Everett*

* In Mr Willis's "Pencillings by the Way," the article in the *North American Review* on "Men and Manners in America," is manifestly attributed to this gentleman as one that could be written by him, and by him alone. That this is a mistake, the present writer is able positively to assert; but he marvels how any one, aware of Mr Everett's high character and talents, could ever dream of laying to his account (whatever opinion might be harboured of the work reviewed) so ineffective—so discreditable a criticism. The writer also happens to know that the

I saw a good deal of, and heard him make a speech of three hours on the Indian question. He was very kind to me, and spoke of writing you.

other statements of Mr Willis, in so far as they regard the author of "Men and Manners," are equally without foundation. It must in charity be presumed that that gentleman was the dupe of a good-humoured joke—intended, perhaps, to trot him out on the national hobby; and, had he not committed the error of publishing to the world what was uttered under the privilege and in the confidence of a private conversation, there was no harm done. Be this as it may, Mr Hamilton never received from any one the review in question; and never expressed to any one any feeling in regard to—what, in point of fact, he never read. For though he meant, and had even pledged himself, to answer any American criticism on his work deserving of attention, an extract from the article in question, which he chanced to meet with in an English provincial (a Kendal?) newspaper, sufficed to satisfy him (as he said) that the attack was such as no gentleman could condescend to notice. He had, therefore, refrained from reading what he was precluded from refuting. The following samples will show that he was right. They may also serve as illustrations of the mendacity of the American newspaper press—as individual confirmations, in this respect, of the general strictures of our author.* Of what, in truth, must we not suppose the daily journals to be capable, in pandering to their promiscuous multitudes, when, addressing a select public, the leading quarterly periodical of the Union, in an elaborate criticism of what it admits to be "the ablest and best written work upon this country which has appeared from the pen of a British traveller;" to be, "in respect of literary execution and general ability, the best British account of this country which has yet been published;" scruples not, or finds it necessary, to sink to such deplorable personalities to found on such unqualified such transparent *falsehoods*.

In reference, and as a rejoinder, to the author's description of the breakfast scene at New York,† we have gravely given as a *fact* (what might, indeed, to those who knew the author, have had some merit, by the rule of contraries, as a fiction)—"the singular fact, that an individual so peculiarly nice in all his habits, and so decidedly averse to 'nastiness' of any kind, to use his own elegant phraseology, should have paid so little attention to the occasional refreshment of his costume during his residence at Bunker's, that his fellow-boarders, if we are rightly informed, actually held a formal meeting on the subject, at which they

* Chap. xxi. p. 444.

† Chap ii. p. 13.

From Washington I returned to Baltimore, where I remained another week. From that I crossed the Alleghany mountains to Wheeling, a journey, in the then state

passed a resolution requesting him to change his linen; and at length, finding his manners incorrigibly offensive, were compelled to abate him as a common nuisance, by requesting the master of the house to deliver them from his company."

Again, apropos of a long account quoted by the reviewer of a Liverpool agricultural dinner, there is the following :—

"If we may trust to the accuracy of the anecdote related in the following paragraph, which rests, however, on merely newspaper authority, it would seem that our author attempted to introduce into this country the agreeable innovation of 'peregrinating amongst decanters,' glasses, and plates, upon the dinner-table, which was practised with so much success at Liverpool, and may perhaps have become general in England. We may remark, *en passant*, that notwithstanding his great complaints of the rapidity with which food is *bolted*—to use another of his choice phrases—in this country, it would seem that on this occasion he dispatched business with much more expedition than his fellow-travellers, and that he was too impatient of their delay even to wait for the retirement of the ladies.

"'Colonel Hamilton, so called, the author of "Men and Manners in America," conducted himself while in this country with less the air of a gentleman or man of good breeding, than any traveller who has visited us for years. From all parts of the country we have anecdotes of his conduct, which reflect upon him the utmost discredit. One of them is related as follows in the *Albany Argus*:—On the passage of the Hudson, in one of our most richly furnished day boats, the table arrangements of which, as well as the whole internal government, are particularly well ordered, Captain H., seated at breakfast on the cushioned seat inside of the table, with ladies on each side of him, rose before a single lady had left the table, and attempted to step upon and across it. He was arrested by the prompt and loud command of the captain of the boat. 'Down, Sir! No man puts his foot upon my table whilst I have the honour to sit at its head.' The Englishman shrank back, chagrined and rebuked. Indeed, such was his mortification, that although he had entered and paid his passage to Albany, he stopped at the first landing, (West Point.) Whether it was on this occasion that, as the *N. Y. Mirror* intimates, he was rebuked by the host of the West Point Hotel for a want of civility in the ladies' drawing-room, we are not informed.'"

On the ground of these unbelieved fabrications, the reviewer rests his marvellous assertions, with their corollaries,—that the author was "coarse and offensive in his manners,"—"that, in conof the roads with snow—of great danger. There I embarked on the Ohio, and came down here in *ten days*, upwards of *two thousand* miles, all river navigation. In no part of the world can the same distance be travelled with equal facility and comfort. The steam-boats are excellent, but the company odious. The Mississippi is most grand. I have been here about three days, and really it is the most disagreeable place I was ever in. No wonder people die by the hundred of yellow fever; there is filth enough to kill a nation. It is all built, too, on the alluvium of the river; and even at this season there is something, to my feelings, unpleasant and unhealthy in the atmosphere. Thank God! I have now reached the furthest extremity of my tour, and the rest of my progress will be homeward. Alexander has been a most steady and useful servant. He hates the Americans; so there is no chance of his staying here, as all the people said he would. I began this letter several days ago, and should be glad were I able to conclude it by saying I was about to quit this *charnel-house* in a day or two. But the roads, I hear, are impassable, owing to the rains, and I must, per force, remain another week at least. I shall certainly go down to see the mouths of the Mississippi, about one hundred miles lower; and the day after to-morrow I go to spend a day or two at a sugar estate, about fifteen miles up the river. After all, this is a wonderful place. Its trade immense; and built where there is not a foot of solid ground for miles. As Coleridge says, there is "water, water every where." They cannot even bury their dead, but build vaults for them above ground. My route backward to New York will be by Mobile, Augusta, Savannah, Charleston, Fayetteville, Richmond, Baltimore, Philadelphia—

sideration of his talents, the cultivated circles in our cities cheerfully overlooked the offensive peculiarities in his personal deportment," &c. &c.—Such is American criticism!

some fifteen hundred miles. I have hitherto enjoyed tolerable health, having been without complaint of any sort, till, in coming down the Mississippi, I slept one night with my cabin window open. The consequence was the *most excruciating* pains upon one side of my face and head, which continued several days. This complaint, I am told, is common here, and is called by the French Creoles " un coup d'air." One must not venture to this country to take any liberty with themselves. If they do, woe betide them. But I must now bid you farewell, my dear William. May God bless you and yours, and believe me ever

Your affectionate Brother,
T. HAMILTON.

To LADY HAMILTON.

QUEBEC, 1st July 1831.

MY DEAR JANET—At New York, about a couple of months ago, I received a letter from you, the only one I have received from Scotland since I left it. I rejoice that you are all well. . . . . I am not quite sure whence it was that I wrote last, but think it was somewhere in the Southern States. If so, many a weary hundred miles of travel have I gone through since then, not unaccompanied with accidents by flood and field, including sundry upsets, being driven for refuge during three days to the hut of an Indian, &c. &c. The most formidable, however, was an attack of fever at Milledgeville, in Georgia. All these, however, passed without permanent consequences of any sort, and I once more reached New York, glad indeed to get out of the country of these southern barbarians. At New York I again spent three weeks, and experienced renewed kindness from my old friends. I then started for Niagara, where I spent a week visiting the Falls, under every different aspect of shade and sunshine, and moonlight and position. I cannot describe them. MOST GRAND! MOST GLORIOUS! is all I can say. No pencil in human fingers, no pen but an inspired one, could convey any idea of this most terrific yet *most beautiful* object. There is nothing on earth's surface to compare with it; so, when you have read this, you will know just as much of the Falls as you did before. From Niagara I crossed Lake Ontario to York, to visit, by invitation, Sir John Colborne, governor of Upper Canada. His secretary, however, had just shot himself the night before, and, of course, I did not see him. I then continued my course along the whole length of this immense lake to the beginning of the St Lawrence, and descended the rapids of that river in a *batteau* to Montreal, a service of some danger, but one in which the beauty of the scenery and of the rapids themselves more than compensated for it all. At Montreal I found Lord Aylmer, the governor-general of both provinces, who was most obliging, and gave me letters to Colonel Cockburn at Quebec, who commands the artillery. Lady Aylmer comes down the day after to-morrow, and has offered me a place in her suite, in a tour she intends making down the St Lawrence from this. She is a clever woman, and a most agreeable one, though somewhat high and decided in manner; and, what is still more to her credit, a great admirer of 'Cyril Thornton.' Of course, bearing letters from the Governor, I have been much noticed here, and was voted an honorary member, on my arrival, of no less than three military messes. I have joined that of the 32d, which has some old friends of mine in its number. So much for the past. Now for the future. My plan is to remain here a few days longer; then return to New York by the route of Lake Champlain; stop a few days at the Springs of Saratoga; perhaps pay a visit to a friend or two on the Hudson river; and then, on the 24th of July or at latest on the 1st of August, embark for Liverpool. You need not, therefore, my dear Janet, write me again in this country; but if you will have a letter lying for me at the Liverpool post-office by the 15th of August at latest, giving me an account of how you all are, &c., you will give me great pleasure. Pray do this, for I have a sort of nervous feeling, which makes me anxious to know how my friends all are before I return. So much, and too much, of myself; but I here see nobody of whom you know any thing, so I am thus in a manner forced, in writing to you, to become to myself my own microcosm. I suppose you have all of late been involved in politics; but of these I will not speak, though I have read every thing lately connected with England with deep and intense interest. Remember me most kindly to William; and, with the warmest anxiety for the welfare of you all, believe me,

Ever, my dear Janet,

Your affectionate Brother,

T. Hamilton.

MEN AND MANNERS
IN AMERICA.

MEN AND MANNERS
IN AMERICA.

BY THE AUTHOR OF CYRIL THORNTON, ETC.

IN TWO VOLUMES.

VOL. I.

Ἴδεν ἄστεα καὶ νόον ἔγνω.

WILLIAM BLACKWOOD, EDINBURGH; AND
T. CADELL, STRAND, LONDON.
M.D.CCC.XXXIII.

TO

WILLIAM WOLRYCHE WHITMORE,

ESQUIRE, M.P.

DEAR WHITMORE,

I INSCRIBE these volumes to you. As a politician, your course has ever been straightforward and consistent, and I know no one who brings to the discharge of his public duties, a mind less biassed by prejudice, or more philosophically solicitous for the attainment of truth. Neither mingling in the asperities of party conflict, nor descending to those arts by which temporary popularity is often purchased at the expense of permanent contempt, you have been wisely content to rest your claims to the gratitude of your country, on a zealous, enlightened, and unobtrusive devotion to her best interests.

Had I been conscious, in what I have written of the United States, of being influenced by any motive incompatible with perfect fairness of purpose, you are perhaps the last person to whose judgment I should venture an appeal. By no one will the arguments I have advanced be more rigidly examined, and the grist of truth more carefully winnowed from the chaff of sophistry and declamation. For this reason, and in testimony of sincere esteem, I now publicly connect your name with the present work. You will at least find in it the conclusions of an independent observer; formed after much deliberation, and offered to the world with that confidence in their justice, which becomes a writer, who, through the medium of the press, pretends to influence the opinions of others.

It was not till more than a year after my return, that I finally determined on publishing the result of my observations in the United States. Of books of travels in America, there seemed no deficiency; and I was naturally unwilling to incur, by the public expression of my opinions, the certainty of giving offence to a people, of whose hospitality I shall always entertain a grateful recollection. I should therefore gladly have remained silent, and devoted those hours which occasionally hang heavy on the hands of an idle gentleman, to the productions of lighter literature, which, if not more attractive to the reader, would certainly have been more agreeable to the taste and habits of the writer.

But when I found the institutions and experience of the United States deliberately quoted in the reformed Parliament, as affording safe precedent for British legislation, and learned that the drivellers who uttered such nonsense, instead of encountering merited derision, were listened to with patience and approbation, by men as ignorant as themselves, I certainly did feel that another work on America was yet wanted, and at once determined to undertake a task which inferior considerations would probably have induced me to decline.

How far, in writing of the institutions of a foreign country, I may have been influenced by the prejudices natural to an Englishman, I presume not to determine. To the impartiality of a cosmopolite I make no pretension. No man can wholly cast off the trammels of habit and education, nor escape from the bias of that multitude of minute and latent predilections, which insensibly affects the judgment of the wisest.

But apart from such necessary and acknowledged influences, I am aware of no prejudice which could lead me to form a perverted estimate of the condition, moral or social, of the Americans. I visited their country with no antipathies to be overcome ; and I doubt not you can bear testimony that my political sentiments were not such, as to make it probable that I would regard with an unfavourable eye the popular character of their government. In the United States I was received with kindness, and enjoyed an intercourse at once gratifying and instructive, with many individuals for whom I can never cease to cherish the warmest sentiments of esteem. I neither left England a visionary and discontented enthusiast, nor did I return to it a man of blighted prospects and disappointed hopes. In the business or ambitions of the world I had long ceased to have any share. I was bound to no party, and pledged to no opinions. I had visited many countries, and may therefore be permitted to claim the possession of such advantages as foreign travel can bestow.

Under these circumstances, I leave it to the ingenuity of others to discover by what probable

—what possible temptation, I could be induced to write in a spirit of unjust depreciation of the manners, morals, or institutions of a people so intimately connected with England, by the ties of interest, and the affinities of common ancestry.

It has been said by some one, that the narrative of a traveller is necessarily a book of inaccuracies. I admit the truth of the apophthegm, and only claim the most favourable construction for his mistakes. The range of a traveller's observations must generally be limited to those peculiarities which float, as it were, on the surface of society. Of the "sunken treasuries" beneath, he cannot speak. His sources of information are always fallible, and at best he can appeal only to the results of an imperfect experience. A great deal which necessarily enters into his narrative, must be derived from the testimony of others. In the common intercourse of society, men do not select their words with that scrupulous precision which they use in a witness-box. Details are loosely given and inaccurately remembered. Events are coloured or distorted by the partialities of the narrator ; minute circumstances are omitted or brought into undue prominence, and the vast and varied machinery by which truth is manufactured into fallacy is continually at work.

From the errors which I fear must still constitute the badge of all our tribe, I pretend to no exemption. But whatever be the amount of its imperfections, the present work is offered to the world without excuse of any sort, for I confess my observations have led to the conclusion, that a book requiring apology is rarely worth it.

Ever, Dear Whitmore,

Very truly yours,

T. H.

Rydal, *8th July*, 1833.

CONTENTS

OF VOLUME FIRST.

CONTENTS

OF VOLUME SECOND.

MEN AND MANNERS

IN AMERICA.

CHAPTER I.

VOYAGE—NEW YORK.

On the morning of the 16th of October, I embarked at Liverpool, on board of the American packet ship, New York, Captain Bennet, bound for the port of the same name. There were twenty-six passengers on board, and though the accommodations were excellent, the cabin, as might be expected, was somewhat disagreeably crowded. Our party consisted of about fifteen or sixteen Americans, some half-dozen countrymen of my own, two or three English, a Swiss, and a Frenchman.

Though the elements of this assemblage were heterogeneous enough, I have great pleasure in remembering that the most perfect harmony prevailed on board. To myself, the whole of my fellow-passengers were most obliging; and for some I contracted a regard, which led me to regret that the period of our arrival in port, was likely to bring with it a lasting cessation of our intercourse.

The miseries of a landsman on board of ship, have afforded frequent matter for pen and pencil. At *best*, a sea voyage is a confinement at once irksome and odious, in which the unfortunate prisoner is compelled for weeks, or months, to breathe the tainted atmosphere of a close and crowded cabin, and to sleep at night in a sort of box, about the size of a coffin for "the stout gentleman." At *worst*, it involves a complication of the most nauseous evils that can afflict humanity,—an utter prostration of power, both bodily and mental,—a revulsion of the whole corporeal machinery, accompanied by a host of detestable diagnostics, which at once convert a well-dressed and well-favoured gentleman, into an object of contempt to himself, and disgust to those around him.

Such are a few of the joys that await a landsman, whom evil stars have led to "go down to the sea in ships, and occupy his business in the great waters." With regard to sailors, the case is different, but not much. Being seasoned vessels, they are, no doubt, exempt from some of those evils, and completely hardened to others, which are most revolting to a landsman. But their Pandora's box can afford to lose a few miseries, and still retain a sufficient stock of all sizes, for any reasonable supply. It may be doubted, too, whether the most ardent sailor was ever so hallucinated by professional enthusiasm, as to pitch his Paradise—wherever he might place his Purgatory—afloat.

On board of the New York, however, I must say, that our sufferings were exclusively those arising from the elements of air and water. Her accommodations were admirable. Nothing had been neglected which could possibly contribute to the comfort of the passengers. In another respect, too, we were fortunate. Our commander had nothing about him, of "the rude and boisterous captain of the sea." In truth, Captain Bennet was not only an adept in all professional accomplishment, but, in other respects, a person of extensive information; and I confess, it was even with some degree of pride, that I learned he had received his nautical education in the British navy. Partaking of the strong sense we all entertained, of his unvarying solicitude for the comfort of his passengers, I am happy also to profess myself indebted to him, for much valuable information relative to the country I was about to visit.

Among the passengers were some whose eccentricities contributed materially to enliven the monotony of the voyage. The most prominent of these was a retired hair-dresser from Birmingham, innocent of all knowledge unconnected with the wig-block, who, having recently married a young wife, was proceeding, accompanied by his fair rib, with the romantic intention of establishing themselves in "some pretty box," in the back-woods of America. As for the lady, she was good-looking, but, being somewhat gratuitously solicitous to barb the arrows of her charms, her chief occupation during the voyage, consisted in adorning her countenance with such variety of wigs of different colours, as unquestionably did excite the marvel, if not the admiration, of the passengers. The billing and cooing of this interesting couple, however, though sanctioned by the laws of Hymen, became at length so public and obtrusive, as, in the opinion of the other ladies, to demand repression; and a request was consequently made, that they would be so obliging for the future, as to reserve their mutual demonstrations of attachment, for the privacy of their own cabin.

Among the passengers too, was Master Burke, better known by the title of the Irish Roscius, who was about to cross the Atlantic with his father and a French music-master, to display his talents on a new field. Though not much given to admire those youthful prodigies, who, for a season or two, are puffed into notice, and then quietly lapse into very ordinary men, I think there can be no question that young Burke is a very wonderful boy. Barely eleven years old, he was already an accomplished and scientific musician, played the violin with first-rate taste and execution, and in his impersonations of character, displayed a versatility of power, and a perception of the deeper springs of human action, almost incredible in one so young. But independently of all this, he became, by his amiable and obliging disposition, an universal favourite on board; and when the conclusion of our voyage brought with it a general separation, I am certain the boy carried with him the best wishes of us all, that he might escape injury or contamination in that perilous profession, to which his talents had been thus early devoted.

We sailed from Liverpool about one o'clock, and in little more than an hour, were clear of the Mersey. On the morning following we were opposite the Tuskar rocks, and a run of two days brought us fairly out into the Atlantic. Then bidding farewell to the bold headlands of the Irish coast, with a flowing sheet we plunged forward into the vast wilderness of waters, which lay foaming before us, and around.

For the first week, all the chances were in our favour. The wind, though generally light, was fair, and the New York—celebrated as a fast sailer—with all canvass set, ran down the distance gallantly.

But, on the seventh day, our good fortune was at an end. The wind came on boisterous and adverse, and our progress for the next fortnight was comparatively small. Many of the party became affected with sea-sickness, and the hopes, to which our early good fortune had given rise, of a rapid passage, were —as other dearer hopes have been by us all,—slowly, but unwillingly, relinquished.

We were yet some five hundred miles to the eastward of the banks of Newfoundland, when, on the 23d day, our spirits were again gladdened by a fair wind. Then it was that the New York gave unquestionable proof that her high character was not unmerited. In the six following days we ran down fifteen hundred miles, and the evening of the twenty-eighth day, found us off Sandy Hook, which forms the entrance to the Bay of New York.

Our misfortunes, however, were not yet at an end. When within a few hours' sail of port, our progress was arrested for four days, by a dense fog. Four more disagreeable days, I never passed. Sun, moon, stars, earth, and ocean, lay hid in impenetrable vapour, and it was only by the constant use of the lead, that the ship could move in safety. The air we breathed seemed changed into a heavier element; we felt like men suddenly smitten with blindness, and it almost seemed, as if the time of chaos had come again, when darkness lay brooding on the face of the deep. The effect of this weather on the spirits of us all, was very remarkable. Even the most jovial of the party became gloomy and morose. Conversation languished, and the mutual benevolence with which we had hitherto regarded each other, had evidently sustained a diminution.

At length, when our patience, hourly sinking, had nearly reached zero, a favourable change took place. About noon on the 17th of November, the mist suddenly rolled upward like a curtain, and with joyful eyes we beheld the coast of New Jersey outstretched before us. Towards evening, we received a pilot, and were visited by several boats employed by the proprietors of the New York newspapers, to procure the earliest intelligence from vessels in the offing. The avidity for news of all kinds, displayed both by these visitors and the American passengers, was rather amusing.

Numerous questions were interchanged, relative to politics and dry goods, shipping and shippers, freights and failures, corn, cotton, constitutions, and commissions. Though in this sort of traffic, as in all others, there was value given on both sides, yet it struck me, that a sincere desire to oblige was generally apparent. Every one seemed happy to enter on the most prolix details for the benefit of his neighbour; and the frequent repetition of the same question, appeared by no means to be attended with the usual consequences on the patience of the person addressed. I certainly could detect nothing of that dogged, and almost sullen brevity, with which, I take it, the communications of Englishmen, in similar circumstances, would have been marked. No one seemed to grudge the trouble necessary to convey a complete comprehension of facts or opinions to the mind of his neighbour, nor to circumscribe his communications, within the limits necessary to secure the gratification of his own curiosity.

We passed Sandy Hook in the night, and, on coming on deck in the morning, were greeted with one of the most beautiful prospects I had ever beheld. We were then passing the Narrows; Long Island on one side, Staten Island on the other, a finely undulating country, hills covered with wood, agreeably interspersed with villas and cottages, and New York on its island, with its vast forest of shipping, looming in the distance.

Such are some of the more prominent features of the scene, by which our eyes were first gladdened, on entering the American waters. A more glorious morning never shone from the heavens. All around was bathed in a flood of sunshine, which seemed brighter when contrasted with the weather under which we had so recently suffered.

I am not aware, that there is any thing very fine in the appearance of New York, when seen from the bay, but, taken in conjunction with the surrounding scenery, it certainly forms a pleasing feature in the landscape. The city stands on the southern extremity of York Island, and enlarging in latitude as it recedes from the apex of a triangle, stretches along the shores of the Hudson and East Rivers, far as the eye can reach. On the right are the heights of

Brooklyn, which form part of Long Island; and across the broad waters of the Hudson, the view is terminated on the left by the wooded shore of New Jersey.

But whatever may be the pictorial defects or beauties of New York, it is almost impossible to conceive a city, better situated for commerce. At no season of the year, can there be any obstruction in its communication with the ocean; and with a fine and navigable river, stretching for nearly two hundred miles into the interior of a fertile country, it possesses natural advantages of no common order. In extent of trade and population, I believe New York already exceeds every other city of the Union; and unquestionably it is yet very far from having gathered all its greatness.

The scene, as we approached the quay, became gradually more animated. Numerous steam-vessels, and boats of all descriptions, were traversing the harbour; and the creaking of machinery, and the loud voices which occasionally reached us from the shore, gave evidence of activity and bustle. About twelve o'clock the ship reached her mooring, and in half an hour I was safely housed in Bunker's Hotel, where I had been strongly recommended to take up my residence. A young American accompanied me to the house, and introduced me to the landlord, who, after some miscellaneous conversation, produced a book, in which I was directed to enrol my name, country, and vocation. This formality being complied with, a black waiter was directed to convey such of my baggage as I had been permitted to bring ashore, to an apartment, and I found myself at liberty to ramble forth, and gratify my curiosity by a view of the town.

In visiting a foreign city, a traveller—especially an English one—usually expects to find, in the aspect of the place and its inhabitants, some tincture of the barbaric. There is something of this, though not a great deal, at New York. The appearance of the population, though not English, is undoubtedly nearer to it than that of any city on the continent of Europe; and but for the number of blacks and people of colour, one encounters in the streets, there is certainly little to remind a traveller that the breadth of an ocean divides him from Great Britain.

The fashions of dress generally adopted by the wealthier classes are those of Paris and London; and the tastes and habits of the people, so far as these appear on the surface, bear a strong resemblance to those of his countrymen. Minute differences, however, are no doubt apparent at the first glance. The aspect and bearing of the citizens of New York, are certainly very distinguishable from any thing ever seen in Great Britain. They are generally slender in person, somewhat slouching in gait, and without that openness of countenance and erectness of deportment to which an English eye has been accustomed. Their utterance, too, is marked by a peculiar modulation, partaking of a snivel and a drawl, which, I confess, to my ear, is by no means laudable on the score of euphony.

Observations of a similar character, are as applicable to the city, as to its inhabitants. The frequent intermixture of houses of brick and framework, was certainly unlike any thing I had ever seen in Europe; and the New-Yorkers have inherited from their Dutch ancestors the fashion of painting their houses of a bright colour, which produces an agreeable effect, and gives to the streets an air of gaiety and lightness which could not otherwise have been attained. The prominent defect of the city, is a want of consistency and compactness, in the structure even of the better streets. There are some excellent houses in them all, but these frequently occur in alternation with mere hovels, and collections of rubbish, which detract materially from the general effect. But the general aspect of New York is unquestionably pleasing. It is full, even to overflow, of business and bustle, and crowded with a population devoting their whole energies, to the arts of money-getting. Such were the first impressions I received in New York.

Having gratified my curiosity with a cursory view of the chief streets, my obliging companion conducted me to the Custom-house, in order to procure a permit for landing my baggage. On arriving there, I was rather surprised to find, that the routine observed, in such matters in this republican country, is in fact more vexatious than in England. In New York, you are first required to swear that the specification given of the contents of your boxes is true; and then, as if no reliance were due to your oath, the officers proceed to a complete search. To the search, however troublesome, unquestionably no objection can be made; but it does appear to be little better than an insulting mockery, to require an oath to which all credit is so evidently denied. The proverb says, that "at lovers' vows Jove laughs;" and if, in America, the deity is supposed to extend his merriment to Custom-house oaths, it surely would be better to abolish a practice, which, to say nothing of the demoralizing influence it cannot fail to exert, is found to have no efficacy in the prevention of fraud. Certainly in no country of Europe is it usual to require an oath, in cases where it is not received as sufficient evidence of the fact deposed to; and why the practice should be different, under a government so popular as that of the United States, it would be difficult to determine.

Custom-house regulations, however, are matters on which most travellers are given to be censorious. In truth, I know nothing so trying to the equanimity of the mildest temper, as the unpleasant ceremony of having one's baggage rummaged over by the rude fists of a revenue-officer. It is in vain reason tells us, that this impertinent poking into our portmanteaus is just and proper; that the privilege is reciprocal between nations, each of which necessarily enjoys the right, of excluding altogether articles of foreign manufacture, or of attaching such conditions to their importation, as it may see fit. All this is very true, but the sense of personal indignity cannot be got over. There is nothing of national solemnity at all apparent in the operation. The investigator of our property is undistinguished by any outward symbol of executive authority. It requires too great an effort of imagination, to regard a dirty Custom-house searcher, as a visible impersonation of the majesty of the law; and in spite of ten thousand unanswerable reasons to the contrary, we cannot help considering his rigid examination of our cloak-bag and shaving-case, rather as an act of individual audacity, than the necessary and perfunctory discharge of professional duty. In short, the *searcher* and *searchee* stand to each other in the relation of *plus* and *minus*, and the latter has nothing for it, but to put his pride in his pocket, and keep down his choler as best he can, with the complete knowledge that being *pro tem.* in the hands of the Philistines, the smallest display of either could only tend to make things worse. It is always my rule, therefore, when possible, to avoid being present at the scene at all; and having, on the present occasion, given directions to my servant, to await the business of inspection, and afterwards to convey the baggage to the hotel, I again committed myself to the guidance of some of my American friends, and commenced another ramble through the city.

As we passed, many of the signs exhibited by the different shops struck me as singular. Of these, "DRY GOOD STORE," words of which I confess I did not understand the precise import, was certainly the most prevalent. My companions informed me that the term *dry goods* is not, as might be supposed, generally applicable to merchandise devoid of moisture, but solely to articles composed of linen, silk, or woollen. "COFFIN WAREHOUSE," however, was sufficiently explanatory of the nature of the commerce carried on within; but had it been otherwise, the sight of some scores of these dismal commodities, arranged in sizes, and ready for immediate use, would have been comment enough. "FLOUR AND FEED STORE," and "OYSTER REFECTORY," were more grateful to the eye and the imagination. "HOLLOW WARE, SPIDERS, and FIRE DOGS," seemed to indicate some novel and anomalous traffic, and carried with it a certain dim and mystical sublimity, of which I shall not venture to divest it, by any attempt at explanation.

I was amused, too, with some of the placards which appeared on the walls. Many of these were political, and one in particular was so unintelligible, as to impose the task of a somewhat prolix commentary on my friends. It ran thus, in sesquipedalian characters,

JACKSON FOR EVER.

GO THE WHOLE HOG!

When the sphere of my intelligence became enlarged with regard to this *affiche*, I learned, that "going the whole hog" is the American popular phrase for Radical Reform, and is used by the Democratic party to distinguish them from the Federalists, who are supposed to prefer less sweeping measures, and consequently *to go* only *a part* of the interesting quadruped in question. The *Go-the-whole-hoggers*, therefore, are politicians determined to follow out Democratic principles to their utmost extent, and with this party, General Jackson is at present an especial favourite. The expression, I am told, is of Virginian origin. In that State, when a butcher kills a pig, it is usual to demand of each customer, whether he will "go the whole hog;" as, by such extensive traffic, a purchaser may supply his table at a lower price, than is demanded of him, whose imagination revels among *prime pieces*, to the exclusion of baser matter.

Before quitting the ship, it had been arranged among a considerable number of the passengers, that we should dine together on the day of our arrival, as a proof of parting in kindness and good-fellowship. Niblo's tavern, the most celebrated eating-house in New York, was the scene chosen for this amicable celebration. Though a little tired with my walks of the morning, which the long previous confinement on board of ship had rendered more than usually fatiguing, I determined to explore my way on foot, and having procured the necessary directions at the hotel, again set forth. On my way, an incident occurred, which I merely mention to show how easily travellers like myself, on their first arrival in a country, may be led into a misconception of the character of the people. Having proceeded some distance, I found it necessary to enquire my way, and accordingly entered a small grocer's shop. "Pray, sir," I said, "can you point out to me the way to Niblo's tavern?" The person thus addressed was rather a gruff-looking man, in a scratch-wig, and for at least half a minute kept eyeing me from top to toe without uttering a syllable. "Yes, sir, I can," he at length replied, with a stare as broad as if he had taken me for the great Katterfelto. Considering this sort of treatment, as the mere ebullition of republican insolence, I was in the act of turning on my heel and quitting the shop, when the man added, "and I shall have great pleasure in showing it you." He then crossed the counter, and accompanying me to the middle of the street, pointed out the land-marks by which I was to steer, and gave the most minute directions for my guidance.

I presume that his curiosity in the first instance was excited by something foreign in my appearance; and that, having once satisfied himself that I was a stranger, he became on that account more than ordinarily anxious to oblige. This incident afforded me the first practical insight into the manners of the people, and was useful both as a precedent for future guidance, and as explaining the source of many of the errors of former travellers. Had my impulse to quit the shop been executed with greater rapidity, I should certainly have considered this man as a brutal barbarian, and perhaps have drawn an unfair inference with regard to the manners and character, of the lower orders of society in the United States.

The dinner at Niblo's,—which may be considered the London Tavern of New York,—was certainly more excellent in point of materiel, than of cookery or arrangement. It consisted of oyster soup, shad, venison,* partridges, grouse, wild-ducks of diffe-

* In regard to game, I adopt the nomenclature in common use in the United States. It may be as well to state, however, that neither the partridges nor the grouse bear any very close resemblance to the birds of the same name in Europe. Their flesh is dry, and comparatively without flavour.

rent varieties, and several other dishes less notable. There was no attempt to serve this chaotic entertainment in courses, a fashion, indeed, but little prevalent in the United States. Soup, fish, flesh and fowl, simultaneously garnished the table; and the consequence was, that the greater part of the dishes were cold, before the guests were prepared to attack them. The venison was good, though certainly very inferior to that of the fallow-deer. The wines were excellent, the company agreeable in all respects, and altogether I do not remember to have passed a more pleasant evening, than that of my first arrival at New York.

CHAPTER II.

NEW YORK.

I HAD nearly completed my toilet on the morning after my arrival, when the tinkling of a large bell gave intimation, that the hour of breakfast was come. I accordingly descended as speedily as possible to the *salle à manger*, and found a considerable party engaged in doing justice to a meal, which, at first glance, one would scarcely have guessed to be a breakfast. Solid viands of all descriptions loaded the table, while, in the occasional intervals, were distributed dishes of rolls, toast, and cakes of buckwheat and Indian corn. At the head of the table, sat the landlady, who, with an air of complacent dignity, was busied in the distribution of tea and coffee. A large bevy of negroes were bustling about, ministering with all possible alacrity, to the many wants which were somewhat vociferously obtruded on their attention. Towards the upper end of the table, I observed about a dozen ladies, but by far the larger portion of the company were of the other sex.

The contrast of the whole scene, with that of an English breakfast-table, was striking enough. Here was no loitering nor lounging; no dipping into newspapers; no apparent lassitude of appetite; no intervals of repose in mastication; but all was hurry, bustle, clamour, and voracity, and the business of repletion went forward, with a rapidity altogether unexampled. The strenuous efforts of the company were of course, soon rewarded with success. Departures, which had begun even before I took my place at the table, became every instant more numerous, and in a few minutes the apartment had become, what Moore beautifully describes in one of his songs, "a banquet-hall deserted." The appearance of the table under such circumstances, was by no means gracious either to the eye or the fancy. It was strewed thickly with the *disjecta membra* of the entertainment. Here, lay fragments of fish, somewhat unpleasantly odoriferous; there, the skeleton of a chicken; on the right, a mustard-pot upset, and the cloth, *passim*, defiled with stains of eggs, coffee, gravy —but I will not go on with the picture. One nasty custom, however, I must notice. Eggs, instead of being eat from the shell, are poured into a wine-glass, and after being duly and disgustingly churned up with butter and condiment, the mixture, according to its degree of fluidity, is forthwith either spooned into the mouth, or drunk off like a liquid. The advantage gained by this unpleasant process, I do not profess to be qualified to appreciate, but I can speak from experience, to its sedative effect on the appetite of an unpractised beholder.

My next occupation was to look over my letters of introduction. Of these I found above thirty addressed to New York, and being by no means anxious to become involved in so wide a vortex of acquaintance, I requested one of my American fellow-passengers to select such, as, from his local knowledge, he imagined might prove of more immediate service to a traveller like myself. In consequence of this arrangement, about half the letters with which the kindness of my friends had furnished me, were discarded, and I can truly say, that the very warm and obliging reception I experienced from those to whom I forwarded introductions, left me no room, to regret the voluntary limitation of their number.

Having despatched my letters, and the morning being wet, I remained at home, busied in throwing together a few memoranda of such matters, as appeared worthy of record. My labours, however, were soon interrupted. Several gentlemen who had heard of my arrival through the medium of my fellow-passengers, but on whose civility I had no claim, did me the honour to call, tendering a welcome to their city, and the still more obliging offer of their services. My letters, too, did not fail of procuring me a plentiful influx of visitors. Numerous invitations followed, and by the extreme kindness of my new friends, free admission was at once afforded me to the best society in New York.

The first impression made by an acquaintance with the better educated order of American gentlemen, is certainly very pleasing. There is a sort of republican plainness and simplicity in their address, quite in harmony with the institutions of their country. An American bows less than an Englishman; he deals less in mere conventional forms and expressions of civility; he pays few or no compliments; makes no unmeaning or overstrained professions; but he takes you by the hand with a cordiality which at once intimates, that he is disposed to regard you as a friend. Of that higher grace of manner, inseparable perhaps from the artificial distinctions of European society, and of which even those most conscious of its hollowness, cannot always resist the attraction, few specimens are of course to be found, in a country like the United States; but of this I am sure, that such a reception as I have experienced in New York, is far more gratifying to a stranger, than the farce of ceremony, however gracefully it may be performed.

Perhaps I was the more flattered by the kindness of my reception, from having formed anticipations of a less pleasing character. The Americans I had met in Europe had generally been distinguished by a certain reserve, and something even approaching to the offensive in manner, which had not contributed to create a prepossession in their favour. It seemed, as if each individual were impressed with the conviction that the whole dignity of his country was concentered in his person; and I imagined them too much given to disturb the placid current of social intercourse, by the obtrusion of national jealousies, and the cravings of a restless and inordinate vanity. It is indeed highly probable, that these unpleasant peculiarities were called into more frequent display, by that air of haughty repulsion, in which too many of my countrymen have the bad taste to indulge; but even from what I have already seen, I feel sure that an American at home, is a very different person from an American abroad. With his foot on his native soil, he appears in his true character; he moves in the sphere, for which his habits and education have peculiarly adapted him, and surrounded by his fellow-citizens, he at once gets rid of the embarrassing conviction, that he is regarded as an individual impersonation of the whole honour of the Union. In England, he is generally anxious to demonstrate by indifference of manner, that he is not dazzled by the splendour which surrounds him, and too solicitously forward in denying the validity of all pretensions, which he fears the world may consider as superior to his own. But in his own country, he stands confessedly on a footing with the highest. His national vanity remains unruffled by opposition or vexatious comparison, and his life passes on in a dreamy and complacent contemplation of the high part, which, in her growing greatness, the United States is soon to assume, in the mighty drama of the world. His imagination is no longer troubled with visions of lords and palaces, and footmen in embroidery and cocked hats; or if he think of these things at all, it is in a spirit far more philosophical, than that with which he once regarded them. Connected with England by commercial relations, by community of literature, and a thousand ties, which it will still require centuries to obliterate, he cannot regard her destinies without deep interest. In the contests in which, by the calls of honour, or by the folly of her rulers, she may be engaged, the reason of an American may be against England, but his heart is always with her. He is ever ready to extend to her sons, the rites of kindness and hospitality, and is more flattered by their praise, and more keenly sensitive to their censure, than is perhaps quite consistent with a just estimate, of the true value of either.

I remember no city which has less to show in the way of *Lions* than New York. The whole interest attaching to it, consists in the general appearance of the place; in the extreme activity and bustle which is everywhere apparent, and in the rapid advances which it has made, and is still making, in opulence and population. In an architectural view, New York has absolutely nothing to arrest the attention. The only building of pretension is the State-House, or City-Hall, in which the courts of law hold their sittings. In form, it is an oblong parallelogram, two stories in height, exclusive of the basement, with an Ionic portico of white marble, which instead of a pediment, is unfortunately surmounted by a balcony. Above is a kind of lantern or pepper-box, which the taste of the architect has led him to substitute for a dome. From the want of simplicity, the effect of the whole is poor, and certainly not improved by the vicinity of a very ugly gaol, which might be advantageously removed to some less obtrusive situation.

The Exchange is a petty affair, and unworthy of a community so large aud opulent as that of New York. With regard to churches, those frequented by the wealthier classes are built of stone, but the great majority are of timber. Their architecture in general is anomalous enough; and the wooden spires, terminating in gorgeous weathercocks, are as gay as the lavish employment of the painter's brush can make them.

But the chief attraction of New York is the Broadway, which runs through the whole extent of the city, and forms as it were the central line from which the other streets diverge to the quays on the Hudson and East River. It is certainly a handsome street, and the complete absence of regularity in the buildings,—which are of all sizes and materials, from the wooden cottage of one story, to the massive brick edifice of five or six,—gives to Broadway a certain picturesque effect, incompatible, perhaps, with greater regularity of architecture. The sides are skirted by a row of stunted and miserable-looking poplars, useless either for shade or ornament, which breaks the unity of the street without compensation of any sort. The shops in Broadway are the depots of all the fashionable merchandise of the city, but somewhat deficient in external attractions, to eyes accustomed to the splendour of display in Regent Street, or Oxford Road. About two o'clock, however, the scene in Broadway becomes one of pleasing bustle and animation. The *trottoirs* are then crowded with gaily dressed ladies, and that portion of the younger population, whom the absence of more serious employment enables to appear in the character of beaux. The latter, however, is small. From the general air and appearance of the people, it is quite easy to gather, that trade in some of its various branches, is the engrossing object of every one, from the youth of fifteen to the veteran of four-score, who, from force of habit, still lags superfluous on the Exchange. There are no morning loungers in New York; and the ladies generally walk unattended; but in the evening, I am told, it is different, and the business of gallantry goes on quite as hopefully, as on our side of the water.

I have observed many countenances remarkable for beauty, among the more youthful portion of the fair promenaders. But unfortunately beauty in this climate is not durable. Like "the ghosts of Banquo's fated line," it comes like a shadow, and so departs. At one or two-and-twenty the bloom of an American lady is gone, and the more substantial materials of beauty follow soon after. At thirty the whole fabric is in decay, and nothing remains but the tradition of former conquests, and anticipations of the period, when her reign of triumph will be vicariously restored in the person of her daughter.

The fashions of Paris reach even to New York, and the fame of Madame Maradan Carson has already transcended the limits of the Old World, and is diffused over the New. I pretend to be something of a judge in such matters, and therefore pronounce *ex cathedrâ*, that the ladies of New York are well dressed, and far from inelegant. The average of height is certainly lower than among my fair countrywomen; the cheek is without colour, and the figure sadly deficient in *en-bon-point*. But with all these disadvantages, I do not remember to have seen more beauty than I have met in New York. The features are generally finely moulded, and not unfrequently display a certain delightful harmony, which reminds one of the *Belle Donne* of St Peter's and the Pincian Mount. The mouth alone is not beautiful; it rarely possesses the charm of fine teeth, and the lips want colour and fulness. The carriage of these fair Americans is neither French nor English, for they have the good sense to adopt the peculiarities of neither. They certainly do not paddle along, with the short steps and affected carriage of a Parisian belle, nor do they consider it becoming, to walk the streets with the stride of a grenadier. In short, though I may have occasionally encountered more grace, than has met my observation since my arrival in the United States, assuredly I have never seen less of external deportment, which the most rigid and fastidious critic could fairly censure.

One of my earliest occupations was to visit the courts of law. In the first I entered, there were two judges on the bench, and a jury in the box, engaged in the trial of an action of assault and battery, committed by one female on another. It is scarcely possible to conceive the administration of justice invested with fewer forms. Judges and barristers were both wigless and gownless, and dressed in garments of such colour and fashion, as the taste of the individual might dictate. There was no mace, nor external symbol of authority of any sort, except the staves which I observed in the hands of a few constables, or officers of the court. In the trial there was no more interest than what the quarrel of two old women, in any country, may be supposed to excite. The witnesses, I thought, gave their evidence with a greater appearance of phlegm and indifference than is usual in our courts at home. No one seemed to think, that any peculiar decorum of deportment was demanded by the solemnity of the court. The first witness examined, held the Bible in one hand, while he kept the other in his breeches pocket, and, in giving his evidence, stood lounging with his arm thrown over the bench. The judges were men about fifty, with nothing remarkable in the mode of discharging their duty. The counsel were younger, and, so far as I could judge, by no means deficient either in zeal for the cause of their clients, or ingenuity in maintaining it. The only unpleasant part of the spectacle,—for I do not suppose that justice could be administered in any country with greater substantial purity,—was the incessant salivation going forward in all parts of the court. Judges, counsel, jury, witnesses, officers, and audience, all contributed to augment the mass of abomination; and the floor around the table of the lawyers presented an appearance, on which even now I find it not very pleasant for the imagination to linger.

Having satisfied my curiosity in this court, I entered another, which I was informed was the Supreme Court of the state. The proceedings here were, if possible, less interesting than those I had already witnessed. The court were engaged in hearing arguments connected with a bill of exchange, and, whether in America or England, a speech on such a subject must be a dull affair; I was therefore on the point of departing, when a jury, which had previously retired to deliberate, came into court, and proceeded in the usual form to deliver their verdict. It was not without astonishment, I confess, that I remarked that three-fourths of the jurymen were engaged in eating bread and cheese, and that the foreman actually announced the verdict with his mouth full, ejecting the disjointed syllables during the intervals of mastication! In truth, an American seems to look on a judge, exactly as he does on a carpenter or coppersmith, and it never occurs to him, that an administrator of justice is entitled to greater respect than a constructor of brass knockers, or the sheather of a ship's bottom. The judge and the brazier are paid equally for their work; and Jonathan firmly believes, that while he has money in his pocket, there is no risk of his suffering from the want either of law or warming pans.

I cannot think, however, that with respect to these matters, legislation in this country has proceeded on very sound or enlightened principles. A very clever lawyer asked me last night, whether the sight of their courts had not cured me of my *John Bullish* predilection for robes, wigs, and maces, and all the other trumpery and irrational devices, for imposing on weak minds. I answered, it had not; nay, so far was the case otherwise, that had I before been disposed to question the utility of those forms to which he objected, what I had witnessed since my arrival in New York, would have removed all doubts on the subject. A good deal of discussion followed, and though each of us persisted in maintaining our own opinion, it is only justice to state, that the argument was conducted by my opponent with the utmost liberality and fairness. I refrain from giving the details of this conversation, because a "protocol" signed only by one of the parties is evidently a document of no weight, and where a casuist enjoys the privilege of adducing the arguments on both sides, it would imply an almost superhuman degree of self-denial, were he not to urge the best on his own, and range himself on the side of the gods, leaving that of Cato to his opponent.

It is a custom in this country to ask, and generally with an air of some triumph, whether an Englishman supposes there is wisdom in a wig; and whether a few pounds of horsehair set on a judge's skull, and plastered with pomatum and powder, can be imagined to bring with it any increase of knowledge to the mind of the person whose cranium is thus disagreeably enveloped? The answer is, No; we by no means hold, either that a head *au naturel*, or that garments of fustian or corduroy, are at all unfavourable to legal discrimination; and are even ready to admit, that in certain genial regions, a judge *in cuerpo*, and seated on a wooden stool, might be as valuable and efficient an administrator of law, as one wigged to the middle, and clad in scarlet and ermine. But whatever American is so deficient in dialectic, as to imagine that this admission involves a surrender of the question in debate, we would beg leave respectfully to remind him, that the schoolmaster is abroad, and recommend him to improve his logic with the least possible delay. If man were a being of pure reason, forms would be unnecessary. But he who should legislate on such an assumption, would afford ample evidence of his own unfitness for the task. Man is a creature of senses and imagination, and even in religion, the whole experience of the world has borne testimony to the necessity of some external rite, or solemnity of observance, to stimulate his devotion, and enable him to concentrate his faculties, for the worship of that awful and incomprehensible

Being, " whose kingdom is, where time and space are not." It is difficult to see on what principle, those who approve the stole of the priest, and cover their generals and admirals with gold lace, can condemn as irrational, all external symbols of dignity, on the part of the judge. Let the Americans at all events be consistent : While they address their judges by a title of honour, let them at least be protected from rudeness, and vulgar familiarity ; and they may, perhaps, be profitably reminded, that the respect exacted in a British court of justice, is homage not to the individual seated on the bench, but to the law, in the person of its minister. Law is the only bond by which society is held together; its administration, therefore, should ever be marked out to the imagination, as well as to the reason of the great body of a nation, as an act of peculiar and paramount solemnity; and when an Englishman sees the decencies of life habitually violated in the very seat of justice, he naturally feels the less disposed to dispense with those venerable forms with which, in his own country, it has been wisely encircled. Our answer therefore is, *that it is precisely to avoid such a state of things as now exists in the American courts,* that the solemnities which invest the discharge of the judicial office in England, were originally imposed, and are still maintained. We regard ceremonies of all sorts, not as things important in themselves, but simply as means conducing to an end. It matters not by what particular process; by what routine of observance; by what visible attributes, the dignity of justice is asserted, and its sanctity impressed on the memory and imagination. But at least let this end, by some means or other, be secured; and if this be done, we imagine there is little chance of our adopting many of the forensic habits, of our friends on this side of the Atlantic.

At New York, the common dinner hour is three o'clock, and I accordingly hurried back to the hotel. Having made such changes and ablutions as the heat of the court-rooms had rendered necessary, I descended to the *bar*, an apartment furnished with a counter, across which supplies of spirits and cigars are furnished to all who desiderate such luxuries. The bar, in short, is the lounging place of the establishment; and here, when the hour of dinner is at hand, the whole inmates of the hotel may be found collected. On the present occasion, the room was so full, that I really found it difficult to get farther than the door. At length a bell sounded, and no sooner did its first vibration reach the ears of the party, than a sudden rush took place towards the diningroom, in which—being carried forward by the crowd—I soon found myself. The extreme precipitation of this movement appeared somewhat uncalled for, as there was evidently no difficulty in procuring places; and on looking round the apartment, I perceived the whole party comfortably seated.

To a gentleman with a keen appetite, the *coup d'œil* of the dinner-table was far from unpleasing. The number of dishes was very great. The style of cookery neither French nor English, though certainly approaching nearer to the latter, than to the former. The dressed dishes were decidedly bad, the sauces being composed of little else than liquid grease, which, to a person like myself, who have an inherent detestation of every modification of oleaginous matter, was an objection altogether insuperable. On the whole, however, it would be unjust to complain. If, as the old adage hath it, "in the multitude of counsellors there is wisdom," so may it be averred, as equally consistent with human experience, that in the multitude of dishes there is good eating. After several unsuccessful experiments, I did discover unobjectionable viands, and made as good a dinner, as the ambition of an old campaigner could desire.

Around, I beheld the same scene of gulping and swallowing, as if for a wager, which my observations at breakfast had prepared me to expect. In my own neighbourhood there was no conversation. Each individual seemed to *pitchfork* his food down his gullet, without the smallest attention to the wants of his neighbour. If you asked a gentleman to help you from any dish before him, he certainly complied, but in a manner that showed you had imposed on him a disagreeable office; and instead of a *slice*, your plate generally returned loaded with a solid massive wedge of animal matter. The New York carvers had evidently never graduated at Vauxhall. Brandy bottles were ranged at intervals along the table, from which each guest helped himself as he thought proper. As the dinner advanced, the party rapidly diminished; before the second course, a considerable portion had taken their departure, and comparatively few waited the appearance of the dessert. Though brandy was the prevailing beverage, there were many also who drank wine, and a small knot of three or four (whom I took to be countrymen of my own) were still continuing the carousal when I left the apartment.

An American is evidently by no means a convivial being. He seems to consider eating and drinking as necessary tasks, which he is anxious to discharge as speedily as possible. I was at first disposed to attribute this singularity to the claims of business, which, in a mercantile community, might be found inconsistent with more prolonged enjoyment of the table. But this theory was soon relinquished, for I could not but observe, that many of the most expeditious bolters of dinner spent several hours afterwards, in smoking and lounging at the bar.

At six o'clock the bell rings for tea, when the party musters again, though generally in diminished force. This meal is likewise provided with its due proportion of solids. The most remarkable was raw hung beef, cut into thin slices, of which,—*horresco referens*,—I observed that even ladies did not hesitate to partake. The tea and coffee were both execrable. A supper, of cold meat, &c., follows at ten o'clock, and remains on the table till twelve, when eating terminates for the day. Such is the unvarying routine of a New York hotel.

On the first Sunday after my arrival, I attended divine service in Grace Church, which is decidedly the most fashionable place of worship in New York. The congregation, though very numerous, was composed almost exclusively of the wealthier class; and the gay dresses of the ladies,—whose taste generally leads to a preference of the brightest colours,—produced an effect not unlike that of a bed of tulips. Nearly in front of the reading desk, a comfortable chair and hassock had been provided for a poor old woman, apparently about fourscore. There was something very pleasing in this considerate and benevolent attention to the infirmities of a helpless and withered creature, who probably had outlived her friends, and was soon about to rejoin them in the grave.

The Episcopal church of America differs little in formula from that of England. The liturgy is the same, though here and there an expression has been altered, not always, I think, for the better. In the first clause of the Lord's Prayer, for instance, the word "which" has been changed into "who," on the score of its being more consonant to grammatical propriety. This is poor criticism, for, it will scarcely be denied, that the use of the neuter pronoun carried with it a certain vagueness and sublimity, not inappropriate in reminding us, that our worship is addressed to a Being incomprehensible, infinite, and superior to all the distinctions applicable to material objects. In truth, the grammatical anomaly so obnoxious to the American critics, is not a blemish, but a felicity. A few judicious retrenchments have also been made in the service, and many of those repetitions which tend sadly to dilute the devotional feeling, by overstraining the attention, have been removed.

Trinity Church, in Broadway, is remarkable as

being the most richly endowed establishment in the Union, and peculiarly interesting, from containing in its cemetery the remains of the celebrated General Hamilton. I have always regarded the melancholy fate of this great statesman with interest. Hamilton was an American, not by birth, but by adoption. He was born in the West Indies, but claimed descent from a respectable Scottish family. It may be truly said of him, that with every temptation to waver in his political course, the path he followed was a straight one. He was too honest, and too independent, to truckle to a mob, and too proud to veil or modify opinions, which, he must have known, were little calculated to secure popular favour. Hamilton brought to the task of legislation, a powerful and perspicacious intellect, and a memory stored with the results of the experience of past ages. He viewed mankind not as a theorist, but as a practical philosopher, and was never deceived by the false and flimsy dogmas of human perfectibility, which dazzled the weaker vision of such men as Jefferson and Madison. In activity of mind, in soundness of judgment, and in the power of comprehensive induction, he unquestionably stood the first man of his age and country. While the apprehensions of other statesmen were directed against the anticipated encroachments of the executive power, Hamilton saw clearly that the true danger menaced from another quarter. He was well aware that democracy, not monarchy, was the rock on which the future destinies of his country were in peril of shipwreck. He was, therefore, desirous that the new Federal Constitution should be framed as much as possible on the model of that of England, which, beyond all previous experience, had been found to produce the result of secure and rational liberty. It is a false charge on Hamilton, that he contemplated the introduction of monarchy, or of the corruptions which had contributed to impair the value of the British constitution; but he certainly was anxious that a salutary and effective check should be found in the less popular of the legislative bodies, on the occasional rash and hasty impulses of the other. He was favourable to a senate chosen for life; to a federal government sufficiently strong to enforce its decrees in spite of party opposition, and the conflicting jealousies of the different States; to a representation rather founded on property and intelligence than on mere numbers; and perhaps of the two evils, would have preferred the tyranny of a single dictator, to the more degrading despotism of a mob.

Hamilton was snatched from his country, in the prime of life and of intellect. Had he lived, it is difficult to foresee what influence his powerful mind might have exercised on the immediate destinies of his country. By his talents and unrivalled powers as an orator, he might have gained fair audience, and some temporary favour, for his opinions. But this could not have been lasting. His doctrines of government in their very nature were necessarily unpopular. The Federalist party from the first occupied a false position. They attempted to convince the multitude of their unfitness for the exercise of political power. This of course failed. The influence they obtained in the period immediately succeeding the revolution, was solely that of talent and character. Being personal, it died with the men, and sometimes before them. It was impossible for human efforts to diminish the democratic impulse given by the revolution, or to be long successful in retarding its increase. In the very first struggle, the Federalists were defeated once and for ever, and the tenure of power by the Republican party has ever since, with one brief and partial exception, continued unbroken.

There is another tomb which I would notice before quitting the churchyard of Trinity. On a slab surmounting an oblong pile of masonry, are engraved the following words:

MY MOTHER.

THE TRUMPET SHALL SOUND AND THE DEAD SHALL ARISE.

This is the whole inscription; and as I read the words I could not but feel it to be sublimely affecting. The name of him who erected this simple monument of filial piety, or of her whose dust it covers, is unpreserved by tradition. Why should that be told, which the world cares not to know? It is enough, that the nameless tenant of this humble grave shall be known, "when the trumpet shall sound and the dead shall arise." Let us trust, that the mother and her child will then be reunited, to part no more.

One of the earliest occupations of a traveller in a strange city, is to visit the theatres. There are three in New York, and I am assured, that both actors and managers prosper in their vocation. Such a circumstance is not insignificant. It marks opulence and comfort, and proves that the great body of the people, after providing the necessaries of life, possess a surplus, which they feel at liberty to lavish on its enjoyments. I have already been several times to the Park Theatre, which is decidedly the most fashionable. The house is very comfortable, and well adapted both for seeing and hearing. On my first visit, the piece was Der Freischutz, which was very wretchedly performed. The farce was new to me, and, I imagine, of American origin. The chief character is a pompous old baronet, very proud of his family, and exceedingly tenacious of respect. In his old age he has the folly to think of marrying, and the still greater folly, to imagine the attractions of his person and pedigree irresistible. As may be anticipated, he is the laughing stock of the piece.

Insult and ridicule follow him in every scene; he is kicked and cuffed to the hearty content of the audience, who return home full of contempt for the English aristocracy, and chuckling at the thought that there are no baronets in America.

My curiosity was somewhat excited by the high reputation which an actor named Forrest has acquired in this country. As a tragedian, in the estimate of all American critics, he stands *primus sine secundo.* To place him on a level with Kean, or Young, or Kemble, or Macready, would here be considered as an unwarranted derogation from his merits. He is a Thespian without blemish and without rival.

I have since seen this *rara avis*, and I confess that the praise so profusely lavished on him does appear to me somewhat gratuitous. He is a coarse and vulgar actor, without grace, without dignity, with little flexibility of feature, and utterly commonplace in his conceptions of character. There is certainly some energy about him, but this is sadly given to degenerate into rant. The audience, however, were enraptured. Every increase of voice in the actor was followed by louder thunders from box, pit, and gallery, till it sometimes became matter of serious calculation, how much longer one's tympanum could stand the crash. I give my impression of this gentleman's merits as an actor the more freely, because I know he is too firmly established in the high opinion of his countrymen, to be susceptible of injury from the criticism of a foreigner, with all his prejudices, inherent and attributive. Perhaps indeed he owes something of the admiration which follows him on the stage, to the excellence of his character in private life. Forrest has realised a large fortune; and I hear from all quarters, that in the discharge of every moral and social duty, he is highly exemplary. His literary talents, I am assured, are likewise respectable.

My fellow-passenger, Master Burke, draws full houses every night of his performance. Each time I have seen him, my estimate of his powers has been raised. In farce he does admirably; but what must be said of the taste of an audience, who can even tolerate the mimicry of a child, in such parts as Lear, Shylock, Richard, and Iago?

No one can be four-and-twenty hours in New

York without hearing the alarm of fire. Indeed, a conflagration here is so very ordinary an occurrence, that it is attended by none of that general anxiety and excitement which follow such a calamity in cities less accustomed to combustion. The New York firemen are celebrated for resolution and activity; and as the exercise of these qualities is always pleasant to witness, I have made it a point to attend all fires since my arrival. The four first were quite insignificant, indeed three of the number were extinguished before my arrival, and I barely got up in time to catch a glimpse of the expiring embers of the fourth. But in regard to the fifth, I was in better luck. Having reached the scene, more than half expecting it would turn out as trumpery an affair as its predecessors, I had at length the satisfaction of beholding a very respectable volume of flame bursting from the windows and roof of a brick tenement of four stories, with as large an accompaniment of smoke, bustle, clamour, and confusion as could reasonably be desired. An engine came up almost immediately after my arrival, and loud cries, and the rattle of approaching wheels from either extremity of the street, gave notice that further assistance was at hand. Some time was lost in getting water, and I should think the municipal arrangements, in regard to this matter, might be better managed. In a few minutes, however, the difficulty was surmounted, and the two elements were brought fairly into collision.

The firemen are composed of young citizens, who, by volunteering this service,—and a very severe one it is,—enjoy an exemption from military duty. Certainly nothing could exceed their boldness and activity. Ladders were soon planted; the walls were scaled; furniture was carried from the house, and thrown from the windows, without apparent concern for the effects its descent might produce on the skulls of the spectators in the street. Fresh engines were continually coming up, and were brought into instant play. But as the power of water waxed, so unfortunately did that of the adverse element; and so far as the original building was concerned, the odds soon became Pompey's pillar to a stick of sealing-wax, on fire.

Day now closed, and the scene amid the darkness became greatly increased in picturesque beauty. At intervals human figures were seen striding through flame, and then vanishing amid the smoke. In the street, confusion became worse confounded. Had the crowd been composed of stentors, the clamour could not have been louder. The inhabitants of the adjoining houses, who, till now, seemed to have taken the matter very coolly, at length became alarmed, when the engines began to play on them, and ejected a torrent of chairs, wardrobes, feather-beds, and other valuable chattels from every available opening. The house in which the fire broke out was now a mere shell; the roof gone, and all the wooden-work consumed. The flames then burst forth in the roof of the house adjoining on the right, but the concentrated play of many engines soon subdued it. All danger was then at an end. The inhabitants began to reclaim the furniture which they had tumbled out into the street, and I have no doubt went afterwards to bed as comfortably as if nothing had happened. I saw several of the inmates of the house that had been burned, and examined their countenances with some curiosity. No external mark of excitement was visible, and I gave them credit for a degree of *nonchalance*, far greater than I should have conceived possible in the circumstances.

On the whole, I have no deduction to make from the praises so frequently bestowed on the New York firemen. The chief defect that struck me, was the admission of the crowd to the scene of action. This caused, and must always cause, confusion. In England, barriers are thrown across the street at some distance, and rigorously guarded by the police and constables. On suggesting this improvement to an American friend, he agreed it would be desirable, but assured me it was not calculated for the meridian of the United States, where exclusion of any kind is always adverse to the popular feeling. On this matter, of course, I cannot judge, but it seems to me clear, that if the exclusion of an idle mob from the scene of a fire, increases the chance of saving property and life, the freedom thus pertinaciously insisted on, is merely that of doing private injury and public mischief.

With regard to the frequency of fires in New York, I confess, that after listening to all possible explanations, it does appear to me unaccountable. I am convinced, that in this single city there are annually more fires than occur in the whole Island of Great Britain. The combustible materials of which the majority of the houses are composed, is a circumstance far from sufficient to account for so enormous a disparity. Can we attribute it to crime? I think not; at least it would require much stronger evidence than has yet been discovered to warrant the hypothesis. In the negligence of servants, we have surer ground. These are generally negroes, and rarely to be depended on in any way, when exempt from rigid *surveillance.* But I am not going to concoct a theory, and so leave the matter as I find it.

CHAPTER III.

NEW YORK—HUDSON RIVER.

The 25th of November, being the anniversary of the evacuation of the city by the British army, is always a grand gala-day at New York. To perpetuate the memory of this glorious event, there is generally a parade of the militia, some firing of cannon and small arms, a procession of the different trades, and the day then terminates as it ought, in profuse and patriotic jollification. But on the present occasion it was determined, in addition to the ordinary cause of rejoicing, to get up a pageant of unusual splendour, in honour of the late Revolution in France. This resolution, I was informed, originated exclusively in the operative class, or *workies*, as they call themselves, in contradistinction to those who live in better houses, eat better dinners, read novels and poetry, and drink old Madeira instead of Yankee rum. The latter and more enviable class, however, having been taught caution by the results of the former French Revolution, were generally disposed to consider the present congratulatory celebration as somewhat premature, but finding it could not be prevented, prudently gave in, and determined to take part in the pageant.

It was arranged, that should the weather prove unfavourable on the 25th, the gala should be deferred till the day following. Nor was this precaution unwise. The morning of the appointed day was as unpropitious, as the prayers of the most pious advocate of legitimacy could have wished. The rain came down in torrents, the streets were flooded ankle deep, and I could not help feeling strong compassion for a party of militia, with a band of music, who with doleful aspect, and drenched to the skin, paraded past the hotel, to the tune of Yankee Doodle. But the morning following was of better promise: the rain had ceased, and though cold and cloudy, it was calm.

About ten o'clock, therefore, I betook myself to a house in Broadway, to which I had been obligingly invited to see the procession. During my progress, every thing gave note of preparation. The shops were closed, and men in military garb, and others decorated with scarfs and ribbons, were seen moving hastily along to their appointed stations. On approaching the route of the procession, the crowd became more dense, and the steps in front of the houses were so completely jammed up with human beings, that it was with difficulty I reached the door of that to which I was invited.

Having at length, however, effected an entrance, I enjoyed the honour of introduction to a large and very pleasant party assembled with the same object as myself, so that, though a considerable time elapsed before the appearance of the pageant, I felt no inclination to complain of the delay. At length, however, the sound of distant music reached the ear; the thunder of drums, the contralto of the fife, the loud clash of cymbals, and first and farthest heard, the spirit-stirring notes of the trumpet.

Ἵππων μ᾽ ὠκυπόδων ἀμφὶ κτύπος οὔατα βάλλει·

On they came, a glorious cavalcade, making

heaven vocal with sound of triumph, and earth beautiful with such colouring as nature never scattered from her pictured urn.

And first appeared, gorgeously caparisoned, a gallant steed bestrode by a cavalier, whose high and martial bearing bespoke him the hero of a hundred fights. The name of this chieftain I was not fortunate enough to learn. Next passed a body of militia, who, if they wished to appear as unlike soldiers as possible, were assuredly most successful. Then came the trades. Butchers on horseback, or drawn in a sort of rustic arbour or shambles, tastefully festooned with sausages. Tailors, with cockades and breast-knots of ribbon, pacing to music, with banners representative of various garments, waving proudly in the wind. Blacksmiths, with forge and bellows. Caravans of cobblers most seducingly appareled, and working at their trade on a locomotive platform, which displayed their persons to the best advantage. And carpenters too,—but the rest must be left to the imagination of the reader; and if he throw in a few bodies of militia, a few bands of music, and a good many most *outré* and unmilitary looking officers, appareled in uniforms apparently of the last century, he will form a very tolerable idea of the spectacle.

I must not, however, omit to notice the fire engines, which formed a very prominent part of the procession, it fortunately happening that no houses were just at that moment in conflagration. These engines were remarkably clean and in high order, and being adorned with a good deal of taste, attracted a large share of admiration. Altogether, it really did seem as if this gorgeous pageant were interminable, and, like a dinner in which there is too large a succession of courses, it was impossible to do equal justice to all its attractions. In the latter case, the fervour with which we demonstrate our admiration of one dish, forces us to disregard the charms of another. If we are not unjust to venison, we must subsequently slight partridge, and then from a whole wilderness of sweets, our waning appetite demands that we should select but one. And thus it was, that I, fervent in my admiration of the butchers, was, in due course, charmed with the carpenters, and subsequently smitten with the singular splendour of the saddlers. But another and another still succeeded, till the eye and tongue of the spectator became literally bankrupt in applause. *Est modus et dulci;* in short, there was too much of it, and one could not help feeling, after three hours spent in gazing, how practicable it was to become satiated with pomp, as well as with other good things.

But tedious as the spectacle was, it did at length pass, and I walked on to Washington Square, in which the ceremonies of the day were to conclude with the delivery of a public oration. On arriving, I found that a large stage, or hustings, had been erected in the square. From the centre of this stage rose another smaller platform, for the accommodation of the high functionaries of the state and city. As even the advanced guard of the procession had not yet given signal of its approach, it was evident that some delay must occur, and I therefore accepted an invitation to one of the houses in the square, where I found a very brilliant concourse of naval and military officers, and other persons of distinction. Among these was the venerable Ex-

President Munroe. It was, of course, not without interest that I gazed on an individual who had played so distinguished a part during the most perilous epoch of American history. He was evidently bent down by the united inroads of age and infirmity; and it was with regret I learned, that to those afflictions, which are the common lot of humanity, had been added those of poverty. The expression of Mr Munroe's countenance was mild, though not, I thought, highly intellectual. His forehead was not prominent, yet capacious and well defined. His eye was lustreless, and his whole frame emaciated and feeble. It was gratifying to witness the respect paid to this aged statesman by all who approached him; and I was delighted to hear the loud demonstrations of reverence and honour, with which his appearance in the street was hailed by the crowd.

Mr Munroe being too feeble to walk even so short a distance, was conveyed to the hustings in an open carriage. His equipage was followed by a *cortège* of functionaries on foot; and accompanying these gentlemen, I was admitted without difficulty to the lower platform, which contained accommodation for about a hundred. Having arrived there, we had still to wait some time for the commencement of the performance, during which some vociferous manifestations of disapprobation were made by the mob, who were prevented from approaching the hustings by an armed force of militia. At length, however, a portly gentleman came forward, and read aloud the address to the French inhabitants of New York, which had been passed at a public meeting. In particular, I observed that his countenance and gestures were directed towards a party of gentlemen of that nation, who occupied a conspicuous station on the stage beneath him. The document was too wordy and prolix, and written in a style of ambitious elaboration, which I could not help considering as somewhat puerile.

While all this was going forward on the hustings, the crowd without were becoming every instant more violent and clamorous; and a couple of boys were opportunely discovered beneath the higher scaffolding, engaged, either from malice or fun, in knocking away its supports, altogether unembarrassed by the consideration, that had their efforts been successful, they must themselves have been inevitably crushed in the fall of the platform.

Notwithstanding these *désagrémens*, the orator—a gentleman named Governor—came forward with a long written paper, which he commenced reading in a voice scarcely audible on the hustings, and which certainly could not be heard beyond its limits. The crowd, in consequence, became still more obstreperous. Having, no doubt, formed high anticipations of pleasure and instruction from the gifted inspiration of this gentleman's eloquence, it was certainly provoking to discover, that not one morsel of it were they destined to enjoy. The orator was, in consequence, addressed in ejaculations by no means complimentary, and such cries as—"Raise your voice, and be damned to you!" "Louder!"—"Speak out!"—"We don't hear a word!" were accompanied by curses which I trust were not deep, in proportion either to their loudness or their number. In vain did Mr Governor strain his throat, in compliance with this unreasonable requisition, but Nature had not formed him either a Hunt or an O'Connell, and the ill-humour of the multitude was not diminished.

At length order seemed at an end. A number of the mob broke through the barricade of soldiers, and, climbing up the hustings, increased the party there in a most unpleasant degree. But this was not all. The dissatisfied crowd below, thought proper to knock away the supports of the scaffolding, and just as Mr Governor was pronouncing a most emphatic period about the slavery of Ireland, down one side of it came with an alarming crash. Fortunately some gentlemen had the good sense to exhort every one to remain unmoved; and from a prudent compliance with this precaution, I believe little injury was sustained by any of the party. For myself, however, being already somewhat tired of the scene, the panic had no sooner ceased, than I took my departure.

Altogether, I must say that the multitude out of earshot had no great loss. The oration appeared a mere trumpery tissue of florid claptrap, which somewhat lowered my opinion with regard to the general standard of taste and intelligence in the American people. On the whole, the affair was a decided failure. What others went to see I know not, but had I not anticipated something better worth looking at, than a cavalcade of artisans mounted on cart-horses, and dressed out in tawdry finery, or the burlesque of military display by bodies of undrilled militia, I should probably have staid at home. I do not say this is in allusion to any deficiency of splendour in the pageant itself. A republic can possess but few materials for display, and in the present case I should not have felt otherwise, had the procession been graced by all the dazzling appendages of imperial grandeur. In truth, I had calculated on a sight altogether different. I expected to see a vast multitude animated by one pervading feeling of generous enthusiasm; to hear the air rent by the triumphant shouts of tens of thousands of freemen, hailing the bloodless dawn of liberty, in a mighty member of the brotherhood of nations. As it was, I witnessed nothing so sublime. Throughout the day, there was not the smallest demonstration of enthusiasm on the part of the vast concourse of spectators. There was no cheering, no excitement, no general expression of feeling of any sort; and I believe the crowd thought just as much of France as of Morocco,—the Cham of Tartary, as of Louis Philippe, King of the French. They looked and laughed indeed at the novel sight of their fellow tradesmen and apprentices tricked out in ribbons and white stockings, and pacing, with painted banners, to the sound of music. But the *moral* of the display, if I may so speak, was utterly overlooked. The people seemed to gaze on the scene before them with the same feeling as Peter Bell did on a primrose; and it was evident enough—if, without irreverence, I may be permitted to parody the fine words of the noblest of contemporary poets,—that in the unexcited imagination of each spectator,

> A butcher on his steed so trim,
> A mounted butcher was to him,
> And he was nothing more.

Such was the source of my disappointment in regard to this splendid festivity. How far it was reasonable, others may decide. I can only say I felt it.

One of the most pleasant evenings I have passed since my arrival, was at a club composed of gentlemen of literary taste, which includes among its members, several of the most eminent individuals of the Union. The meetings are weekly, and take place at the house of each member in succession. The party generally assembles about eight o'clock; an hour or two is spent in conversation; supper follows; and after a moderate, though social potation, the meeting breaks up. I had here the honour of being introduced to Mr Livingston, lieutenant-governor of the State, Mr Gallatin, Mr Jay, and several other gentlemen of high accomplishment.

Mr Gallatin I regarded with peculiar interest. His name was one with which I had been long familiar. Born in Switzerland, he became a citizen of the United States, soon after the Revolution, and found there a field, in which, it was not probable that talents like his, would remain long without high and profitable employment. I believe it was in the cabinet of Mr Jefferson that Mr Gallatin commenced his career as a statesman. Since then, much of his life has been passed either in high offices at home, or as minister to some of the European Courts; and the circumstance of his foreign birth rendering him ineligible to the office of President, this veteran statesman and diplomatist, wisely judging that there should be 'some space between the *cabinet* and grave,' has retired from political life, and finds exercise for his yet unbroken energies in the calmer pursuits of literature.

In his youth Mr Gallatin must have been handsome. His countenance is expressive of great sagacity. He is evidently an acute thinker, and his conversation soon discovered him to be a ruthless exposer of those traditionary or *geographical* sophisms, in politics and religion, by which the mind of whole nations has been frequently obscured, and from the influence of which, none perhaps are entirely exempt. Mr Gallatin speaks our language with a slight infusion of his native accent, but few have greater command of felicitous expression, or write it with greater purity.

An evening passed in such company, could not be other than delightful. There was no monopoly of conversation, but its current flowed on equably and agreeably. Subjects of literature and politics were discussed with an entire absence of that bigotry and dogmatism, which sometimes destroy the pleasure of interchange of opinion, even between minds of high order. For myself, I was glad to enjoy an opportunity of observing the modes of thinking peculiar to intellects of the first class, in this new and interesting country, and I looked forward to nothing with more pleasure, than availing myself of the obliging invitation to repeat my visits at the future meetings of the Club.

Having already passed a fortnight in one unbroken chain of engagements in this most hospitable city, I determined to give variety to the tissue of my life, by accepting the very kind and pressing invitation of Dr Hosack, to visit him at his country-seat on the banks of the Hudson. The various works of this gentleman have rendered his name well known in Europe, and procured his admission to the most eminent Philosophical Institutions in England, France, and Germany. For many years, he enjoyed as a physician the first practice in New York, and has recently retired from the toilsome labours of his profession, with the reputation of great wealth, and the warm esteem of his fellow-citizens.

At eight o'clock in the morning, therefore, of a day which promised to turn out more than usually raw and disagreeable, I embarked in the steam-boat North America, and proceeded up the river to Hyde-Park, about eighty miles distant. I had anticipated much enjoyment from the beautiful scenery on the Hudson, but the elements were adverse. We had scarcely left the quay, when the lowering clouds began to discharge their contents in the form of snow, and the wind was so piercingly cold that I found it impossible, even with all appliances of cloaks and great-coats, to remain long on deck. Every now and then, however, I reascended from below, to see as much as I could, and when nearly half frozen, returned to enjoy the scarcely less interesting prospect of the cabin stove.

Of course, it was impossible, under such circumstances, to form any just estimate of scenery; but still the fine objects which appeared occasionally glimmering through the mist, were enough to convince me, that seen under more favourable auspices, my expectations, highly as they had been excited, were not likely to encounter disappointment. That portion of the scenery in particular, distinguished by the name of the Highlands, struck me, as combining the elements of the grand and beautiful, in a very eminent degree. I remember nothing on the Rhine at all equal to it. The river at this place has found a passage through two ranges of mountains, evidently separated by some convulsion of nature, and which, in beauty and variety of form, and grandeur of effect, can scarcely be exceeded.

But the vessel in which this little voyage was performed, demands some notice, even amid scenery fine as that along which it conducted us with astonishing rapidity. Its dimensions seemed gigantic. Being intended solely for river navigation, the keel is nearly flat, and the upper portion of the vessel is made to project beyond the hull to a very considerable distance on either side. When standing at the stern, and looking forward, the extent of accommodation appears enormous, though certainly not more than is required for the immense number of passengers who travel daily between New York and Albany. Among other unusual accommodations on deck, I was rather surprised at observing a barber's shop, in which,—judging from the state of the visages of my fellow-passengers,—I have no doubt that a very lucrative trade is carried on.

The accommodation below was scarcely less worthy of note. It consisted of two cabins, which I guessed, by pacing them, to be an hundred and fifty feet in length. The sternmost of these spacious apartments is sumptuously fitted up with abundance of mirrors, ottomans, and other appurtenances of luxury. The other, almost equally large, was very inferior in point of decoration. It seemed intended for a sort of tippling-shop, and contained a *bar*, where liquors of all kinds, from Champagne to small beer, were dispensed to such passengers as have inclination to swallow, and money to pay for them. The sides of both of these cabins were lined with a triple row of sleeping-berths; and as the sofas and benches were likewise convertible to a similar purpose, I was assured, accommodation could be easily furnished for about five hundred.

The scene at breakfast was a curiosity. I calculated the number of masticators at about three hundred, yet there was no confusion, and certainly no scarcity of provision. As for the waiters, their name might have been *Legion*, for they were many, and during the whole entertainment, kept skipping about with the most praiseworthy activity, some collecting money, and others engaged in the translation of cutlets and coffee. The proceedings of the party *in re* breakfast, were no less brief and compendious afloat, than I had observed them on shore. As for *eating*, there was nothing like it discoverable on board the North America. Each man seemed to *devour*, under the uncontrollable impulse of some sudden hurricane of appetite, to which it would be difficult to find any parallel beyond the limits of the Zoological Gardens. A few minutes did the business. The clatter of knives and voices, vociferous at first, speedily waxed faint and fainter, plates, dishes, cups, and saucers disappeared as if by magic, and every thing connected with the meal became so suddenly invisible, that but for internal evidence, which the hardiest sceptic could scarcely have ventured to discredit, the breakfast in the North America might have passed for one of those gorgeous, but unreal visions, which, for a moment, mock the eye of the dreamer, and then vanish into thin air.

The steamer made several brief stoppages at villages on the river, for the reception and discharge of goods or passengers. From the large warehouses which these generally contained, they were evidently places of considerable deposit for the agricultural produce of the neighbouring country. They were built exclusively of wood, painted of a white colour; and, certainly, for their population, boasted an unusual number of taverns, which gave notice of their hospitality, on signboards of gigantic dimensions. The business to be transacted at these places occasioned but little loss of time. Every arrangement had evidently been made to facilitate despatch, and by two o'clock I found myself fairly ashore at Hyde Park, and glad to seek shelter in the landing-house from the deluge of snow, which had already whitened the whole surface of the country.

I had just begun to question the landlord about the possibility of procuring a conveyance to the place of my destination, when Dr Hosack himself appeared, having obligingly brought his carriage for my conveyance. Though the drive from the landing-place led through a prettily variegated country, I was not much in the humour to admire scenery, and looked, I fear, with more indifference on the improvements past and projected, to which the Doctor directed my attention, than would have been consistent with politeness in a warmer and more comfortable auditor. The distance, however, was little more than a mile, and, on reaching the house, the disagreeables of the journey were speedily forgotten in the society of its amiable inmates, and the enjoyment of every convenience which wealth and hospitality could supply. Dr Hosack had received his professional education in Scotland, and passed a considerable portion of his early life there. I was fortunately enabled to afford him some information relative to the companions of his early studies, many of whom have since risen to eminence, while others, perhaps not less meritorious, have lived and died undistinguished. In return, the Doctor was good enough to favour me, by communicating much valuable knowledge on the state of science and the arts in the United States, which I must have found great difficulty in obtaining from other sources.

There is this advantage in the pursuit of science, that it tends to generate liberality of sentiment, and destroy those prejudices which divide nations far more effectually than any barrier of nature. Science is of no country, and its followers, wherever born, constitute a wide and diffusive community, and are linked together by ties of brotherhood and interest, which political hostility cannot sever. These observations were particularly suggested by my intercourse with Dr Hosack. Though our conversation was excursive, and embraced a vast variety of topics fairly debateable between an American and an Englishman, I could really detect nothing of national prejudice in his opinions. He uniformly spoke of the great names of Europe with admiration and respect, and his allusions to the achievements of his countrymen in arts, arms, science, or philosophy, betrayed nothing of that vanity and exaggeration, with which, since my arrival, I had already become somewhat familiar.

The following morning was bright and beautiful.

The snow, except in places where the wind had drifted it into wreaths, had entirely disappeared; and after breakfast, I was glad to accept the invitation of my worthy host, to examine his demesne, which was really very beautiful and extensive. Nothing could be finer than the situation of the house. It stands upon a lofty terrace, overhanging the Hudson, whose noble stream lends richness and grandeur to the whole extent of the foreground of the landscape. Above, its waters are seen to approach from a country finely variegated, but unmarked by any peculiar boldness of feature. Below, it is lost among a range of rocky and wooded eminences of highly picturesque outline. In one direction alone, however, is the prospect very extensive, and in that, (the southwest,) the Catskill Mountains, sending their bald and rugged summits far up into the sky, form a glorious framework for the picture.

We drove through a finely-undulating country, in which the glories of the ancient forest have been replaced by bare fields, intersected by hideous zigzag fences. God meant it to be beautiful, when He gave such noble varieties of hill and plain, wood and water; but man seemed determined it should be otherwise. No beauty which the axe could remove was suffered to remain; and wherever the tide of population reached, the havoc had been indiscriminate and unsparing.

Yet, of this, it were not only useless, but ridiculous to complain. Such changes are not optional, but imperative. The progress of population necessarily involves them, and they must be regarded only as the process by which the wilderness is brought to minister to the wants and enjoyments of civilized man. The time at length comes, when another and a higher beauty replaces that which has been destroyed. It is only the state of transition which it is unpleasant to behold; the particular stage of advancement in which the wild grandeur of nature has disappeared, and the charm of cultivation has not yet replaced it.

Dr Hosack was a farmer, and took great interest in the laudable, but expensive amusement of improving his estate. He had imported sheep and cattle from England, of the most improved breeds, and in this respect promised to be a benefactor to his neighbourhood. I am not much of a farmer, and found the Doctor sagacious about long horns and short legs, in a degree which impressed me with a due consciousness of my ignorance. The farm offices were extensive and well arranged, and contained some excellent horses. A pair of powerful carriage-horses, in particular, attracted my admiration. In this country these fine animals cost only two hundred dollars. In London, I am sure, that under Tattersall's hammer, they would not fetch less than three hundred guineas.

But America is not the place for a gentleman farmer. The price of labour is high, and besides, it cannot always be commanded at any price. The condition of society is not yet ripe for farming on a great scale. There will probably be no American Mr Coke for some centuries to come. The Transatlantic Sir John Sinclairs are yet *in ovo*, and a long period of incubation must intervene, before we can expect them to crack the shell. As things at present stand, small farmers could beat the great ones out of the field. What a man produces by his own labour, and that of his family, he produces cheaply. What he is compelled to hire others to perform, is done expensively. It is always the interest of the latter to get as much, and give as little labour in exchange for it as they can. Then arises the necessity of bailiffs and overseers, fresh mouths to be fed and pockets to be filled, and the owner may consider himself fortunate if these are content with devouring the profits, without swallowing the estate into the bargain.

Having passed two very pleasant days with my kind and hospitable friends, I again took steam on my return to New York. Dr Hosack was good enough to accompany me on board, and introduce me to a family of the neighbourhood, who were returning from their summer residence to pass the winter in the city. In its members, was included one of the most intelligent and accomplished ladies I have ever met in any country. The voyage, therefore, did not appear tedious, though the greater part of it was performed in the dark. About ten o'clock the steam-boat was alongside the quay, and I speedily found myself installed in my old quarters in Bunker's hotel.

CHAPTER IV.

NEW YORK.

Professor Griscomb, a member of the Society of Friends, was obliging enough to conduct me over a large seminary placed under his immediate superintendence. The general plan of education is one with which, in Scotland at least, we are familiar, and I did not remark that any material improvement had followed its adoption in the United States. To divide boys into large classes of fifty or a hundred, in which, of course, the rate of advancement of the slowest boy must regulate that of the cleverest and most assiduous, does not, I confess, appear a system founded on very sound or rational principles. On this plan of retardation, it is, of course, necessary to discover some employment for the boys, whose talents enable them to outstrip their fellows; and this is done by appointing them to the office of monitor, or teacher, of a subdivision of the class. This mode of communicating knowledge has its advantages and its faults. It is no doubt beneficial to the great body of the class, who are instructed with greater facility, and less labour to the master. But the monitors are little better than scapegoats, who, with some injustice, are made to pay the whole penalty of the comparative dulness of their companions. The system, however, I have been assured, both in this country and in England, is found to work well, and I have no doubt it does so in respect to the *average* amount of instruction imparted to the pupils. But the principle of sacrificing the clever few, for the advancement of the stupid many, is one, I still humbly conceive, to be liable to strong objections. Of establishments on this principle, I have seen none more successful than that of Professor Griscomb. Every thing which zeal and talent on the part of the master could effect, had obviously been done; and on the part of the scholars, there was assuredly no want of proficiency in any branch of knowledge adapted to their age and capacity.

A striking difference exists between the system of rewards and punishments adopted in the schools of the United States, and in those of England. In the former, neither personal infliction, nor forcible coercion of any kind, is permitted. How far such a system is likely to prove successful, I cannot yet form an opinion, but judging solely from the seminary under Dr Griscomb, I should be inclined to augur favourably of its results. It has always, however, appeared strange to me, that the Americans should betray so strong an antipathy to the system of the public schools of England. There are no other establishments, perhaps, in our country, so entirely republican both in principle and practice. Rank is there allowed no privileges, and the only recognised aristocracy is that of personal qualities. Yet these schools are far from finding favour in American eyes. The system of fagging, in particular, is regarded with abhorrence; and since my arrival, I have never met any one who could even speak of it with patience. The state of feeling on this matter in the two countries presents this curious anomaly: A young English nobleman is sent to Westminster or Winchester to brush coats and wash tea-cups, while the meanest American storekeeper would redden with virtuous indignation at the very thought of the issue of his loins contaminating his plebeian blood by the discharge of such functions.

This difference of feeling, however, seems to admit of easy explanation. In England, the menial offices in question form the duties of *freemen;* in America, even in those States where slavery has been abolished, domestic service being discharged by Negroes, is connected with a thousand degrading associations. So powerful are these, that I have never yet conversed with an American who could understand that there is nothing intrinsically disgraceful in such duties; and their being at all considered so, proceeds entirely from a certain confusion of thought, which connects the office with the manners and character of those by whom it is discharged. In a country where household services are generally performed by persons of respectable character, on a level, in point of morals and acquirement, with other handicraftsmen, it is evident that such prejudice could exist in no material degree. But it certainly could not exist *at all* in a country, where for a certain period such services were performed by *all*, including every rank below royalty. Let the idea of personal degradation, therefore, be wholly abstracted, and then the question will rest on its true basis, namely, whether such discipline as that adopted in our public schools, be favourable to the improvement of the moral character or not?

In England, the system is believed from long experience to work practically well. No man will say, that British gentlemen, formed under the discipline of these institutions, are deficient in high bearing, or in generous spirit; nor will it readily be considered a disadvantage, that those who are afterwards to wield the united influence of rank and wealth, should, in their early years, be placed in a situation, where their personal and moral qualities alone can place them even on an equality with their companions.

It is very probable, indeed, that a system suited to a country, in which gradation of ranks forms an integral part of the constitution, may not be adapted to another, which differs so widely in these respects, as the United States. Here, there is no pride of birth or station to be overcome; and whether, under circumstances so different, the kind of discipline in question might operate beneficially or otherwise, is a point on which I certainly do not presume to decide. I only assert my conviction, that in this country it has never yet been made the subject of liberal and enlightened discussion, and therefore that the value of Transatlantic opinion with regard to it is absolutely null. The conclusion adopted may be right, but the grounds on which it is founded are evidently wrong.

Having resolved to devote the day to the inspection of schools, I went from that under the superintendence of Professor Griscomb, to another for the education of children of colour. I here found about a hundred boys, in whose countenances might be traced every possible gradation of complexion between those of the swarthy Ethiop and florid European. Indeed several of the children were so fair, that I certainly never should have discovered the lurking taint of African descent. In person they were clean and neat, and though of course the offspring of the very lowest class of the people, there was nothing in their dress or appearance indicative of abject poverty. The master struck me as an intelligent and benevolent man. He frankly answered all my questions, and evidently took pride in the proficiency of his pupils.

It has often happened to me, since my arrival in this country, to hear it gravely maintained by men of education and intelligence, that the Negroes were an inferior race, a link as it were between man and the brutes. Having enjoyed few opportunities of observation on people of colour in my own country, I was now glad to be enabled to enlarge my knowledge on a subject so interesting. I therefore requested the master to inform me whether the results of his experience had led to the inference, that the aptitude of the Negroe children for acquiring knowledge was inferior to that of the whites. In reply, he assured me they had not done so; and, on the contrary, declared, that in sagacity, perseverance, and capacity for the acquisition and retention of knowledge, his poor despised scholars were equal to any boys he had ever known. "But alas, sir!" said he, "to what end are these poor creatures taught acquirement, from the exercise of which they are destined to be debarred, by the prejudices of society? It is surely but a cruel mockery to cultivate talents, when in the present state of public feeling, there is no field open for their useful employment. Be his acquirements what they may, a Negroe is still a Negroe, or, in other words, a creature marked out for degradation, and exclusion from those objects which stimulate the hopes and powers of other men."

I observed, in reply, that I was not aware that, in those States in which slavery had been abolished, any such barrier existed as that to which he alluded. "In the State of New York, for instance," I asked, "are not all offices and professions open to the man of colour as well as to the white?"

"I see, sir," replied he, "that you are not a native of this country, or you would not have asked such a question." He then went on to inform me, that the exclusion in question did not arise from any legislative enactment, but from the tyranny of that prejudice, which, regarding the poor black as a being of inferior order, works its own fulfilment in making him so. There was no answering this, for it accorded too well with my own observations in society, not to carry my implicit belief.

The master then proceeded to explain the system of education adopted in the school, and subsequently afforded many gratifying proofs of the proficiency of his scholars. One class were employed in navigation, and worked several complicated problems with great accuracy and rapidity. A large proportion were perfectly conversant with arithmetic, and not a few with the lower mathematics. A long and rigid examination took place in geography, in the course of which questions were answered with facility, which I confess would have puzzled me exceedingly, had they been addressed to myself.

I had become so much interested in the little party-coloured crowd before me, that I recurred to our former discourse, and enquired of the master, what would probably become of his scholars on their being sent out into the world? Some trades, some description of labour of course were open to them, and I expressed my desire to know what these were. He told me they were few. The class studying navigation, were destined to be sailors; but let their talents be what they might, it was impossible they could rise to be officers of the paltriest merchantman that entered the waters of the United States. The office of cook or steward was indeed within the scope of their ambition; but it was just as feasible for the poor creatures to expect to become Chancellor of the State, as mate of a ship. In other pursuits it was the same. Some would become stone-masons, or bricklayers, and to the extent of carrying a hod, or handling a trowel, the course was clear before them; but the office of master-bricklayer was open to them in precisely the same sense as the Professorship of Natural Philosophy. No white artificer would serve under a coloured master. The most degraded Irish emigrant would scout the idea with indignation. As carpenters, shoemakers, or tailors, they were still arrested by the same barrier. In either of the latter capacities, indeed, they might work for people of their own complexion, but no *gentleman* would ever think of ordering garments of any sort from a *schneider* of cuticle less white than his own. Grocers they might be, but then who could conceive the possibility of a respectable household matron purchasing tea or spiceries from a vile "Nigger?" As barbers, they were more fortunate, and in that capacity might even enjoy the privilege of taking the President of the United States by the nose. Throughout the Union, the department of domestic service peculiarly belongs to them, though recently they are beginning to find rivals in the Irish emigrants, who come annually in swarms like locusts.

On the whole, I cannot help considering it a mistake to suppose, that slavery has been abolished in the Northern States of the Union. It is true, indeed, that in these States the power of compulsory labour no longer exists; and that one human being within their limits, can no longer claim property in the thews and sinews of another. But is this all that is implied in the boon of freedom? If the word mean any thing, it must mean the enjoyment of equal rights, and the unfettered exercise in each individual of such powers and faculties as God has given him. In this true meaning of the word, it may be safely asserted, that this poor degraded caste are still slaves. They are subjected to the most grinding and humiliating of all slaveries, that of universal and unconquerable prejudice. The whip, indeed, has been removed from the back of the Negro, but the chains are still on his limbs, and he bears the brand of degradation on his forehead. What is it but mere abuse of language to call him *free*, who is tyrannically deprived of all the motives to exertion which animate other men? The law, in truth, has left him in that most pitiable of all conditions, *a masterless slave*.

It cannot be denied, that the Negro population are still compelled, *as a class*, to be the hewers of wood, and drawers of water, to their fellow-citizens. *Citizens!* there is indeed something ludicrous in the application of the word to these miserable Pariahs. What privileges do they enjoy as such? Are they admissible upon a jury? Can they enroll themselves in the militia? Will a white man eat with them, or extend to them the hand of fellowship? Alas! if these men, so irresistibly manacled to degradation, are to be called *free*, tell us, at least, what stuff are slaves made of!

But on this subject, perhaps, another tone of expression—of thought, there can be no other—may be more judicious. I have already seen abundant proofs, that the prejudices against the coloured portion of the population, prevail to an extent, of which an Englishman could have formed no idea. But many enlightened men, I am convinced, are above them. To these I would appeal. They have already begun the work of raising this unfortunate race from the almost brutal state to which tyranny and injustice had condemned it. But let them not content themselves with such delusive benefits as the extension of the right of suffrage, recently conferred by the Legislature of New York.* The opposition

* The Legislature of New York, in 1829, extended the right of suffrage to men of colour, *possessed of a clear freehold estate, without encumbrance, of the value of* 250 *dollars.* A very safe concession no doubt, since to balance the *black interest,* the same right of suffrage was granted to *every* white male of twenty-one years, who has been one year in the State. It might be curious to know how many coloured voters became qualified by this enactment. They must indeed have been *rari nantes in gurgite vasto* of the election.

to be overcome, is not that of *law*, but of *opinion*. If in unison with the ministers of religion, they will set their shoulders to the wheel, and combat prejudice with reason, ignorance with knowledge, and pharisaical assumption with the mild tenets of Christianity, they must succeed in infusing a better tone into the minds and hearts of their countrymen. It is true, indeed, the victory will not be achieved in a day, nor probably in an age, but assuredly it will come at last. In achieving it, they will become the benefactors, not only of the Negro population, but of their fellow-citizens. They will give freedom to both; for the man is really not more free whose mind is shackled by degrading prejudice, than he who is its victim.

As illustrative of the matter in hand, I am tempted here to relate an anecdote, though somewhat out of place, as it did not occur till my return to New York in the following Spring. Chancing one day at the Ordinary at Bunker's, to sit next an English merchant from St Domingo; in the course of conversation, he mentioned the following circumstances. The son of a Haytian general, high in the favour of

Boyer, recently accompanied him to New York, which he came to visit for pleasure and instruction. This young man, though a mulatto, was pleasing in manner, and with more intelligence than is usually to be met with in a country in which education is so defective. At home, he had been accustomed to receive all the deference due to his rank, and when he arrived in New York, it was with high anticipations of the pleasure that awaited him in a city so opulent and enlightened.

On landing, he enquired for the best hotel, and directed his baggage to be conveyed there. He was rudely refused admittance, and tried several others with similar result. At length he was forced to take up his abode in a miserable lodging-house kept by a Negro woman. The pride of the young Haytian, (who, sooth to say, was something of a dandy, and made imposing display of gold chains and brooches,) was sadly galled by this, and the experience of every hour tended further to confirm the conviction, that, in this country, he was regarded as a degraded being, with whom the meanest white man would hold it disgraceful to associate. In the evening he went to the theatre, and tendered his money to the box-keeper. It was tossed back to him, with a disdainful intimation, that the place for persons of his colour was the upper gallery.

On the following morning, my countryman, who had frequently been a guest at the table of his father, paid him a visit. He found the young Haytian in despair. All his dreams of pleasure were gone, and he returned to his native island by the first conveyance, to visit the United States no more.

This young man should have gone to Europe. Should he visit England, he may feel quite secure, that if he have money in his pocket, he will offer himself at no hotel, from Land's End to John O'-Groat's house, where he will not meet a very cordial reception. Churches, theatres, operas, concerts, coaches, chariots, cabs, vans, waggons, steam-boats, railway carriages and air balloons, will all be open to him as the daylight. He may repose on cushions of down or of air, he may charm his ear with music, and his palate with luxuries of all sorts. He may travel *en prince* or *en roturier*, precisely as his fancy dictates, and may enjoy even the honours of a crowned head, if he will only pay like one. In short, so long as he carries certain golden ballast about with him, all will go well. But, when that is done, God help him. He will then become familiar with the provisions of the vagrant act, and Mr Roe or Mr Ballantine will recommend exercise on the treadmill, for the benefit of his constitution. Let him but show his nose abroad, and a whole host of parish overseers will take alarm. The new police will bait him like a bull; and should he dare approach even the lowest eating-house, the master will shut the door in his face. If he ask charity, he will be told to work. If he beg work, he will be told to get about his business. If he steal, he will be found a free passage to Botany Bay, and be dressed gratis on his arrival, in an elegant suit of yellow. If he rob, he will be found a free passage to another world, in which, as there is no paying or receiving in payment, we may hope that his troubles will be at an end for ever.

CHAPTER V.

NEW YORK.

HAVING moved, since my arrival, in a tolerably wide circle, I now feel qualified to offer some observations on the state of society in New York. The houses of the better order of citizens, are generally of brick, sometimes faced with stone or marble, and in the allotment of the interior very similar to tenements of the same class in England. The dining and drawing-rooms are uniformly on the ground floor, and communicate by folding doors, which, when dinner is announced, are thrown open for the transit of the company. The former of these apartments, so far as my observation has carried me, differs nothing in appearance from an English one. But the drawing-rooms in New York certainly strike me as being a good deal more primitive in their appliances than those of the more opulent classes in the old country. Furniture in the United States is apparently not one of those articles in which wealth takes pride in displaying its superiority. Every thing is comfortable, but every thing is plain. Here are no buhl tables, nor or-molu clocks, nor gigantic mirrors, nor cabinets of Japan, nor draperies of silk or velvet; and one certainly does miss those thousand elegancies, with which the taste of British ladies delights in adorning their apartments. In short, the appearance of an American mansion is decidedly republican. No want remains unsupplied, while nothing is done for the gratification of a taste for expensive luxury.

This is as it should be. There are few instances of such opulence in America as would enable its owner, without inconvenience, to lavish thousands on pictures, ottomans, and china vases. In such a country, there are means of profitable outlay for every shilling of accumulated capital, and the Americans are too prudent a people to invest in objects of mere taste, that which, in the more vulgar shape of cotton or tobacco, would tend to the replenishing of their pockets. And, after all, it is better, perhaps, to sit on leather or cotton, with a comfortable balance at one's banker's book, than to lounge on damask, and tread on carpets of Persia, puzzling our brains about the budget and the ways and means.

One cause of the effect just noticed, is unquestionably the absence of the law, or rather the custom of primogeniture. A man whose fortune, at his death, must be divided among a numerous family in equal proportions, will not readily invest any considerable portion of it, in such inconvertible objects as the productions of the fine arts, and still less in articles of mere household luxury, unsuited to the circumstances of his descendants. It will rarely happen that a father can bequeath to each of his children enough to render them independent. They have to struggle into opulence as best they may; and assuredly, to men so circumstanced, nothing could be more inconvenient and distasteful, than to receive any part of their legacies, in the form of pictures, or scagliola tables, instead of Erie canal shares, or bills of the New York Bank.

Another circumstance, probably not without its effect in recommending both paucity and plainness of furniture, is the badness of the servants. These are chiefly people of colour, habituated from their cradle to be regarded as an inferior race, and consequently sadly wanting both in moral energy and principle. Every lady with whom I have conversed on the subject, speaks with envy of the superior comforts and facilities of an English establishment. A coloured servant, they declare, requires perpetual supervision. He is an executive, not a deliberative being. Under such circumstances the drudgery that devolves on an American matron, I should imagine to be excessive. She must direct every operation that is going on from the garret to the cellar. She must be her own housekeeper; superintend all the outgoings and comings in, and interfere in a thousand petty and annoying details, which, in England, go on like clock-work, out of sight and out of thought.

If it fare so with the mistress of an establishment, the master has no sinecure. A butler is out of the question. He would much rather know that the keys of his cellar were at the bottom of the Hudson, than in the pocket of black Cæsar, with a fair opportunity of getting at his *Marston* or his *Bingham.* Few of the coloured population have energy to resist temptation. The dread of punishment has been removed as an habitual motive to exertion, but the sense of inextinguishable degradation yet remains.

The torment of such servants has induced many families in New York to discard them altogether, and supply their places with natives of the Emerald Isle. It may be doubted, whether the change has generally been accompanied by much advantage. Domestic service in the United States, is considered as degrading by all untainted by the curse of African descent. No native American could be induced to it, and popular as the present President may be, he would probably not find one of his constituents, whom any amount of emolument would induce to brush his coat, or stand behind his carriage. On their arrival in this country, therefore, the Scotch and English, who are not partial to being looked down upon by their neighbours, very soon get hold of this prejudice; but he of that terrestrial paradise, "first flower of the earth, and first gem of the sea," has no such scruples. Landing often at the quay of New York, without hat, shoes, and sometimes less dispensable garments, he is content to put his pride in his pocket, where there is always ample room for its accommodation. But even with him domestic service is only a temporary expedient. The moment he contrives to scrape together a little money, he bids his master good morning, and, fired with the ambition of farming or storekeeping, starts off for the back country.

The nuisance of this is, that no white servant is ever stationary in a place. He comes a mere clod-pole, and is no sooner taught his duty, and become an useful member of the house, than he accepts the Chiltern Hundreds, and a new writ must forthwith be issued for a tenant of the pantry. Now, though annual elections may be very good things in the body *politic*, the most democratic American will probably admit, that in the body *domestic*, the longer the members keep their seats the better. Habits of office are of some value in a valet, as well as in a secretary of state, and how these are to be obtained by either functionary, as matters are at present ordered in this country, I profess myself at a loss to understand.

When you enter an American house, either in quality of casual visitor or invited guest, the servant never thinks of ushering you to the company; on the contrary, he immediately disappears, leaving you to explore your way, in a navigation of which you know nothing, or to amuse yourself in the passage by counting the hat-pegs and umbrellas. In a strange house, one cannot take the liberty of bawling for assistance, and the choice only remains of opening doors on speculation, with the imminent risk of intruding on the bedroom of some young lady, or of cutting the gordian knot by escaping through the only one you know any thing about. I confess, that the first time I found myself in this unpleasant predicament, the latter expedient was the one I adopted, though I fear not without offence to an excellent family, who, having learned the fact of my admission, could not be supposed to understand the motive of my precipitate retreat.

On the whole, the difference is not striking, I

should imagine, between the social habits of the people of New York, and those prevalent in our first-rate mercantile cities. In both, the faculties are exerted in the same pursuits; in both, the dominant aristocracy is that of wealth; and in both, there is the same grasping at unsubstantial and unacknowledged distinctions.

It is the fashion to call the United States the land of liberty and equality. If the term equality be understood simply as implying, that there exists no privileged order in America, the assertion, though not strictly true,* may pass. In any wider acceptation it is mere nonsense. There is quite as much practical equality in Liverpool as New York. The magnates of the Exchange do not strut less proudly in the latter city than in the former; nor are their wives and daughters more backward in supporting their pretensions. In such matters legislative enactments can do nothing. Man's vanity, and the desire of distinction inherent in his nature, cannot be

* Not strictly true, because in many of the States the right of suffrage is made dependent on a certain qualification in property. In Virginia, in particular, this qualification is very high.

repressed. If obstructed in one outlet, it will only gush forth with greater vehemence at another. The most contemptible of mankind has some talent of mind or body, some attraction—virtue—accomplishment—dexterity—or gift of fortune,—in short, something real or imaginary, on which he arrogates superiority to those around him. The rich man looks down upon the poor, the learned on the ignorant, the orator on him unblessed with the gift of tongues, and " he that is a true-born gentleman, and stands upon the honour of his birth," despises the *roturier*, whose talents have raised him to an estimation in society perhaps superior to his own.

Thus it is with the men, and with the fairer sex assuredly it is not different. No woman, conscious of attraction, was ever a republican in her heart. Beauty is essentially despotic—it uniformly asserts its power, and never yet consented to a surrender of privilege. I have certainly heard it maintained in the United States, that all men were equal, but never did I hear that assertion from the lips of a lady. On the contrary, the latter is always conscious of the full extent of her claims to preference and admiration, and is never satisfied till she feels them to be acknowledged. And what zephyr is too light to fill the gossamer sails of woman's vanity! The form of a feature, the whiteness of a hand, the shade of a ringlet, a cap, a feather, a trinket, a smile, a motion—all, or any of these, or distinctions yet finer and more shadowy, if such there be—are enough, here as elsewhere, to constitute the sign and shibboleth of her fantastic supremacy. It is in vain, therefore, to talk of female republicans; there exists, and can exist, no such being on either side of the Atlantic, for human nature is the same on both.

In truth, the spirit of aristocracy displays itself in this commercial community in every variety of form. One encounters it at every turn. T'other night, at a ball, I had the honour to converse a good deal with a lady, who is confessedly a star of the first magnitude in the hemisphere of fashion. She enquired what I thought of the company. I answered, "that I had rarely seen a party in any country in which the average of beauty appeared to me to be so high."

"Indeed!" answered my fair companion, with an

expression of surprise; "it would seem that you English gentlemen are not difficult to please; but does it strike you, that the average is equally high as regards air, manner, fashion?"

"In regard to such matters," I replied, "I certainly could not claim for the party in question any remarkable distinction; but that, in a scene so animated, and brilliant with youth, beauty, and gaiety of spirit, I was little disposed to play the critic."

"Nay," replied my opponent, for the conversation had already begun to assume something of the form of argument, "it surely requires no spirit of rigid criticism, to discriminate between such a set of vulgarians, as you see collected here, and ladies who have been accustomed to move in a higher and better circle. Mrs ——— is an odd person, and makes it a point to bring together at her balls all the riff-raff of the place—people whom, if you were to remain ten years in New York, you would probably never meet any where else. I assure you, there are not a dozen girls in this room that I should think of admitting to my own parties."

Thus driven from the field, I ventured to direct

her notice to several elegant and pretty girls, about whom I asked some questions. Their attractions, however, were either not admitted, or when these were too decided to allow of direct negation, the subject was ingeniously evaded. If I talked of a pretty foot, I was told its owner was the daughter of a tobacconist. If I admired a graceful dancer, I was assured (what I certainly should not have discovered) that the young lady was of vulgar manners, and without education. Some were so utterly unknown to fame, that the very names, birth, habits, and connexions, were buried in the most profound and impenetrable obscurity. In short, a Count of the Empire, with his sixteen quarterings, probably would not have thought, and certainly would not have spoken, with contempt half so virulent of these fair plebeians. The reader will perhaps agree, that there are more *exclusives* in the world than the lady-patronesses of Almack's.

I shall now give an instance of the estimation in which wealth is held in this commercial community. At a party a few evenings ago, the worthy host was politely assiduous in introducing me to the more prominent individuals who composed it. Unfortunately, he considered it necessary to preface each repetition of the ceremony with some preliminary account of the pecuniary circumstances of the gentleman, the honour of whose acquaintance was about to be conferred on me. "Do you observe," he asked, "that tall thin person, with a cast in his eye, and his nose a little cocked? Well, that man, not three months ago, made an hundred thousand dollars by a single speculation in tallow. You must allow me to introduce you to him."

The introduction passed, and my zealous cicerone again approached, with increased importance of aspect—"A gentleman," he said, "worth at least half a million, had expressed a desire to make my acquaintance." This was gratifying, and, of course, not to be denied. A third time did our worthy entertainer return to the charge, and before taking my departure, I had the honour of being introduced to an individual, who was stated to be still more opulent than his predecessors. Had I been presented to so many bags of dollars, instead of to their possessors, the ceremony would have been quite as interesting, and perhaps less troublesome.

The truth is, that in a population wholly devoted to money-getting, the respect paid to wealth is so pervadingly diffused, that it rarely occurred to any one, that it was impossible I should feel the slightest interest in the private circumstances of the gentlemen with whom I might chance to form a transient acquaintance. It is far from my intention, however, to assert, that many of the travelled and more intelligent order of Americans could be guilty of such *sottises* as that to which I have alluded. But it is unquestionably true, that the tone of conversation, even in the best circles, is materially lowered by the degree in which it is engrossed by money and its various interests. Since my arrival, I have received much involuntary instruction in the prices of corn, cotton, and tobacco. I am already well informed as to the reputed pecuniary resources of every gentleman of my acquaintance, and the annual amount of his disbursements. My stock of information as to bankruptcies and dividends is very respectable; and if the manufacturers of Glasgow and Paisley knew only half as well as I do, how thoroughly the New York market is glutted with their goods, they assuredly would send out no more on speculation.

The usual dinner hour at New York is three o'clock, and as the gentlemen almost uniformly return to the discharge of business in the evening, it may be presumed that dinner parties are neither convenient to the entertainer nor the guests. Though not uncommon, therefore, they are certainly less frequent than among individuals of the same class in England. This circumstance has, perhaps, wrought some change in their character, and deprived them of that appearance of easy and habitual hospitality, for the absence of which, additional splendour or profusion can afford but imperfect compensation. When a dinner party is given in this country, it is always on a great scale. Earth, and air, and ocean, are ransacked for their products. The whole habits of the family are deranged. The usual period of the meal is postponed for several hours; and considering the materials of which an American *ménage* is composed, it is not difficult to conceive the bustle and confusion participated by each member of the establishment, from Peter, the saffron-coloured groom of the chambers, to Silvia, the black kitchen wench.

In the ordinary routine, therefore, of American intercourse, visiting seldom commences till the evening, when the wealthier members of the community almost uniformly open their houses for the reception of company. Of this hospitable arrangement I have frequently taken advantage. On such occasions little ceremony is observed. Each guest enters and departs when he thinks proper, without apology or explanation. Music and conversation are the usual entertainments—some slight refection is handed round, and before midnight the party has broken up.

This facility of intercourse is both pleasant and convenient to a stranger like myself. It affords valuable opportunities for the observation of manners; and it is pleasing to be admitted within the charmed circle, which many of my predecessors have found it difficult, if not impossible, to overpass.

The formalities of a New York dinner do not differ much from those of an English one. Unfortunately, it is not here the fashion to invite the fairer part of creation to entertainments so gross and substantial, and it rarely happens that any ladies are present on such occasions, except those belonging to the family of the host. The party, however, is always enlivened by their presence at the tea-table, and then comes music, and perhaps dancing, while those who, like myself, are disqualified for active participation in such festivities, talk with an air of grave authority, of revolutions in Europe, the prospects of war or peace, Parliamentary Reform, and other high and interesting matters.

Before dinner, the conversation of the company assembled in the drawing-room is here, as elsewhere, generally languid enough; but a change suddenly comes over the spirit of their dream: The folding-doors which communicate with the dining-room are thrown open, and all paradise is at once let in on the soul of a gourmand. The table, instead of displaying, as with us, a mere beggarly account of fish and soup, exhibits an array of dishes closely wedged in triple column, which it would require at least an acre of mahogany to deploy into line. Plate, it is true, does not contribute much to the splendour of the prospect, but there is quite enough for comfort, though not perhaps for display. The lady of the mansion is handed in form to her seat, and the entertainment begins. The domestics, black, white, snuff-coloured, and nankeen, are in motion; plates vanish and appear again as if by magic; turtle, cold-blooded by nature, has become hot as Sir Charles Wetherell, and certainly never moved so rapidly before. The flight of ham and turkey is unceasing; venison bounds from one end of the table to the other, with a velocity never exceeded in its native forest; and the energies of twenty human beings are all evidently concentrated in one common occupation.

During soup and fish, and perhaps the first slice of the haunch, conversation languishes, but a glass or two of Champagne soon operates as a corrective. The eyes of the young ladies become more brilliant, and those of elderly gentlemen acquire a certain benevolent twinkle, which indicates, that for the time being they are in charity with themselves and all mankind.

At length the first course is removed, and is succeeded by a whole wilderness of sweets. This, too, passes, for it is impossible, alas! to eat for ever. Then come cheese and the dessert; then the departure of the ladies; and Claret and Madeira for an hour or twain are unquestioned lords of the ascendant.

The latter is almost uniformly excellent. I have never drank any Madeira in Europe at alle qualling what I have frequently met in the United States. *Gourmets* attribute this superiority partly to climate, but in a great measure to management. Madeira, in this country, is never kept as with us, in a subterranean vault, where the temperature throughout the year is nearly equal. It is placed in the attics, where it is exposed to the whole fervour of the summer's heat, and the severity of winter's cold. The effect on the flavour of the wine is certainly remarkable.

The Claret is generally good, but not better than in England; Port is used by the natives only as a medicine, and is rarely produced at table except in compliment to some English stranger, it being a settled canon, here as elsewhere, that every Englishman drinks Port. I have never yet seen fine Sherry, probably because that wine has not yet risen into esteem in the United States.

The gentlemen in America pique themselves on their discrimination in wine, in a degree which is not common in England. The ladies have no sooner risen from table, then the business of winebibbing commences in good earnest. The servants still remain in the apartment, and supply fresh glasses to the guests as the successive bottles make their appearance. To each of these a history is attached, and the vintage, the date of importation, &c., are all duly detailed; then come the criticisms of the company, and as each bottle produced contains wine of a different quality from its predecessor, there is no chance of the topic being exhausted. At length, having made the complete tour of the cellar, proceeding progressively from the commoner wines to those of finest flavour, the party adjourns to the drawing-room, and, after coffee, each guest takes his departure without ceremony of any kind.

It would be most ungrateful were I not to declare, that I have frequently found these dinner parties extremely pleasant. I admit that there is a plainness and even bluntness in American manners, somewhat startling at first to a sophisticated European. Questions are asked with regard to one's habits, family, pursuits, connexions, and opinions, which are never put in England, except in a witness box, after the ceremony of swearing on the four Evangelists. But this is done with the most perfect *bonhommie*, and evidently without the smallest conception, that such examination can possibly be offensive to the patient. It is scarcely fair to judge one nation by the conventional standard of another; and travellers who are tolerable enough of the peculiarities of their continental neighbours, ought in justice, perhaps, to make more allowance than they have yet done, for those of Brother Jonathan. Such questions, no doubt, would be sheer impertinence in an Englishman, because, in putting them, he could not but be aware, that he was violating the established courtesies of society. They are not so in an American, because he has been brought up with different ideas, and under a social *regime* more tolerant of individual curiosity, than is held in Europe to be compatible with good manners. Yet, after all, it must be owned, that it is not always pleasant, to feel yourself the object of a scrutiny, often somewhat coarsely conducted, and generally too apparent to be mistaken. I do assert, however, that in noo ther country I have ever visited, are the charities of life so readily and so profusely opened to a stranger as in the United States. In no other country will he receive attentions so perfectly disinterested and benevolent; and in none, when he seeks acquaintances, is it so probable that he will find friends.

It has been often said,—indeed said so often as to have passed into a popular apophthegm, that a strong prejudice against Englishmen exists in America. Looking back on the whole course of my experience in that country, I now declare, that no assertion more utterly adverse to truth, was ever palmed by prejudice or ignorance, on vulgar credulity. That a prejudice exists, I admit, but instead of being *against* Englishmen, as compared with the natives of other countries, it is a prejudice in *their favour*. The Americans do not weigh the merits of their foreign visitors in an equal balance. They are only too apt to throw their own partialities into the scale of the Englishman, and give it a preponderance to which the claims of the individual have probably no pretensions.

I beg, however, to be understood. Of the vast multitude of English whom the extensive commercial intercourse between the countries draws to the United States, few, indeed, are persons of liberal acquirement, or who have been accustomed to mix in good society in their own country. Coming to the United States on the pursuits of business, they are, of course, left to the attentions of those gentlemen with whom their professional relations bring them more particularly in contact. Admitting, for argument's sake, that all those persons were entirely unexceptionable both in manners and morals, their mere number, which is very great, would, in itself, operate as an exclusion. That they are hospitably received, I have no doubt, nor have I any that they meet with every attention and facility which commercial men can expect in a commercial community.

But when an English gentleman, actuated by motives of liberal curiosity, visits their country, he is received in a different manner, and with very different feeling. Once assured of his respectability, he is admitted freely into society, and I again assert that he will meet a benevolent interest in promoting his views, which a traveller may in vain look for in other countries. I should be wrong in saying, however, that all this takes place without some scrutiny. Of whatever solecisms of deportment they are themselves guilty, the Americans are admirable, and, perhaps, not very lenient, judges of manners in others. They are quite aware of high breeding when they see it, and draw conclusions with regard to the pretensions of their guests from a thousand small circumstances apparent only to very acute observation. With them vulgar audacity will not pass for polished ease; nor will fashionable exterior be received for more than it is worth. I know of no country in which an impostor would have a more difficult game to play in the prosecution of his craft, and should consider him an accomplished deceiver, were he able to escape detection amid observation so vigilant and acute.

In admitting that the standard of manners in the United States is somewhat lower than in England, I wish to be understood as speaking exclusively of the higher circles in the latter country. I am not aware, that bating a few peculiarities, the manners of the first-rate merchants of New York, are at all inferior to those either of Liverpool or any other of our great commercial cities. I am certain that they are not inferior to any merchants in the world, in extent of practical information, in liberality of sentiment, and generosity of character. Most of them have been in England, and from actual observation have formed notions of our national character and advantages, very different from the crude and ignorant opinions, which, I must say, are entertained by the great body of their countrymen. Were it admissible to form general conclusions of the American character, from that of the best circle in the greater Atlantic cities of the Union, the estimate would be high indeed.

Unfortunately, however, the conclusions drawn from premises so narrow, would be sadly erroneous. The observations already made are applicable only to a very small portion of the population, composed almost entirely of the first-rate merchants and lawyers. Beyond that, there is a sad change for the worse. Neither in the manners nor in the morals of the great body of traders, is there much to draw approbation from an impartial observer. Comparing them with the same classes in England, one cannot but be struck with a certain resolute and obtrusive cupidity of gain, and a laxity of principle as to the means of acquiring it, which I should be sorry to believe formed any part of the character of my countrymen. I have heard conduct praised in conversation at a public table, which in England would be attended, if not with a voyage to Botany Bay, at least with total loss of character. It is impossible to pass an hour in the bar of the hotel, without being struck with the tone of callous selfishness which pervades the conversation, and the absence of all pretension to pure and lofty principle. The only restraint upon these men is the law, and he is evidently considered the most skilful in his vocation, who contrives to overreach his neighbour, without incurring its penalties.

It may probably be urged, that in drawing these harsh conclusions, I judge ignorantly, since, having no professional connexion with trade or traders, I cannot be supposed to know from experience any thing of the actual character of their commercial transactions. To this I reply, that my judgment has been formed on much higher grounds than the experience of any individual could possibly afford. If I am cheated in an affair of business, I can appeal but to a single case of fraud. I can only assert, that a circumstance has happened in America, which might have happened in any country of Europe. But when a man publicly confesses an act of fraud, or applauds it in another, two conclusions are fairly deducible. First, that the narrator is a person of little principle; and, second, that he believes his audience to be no better than himself. Assuredly, no man will confess any thing, which he imagines may, by possibility, expose him to contempt; and the legitimate deduction from such details extends not only to the narrator of the anecdote, but to the company who received it without sign of moral indignation.

It may be well, however, to explain, that the preceding observations have not been founded exclusively on the population of New York. The company in a hotel, is generally composed of persons from all States in the Union ; and it may be, that the standard of probity is somewhat higher in this opulent and commercial city, than in the poorer and more remote settlements. For the last three weeks I have been daily thrown into the company of about an hundred individuals, fortuitously collected. A considerable portion of these are daily changing, and it is perhaps not too much to assume that, as a whole, they afford a fair average specimen of their class. Without, therefore, wishing to lead the reader to any hasty or exaggerated conclusion, I must in candour state, that the result of my observations has been to lower considerably the high estimate I had formed of the moral character of the American people.

Though I have unquestionably met in New York with many most intelligent and accomplished gentlemen, still I think the fact cannot be denied, that the average of acquirement resulting from education is a good deal lower in this country than in the better circles of England. In all the knowledge which must be taught, and which requires laborious study for its attainment, I should say the Americans are considerably inferior to my countrymen. In that knowledge, on the other hand, which the individual acquires for himself by actual observation, which bears an immediate marketable value, and is directly available in the ordinary avocations of life, I do not imagine the Americans are excelled by any people in the world. They are consequently better fitted for analytic than synthetic reasoning. In the former process they are frequently successful. In the latter, their failure sometimes approaches to the ludicrous.

Another result of this condition of intelligence is, that the tone even of the best conversation is pitched in a lower key than in England. The speakers evidently presume on an inferior degree of acquirement in their audience, and frequently deem it necessary to advance deliberate proof of matters, which in the old country would be taken for granted. There is certainly less of what may be called floating intellect in conversation. First principles are laboriously established, and long trains of reasoning terminate, not in paradox, but in commonplace. In short, whatever it is the obvious and immediate interest of Americans to know, is fully understood. Whatever is available rather in the general elevation of the intellect, than in the promotion of individual ambition, engrosses but a small share of the public attention.

In the United States one is struck with the fact, that there exist certain doctrines and opinions which have descended like heirlooms from generation to generation, and seem to form the subject of a sort of national entail, most felicitously contrived to check the natural tendency to intellectual advancement in the inheritors. The sons succeed to these opinions of their father, precisely as they do to his silver salvers, or gold-headed cane; and thus do certain dogmas, political and religious, gradually acquire a sort of prescriptive authority, and continue to be handed down, unsubjected to the test of philosophical examination. It is at least partially attributable to this cause, that the Americans are given to deal somewhat too extensively in broad and sweeping aphorisms. The most difficult problems of legislation are here treated as matters on which it were an insult on the understanding of a schoolboy, to suppose that he could entertain a doubt. Enquire their reasons for the inbred faith, of which they are the dark though vehement apostles, and you get nothing but a few shallow truisms, which absolutely afford no footing for the conclusions they are brought forward to establish. The Americans seem to imagine themselves imbued with the power of *feeling* truth, or, rather, of getting at it by intuition, for by no other process can I yet discover that they attempt its attainment. With the commoner and more vulgar truths, indeed, I should almost pronounce them too plentifully stocked, since in these, they seem to imagine, is contained the whole valuable essence of human knowledge. It is unquestionable, that this character of mind is most unfavourable to national advancement; yet it is too prominent not to find a place among the features which distinguish the American intellect from that of any other people with whom it has been my fortune to become acquainted.

To-morrow it is my intention to proceed to Boston; I shall leave the public establishments, &c.

of New York unvisited till my return; being anxious, during the first period of my residence, to confine my attention to the more prominent and general features which distinguish this interesting community.

CHAPTER VI.

VOYAGE—PROVIDENCE—BOSTON.

At four o'clock, P.M. on the 8th of December, I embarked on board the steam-boat Chancellor Livingstone, and in a few minutes the vessel was under weigh. Her course lay up the East River, and along the channel which divides Long Island from the mainland. I had heard much of a certain dangerous strait, called Hell Gate, formed by the projection of huge masses of rock, which obstruct the passage of the river, and diverting the natural course of the current, send its waters spinning round in formidable eddies and whirlpools. At high water—as it happened to be when we passed it—this said portal had no very frightful aspect. The stream was rapid, to be sure, but a double engine of ninety horse power was more than a match for it; and the Chancellor, in spite of its terrors, held on his course rejoicing, with little apparent diminution of velocity. Vessels, however, have been wrecked here, and a canal is spoken of, by which its dangers may be avoided.

The accommodations on board were such, as to leave the most querulous traveller no excuse for grumbling. The cabin, to be sure, with two huge red-hot stoves in it, was of a temperature which a salamander must have admired exceedingly, but the atmosphere, composed of the discarded breath of about an hundred passengers, still retained a sufficient portion of oxygen to support life. The hour of tea came, and all the appetite on board was mustered on the occasion. The meal passed speedily as heart could desire; but the mingled odour of fish, onions, and grease, was somewhat more permanent. Whether it improved the atmosphere, or not, is a point which I could not settle to my own satisfaction at the time, and must now, I fear, remain for ever undecided.

It was impossible, in such circumstances, to think of bed. The very thought of blankets was distressing. I had no book; and as for conversation, I could hear none in which I was at all qualified to bear a part. I therefore ordered my writing-box, adjusted a new Bramah, and of the words that flowed from it, he that has read the preceding pages is already in possession.

If I wrote in bad humour there was really some excuse for it. Close to my right were two loud polemics, engaged in fierce dispute on the Tariff bill. On my left was an elderly gentleman, without shoes or slippers, whose cough and expectoration were somewhat less melodious than the music of the spheres. In the berth immediately behind, lay a passenger, whose loud snoring proclaimed him as happy as a complete oblivion of all worldly cares could make him. Right opposite was a gentleman without breeches, who, before jumping into bed, was detailing to a friend the particulars of a lucky hit he had just made in a speculation in train oil. And beside me, at the table, sat a Baptist clergyman, reading, *sotto voce*, a chapter of Ezekiel, and casting, at the conclusion of each verse, a glance of furtive curiosity at my paper.

It may be admitted, that such are not the items which go to the compounding of a paradise. But the enjoyment of travelling, like other pleasures, must be purchased at some little expense; and he whose good-humour can be ruffled by every petty inconvenience he may chance to encounter, had unquestionably better remain at home. For myself, I beg it therefore to be understood, that in detailing the petty and transient annoyances connected with my journey, I do so, not as matters by which my tranquillity was materially affected, but as delineations naturally belonging to a picture of society, and without which it would be incomplete. A tourist in the United States, will find no occasion for the ardour, the perseverance, or the iron constitution of a Lander; and yet he will do well to remember, that travellers, like players at bowls, must occasionally expect rubbers.

But I have dwelt too much on the disagreeables of the voyage, without giving the *per contra* side of the account. There was a fair breeze and a smooth sea; and an Irish steward, who was particularly active in my behalf, and made my berth very comfortable, by the fraudulent abstraction of sundry pillows from those of my American neighbours. This he has done—he told my servant so—because I am from the old country; and yet one would suppose, that on such a man the claim of mere national affinity could have little influence. I talked a good deal with him about his former circumstances, and soon collected, that what is called *living* in Ireland, is usually entitled *starving* in other countries. Though rather chary of confession, I gathered, too, that the world was not his friend, nor the world's laws, and that he came to the United States to avoid a gaol, and without a shilling in his pocket. The day on which he left Ireland should be marked in his annals with a white stone. He now enjoys a comfortable situation—confesses he can save money; eats and drinks well; is encased in warm clothing; is troubled very little with the tax-gatherer, and not at all with the tithe-proctor. And what is there in the countenance of an Englishman, that it should excite in such a man the feeling of benevolence and kindred? In his memory, one would suppose, the past would be linked only with suffering, while the present is undoubtedly associated with the experience of a thousand comforts, to which, in his days of vassalage and white-boyism, his imagination never ventured to soar. Yet, believe the man, and he regrets having left home! He thinks he could have done as well in Ireland. He has no fault to find with America—it is a good country, enough for a poor man. Whisky is cheaper here, and so is bread and *mate;* but then his *ould* mother,—and his sisters,—and Tim Regan, he would like to see them again; and, please God, if he ever can afford it, he will return, and have his bones laid in the same churchyard with theirs.

But if Pat ever get back to Ireland, I venture to prophesy that his stay will not be long there. At present, his former privations are more than half-forgotten; but let him once again encounter them, and the difference between the country of his birth and that of his adoption, will become more apparent than argument could now make it. On the whole, it was pleasing to observe, that while time and distance obliterate the misfortunes of life, their tendency is to strengthen its charities.

On the following morning, about eleven o'clock,

we reached Providence, and found eight or ten stage-coaches waiting on the quay to convey the passengers to Boston. Though I carried letters of introduction to several gentlemen in Providence, it had not been my intention to remain there, and I had accordingly, before landing, secured places in one of these vehicles. But in the hurry and bustle of scrambling for seats and coaches, and with the sight of eight large human beings already cooped up in that by which I must have travelled, I began to waver in my resolution, and at length resolved to sacrifice the money I had paid, and take the chances of better accommodation, and a more agreeable party, on the day following. Besides, the weather was raw and gusty, and I had been drenched from the knee downward in wading through the masses of half-melted snow, which covered the landing-place. The idea, therefore, of a comfortable Providence hotel, naturally found more favour in my imagination, than an eight hours' journey to Boston, in such weather, such company, and such conveyance as I could reasonably anticipate.

On reaching the hostelry, however, its external appearance was far from captivating. There was no sign-board, nor did the house display any external symbol of the hospitality within. Below was a range of shops, and the only approach was by a narrow stair, which might have passed for clean in Rome, but would have been considered dirty in England. On entering, I stood for some time in the passage, and though I enquired at several members of the establishment, who brushed past me, whether I could have accommodation, no answer was vouchsafed. At length, advancing to the bar, I observed the landlord, who was evidently too busily engaged in mixing brandy and water for a party of smokers, to have any attention to bestow on a stranger like myself. I, therefore, addressed a woman whom I observed to look towards me with something of cold enquiry in her expression, and again begged to know whether I could be accommodated for the night. The question was not more fortunate than its predecessors in drawing forth a response, nor was it till some minutes had elapsed, that, during a fortunate intermission of the demand for spirits, my enquiries were at length attended to, and satisfactorily answered.

Matters now went on more promisingly. I found that I could not only be supplied, with every thing within the scope of reasonable expectation, but with a luxury I had not ventured to anticipate,—a private parlour, communicating with a very comfortable bed-room, and accompanied with the privilege of commanding my own hours.

Having changed my dress, and given a few directions about dinner, I sallied forth to view the city. Providence is the capital of the State of Rhode Island, and contains about 25,000 inhabitants. It stands at the foot and on the brow of a hill, which commands a complete view of the fine bay. The great majority of the houses are built of wood, interspersed, however, with tenements of brick, and a few which are at least fronted with stone. It contains considerable cotton manufactories, which—boasting no knowledge of such matters—I was not tempted to visit. The college appears a building of some extent, and is finely situated on the summit of a neighbouring height. The roads were so obstructed by snow, as to render climbing the ascent a matter of more difficulty than I was in the humour to encounter; and so it was decreed, that Brown's College should remain by me unvisited.

The first settlement of Providence is connected with a melancholy instance of human inconsistency. The Pilgrim Fathers, as they are called, had left their country, to find in the wilds of the New World that religious toleration which had been denied them in the Old. But no sooner had these victims of persecution established themselves in New England, than, in direct and flagrant violation, not only of all moral consistency, but of the whole scope and spirit of the Christian religion, they became *persecutors* in their turn. Socinians and Quakers,—all, in short, who differed from them in opinion, were driven forth with outrage and violence. Among the number was Roger Williams, a Puritan clergyman, who ventured to expose what he considered "evidence of backsliding" in the churches of Massachusetts. The clergy at first endeavoured to put him down by argument and remonstrance; the attempt failed, and it was then determined that the civil authority should free the orthodox population from the dangerous presence of so able and sturdy a polemic. Roger Williams was banished, and, followed by a few of his people, continued to wander in the wilderness, till, coming to a place called by the Indians Mooshausic, he there pitched his tabernacle, and named it Providence.

Such are a few of the circumstances connected with the first establishment of the State of Rhode Island. The light in which they exhibit human nature is not flattering; yet they only afford another proof, if such were wanted, of the natural connexion between bigotry and persecution, and that the victims of political or religious oppression, too often want only the power to become its ministers.

The only building which makes any pretension to architectural display is the arcade, faced at either extremity with an Ionic portico. Judging by the eye, the shaft of the columns is in the proportion of the Grecian Doric, an order beautiful in itself, but which, of course, is utterly barbarized by an Ionic entablature. By the way, I know not any thing in which the absence of taste in America is more signally displayed than in their architecture. The country residences of the wealthier citizens are generally adorned with pillars, which often extend from the basement to the very top of the house, (some three or four stories,) supporting, and pretending to support, nothing. The consequence is, that the proportions of these columns are very much those of the stalk of a tobacco-pipe, and it is difficult to conceive any thing more unsightly. Even in the public buildings, there is often an obtrusive disregard of every recognised principle of proportion, and clamorous demands are made on the admiration of foreigners, in behalf of buildings which it is impossible to look upon without instant and unhesitating condemnation.

In a seaport one generally takes a glance at the harbour, to draw some conclusions, however uncertain, with regard to the traffic of the place. The guide-books declare, that Providence has a good deal of foreign commerce. It may be so, but in the bay I could only count two square-rigged vessels, and something under a score of sloops and schooners.

I must not forget to mention, having witnessed to-day the progress of an operation somewhat singular in character. This was nothing less than raising a large tenement, for the purpose of introducing another story below. The building was of frame-work, with chimneys of brick, and consisted of two houses connected by the gable. The lower part of one was occupied as a warehouse, which seemed well filled with casks and cotton-bags. I stood for some time to observe the progress of the work. The process adopted was this: The building was first raised by means of a succession of wedges inserted below the foundation. Having thus gained the requisite elevation, it was maintained there by supports at each corner, and by means of screws pressing laterally on the timbers. At the time I saw it, the building had been raised about five feet into the air, and the only mode of ingress or egress was by ladders. On looking with some curiosity at the windows, I soon gathered enough to convince me that the inhabitants were engaged in their usual domestic avocations, without being at all disturbed by their novel position in the atmosphere. As for the warehouse, the business of buying and selling had apparently encountered no interruption. On the whole, the operation, though simple, struck me as displaying a very considerable degree of mechanical ingenuity.

Having finished my ramble, I returned to the inn, where a very tolerable dinner awaited my appearance. It was the first time I had dined alone since leaving England, and, like my countrymen generally, I am disposed to attach considerable importance to the privilege of choosing my dinner, and the hour of eating it. It is only when alone that one enjoys the satisfaction of feeling that he is a distinct unit in creation, a being *totus, teres, atque rotundus.* At a public ordinary he is but a fraction, a decimal at most, but very probably a centesimal of a huge masticating monster, with the appetite of a Mastodon or a Behemoth. He labours under the conviction, that his meal has lost in dignity what it has gained in profusion. He is consorted involuntarily with people to whom he is bound by no tie but that of temporary necessity, and with whom, except the immediate impulse of brutal appetite, he has probably nothing in common. A man, like an American, thus diurnally mortified and abased from his youth upwards, of course knows nothing of the high thoughts which visit the imagination of the solitary, who, having finished a good dinner, reposes with a full consciousness of the dignity of his nature, and the high destinies to which he is called. The situation is one which naturally stimulates the whole inert mass of his speculative benevolence. He is at peace with all mankind, for he reclines on a well-stuffed sofa, and there are wine and walnuts on the table. He is on the best terms with himself, and recalls his own achievements in arms, literature, or philosophy, in a spirit of the most benign complacency. If he look to the future, the prospect is bright and unclouded. If he revert to the past, its "written troubles," its failures and misfortunes, are erased from the volume, and his memories are exclusively those of gratified power. He is in his slippers, and comfortable *robe-de-chambre*, and what to him, at such a moment, are the world and its ambitions? I appeal to the philosopher, and he answers—Nothing!

It was in such condition of enjoyment, physical and intellectual, that I was interrupted by the entrance of my servant, to inform me that he had just met Captain Bennet on the stair, who, learning that I was at dinner, had obligingly expressed his intention of favouring me with a visit at the conclusion of my meal. I immediately returned assurance, that nothing could afford me greater pleasure; and in a few minutes I had the satisfaction of exchanging a friendly grasp with this kind and intelligent sailor. In the course of our *tête-à-tête*, he informed me that he was travelling from his native town, New Bedford, to Boston, in company with Mrs Bennet, to whom he was good enough to offer me the privilege of an introduction. I accordingly accompanied the Captain to his apartment, where I passed a pleasant evening, and retired, gratified by the intelligence that they were to proceed on the following morning by the same vehicle in which I had already secured places. To travel with Captain Bennet was, in truth, not only a pleasure, but an advantage, for being a New Englander, he was enabled, in the course of our journey, to communicate many particulars with regard to his native province, which, though most useful in directing the opinions of a traveller, could scarcely, perhaps, have fallen within the immediate sphere of his observations.

On the following morning we were afoot betimes, and after a tolerable breakfast at a most unchristian hour, left Providence at seven o'clock, and I enjoyed my first introduction to an American stage-coach. Though what an Englishman accustomed to the luxuries of "light-post coaches," and Macadamised roads, might not unreasonably consider a wretched vehicle, the one in question was not so utterly abominable as to leave a Frenchman or an Italian any fair cause of complaint. It was of ponderous proportions, built with timbers, I should think about the size of those of an ordinary waggon, and was attached by enormous straps to certain massive irons, which nothing in the motion of the carriage could induce the traveller to mistake for *springs*. The sides of this carriage were simply curtains of leather, which, when the heat of the weather is inconvenient, can be raised to admit a freer ventilation. In winter, however, the advantages of this contrivance are more than apocryphal. The wind penetrates through an hundred small crevices, and with the thermometer below zero, this freedom of circulation is found not to add materially to the pleasures of a journey. The complement of passengers inside was nine, divided into three rows, the middle seat being furnished with a strap, removable at pleasure, as a back support to the sitters. The driver also receives a companion on the box, and the charge for this place is the same as for those in the interior. The whole machine indeed was exceedingly clumsy, yet perhaps not more so, than was rendered necessary by the barbarous condition of the road on which it travelled. The horses, though not handsome, were strong, and apparently well adapted for their work, yet I could not help smiling, as I thought of the impression the whole *set out* would be likely to produce on an English road. The flight of an air balloon would create far less sensation. If exhibited as a specimen of a fossil carriage, buried since the Deluge, and lately discovered by Professor Buckland, it might pass without question as the family-coach in which Noah conveyed his establishment to the ark. Then the Jehu! A man in rusty black, with the appearance of a retired grave-digger. Never was such a coachman seen within the limits of the four seas.

Though the distance is only forty miles, we were eight hours in getting to Boston. The road, I remember to have set down at the time, as the very worst in the world, an opinion, which my subsequent experience as a traveller in the United States, has long since induced me to retract. It abounded in deep ruts, and huge stones which a little exercise of the hammer might have converted into excellent material. English readers may smile when one talks seriously of the punishment of being jolted in a stage-coach, but to arrive at the end of a journey with bruised flesh and aching bones, is, on the whole, not particularly pleasant. For myself, I can truly say, that remembering all I have occasionally endured in the matter of locomotion on the American continent, the martyr to similar sufferings shall always enjoy my sincere sympathy. On the present occasion, to say nothing of lateral concussion, twenty times at least was I pitched up with violence against the roof of the coach, which, being as ill provided with stuffing as the cushions below, occasioned a few changes in my phrenological developements. One of the passengers, however,—a grave valetudinarian—assured me, that such unpleasant exercise was an admirable cure for dyspepsy, and that when suffering under its attacks, he found an unfailing remedy in being jolted over some forty or fifty miles of such roads as that we now travelled. At the moment, I certainly felt more inclined to pity him for the remedy than the disease.

There had been thaw during the night, and the greater part of the snow had disappeared. The country through which we passed was prettily varied in surface, but the soil was poor and stony, and the extent to which wood had been suffered to grow on land formerly subjected to the plough, showed it had not been found to repay the cost of tillage. About four miles from Providence, we passed the village of Pawtucket. It is one of the chief seats of the cotton manufacture in the United States. The aspect of the place was not unpleasing, and I counted about a dozen factories of considerable size. The houses of the workmen had a clean and comfortable appearance. I was informed, however, by my fellow-travellers, that, within the last eighteen months, every establishment in the place had become bankrupt; a proof, I should imagine, that the success of the Tariff system has not been very brilliant.

During our journey there was a good deal of conversation in the coach, in which, I was physically too uneasy to bear any considerable part. I was amused, however, at the astonishment of a young Connecticut farmer, when Captain Bennet informed him, that in England, the white birch-tree—which, in this part of the world, is regarded as a noxious weed—is protected in artificial plantations with great care. He was evidently incredulous, though he had before made no difficulty in believing the numerous absurdities, in law, polity, and manners attributed, whether with truth or otherwise, to my countrymen. But to plant the white birch-tree! This, indeed, was beyond the limits of belief.

The road, as we approached Boston, lay through a more populous country, and we passed a height, which commanded a fine view of the bay. At length, entering on a long street, I found myself again surrounded by the busy hum of a great city. The first impression was decidedly favourable. There is in Boston less of that rawness of outline, and inconsistency of architecture, which had struck me in New York. The truth is, that the latter has increased so rapidly, that nine-tenths of the city have been built within the last thirty years, and probably one half of it within a third of the period. In Boston, both wealth and population have advanced at a slower pace. A comparatively small portion of the city is new, and the hand of time has somewhat mellowed even its deformities, contributing to render that reverend which was originally rude.

There is an air of gravity and solidity about Boston; and nothing gay or flashy, in the appearance of her streets, or the crowd who frequent them. New York is a young giantess, weighing twenty stone, and yet frisky withal. Boston, a matron of stayed and demure air, a little past her prime perhaps, yet showing no symptom of decay. The former is brisk, bustling, and annually outgrowing her petticoats. The latter, fat, fair, and forty, a great breeder, but turning her children out of doors, as fast as she produces them. But it is an old and true apophthegm, that similes seldom run on all fours, and therefore it is generally prudent not to push them too far.

Most gratifying is it to a traveller in the United States, when, sick to death of the discomforts of the road, he finds himself fairly housed in the Tremont Hotel. The establishment is on a large scale, and admirably conducted. I had no difficulty in procuring a small but very comfortable suite of apartments, deficient in nothing which a single gentleman could require. What is more, I enjoyed the blessing of rational liberty, had command of my own hours and motions, in short, could eat, drink, or sleep, at what time, in what manner, and on what substances I might prefer.

The truth is, that instead of being free, a large proportion of the American people live in a state of the most degrading bondage. No liberty of tongue can compensate for vassalage of stomach. In their own houses, perhaps, they may do as they please, though I much doubt whether any servants would consent to live in a family who adopted the barbarous innovation of dining at six o'clock, and breakfasting at eleven. But on the road, and in their hotels, they are assuredly any thing but freemen. Their hours of rest and refection are there dictated by Boniface, the most rigorous and iron-hearted of despots. And surely never was monarch blessed with more patient and obedient subjects! He feeds them in droves like cattle. He rings a bell, and they come like dogs at their master's whistle. He places before them what he thinks proper, and they swallow it without grumbling. His decrees are as those of fate, and the motto of his establishment is, "Submit or starve."

No man should travel in the United States without one of Baraud's best chronometers in his fob. In no other country can a slight miscalculation of time be productive of so much mischief. Woe to him whose steps have been delayed by pleasure or business, till the fatal hour has elapsed, and the dinner-cloth been removed. If he calculate on the emanation from the kitchen of smoking chop or spatchcock, he will be grievously deceived. Let him not look with contempt on half-coagulated soup, or fragments of cold fish, or the rhomboid of greasy pork, which has been reclaimed from the stock-barrel for his behoof. Let him accept in meekness what is set before him, or be content to go dinnerless for the day. Such are the horns of the dilemma, and he is free as air to choose on which he will be impaled.*

On the morning following my arrival, I despatched my letters of introduction, and walked out to see the city. Of its appearance, I have already said something, but have yet a little more to say. Boston stands on an undulating surface, and is surrounded

* It is fair, however, to state, that in the hotels in the greater cities, private apartments can generally be obtained. The charge for these is about as high as in London, and the privilege of separate meals is also to be paid for. To give the reader some idea of the expense of such mode of living in the United States, I may state, that in New York, with nothing but an inferior bedroom, and living at the public table, the charge for myself and servant was eighteen dollars a-week. At Boston, with three excellent rooms, and the privilege of private meals, it amounted, including every thing except wine, to thirty-five. At Philadelphia, I paid twenty-six dollars; at Baltimore, twenty-eight; at Washington, forty; the extent of accommodation nearly equal in all.

It is the invariable custom in the United States to charge by the day or week; and travellers are thus obliged to pay for meals whether they eat them or not. For a person who, like myself, rarely dined at home, I remember calculating the charge to be higher than in Long's, or the Clarendon.

on three sides by the sea. The harbour is a magnificent basin, encircled by a beautiful country, rising in gentle acclivities, and studded with villas. There is nothing very handsome about the town, which is rather English in appearance, and might in truth be easily mistaken for one of our more populous seaports. A considerable number of the buildings are of granite, or, more properly speaking, of sienite, but brick is the prevailing material, and houses of framework are now rarely to be met with in the streets inhabited by the better orders. The streets are narrow, and often crooked, yet, as already stated, they exhibit more finish and cleanliness than are to be found in New York. In architecture, I could discover little to admire. The State-house stands on an eminence commanding the city; it is a massive square building, presenting in front a piazza of rusticated arches, surmounted by a gratuitous range of Corinthian columns, which support nothing. The building in front has a small attic with a pediment, and from the centre rises a dome, the summit of which is crowned by a square lantern.

The Tremont hotel, and a church in the same

street, are likewise pointed out to strangers as worthy of all the spare admiration at their disposal. The latter is a plain building, rather absurdly garnished, along its whole front, with a row of Ionic columns, stuck in close to the wall, which they are far from concealing; and, to increase the deformity, above these columns rises a naked square tower, intended, I presume, for a belfry.

An anecdote connected with this place of worship, however, is worth preserving: It was formerly called the King's Chapel, and belonged to a congregation holding the tenets of the Church of England. In this state of things a rich old gentleman died, bequeathing, by his last testament, a considerable sum, to be expended in defraying the charge of a certain number of annual discourses "on the Trinity." The testator having lived and died in the communion of the Church of England, of course no doubt could be entertained of his intention in the bequest; but the revolution took place, and, at the restoration of peace, the congregation of the King's Chapel were found to have cast off both king and creed, and become not only Republicans in politics, but Unitarians in religion. Under these circumstances, what was to be done with the legacy? This did not long remain a moot point. It was discovered that an Unitarian could preach sermons *on* the Trinity as well as the most orthodox Athanasian that ever mounted a pulpit; and the effect of the testator's zeal for the diffusion of pure faith, has been to encourage the dissemination of doctrines, which of course he regarded as false and damnable! The old gentleman had better have left his money to his relations.

I have been too well satisfied with the good living of the Tremont hotel, not to feel grieved to be compelled to speak disparagingly of its architecture. I beg to say, however, that I allude to it only because I have heard its construction gravely praised by men of talent and intelligence, as one of the proudest achievements of American genius. The edifice is of fine sienite, and I imagine few parts of the world can supply a more beautiful material for building. In front is a Doric portico of four columns, accurately proportioned, but, as usual, without pediment. These have not sufficient projection, and seem as if they had been thrust back upon the walls of the building by the force of some gigantic steam-engine. The dining-hall, which is here the chief object of admiration, is defective, both in point of taste and proportion. The ceiling, in the first place, is too low; and then the ranges of Ionic columns, which extend the whole length of the apartment, are mingled with Antæ of the Composite order; thus defacing, by the intermixture of a late Roman barbarism, the purer taste of Greece. But it were mere waste of time and patience to enlarge on such matters.

My letters of introduction soon fructified into a plentiful harvest of visits and invitations. I discerned, or thought I discerned, some difference of manner between the gentlemen of Boston and those of New York. For the first five minutes, perhaps, the former seemed less pleasing, but my opinion in this respect soon changed, and I certainly now class many of my Boston friends, not only among the most liberal and enlightened, but among the most agreeable men, I had the good fortune to encounter in my tour.

My first visit was to a club, not professedly literary, but which numbered among its members many of the most eminent individuals of the State. Nothing could exceed the kindness of my reception. Several gentlemen, on learning my objects in visiting their city, obligingly professed their readiness to promote them by every means in their power, and I soon found that hospitality to strangers was by no means an exclusive attribute of New York.

The day following being Sunday, I attended morning service in one of the Episcopal churches. It was performed with great propriety to a congregation generally composed of the better orders. In the evening I accompanied an amiable family to a church, of which the celebrated Dr Channing is the pastor. The Doctor, I learned, was then at Havannah, where he had accompanied Mrs Channing, whose health required a milder winter climate than that of New England. The tenets of the congregation are Unitarian, and the service is that of the Church of England, with the omission of all expressions which attribute divinity to our Saviour. Yet this, if not asserted, is not denied. It seems to have been the object to establish a service in which all sects and classes of Christians may conscientiously join, and which affirms nothing in regard to those points which afford matter of controversy to Theologians.

Though the intentions of the framers of this service were obviously good, I am not sure that they have been guided by very just or philosophical views of the infirmities of human nature. The great benefit to be derived from public worship, is connected with the feeling of fellowship with those by whom we are surrounded, and that diffusive sentiment of charity and brotherhood, arising from community of faith. In the presence of God it is indeed proper that all minor differences should be forgotten; but when these differences extend beyond a certain limit, and embrace the more sacred points of belief, I can understand no benefit which can arise from the common adoption of a liturgy so mutilated, as to exclude all expression of that faith and those doctrines, which Christians in general regard as the very keystone of their hope. The value of prayer, perhaps, consists less in any influence it can be supposed to have on the decrees of an eternal and immutable Being, than in that which it exercises over the heart and feelings of the worshipper. To exert this influence, it must be felt to be appropriate to our individual wants and necessities. It must not deal in vague generalities, nor petition only for those blessings in which the great body of mankind possess an equal interest. Like material objects, the human feelings become uniformly weakened by extension. We cannot pray for the whole of our species with the same earnestness that we petition for the prosperity of our country, and our supplications in behalf of our family are yet more ardent. There is a gradation of fervour for each link of the chain as it approaches nearer to ourselves, and it is only, perhaps, in imploring mercy for some one individual, that our feelings reach their climax of intensity. I have no faith in the efficacy of a system of devotion founded on the abstract principles of philosophy. The religious worship of mankind must be accommodated to their infirmities. The prayer which is adapted to all sects can evidently express the faith or sentiments of none.

The liturgy was plainly, but effectively, read by the Rev. Mr Greenwood, whom I had the pleasure of ranking among my acquaintance. The sermon was elegant, but somewhat cold and unemphatic. Indeed, how could it be otherwise? An Unitarian is necessarily cut off from all appeals to those deeper sources of feeling, which, in what is called Evangelical preaching, are found to produce such powerful effects. No spirit was ever strongly moved by a discourse on the innate beauty of virtue, or arguments in favour of moral purity drawn from the harmony of the external world. The inference that man should pray, because the trees blossom and the birds sing, is about as little cogent in theory as the experience of mankind has proved it in practice. The *sequitur* would be quite as good, were it asserted that men should wear spectacles because bears eat horse-flesh, and ostriches lay eggs in the sand. But, admitting the conclusion to be clear as the daylight, the disease of human depravity is too strong to be overcome by the administration of such gentle alteratives. Recourse must be had to stronger medicines, and these, unfortunately, the chest of the Unitarian does not furnish.

Boston is the metropolis of Unitarianism. In no

other city has it taken root so deeply, or spread its branches so widely. Fully half of the population, and more than half of the wealth and intelligence of Boston, are found in this communion. I was at one time puzzled to account for this; but my journey to New England has removed the difficulty. The New Englanders are a cold, shrewd, calculating, and ingenious people, of phlegmatic temperament, and perhaps have in their composition less of the stuff of which enthusiasts are made, than any other in the world. In no other part of the globe, not even in Scotland, is morality at so high a premium. Nowhere is undeviating compliance with public opinion so unsparingly enforced. The only lever by which people of this character can be moved, is that of argument. A New Englander is far more a being of reason than of impulse. Talk to him of what is high, generous, and noble, and he will look on you with a vacant countenance. But tell him of what is just, proper, and essential to his own well-being or that of his family, and he is all ear. His faculties are always sharp; his feelings are obtuse.

Unitarianism is the democracy of religion. Its

creed makes fewer demands on the faith or the imagination, than that of any other Christian sect. It appeals to human reason in every step of its progress, and while it narrows the compass of miracle, enlarges that of demonstration. Its followers have less bigotry than other religionists, because they have less enthusiasm. They refuse credence to the doctrine of one grand and universal atonement, and appeal to none of those sudden and preternatural impulses which have given assurance to the pious of other sects. An Unitarian will take nothing for granted but the absolute and plenary efficacy of his own reason in matters of religion. He is not a fanatic, but a dogmatist; one who will admit of no distinction between the incomprehensible and the false.

With such views of the Bostonians and their prevailing religion, I cannot help believing, that there exists a curious felicity of adaptation in both. The prosperity of Unitarianism in the New England States, seems a circumstance, which a philosophical observer of national character, might, with no great difficulty, have predicted. Jonathan chose his religion, as one does a hat, because it fitted him. We believe, however, that his head has not yet attained its full size, and confidently anticipate that its speedy enlargement will erelong induce him to adopt a better and more orthodox covering.

One of my first morning's occupations was to visit Cambridge University, about three miles distant. In this excursion I had the advantage of being accompanied by Professor Ticknor, who obligingly conducted me over every part of the establishment. The buildings, though not extensive, are commodious; and the library—the largest in the United States—contains about 30,000 volumes; no very imposing aggregate. The academical course is completed in four years, at the termination of which the candidates for the degree of Bachelor of Arts are admitted to that honour, after passing the ordeal of examination. In three years more, the degree of Master may—as in the English Universities—be taken as matter of course. There are three terms in the year, the intervals between which amount to about three months. The number of students is somewhat under two hundred and fifty. These have the option of either living *more academico* in the college, or of boarding in houses in the neighbourhood. No religious tenets are taught; but the regnant spirit is unquestionably Unitarian. In extent, in opulence, and in number of students, the establishment is not equal even to the smallest of our Scottish Universities.

On leaving Cambridge, we drove to Bunker's Hill, celebrated as the spot on which the first collision took place between the troops of the mother-country and her rebellious colonists. It is a strong position, and if duly strengthened by intrenchments, might be defended against an enemy of much superior force. On the summit of this height, a monument to the memory of Washington was in progress. A more appropriate site could not have been selected. But tributes of stone or brass are thrown away upon Washington. *Si monumentum quæris, circumspice.*

Our next visit was to the navy-yard, an establishment of considerable extent. There were two seventy-fours on the stocks, and, if I remember rightly, a frigate and a sloop. A dry-dock had nearly been completed of size sufficient to receive the largest line-of-battle ship. Commodore Morris, the commandant, was obligingly communicative, and, in the course even of a short conversation, afforded abundant proof, that his acquirements were very far from being exclusively professional.

On the day following, I went, accompanied by a very kind friend, to see the State-prison at Charleston. The interesting description given by Captain Hall of the prison at Sing-Sing had raised my curiosity, and I felt anxious to inspect an establishment, conducted on the same general principle, and with some improvements in detail. It was difficult to conceive, that a system of discipline so rigid could be maintained, without a degree of severity, revolting to the feelings. That hundreds of men should live together for years in the daily association of labour, under such a rigorous and unbroken system of restraint, as to prevent them during all that period from holding even the most trifling intercourse, seemed a fact so singular, and in such direct opposition to the strongest propensities of human nature, as to require strong evidence to establish its credibility. I was glad to take advantage, therefore, of the first opportunity to visit the prison at Charleston, and the scene there presented, was unquestionably one of the most striking I have ever witnessed. Pleasant it was not, for it cannot be so to witness the degradation and sufferings of one's fellow-creatures.

In no part of the establishment, however, was there any thing squalid or offensive. The gaoler—one expects hard features in such an official—was a man of mild expression, but of square and sinewy frame. He had formerly been skipper of a merchantman, and it was impossible to compliment him on the taste displayed in his change of profession. Before proceeding on the circuit of the prison, he communicated some interesting details in regard to its general management, and the principles on which it was conducted.

The prisoners amounted to nearly three hundred; the keepers were only fourteen. The disparity of force, therefore, was enormous; and as the system adopted was entirely opposed to that of solitary confinement, it did, at first sight, seem strange that the convicts—the greater part of whom were men of the boldest and most abandoned character—should not take advantage of their vast physical superiority, and, by murdering the keepers, regain their liberty. A cheer, a cry, a signal, would be enough; they had weapons in their hands, and it required but a momentary effort of one-tenth of their number, to break the chains of perhaps the most galling bondage to which human beings were ever subjected.

In what then consisted the safety of the goaler and his assistants? In one circumstance alone. In a *surveillance* so strict and unceasing, as to render it physically impossible, by day or night, for the prisoners to hold the slightest communication, without discovery. They set their lives upon this cast. They knew the penalty of the slightest negligence, and they acted like men who knew it.

The buildings enclose a quadrangle of about two hundred feet square. One side is occupied by a building, in which are the cells of the prisoners. It contains three hundred and four solitary cells, built altogether of stone, and arranged in four stories. Each cell is secured by a door of wrought iron. On the sides where the cell-doors present themselves, are stone galleries, three feet wide, supported by cast-iron pillars. These galleries extend the whole length of the building, and encircle three sides of these ranges of cells. The fourth presents only a perpendicular wall, without galleries, stairs, or doors. Below, and exterior to the cells and galleries, runs a passage nine feet broad, from which a complete view of the whole can be commanded.

The cells have each a separate ventilator. They are seven feet long, three feet six inches wide, and contain each an iron bedstead. On one side considerably elevated, is a safety watch-box, with an alarum-bell, at the command only of the gaoler on duty. In front of the building, or rather between the building and the central quadrangle, is the kitchen, communicating, by doors and windows, with a passage, along which the prisoners must necessarily travel in going to, or returning from their cells. Adjoining is a chapel, in which the convicts attend prayers twice a-day.

In regard to the system of discipline enforced in this interesting establishment, it may be better described in other words than my own. The following is an extract from the annual report of the Boston Prison Discipline Society:—"From the locking up at night till daylight, all the convicts, except an average of about five in the hospital, are in the new building, in separate cells, and in cells so arranged, that a sentinel on duty can preserve entire silence among three hundred. The space around the cells being open from the ground to the roof, in front of four stories of cells, in a building two hundred feet in length, furnishes a perfect sounding gallery, in which the sentinel is placed, who can hear a whisper from the most distant cell. He can, therefore, keep silence from the time of locking up at night to the time of unlocking in the morning, which, at some seasons of the year, makes more than one half of all the time, which is thus secured from evil communication. From the time of unlocking in the morning, about twelve minutes are occupied in a military movement of the convicts, in companies of thirty-eight, with an officer to each company, in perfect silence, to their various places of labour. At the end of that period, it is found that there is a place for every man, and every man in his place. This is as true of the officers as of the convicts. If an officer have occasion to leave his place, the system requires that a substitute be called; if a convict have occasion to leave his place, there is a token provided for each shop, or for a given number of men, so that from this shop or number only one convict can leave his place at a time. The consequence is, that with the exception of those who have the tokens in their hands, any officer of the institution may be certain of finding, during the hours of labour, a place for every man, and every man in his place. There is, however, a class of men, consisting of ten or twelve, called *runners* and *lumpers*, whose duty consists in moving about the yard. But even their movements are in silence and order. Consequently, during the hours of labour, the convicts are never seen moving about the yard promiscuously, or assembled in little groups, in some hiding-places of mischief, or even two and two in common conversation. All is order and silence, except the busy noise of industry during the hours of labour.

"The hours of labour in the morning vary a little with the season of the year, but amount at this season to nearly two hours, from the time of unlocking in the morning till breakfast. When the hour for breakfast comes, almost in an instant the convicts are all seen marching in solid and silent columns, with the lock-step, under their respective officers, from the shops to the cells. On their way to the cells they pass the cookery, where the food, having been made ready, is handed to them as they pass along; and at the end of about twelve minutes, from the time of ringing the bell for breakfast, all the convicts are in their cells eating their breakfasts, silently and alone. One officer only is left in charge to preserve silence, and the others are as free from solicitude and care, till the hour for labour returns, as other citizens.

"When the time of labour again returns, which is at the end of about twenty-five minutes, almost in an instant the whole body of convicts are again seen marching as before to their places of labour. On their way to the shops, they pass through the chapel and attend prayers. The time from breakfast till dinner passes away like the time for labour before breakfast, all the convicts being found in their places industriously employed, in silence. The time assigned for dinner is filled up in the same manner as the time assigned for breakfast; and the time for labour in the afternoon in the same manner as the time for labour in the morning; and when the time for evening prayers has come, at the ringing of the bell, all the convicts, and all the officers not on duty elsewhere, are seen marching to the chapel, where the chaplain closes the day with reading the Scriptures and prayer. After which the convicts march with perfect silence and order to their cells, taking their supper as they pass along. In about five-and-twenty minutes from the time of leaving their labour, the convicts have attended prayers in the chapel, taken their supper, marched to their cells with their supper in their hands, and are safely locked up for the night. This is the history of a day at Charleston; and the history of a day is the history of a year, with the variations which are made on the Sabbath, by dispensing with the hours of labour, and substituting the hours for instruction in the Sabbath-School, and the hours for public worship."

We had hardly time to examine the arrangement of the cells when the dinner-bell sounded, and issuing out into the quadrangle, the whole prisoners marched past in imposing military array. In passing the kitchen, each man's dinner was thrust out on a sort of ledge, from which it was taken without any interruption of his progress. In less than two minutes they were in their "deep solitudes and awful cells," and employed in the most agreeable duty of their day—dinner. I again entered the building, to listen for the faintest whisper. None was to be heard; the silence of the desert could not be deeper. In about half an hour another bell rang, and the prisoners were again a-foot. The return to labour differed in nothing from the departure from it; but the noise of saws, axes, and hammers, soon showed they were now differently employed.

The gaoler next conducted us through the workshops. Each trade had a separate apartment. The masons were very numerous; so were the carpenters and coopers. The tailors were employed in making clothes for their companions in misfortune, and the whole establishment had the air rather of a well-conducted manufactory than of a prison. There was nothing of deep gloom, but a good deal of callous indifference generally observable in the countenances of the convicts. In some, however, I thought I did detect evidence of overwhelming depression. Yet this might be imagination, and when I pointed out the individuals to the gaoler, he assured me I was mistaken.

The prisoners are allowed to hold no intercourse of any kind, with the world beyond the walls which enclose them. It is a principle invariably adhered to, that they shall be made to feel, that during their confinement—and many are confined for life—they are beings cut off even from the commonest sympathies of mankind. I know not but that severity in this respect has been carried too far. If they are again to be turned out upon society, is it not injudicious, as it is cruel policy, to trample on the affections even of these depraved and guilty beings, and to send them forth with every tie broken which might have acted as a motive to reformation? What can be expected from men so circumstanced, but that they will renew their former courses, or plunge into guilt yet deeper. On the other hand, if they are to be immured for life, the punishment can be considered little better than a gratuitous barbarity. But the great evil is, that on the utterly abandoned it falls lightly. It is the heart guilty, yet not hardened in guilt, which is still keenly alive to the gentler and purer affections, that it crushes with an oppression truly withering. And can no penalty be discovered more appropriate for the punishment of the sinner, than one which falls directly and exclusively on the only generous sympathies which yet link him to his fellow-men? Why should he be treated like a brute, whose very sufferings prove him to be a man?

The whole produce of the labour of the prisoners belongs to the state. No portion of it is allowed to the prisoner on his discharge. This regulation may be judicious in America, where the demand for labour is so great, that every man may, at any time, command employment; but in Great Britain it is different, and there to turn out a convict on the world, penniless, friendless, and without character, would be to limit his choice to the alternative of stealing or starving.

Of course, a system of discipline so rigorous could not be enforced without a power of punishment, almost arbitrary, being vested in the gaoler. The slightest infraction of the prison rules, therefore, is uniformly followed by severe infliction. There is no pardon, and no impunity for offenders of any sort; and here, as elsewhere, the certainty of punishment following an offence is found very much to diminish the necessity for its frequency. There is great evil, however, in this total irresponsibility on the part of the gaoler. There is no one to whom the convict, if unjustly punished, can complain, and a power is intrusted to an uneducated man, possibly of strong passions, which the wisest and best of mankind would feel himself unfit to exercise. I cannot help thinking, therefore, that a board of inspectors should assemble at least monthly at the prison, in order to hear all complaints that may be made against the gaoler. There is no doubt that this unpopular functionary would be subject to many false and frivolous accusations. The latter, however, may always be dismissed without trouble of any sort, but all plausible charges should receive rigid and impartial examination. The circumstances connected with the Charleston prison are precisely the most favourable for the attainment of truth. There can be no concert among the witnesses to be examined, no system of false evidence got up, no plotting, no collusion. Here coincidence of testimony could be explained only on the hypothesis of its truth; and this circumstance must be quite as favourable to the gaoler as to the prisoners. The former could never want the means of vindication, if falsely impeached.

I had a good deal of conversation with the gaoler in regard to the effects produced by the system on the morals of the convicts. He at once admitted that any material improvement of character in full-grown offenders was rarely to be expected, but maintained that the benefit of the Charleston system, even in this respect, was fully greater than had been found to result from any other plan adopted in the United States. His experience had not led him to anticipate much beneficial consequence from the system of solitary confinement. He had seen it often tried, but the prisoners on their liberation had almost uniformly relapsed into their former habits of crime. One interesting anecdote which occurred under his own observation, I shall here record.

Many years ago, long before the establishment of the present prison system, a man of respectable connexions, but of the most abandoned habits, was convicted of burglary, and arrived at Charleston jail, under sentence of imprisonment for life. His spirit was neither humbled by the punishment nor the disgrace. His conduct towards the keepers was violent and insubordinate, and it was soon found necessary, for the maintenance of discipline, that he should be separated from his fellow-prisoners, and placed in solitary confinement. For the first year he was sullen and silent, and the clergyman who frequently visited him in his cell, found his mind impervious to all religious impression. But by degrees a change took place in his deportment. His manner became mild and subdued; he was often found reading the Scriptures, and both gaoler and chaplain congratulated themselves on the change of character so manifest in the prisoner. He spoke of his past life, and the fearful offences in which it had abounded, with suitable contrition, and expressed his gratitude to God, that, instead of being snatched away in the midst of his crimes, time had been afforded him for repentance, and the attainment of faith in that grand and prevailing atonement, by the efficacy of which even the greatest of sinners might look for pardon.

Nothing in short could be more edifying than this man's conduct and conversation. All who saw him became interested in the fate of so meek a Christian, and numerous applications were made to the Governor of the State for his pardon. The Governor, with such weight of testimony before him, naturally inclined to mercy, and in a few weeks the man would have been undoubtedly liberated, when one day, in the middle of a religious conversation, he sprang upon the keeper, stabbed him in several places, and having cut his throat, attempted to escape.

The attempt failed. The neophyte in morality was brought back to his cell, and loaded with heavy irons. In this condition he remained many years, of course without the slightest hope of liberation. At length, his brother-in-law, a man of influence and fortune in South Carolina, made application to the authorities of Massachusetts on his behalf. He expressed his readiness to provide for his unfortunate relative, and, if liberated, he promised, on his arrival in Charleston, to place him in a situation above all temptation to return to his former crimes.

This offer was accepted; the prisoner was set at liberty, and the goaler, who told me the anecdote, was directed to see him safely on board of a Charleston packet, in which due provision had been made for his reception. His imprisonment had extended to the long period of twenty years, during which he had never once breathed the pure air of heaven, nor gazed on the sun or sky. In the interval, Boston, which he remembered as a small town, had grown into a large city. Its advance in opulence had been still more rapid. In every thing there had been a change. The appearance, manners, habits, thoughts, prejudices, and opinions of the generation then living, were different from all to which he had been accustomed. Nor was the aspect of external objects less altered. Streets of framework cottages had been replaced by handsome squares, and stately edifices of brick. Gay equipages, such as he never remembered, met his observation at every turn. In short, he felt like the inhabitant of another planet, suddenly cast into a world of which he knew nothing.

My informant—I wish I could give the story in his own words—described well and feelingly the progress of the man's impressions. A coach had been provided for his conveyance to the packet. On first entering it he displayed no external symptom of emotion; but as the carriage drove on, he gazed from the window, endeavouring to recognise the features of the scenery. But in vain; he looked for marsh and forest, and he beheld streets; he expected to cross a poor ferry, and the carriage rolled over a magnificent bridge; he looked for men as he had left them, and he saw beings of aspect altogether different. Where were the great men of the State-house and the Exchange—the aristocracy of the dollar bags—the Cincinnati of the Revolution, who brought to the counting-house the courtesies of the camp and the parade, and exhibited the last and noblest specimens of the *citizen gentleman?* They had gone down to their fathers full of years and of honour, and their descendants had become as the sons of other men. Queues, clubs, periwigs, shoe-buckles, hair-powder, and cocked hats, had fled to some other and more dignified world. The days of dram-drinking and tobacco-chewing, of gaiters, trowsers, and short crops, had succeeded. The latter circumstances, indeed, might not have occasioned the poor relieved convict any great concern, but the whole scene was too much for him to bear unmoved. His spirit was weighed down by a feeling of intense solitude, and he burst into tears.

The remainder of the story may be told in a few words. He reached Charleston, where his brother placed him in a respectable boarding-house, and supplied him with necessaries of every kind. His conduct for the first year was all that could be desired. But at length in an evil hour he was induced to visit New York. He there associated with profligate companions, and relapsing into his former habits, was concerned in a burglary, for which he was tried and convicted. He is now in the prison at Sing-Sing, under sentence of imprisonment for life, and from death only can he hope for liberation.

The gaoler told me this anecdote, as a proof how little amendment of the moral character is to be expected from solitary confinement. The case undoubtedly is a strong one, yet, of all the systems of punishment hitherto devised, the entire isolation of the criminal from his fellow-men,—if judicious advantage be taken of the opportunities it affords, and the state of mind which it can scarcely fail to produce,—seems that which is most likely to be attended with permanent reformation. The great objection to the Auburn and Charleston system, is, that the prisoners are treated like brutes, and any lurking sense of moral dignity is destroyed. Each individual is not only degraded in his own eyes, but in those of his companions; and it appears impossible that a criminal, once subjected to such treatment, should ever after be qualified to discharge, with advantage to his country, the duties of a citizen. Solitary confinement, on the other hand, has necessarily no such consequence; it at once obviates all occasion for corporal punishment, and for the exercise of arbitrary and irresponsible power on the part of the gaoler. The prisoner, on his liberation, is restored to society, humbled, indeed, by long suffering, yet not utterly degraded below the level of his fellow-creatures.

On the whole, the system of discipline I have witnessed at Charleston must be considered as a curious experiment, illustrating the precise degree of coercion necessary to destroy the whole influence of human volition, and reduce man to the condition of a machine. How far it accomplishes the higher objects contemplated in the philosophy of punishment, is a question which demands more consideration than I have at present time or inclination to bestow on it. I anticipate, however, having occasion to return to the subject, in narrating my visit to the Penitentiary at Philadelphia.

CHAPTER VII.

BOSTON.

The New England States are the great seat of manufactures in the Union; and in Boston especially, it is impossible to mix at all in society without hearing discussions on the policy of the Tariff Bill. I was prepared to encounter a good deal of bigotry on this subject, but on the whole found less than I expected. Of course, here, as elsewhere, men will argue strenuously and earnestly on the policy of a measure, with which they know their own interests to be inseparably connected; but both the advocates and opponents of the Tariff are to be found mingled very sociably at good men's feasts, and I have not been able to discover that antagonism of opinion has been in any degree productive of hostility of feeling.

On this question, as on many others, the weight of numbers is on one side, and that of sound argument on the other. It is the observation, I think, of Hobbes, that were it to become the interest of any portion of the human race to deny the truth of a proposition in Euclid, by no power of demonstration could it ever after command universal assent. This may be going too far, but we know how difficult it is, in the less certain sciences, to influence the understanding of those in favour of a conclusion, whose real or imagined interests must be injuriously affected by its establishment. Truths cease to be palpable when they touch a man's prejudices or his pocket, and patriotism is generally found at a premium or a discount, precisely as it happens to be connected with profit or loss.

It was not to be expected, therefore, that a question affecting the various and conflicting interests of different classes of men should be discussed in a very calm or philosophical spirit. "The American system," as it is called, was strenuously supported by the rich northern merchants, who expected to find in manufactures a new and profitable investment for their capital; and by the farmers, who expected to realize better prices for their wool and corn than could be commanded in the English market. It was opposed with at least equal vehemence by the planters of the Southern States, who regarded England as their best customer, and who must have been the chief sufferers had these measures of restriction been met by retaliation. Of course, as no manufactures of any kind exist south of the Potomac, the inhabitants of that extensive region were by no means satisfied of the justice of a policy, which, by increasing the price of all foreign commodities, had the effect of transferring money from their pockets to those of the New England monopolists. The Tariff Bill encountered strong opposition in both houses of the Legislature, but the representatives of the Western States having declared in its favour, it eventually passed, though by narrow majorities, and became law.

The passing of this bill inflicted a deep wound on the stability of the Union. The seeds of dissension among the different States had long been diffused, and now began to exhibit signs of rapid and luxuriant growth. The inhabitants of the Southern States were almost unanimous against the law. Their representatives not only protested loudly against its injustice, but declared, that in imposing duties, not for the sake of revenue but protection, Congress had wantonly exceeded its powers, and violated one of the fundamental principles of the constitution. Thus arose the celebrated doctrine of *nullification*, or, in other words, the assertion of an independent power in each State of the Union, to decide for itself on the justice of the measures of the Federal government, and to declare null, within its own limits, any act of the Federal Congress which it may consider as an infraction of its separate rights.

To this great controversy, affecting in its very principle the cohesion of the different states, I shall not at present do more than allude. It does, however, appear abundantly clear, that if there ever was a country in which it is injudicious to trammel industry with artificial restrictions, that country is the United States. Covering a vast extent of fertile territory, and advancing in wealth and population with a rapidity altogether unparalleled, it seems only necessary to the happiness and prosperity of this favoured people, that they should refrain from counteracting the beneficence of nature, and tranquilly enjoy the many blessings which she has placed within their reach. But this, unfortunately, is precisely what American legislators are not inclined to do. They seem determined to have a prosperity of their own making; to set up rival Birminghams and Manchesters; and in spite of " nature and their stars," to become, without delay, a great manufacturing, as well as a great agricultural nation.

But such things as Birmingham and Manchester are not to be created by an act of Congress. They can arise only under a vast combination of favourable circumstances, the approach of which may be retarded, but cannot possibly be accelerated, by a system of restrictions. They would undoubtedly have arisen far sooner in England, but for the ignorant adoption of the very policy which the Americans have now thought it expedient to imitate. But there is this excuse at least for our ancestors: The policy they adopted was in the spirit of their age. They did not seek to revive the exploded dogmas of a country or a period less enlightened than their own; and it can only be charged against them, that in seeking to gain a certain object, with but few and scattered lights to guide their footsteps, they went astray.

But to such palliation the conduct of the American legislators has no claim. With the path before them clear as daylight, they have preferred entangling themselves in thickets and quagmires. Like children, they have closed their eyes, and been content to believe that all is darkness. Living in one age, they have legislated in the spirit of another, and their blunders want even the merit of originality. They have exchanged their own comfortable clothing for the cast-off garments of other men, and strangely appeal to their antiquity as evidence of their value.

The appeal to English precedent may have some weight as an *argumentum ad hominem*, but as an *argumentum veritatis* it can have none. We cheerfully admit, that there is no absurdity so monstrous, as to want a parallel in the British statute-book. We only hope that we are outgrowing our errors, and profiting, however tardily, by our own experience and that of the world. But even this praise the advocates of American monopoly are not inclined to allow us. They charge us with bad faith in our commercial reforms; with arguing on one side, and acting on the other; and allege, that our statesmen, with the words *free trade* constantly on their lips, are still guided in their measures, by the spirit of that antiquated policy, which they so loudly condemn.

Enough of allowance, however, has not been made for the difficulties of their situation. Our legislators, it should be remembered, had to deal with vast interests, which had grown up under the exclusive system so long and rigidly adhered to. Any great and sudden change in our commercial policy would have been ruinous and unjust. It was necessary that the transition should be gradual, even to a healthier regimen; that men's opinions should be conciliated, and that time should be afforded for the adjustment of vested interests to the new circumstances of competition which awaited them. The question was far less as to the truth or soundness of certain abstract doctrines of political economy, than by what means changes affecting the disposition of the whole capital of the country, could be introduced with least injury and alarm.

Those only who have minutely followed the public life of Mr Huskisson during the last ten years, can duly estimate the magnitude of the obstacles with which at every step of his progress he had to contend. In truth, we know not any portion of history which would better repay the study of American statesmen. They will there acquire some knowledge of the difficulties, which assuredly, sooner or later, they will be compelled to encounter. They will learn, that a system of prohibition cannot be abandoned with the same ease with which it was originally assumed. Their first advance in the course on which they have entered may be prosperous, but their retreat must necessarily be disastrous. They will have to endure the reproaches of the bankrupt manufacturers. They will have the punishment of beholding a large proportion of the capital of their country irrecoverably lost. They will be assailed by the clamour and opposition of men of ruined fortunes and disappointed hopes, and while they lament the diminution of their country's prosperity, even their self-love will scarcely secure them from the conviction of its being attributable solely to their own selfish and ignorant policy.

In no country in the world, perhaps, could the prohibitory system be tried with less prospect of success than in the United States. The vast extent of territory alone presents an insuperable obstacle to its enforcement. The statesmen of England had no such difficulty to struggle with. They had to legislate for a small, compact, and insular country, in which there existed no such diversity of climate or of interest as to create much inequality of pressure in any scheme, however unreasonable, of indirect taxation. In England, there are no provincial jealousies to be reconciled, no rivalries or antipathies between different portions of the kingdom, and the facilities of communication are already so great as to give promise that the word *distance* will be speedily erased from our vocabulary.

But in America all this is different. Those err egregiously who regard the population of the United States as an uniform whole, composed throughout of similar materials, and whose patriotic attachment embraces the whole territory between the Mississippi and the Penobscot. An American is not a being of strong *local* attachments, and the slightest temptation of profit is always strong enough to induce him to quit his native State, and break all the ties which are found to operate so powerfully on other men. Entire disparity of circumstances and situation between the Northern and Southern States have, besides, produced considerable alienation of feeling in their inhabitants; and disputes, arising from differences of soil and climate, are evidently beyond the control of legislative interference. The Georgian or Carolinian, therefore, lives in a state of the most profound indifference with regard to the prosperity of New England, or rather, perhaps, is positively jealous of any increase of wealth or population, by which that portion of the Union may acquire additional influence in the national councils. To the people of the Southern States, therefore, any indirect taxation, imposed for the benefit of the Northern, must be doubly odious. The former wish only to buy where they can buy cheapest, and to sell where they can find the best market for their produce. Besides, they are violent and high-spirited, strong republicans, and averse from any unnecessary exercise of power on the part of the Federal government. England is their great customer, and the planter can entertain no reasonable hope of opulence which is not founded on her prosperity. Such are the discordant materials with which Congress has to deal, and which visionary legislators have vainly attempted to unite in cordial support of "the American system."

It is obvious, that a legislature which enters on a system of protection-duties, assumes the exercise of a power with which no wise men would wish to be intrusted, and which it is quite impossible they can exercise with advantage. They, in fact, assume the direction of the whole industry and capital of the country; dictate in what channels they shall flow; arbitrarily enrich one class at the expense of another; tax the many for the benefit of the few, and, in short, enter on a policy, which, if followed by other countries, would necessarily put a stop to all commerce, and throw each nation on its individual resources. There can be no *reductio ad absurdum* more complete. The commercial intercourse of nations would be annihilated were there a dozen governments in the world actuated by a cupidity so blind and uncalculating. It is, besides, impossible that any system of protection can *add* any thing to the productive industry of a people. The utmost it can effect is the transference of labour and capital from one branch of employment to another. It simply holds out a bribe to individuals to divert their industry from the occupations naturally most profitable, to others which are less so. This cannot be done without national loss. The encouragement which is felt in one quarter, must be accompanied by at least equal depression in another. The whole commercial system is made to rest on an insecure and artificial foundation, and the capital of the country, which has been influenced in its distribution, by a temporary and contingent impulse, may, at any moment, be paralysed by a change of system.

It is impossible, therefore, as matters now stand in America, that the manufacturing capitalists can look with any feeling of security to the future. They know, that the sword which is suspended over them hangs only by a hair, and may fall at any time. A large portion of the Union are resolutely, and almost unanimously, opposed to the continuance of the system. The monopolists, therefore, can ground their speculations on no hope but that of large and *immediate* profits, and the expectation, that should the present Tariff continue in force but a few years, they will, in that period, not only have realized the original amount of their investments, but a return sufficiently large to compensate for all the hazards of the undertaking. It is from the pockets of their fellow-subjects that they look for this enormous reimbursement; and, in a general point of view, perhaps, it matters little how much of the wealth of Virginia and the Carolinas may be transferred to New England, since the aggregate of national opulence would continue unchanged. One great and unmitigated evil of the Tariff-tax, however, consists in this, that while it is unjust and oppressive in its operation, it destroys far more capital than it sends into the coffers either of the Government or of individuals. All that portion of increased price which proceeds from increased difficulty of production in any article, is precisely so much of the national capital annihilated without benefit of any sort.

But, in truth, the exclusion of British goods from the Union is impossible. The extent of the Canadian frontier is so great, that the vigilance of a million of custom-house officers could not prevent their introduction. A temptation high in exact proportion to the amount of the restrictive duty, is held out to every trader; or in other words, the government which enforces the impost, offers a premium for its evasion. If Jonathan,—which we much doubt,—is too honest to smuggle, John Canadian is not; and the consequence simply is, that the United States are supplied with those goods from Montreal, which, under other circumstances, would have been directly imported. I remember walking through some warehouses in New York with an eminent merchant of that city; and on remarking the vast profusion of British manufactures everywhere apparent, he significantly answered, "Depend upon it, you have seen many more goods to-day than ever passed the Hook." In this matter, therefore, there exists no discrepancy between reason and experience. The trade between the countries still goes on with little, if any diminution. It has only been diverted from its natural and wholesome channel; taken from the respectable merchant, and thrown into the hands of the smuggler.

Among the body of the people there exists more ignorance as to the nature and effects of commerce, than might have been expected in a nation so generally commercial. I believe the sight of the vast importations from Britain, which fill the warehouses in every seaport, is accompanied with a feeling not unallied to envy. They would pardon us for our king and our peers, our palaces and our parade, far sooner than for our vast manufactories, which deluge the world with their produce. Such feelings are the consequence of ignorant and narrow views. In truth, every improvement in machinery which is made in Leeds or Manchester is a benefit to the world. By its agency the price of some commodity has been lowered, and an article, perhaps essential to comfort, is thus brought within the reach of millions to whom it must otherwise have been inaccessible.

Any sentiment of jealousy arising from the diffusion of British manufactures in their own country is no less absurd. Every increase of importation is, in fact, an evidence of increased opulence and prosperity in the importing country. Not a bale of goods is landed at the quay of New York, without an equal value of the produce of the country being exported to pay for it. Commerce is merely a barter of equivalents, and carries this advantage, that both parties are enriched by it. Thus, a piece of muslin may be more valuable in America than a bag of cotton; while, in England, the superiority of value is on the side of the latter. It is evident, therefore, that if these two articles be exchanged, both parties are gainers; both receive a greater value than they have given, and the mass of national opulence, both in England and America, has received a positive increase. A commerce which is not mutually advantageous cannot be continued. No Tariff bill, no system of restriction, is required to put a stop to it. Governments have no reason to concern themselves about the balance of trade. They may safely leave that to individual sagacity, and devote their attention to those various interests in which legislation may at least possibly be attended with benefit.

But formidable as the difficulties are which surround the supporters of the prohibitory system, another is approaching, even of greater magnitude. In two years the national debt will be extinguished, and the Federal government will find itself in possession of a surplus revenue of 12,000,000 of dollars, chiefly the produce of the Tariff duties. The question will then arise, how is this revenue to be appropriated. If divided among the different states, the tranquillity of the Union will be disturbed by a thousand jealousies, which very probably would terminate in its dissolution. Besides, such an appropriation is confessedly unconstitutional, and must arm the government with a power never contemplated at its formation. To apply the surplus in projects of general improvement, under direction of Congress, would increase many of the difficulties, while it obviated none. In short, there is no escaping from the dilemma; and, singular as it may seem to an Englishman, the Tariff will probably be extinguished by a sheer plethora of money. The most enlightened statesmen unite in the conviction, that there is but one course to be pursued, and that is, to reduce the duties to a fair system of revenue; to extract from the pockets of the people what is sufficient for the necessary expenses of the government, and no more. It is singular, that the wealth of a nation, which in other countries is found to generate corruption, should, in the United States, be the means of forcing the government to return to the principles of sound and constitutional legislation.

I am aware there is nothing new in all this, nor is it possible perhaps to be very original on a subject which has been so often and so thoroughly discussed. It ought perhaps in justice to be stated, that the majority of the gentlemen among whom I moved in Boston, were opposed to the Tariff, and that I derived much instruction both from their conversation and writings. The great majority of the mercantile population, however, are in favour of the prohibitory system, though I could not discover much novelty in the arguments by which they support it. To these, however, I shall not advert, and gladly turn from a subject, which I fear can possess little interest for an English reader.

A traveller has no sooner time to look about him in Boston, than he receives the conviction that he is thrown among a population of a character differing in much from that of the other cities of the Union. If a tolerable observer, he will immediately remark that the lines of the forehead are more deeply indented; that there is more hardness of feature; a more cold and lustreless expression of the eye; a more rigid compression of the lips, and that the countenance altogether is of a graver and more meditative cast. Something of all this is apparent even in childhood; as the young idea shoots, the peculiarities become more strongly marked; they grow with his growth and strengthen with his strength, and it is only when the New Englander is restored to his kindred dust that they are finally obliterated. Observe him in every different situation; at the funeral, and the marriage-feast; at the theatre, and the conventicle; in the ball-room, and on the exchange, and you will set him down as of God's creatures the least liable to be influenced by circumstances appealing to the heart or imagination.

The whole city seems to partake of this peculiar character, and a traveller coming from New York is especially struck with it. It is not that the streets of Boston are less crowded, the public places less frequented, or that the business of life is less energetically pursued. In all these matters, to the eye of a stranger there is little perceptible difference. But the population is evidently more orderly; the conventional restrictions of society are more strictly drawn, and even the lower orders are distinguished by a solemnity of demeanour, not observable in their more southern neighbours. A shopkeeper weighs coffee or measures tape with the air of a philosopher; makes observations on the price or quality with an air of sententious sagacity; subjects your coin to a sceptical scrutiny, and as you walk off with your parcel in your pocket, examines you from top to toe, in order to gain some probable conclusion as to your habits or profession.

Boston is quiet, but there is none of the torpor of

still life about it. Nowhere are the arts of money getting more deeply studied or better understood. There is here less attempt than elsewhere to combine pleasure and business, simply because to a New Englander business *is* pleasure—indeed the only pleasure he cares much about. An English shopkeeper is a tradesman all morning, but a gentleman in the evening. He casts his slough like a snake, and steps into it again, only when he crosses the counter. Tallow, *dry goods*, and tobacco are topics specially eschewed in the drawing-rooms of Camberwell and Hackney, and all talk about sales and bankruptcies is considered a violation of the *bienséances* at Broadstairs and Margate. In short, an English tradesman is always solicitous to *cut the shop* whenever he can do so with impunity, and it often happens that an acute observer of manners can detect a man's business rather by the topics he betrays anxiety to avoid, than those on which he delivers his opinion.

There is some folly in all this, but there is likewise some happiness. Enough, and too much, of man's life is devoted to business and its cares, and it is well that at least a portion of it should be given to enjoyment, and the cultivation of those charities, which constitute the redeeming part of our nature. The follies of mankind have at least the advantage of being generally social, and connected with the happiness of others as well as with our own. But the pursuits of avarice and ambition are selfish; their object is the attainment of solitary distinction, and the depression of competitors is no less necessary to success, than the positive elevation of the candidate. The natural sympathies of humanity are apt to wither in the hearts of men engrossed by such interests. Even the vanities and follies of life have their use in softening the asperities of contest, and uniting men in their weakness, who would willingly stand apart in their strength. It is good, therefore, that the lawyer should sometimes forget his briefs, and the merchant his "argosies," and his money-bags; that the poor man should cast off the memory of his sweat and his sufferings, and find even in frivolous amusements, a Sabbath of the sterner passions.

But such Sabbath the New Englander rarely knows. Wherever he goes the coils of business are around him. He is a sort of moral Laocoon, differing only in this, that he makes no struggle to be free. Mammon has no more zealous worshipper than your true Yankee. His homage is not merely that of the lip, or of the knee; it is an entire prostration of the heart; the devotion of all powers, bodily and mental, to the service of the idol. He views the world but as one vast exchange, on which he is impelled, both by principle and interest, to over-reach his neighbours if he can. The thought of business is never absent from his mind. To him there is no enjoyment without traffic. He travels snail-like, with his shop or his counting-house on his back, and, like other hawkers, is always ready to open his budget of little private interests for discussion or amusement. The only respite he enjoys from the consideration of his own affairs, is the time he is pleased to bestow on prying into yours. In regard to the latter, he evidently considers that he has a perfect right to unlimited sincerity. There is no baffling him. His curiosity seems to rise in proportion to the difficulty of its gratification: He will track you through every evasion, detect all your doublings, or, if thrown out, will hark back so skilfully on the scent, that you are at length fairly hedged in a corner, and are tempted to exclaim, in the words of the most gifted of female poets,—

> "The devil damn thy question-asking spirit;
> For when thou takest a notion by the skirt,
> Thou, like an English bull-dog, keepest thy hold,
> And wilt not let it go."

Their puritan descent has stamped a character on the New Englanders, which nearly two centuries have done little to efface. Among their own countrymen they are distinguished for their enterprise, prudence, frugality, order, and intelligence. Like the Jews, they are a marked people, and stand out in strong relief from the population which surrounds them. I imagine attachment to republicanism is less fervent in this quarter of the Union than in any other. The understanding of a Yankee is not likely to be run away with by any political plausibilities, and concerns itself very little about evils which are merely speculative. He is content when he feels a grievance to apply a remedy, and sets about the work of reform, with none of that revolutionary fury, which has so often marred the fairest prospects of the philanthropist. Since the establishment of their independence, the representatives of these States have almost uniformly advocated in Congress the principles of Washington, Hamilton, and Adams, and rather regarded with apprehension the democratic tendencies of the constitution, than the dangers which might result from increase of power on the part of the executive.

This is the more remarkable, as the constitutions of most of the New England States are in truth republican in a degree verging on democracy. In New Hampshire, the governor, council, senators, and representatives are all elected annually by the people. In Vermont, there is only one Legislative Body, which, along with the governor and council, and *judges*, is chosen annually. Rhode Island, strange to say, has no written constitution at all, and the inhabitants find it very possible to live in perfect comfort and security without one. The custom is, however, to have a governor, senate, and representatives, who are chosen annually. The appointment of judges is likewise annual. In Massachusetts, the governor and Legislative Bodies are annually chosen — the judges, however, hold their offices *ad vitam aut culpam*. In the States of Maine and Connecticut, the Executive and Legislative Bodies are appointed annually; the Judiciary, however, is permanent. In all these states, the right of suffrage, with some few restrictions in regard to paupers, &c. is universal.

In contrast with this, it may be curious to take a glance at the constitution of Virginia, the native state of Washington, Jefferson, Madison, and Munroe, which has always been remarkable in the Federal Congress for the assertion of the highest and purest principles of republicanism. It must be observed, however, that until 1829, the right of suffrage depended on a much higher territorial qualification than at present. In that year, the constitution was remodelled and liberalized by a convention of the inhabitants.

There are in Virginia two Legislative Bodies. The members of the Lower House are chosen annually, the senators every *four* years. These houses, by a joint vote, elect the governor, who remains in office *three* years. The judges are during good behaviour, or until removed by a concurrent vote of both houses, two-thirds being required to constitute the necessary majority. The right of suffrage is vested in every citizen possessed of a freehold of the value of twenty-five dollars, or who has a life-interest in land of the value of fifty dollars, or who shall own or occupy a leasehold estate of the annual value of two hundred dollars, &c.

There is thus presented the anomaly of the most democratic state of the Union adhering to a constitution comparatively aristocratic, and appending to the right of suffrage a high territorial qualification; while the New England States, with institutions more democratic than have ever yet been realized in any other civilized community, are distinguished as the advocates of a strong federal legislature, a productive system of finance, the establishment of a powerful navy, and such liberal expenditure at home and abroad, as would tend to ensure respect and influence to the government.

The truth seems to be, that the original polity of these States partook of the patriarchal character, and has not yet entirely lost its hold on the feelings of the people. It was easy to maintain order in a country where there was little temptation to crime; where, by a day's labour, a man could earn the price of an acre of tolerable land, and becoming a territorial proprietor, of course, immediately partook of the common impulse, to maintain the security of property. Add to this the character of the people; their apathetic temperament, their habits of parsimony, the religious impressions communicated by their ancestors, and, above all, the vast extent of fertile territory which acted as an escape-valve for the more daring and unprincipled part of the population, and we shall have reasons enough, I imagine, why the New Englanders could bear, without injury, a greater degree of political liberty than perhaps any other people in the world.

But though the New Englanders had little apprehension of glaring violations of law within their own territory, they had evidently no great confidence in the wisdom and morality of their neighbours. They were, therefore, in favour of a federal legislature, strong enough to command respect, and maintain order throughout the Union. Forming a small minority of the confederated States, yet for long subsequent to the Revolution, possessing by far the greater share of the national capital, they felt that they had more to lose than those around them, and were consequently more solicitous to strengthen the guarantees of public order. They would, therefore, have been better satisfied had greater influence been given to property, and would gladly have seen the senate so constituted, as to act as a check on the hasty impulses of the more popular chamber. Within their own limits there was no risk of domestic disturbance. The most wealthy capitalist felt, that from the citizens of his own province, he had nothing to apprehend. But it was to the federal legislature alone, that they could look for security from without, and they were naturally anxious that this body should be composed of men with a deep interest in the stability of the Union, and representing rather the deliberate opinions of their more intelligent constituents, than the hasty and variable impressions of the ignorant and vulgar.

The New England states have something approaching to a religious establishment. In Massachusetts,

Vermont, New Hampshire, and Connecticut, the law requires each town to provide, by taxation, for the support of the *Protestant* religion, leaving, however, to every individual, the choice of the particular sect to which he will contribute. In the other States of the Union, every person is at liberty to act as he pleases in regard to religion, which is regarded solely as a relation between man and his Maker, and any compulsory contribution would be considered a direct encroachment on personal liberty. But if Christianity be a public benefit; if it tend to diminish crime and encourage the virtues essential to the prosperity of a community, it is difficult to see on what grounds its support and diffusion should not form part of the duties of a legislature.

In these States, the education of the people is likewise the subject of legislative enactment. In Massachusetts, public schools are established in every district, and supported by a tax levied on the public. In Connecticut they are maintained in another manner. By the charter of Charles the Second, this colony extended across the Continent to the Pacific, within the same parallels of latitude which bound it on the East. It therefore included a large portion of the present States of Pennsylvania and Ohio, which being sold, produced a sum amounting to L.270,000 sterling, the interest of which is exclusively devoted to the purposes of education throughout the State. This fund is now largely increased, and its annual produce, I believe, is greater than the whole income of the State arising from taxation.

In these public schools every citizen has not only a right to have his children educated, but, as in some parts of Germany, he is compelled by law to exercise it. It is here considered essential to the public interest that every man should receive so much instruction as shall qualify him for a useful member of the State. No member of society can be considered as an isolated and abstract being, living for his own pleasure, and labouring for his own advantage. In free States, especially, every man has important political functions, which affect materially not only his own well-being but that of his fellow-citizens; and it is surely reasonable to demand that he shall at least possess such knoweledge as shall render it possible for him to discharge his duties with advantage to the community. The policy which attempts to check crime by the diffusion of knowledge, is the offspring of true political wisdom. It gives a security to person and property, beyond that afforded by the law, and looks for the improvement of the people, not to the gibbet and the prison, but to increased intelligence, and a consequently keener sense of moral responsibility.

Speaking generally, it may be said that every New Englander receives the elements of education. Reading and writing, even among the poorest class, are universally diffused; arithmetic, I presume, comes by instinct among this guessing, reckoning, expecting, and calculating people. The school-master has long been abroad in these States, deprived, it is true, of his rod and ferule, but still most usefully employed. Up to a certain point he has done wonders; he has made his scholars as wise as himself, and it would be somewhat unreasonable to expect more. If it be considered desirable, however, that the present range of popular knowledge should be enlarged, the question then arises, who shall teach the schoolmaster? Who shall impress a pedagogue (on the best terms with himself, and whose only wonder is, " that one small head should carry all he knows,") with a due sense of his deficiencies, and lead him to admit that there are more things between heaven and earth than are dreamt of in his philosophy? A New Englander passes through the statutory process of education, and enters life with the intimate conviction that he has mastered, if not the *omne scibile*, at least every thing valuable within the domain of intellect. It never occurs to him as possible, that he may have formed a wrong conclusion on any question, however intricate, of politics or religion. He despises all knowledge abstracted from the business of the world, and prides himself on his stock of practical truths. In mind, body, and estate, he believes himself the first and noblest of God's creatures. The sound of triumph is ever on his lips, and, like a man who has mounted the first step of a ladder, it is his pride to look down on his neighbours, whom he overtops by an inch, instead of directing his attention to the great height yet to be surmounted.

This folly, indeed, is not peculiar to the New Englander, though in him it is more strongly marked than in the inhabitants of the other States. It enters into the very essence of his character; it is part and parcel of him, and its eradication would involve an entire change of being. "A blessing be on him who first invented sleep," says Sancho Panza, "for it covers a man all over like a cloak." And even so Jonathan may bless his vanity. He is encased in it from top to toe; it is a panoply of proof, which renders him invulnerable equally to ridicule and argument

If to form a just estimate of ourselves and others, be the test of knowledge, the New Englander is the most ignorant of mankind. There is a great deal that is really good and estimable in his character, but, after all, he is not absolutely the ninth wonder of the world. I know of no benefit that could be conferred on him equal to convincing him of this truth. He may be assured that the man who knows nothing, and is aware of his ignorance, is a wiser and more enviable being than he who knows a little, and imagines that he knows all. The extent of our ignorance is a far more profitable object of contemplation than that of our knowledge. Discontent with our actual amount of acquirement is the indispensable condition of possible improvement. It is to be wished that Jonathan would remember this. He may rely on it, he will occupy a higher place in the estimation of the world, whenever he has acquired the wisdom to think more humbly of himself.

The New England free-schools are establishments happily adapted to the wants and character of the people. They have been found to work admirably, and too much praise cannot be bestowed on the enlightened policy which, from the very foundation of the colony, has never once lost sight of the great object of diffusing education through every cottage within its boundaries. It will detract nothing from the honour thus justly due, to mention that the establishment of district schools was not an original achievement of New England intelligence. The parish-schools of Scotland (to say nothing of Germany) had existed long before the pilgrim fathers ever knelt in worship beneath the shadows of the hoary forest trees. The principle of the establishments in both countries is the same, the only difference is in the details. In Scotland the land-owners of each parish contribute the means of education for the body of the people. The schoolhouse and dwelling-house of the master are provided and kept in repair by an assessment on the land, which is likewise burdened with the amount of his salary.

It has been an object, however, wisely kept in view, that instruction at these seminaries shall not be wholly gratuitous. There are few even of the poorest order in Scotland who would not consider it a degradation to send their children to a charity school, and the feeling of independence, is perhaps the very last which a wise legislator will venture to counteract. It is to be expected, too, that when the master depends on the emolument to be derived from his scholars, he will exert himself more zealously than when his remuneration arises from a source altogether independent of his own efforts. The sum demanded from the scholars, however, is so low, that instruction is placed within the reach of the poorest cottager; and instances are few indeed, in which a child born in Scotland is suffered to grow up without sufficient instruction to enable him to discharge respectably the duties of the situation he is destined to fill.

When Mr Brougham, however, brought forward in the British Parliament his plan of national education, which consisted mainly in the establishment throughout the kingdom of parish-schools, similar to those in Scotland, one of the most eminent individuals of the Union* did not hesitate to arrogate the whole merit of the precedent for New England. I have more than once since my arrival heard Mr Brougham accused of unworthy motives, in not publicly confessing that his whole project was founded on the example set forth for imitation in this favoured region. It was in vain that I pleaded the circumstances above stated, the company were evidently determined to believe their own schools without parallel in the world, and the Lord Chancellor will assuredly go down to his grave unabsolved from this weighty imputation.

In character there are many points of resemblance between the Scotch and New Englanders. There is

* Mr Webster, in his speech delivered at Plymouth, in commemoration of the first settlement of New England.

the same sobriety, love of order, and perseverance in both; the same attachment to religion, mingled with more caution in Sanders, and more enterprise in Jonathan. Both are the inhabitants of a poor country, and both have become rich by habits of steady industry and frugality. Both send forth a large portion of their population to participate in the wealth of more favoured regions. The Scot, however, never loses his attachment to his native land. It has probably been to him a rugged nurse, yet, wander where he will, its heathy mountains are ever present to his imagination, and he thinks of the bleak muirland cottage in which he grew from infancy to manhood, as a spot encircled by a halo of light and beauty. Whenever fortune smiles on him, he returns to his native village, and the drama of his life closes where it commenced.

There is nothing of this local attachment about the New Englander. His own country is too poor and too populous to afford scope for the full exercise of his enterprise and activity. He therefore shoulders his axe, and betakes himself to distant regions; breaks once and for ever all the ties of kindred and connexion, and without one longing lingering look, bids farewell to all the scenes of his infancy.

In point of morality, I must be excused for giving the decided preference to my countrymen. The Scotch have established throughout the world a high character for honesty, sobriety, and steady industry. Jonathan is equally sober and industrious, but his reputation for honesty is at a discount. The whole Union is full of stories of his cunning frauds, and of the impositions he delights to perpetrate on his more simple neighbours. Whenever his love of money comes in competition with his zeal for religion, the latter is sure to give way. He will insist on the scrupulous observance of the Sabbath, and cheat his customer on the Monday morning. His life is a comment on the text, *Qui festinat ditescere, non erit innocens.* The whole race of Yankee pedlars, in particular, are proverbial for dishonesty. These go forth annually in thousands to lie, cog, cheat, swindle, in short, to get possession of their neighbour's property, in any manner it can be done with impunity. Their ingenuity in deception is confessedly very great. They warrant broken watches to be the best time-keepers in the world; sell pinchbeck trinkets for gold; and have always a large assortment of wooden nutmegs, and stagnant barometers. In this respect they resemble the Jews, of which race, by the by, I am assured, there is not a single specimen to be found in New England. There is an old Scotch proverb, "Corbies never pick out corbies' een."

The New Englanders are not an amiable people. One meets in them much to approve, little to admire, and nothing to love. They may be disliked, however, but they cannot be despised. There is a degree of energy and sturdy independence about them, incompatible with contempt. Abuse them as we may, it must still be admitted they are a singular and original people. Nature, in framing a Yankee, seems to have given him double brains, and half heart.

Wealth is more equally distributed in the New England states, than perhaps in any other country of the world. There are here no overgrown fortunes. Abject poverty is rarely seen, but moderate opulence everywhere. This is as it should be. Who would wish for the introduction of the palace, if it must be accompanied by the Poor's-house?*

There are few beggars to be found in the streets of Boston, but some there are, both there and at New York. These, however, I am assured, are all foreigners, or people of colour, and my own observations go to confirm the assertion. Nine-tenths of those by whom I have been importuned for charity, were evidently Irish. The number of negroes in Boston is comparatively small. The servants, in the better houses at least, are generally whites, but I have not been able to discover that the prejudices which, in the other States, condemn the poor African to degradation, have been at all modified or diminished by the boasted intelligence of the New Englanders.

* The observations on the New England character in the present chapter, would perhaps have been more appropriately deferred till a later period of the work. Having written them, however, they must now stand where chance has placed them. I have only to beg they may be taken, not as the hasty impressions received during a few days or weeks residence in Boston, but as the final result of my observations on this interesting people, both in their own states, and in other portions of the Union.

This observation is equally applicable to the opinions expressed in different parts of these volumes, and I must request the reader to be good enough to bear it in mind.

Though the schoolmaster has long exercised his vocation in these States, the fruit of his labours is but little apparent in the language of his pupils. The amount of bad grammar in circulation is very great; that of barbarisms enormous. Of course, I do not now speak of the operative class, whose massacre of their mother-tongue, however inhuman, could excite no astonishment; but I allude to the great body of lawyers and traders; the men who crowd the exchange and the hotels; who are to be heard speaking in the courts, and are selected by their fellow-citizens to fill high and responsible offices. Even by this educated and respectable class, the commonest words are often so transmogrified as to be placed beyond the recognition of an Englishman. The word *does* is split into two syllables, and pronounced *do-es*. *Where*, for some incomprehensible reason, is converted into *whare*, *there* into *thare;* and I remember, on mentioning to an acquaintance that I had called on a gentleman of taste in the arts, he asked, "Whether he *shew* (showed) me his pictures." Such words as oratory and dilatory, are pronounced with the penult syllable, long and accented; missionary becomes *missionairy*, angel, *ângel*, danger, *dânger*, &c.

But this is not all. The Americans have chosen arbitrarily to change the meaning of certain old and established English words, for reasons which they cannot explain, and which I doubt much whether any European philologist could understand. The word *clever* affords a case in point. It has here no connexion with talent, and simply means pleasant or amiable. Thus a good-natured blockhead in the American vernacular, is a *clever* man, and having had this drilled into me, I foolishly imagined that all trouble with regard to this word at least, was at an end. It was not long, however, before I heard of a gentleman having moved into a *clever* house, of another succeeding to a *clever* sum of money, of a third embarking in a *clever* ship, and making a *clever* voyage, with a *clever* cargo; and of the sense attached to the word in these various combinations, I could gain nothing like satisfactory explanation.

With regard to the meaning intended to be conveyed by an American in conversation, one is sometimes left utterly at large. I remember, after conversing with a very plain, but very agreeable lady, being asked whether Mrs —— was not *a very fine woman.* I believe I have not more conscience than my neighbours in regard to a compliment, but in the present case there seemed something so ludicrous in the application of the term, that I found it really impossible to answer in the affirmative. I therefore ventured to hint, that the personal charms of Mrs —— were certainly not her principal attraction, but that I had rarely enjoyed the good fortune of meeting a lady more pleasing and intelligent. This led to an explanation, and I learned that in the dialect of this country, the term *fine woman* refers exclusively to the intellect.

The privilege of barbarizing the King's English is assumed by all ranks and conditions of men. Such words as *slick*, *hedge*, and *boss*, it is true, are rarely used by the better orders; but they assume unlimited liberty in the use of "expect," "reckon," "guess," "calculate," and perpetrate conversational anomalies with the most remorseless impunity. It were easy to accumulate instances, but I will not go on with this unpleasant subject; nor should I have alluded to it, but that I feel it something of a duty to express the natural feeling of an Englishman, at finding the language of Shakspeare and Milton thus gratuitously degraded. Unless the present progress of change be arrested, by an increase of taste and judgment in the more educated classes, there can be no doubt that, in another century, the dialect of the Americans will become utterly unintelligible to an Englishman, and that the nation will be cut off from the advantages arising from their participation in British literature. If they contemplate such an event with complacency, let them go on and prosper; they have only to "*progress*" in their present course, and their grandchildren bid fair to speak a jargon as novel and peculiar as the most patriotic American linguist can desire.

CHAPTER VIII.

NEW ENGLAND.

Having directed the attention of the reader to some of the more prominent defects of the New England character, it is only justice to add, that in Boston at least, there exists a circle almost entirely exempt from them. This is composed of the first-rate merchants and lawyers, leavened by a small sprinkling of the clergy, and, judging of the quality of the ingredients, from the agreeable effect of the mixture, I should pronounce them excellent. There is much taste for literature in this circle; much liberality of sentiment, a good deal of accomplishment, and a greater amount, perhaps, both of practical and speculative knowledge, than the population of any other mercantile city could supply. In such society it is possible for an Englishman to express his opinions without danger of being misunderstood, and he enjoys the advantage of free interchange of thought, and correcting his own hasty impressions by comparison with the results of more mature experience and sounder judgment.

It certainly struck me as singular, that while the great body of the New Englanders are distinguished above every other people I have ever known by bigotry and narrowness of mind, and an utter disregard of those delicacies of deportment which indicate benevolence of feeling, the higher and more enlightened portion of the community should be peculiarly remarkable for the display of qualities precisely the reverse. Nowhere in the United States will the feelings, and even prejudices of a stranger, meet with such forbearance as in the circle to which I allude. Nowhere are the true delicacies of social intercourse more scrupulously observed, and nowhere will a traveller mingle in society, where his errors of opinion will be more rigidly detected or more charitably excused. I look back on the period of my residence in Boston with peculiar pleasure. I trust there are individuals there who regard me as a friend, and I know of nothing in the more remote contingencies of life, which I contemplate with greater satisfaction, than the possibility of renewing in this country, with at least some of the number, an intercourse which I found so gratifying in their own.

In externals, the society of Boston differs little from that of New York. There is the same routine of dinners and parties, and in both the scale of expensive luxury seems nearly equal. In Boston, however, there is more literature, and this circumstance has proportionally enlarged the range of conversation. An Englishman is a good deal struck in America with the entire absence of books, as articles of furniture. The remark, however, is not applicable to Boston. There, works of European literature, evidently not introduced for the mere purpose of display, are generally to be found, and even the drawing-room sometimes assumes the appearance of a library.

The higher order of the New Englanders offers no exception to that grave solemnity of aspect, which is the badge of all their tribe. The gentlemen are more given than is elsewhere usual, to the discussion of abstract polemics, both in literature and religion. There is a moral pugnacity about them, which is not offensive, because it is never productive of any thing like wrangling, and is qualified by a very large measure of philosophical tolerance. The well-informed Bostonian is a calm and deliberative being. His decision, on any point, may be influenced by interest, but not by passion. He is rarely contented, like the inhabitants of other states, with taking the plain and broad features of a case; he enters into all the refinements of which the subject is capable, discriminates between the plausible and the true, establishes the precise limits of fact and probability, and with unerring accuracy fixes on the weak point in the argument of his opponent. Of all men he is the least liable, I should imagine, to be misled by any general assertion of abstract principle. He uniformly carries into the business of common life a certain practical good sense, and never for a moment loses sight of the results of experience. In politics he will not consent to *go the whole hog*, or, in other words, to hazard a certain amount of present benefit, for the promise, however confident, of new and untried advantages.

Of the ladies of Boston I did not see much, and can therefore only speak in doubtful terms of the amount of their attractions. Unfortunately it is still less the fashion, than at New York, to enliven the dinner-table with their presence, and, during my stay, I was only present at one ball. But the impression I received was certainly very favourable. These fair New Englanders partake of the endemic gravity of expression, which sits well on them, because it is natural. In amount of acquirement, I believe they are very superior to any other ladies of the Union. They talk well and gracefully of novels and poetry, are accomplished in music and the living languages, and though the New York ladies charge them with being *dowdyish* in dress, I am not sure that their taste in this respect is not purer, as it certainly is more simple, than that of their fair accusers.

The habits of the Bostonians are, I believe, more domestic than is common in the other cities of the Union. The taste for reading contributes to this, by rendering both families and individuals less dependent on society. A strong aristocratic feeling is apparent in the families of older standing. The walls of the apartments are often covered with the portraits of their ancestors, armorial bearings are in general use, and antiquity of blood is no less valued here than in England. The people, too, display a fondness for title somewhat at variance with their good sense in other matters. The governor of Massachusetts receives the title of Excellency. The President of the United States claims no such honour. The members of the Federal Senate are addressed generally in the northern states, with the prefixture of Honourable, but the New Englanders go further, and extend the same distinction to the whole body of representatives, a practice followed in no other part of the Union.

Such trifles often afford considerable insight to the real feelings of a people. Nowhere are mere nominal distinctions at so high a premium as in this republican country. Military titles are caught at with an avidity, which to an Englishman appears absolutely ridiculous. The anomaly of learned majors at the bar addressing learned colonels or generals on the bench is not uncommon, and as the privates of militia enjoy the privilege of electing their officers, of course the principle of choice is by no means the possession of military knowledge. In a thinly-peopled country, where candidates of a better class are not to be had, it must often happen, that the highest military rank is bestowed on men of the very lowest station in society. This circumstance, it might be expected, would bring this class of honours into disrepute, and that, like the title of knight-bachelor in England, they would be avoided by the better order of citizens. This, however, is by no means the case. Generals, colonels, and majors, swarm all over the Union, and the titular distinction is equally coveted by the President and the senator, the judge on the bench and the innkeeper at the bar.

There is far more English feeling in Boston than I was prepared to expect. The people yet feel pride in the country of their forefathers, and even retain somewhat of reverence for her ancient institutions. At the period of my visit, the topic of Parliamentary Reform was naturally one of peculiar interest. The revolution in France had communicated a strong impulse to opinion in England, and the policy to be adopted by the ministry in regard to this great question, was yet unknown. The subject, therefore, in all its bearings, was very frequently discussed in the society of Boston. It was one on which I had anticipated little difference of opinion among the citizens of a republic. Admitting that their best wishes were in favour of the prosperity of Britain, and the stability of her constitution, I expected that their judgment would necessarily point to great and immediate changes in a monarchy confessedly not free from abuse. For myself, though considered, I believe, as something of a Radical at home, I had come to the United States prepared to bear the imputation of Toryism among a people whose ideas of liberty were carried so much further than my own.

In all these anticipations I was mistaken. Strange to say, I found myself quite as much a Radical in Boston, and very nearly as much so in New York, as I had been considered in England. It was soon apparent that the great majority of the more enlightened class in both cities, regarded any great and sudden change in the British institutions as pregnant with the most imminent danger. In their eyes the chance of ultimate advantage was utterly insignificant, when weighed against the certainty of immediate peril. "You at present," they said, "enjoy more practical freedom than has ever in the whole experience of mankind been permanently secured to a nation by any institutions. Your government, whatever may be its defects, enjoys at least this inestimable advantage, that the habits of the people are adapted to it. This cannot be the case in regard to any change, however calculated to be ultimately beneficial. The process of moral adaptation is ever slow and precarious, and the experience of the world demonstrates that it is far better that the intelligence of a people should be in advance of their institutions, than that the institutions should precede the advancement of the people. In the former case, however theoretically bad, their laws will be practically modified by the influence of public opinion; in the latter, however good in themselves, they cannot be secure or beneficial in their operation. We speak as men whose opinions have been formed from experience, under a government, popular in the widest sense of the term. As friends, we caution you to beware. We pretend not to judge whether change be necessary. If it be, we trust it will at least be gradual; that your statesmen will approach the work of reform, with the full knowledge that every single innovation will occasion the necessity of many. The appetite for change in a people grows with what it feeds on. It is insatiable. Go as far as you will, at some point you must stop, and that point will be short of the wish of a large portion—probably of a numerical majority—of your population. By no concession does it appear to us that you can avert the battle that awaits you. You have but the choice whether the great struggle shall be for reform or property."

I own I was a good deal surprised by the prevalence of such opinions among the only class of Americans whose judgment as to matters of government, could be supposed of much value. As it was my object to acquire as much knowledge as possible with regard to the real working of the American constitution on the habits and feelings of the people; I was always glad to listen to political discussion between enlightened disputants. This carried with it at least the advantage of affording an indication to the prevailing tone of thought and opinion, in a condition of society altogether different from any within the range of European experience. At present I have only alluded to the subject of politics at all, as illustrative of a peculiar feature in the New England character. At a future period, I shall have occasion to view the subject under a different aspect.

The comparative diffusion of literature in Boston, has brought with it a taste for the fine arts. The better houses are adorned with pictures; and in the Athenæum—a public library and reading-room—is a collection of casts from the antique. Establishments for the instruction of the people in the higher branches of knowledge, are yet almost unknown in the United States, but something like a Mechanics' Institute has at length been got up in Boston, and I went to hear the introductory lecture. The apartment, a large one, was crowded by an audience whose appearance and deportment were in the highest degree orderly and respectable. The lecture was on the steam-engine, the history, principle, and construction of which were explained most lucidly by a lecturer, who belonged, I was assured, to the class of operative mechanics.

Boston can boast having produced some eminent artists, at the head of whom is Mr Alston, a painter, confessedly of fine taste, if not of high genius. His taste, however, unfortunately renders him too fastidious a critic on his own performances, and he has now been upwards of ten years in painting an historical subject, which is yet unfinished. This surely is mere waste of life and labour. Where a poet or painter has a strong grasp of his subject, he finds no difficulty in embodying his conceptions. The idea which requires years of fostering, and must be cherished and cockered into life, is seldom worth the cost of its nurture. Mr Alston should remember that a tree is judged by the quantity as well as by the quality of its fruit. Had Raphael, Rubens, or Titian, adopted such a process of elaboration, how many of the noblest specimens of art would have been lost to the world!

I had the pleasure of becoming acquainted with Mr Harding, a painter of much talent, and very considerable genius. His history is a singular one. During the last war with Great Britain, he was a private soldier, and fought in many of the battles on the frontier. At the return of peace, he exchanged the sword for the pallet, and without instruction of any kind, attained to such excellence, that his pictures attracted much notice, and some little encouragement. But America affords no field for the higher walks of art, and Harding, with powers of the first order, and an unbounded enthusiasm for his profession, is not likely, I fear, to be appreciated as he deserves. Some years ago he visited England, where his talents were fast rising into celebrity, but the strength of the *amor patriæ* unfortunately determined him to return to his native land. I say unfortunately, because in England he could scarcely have failed of attaining both wider fame, and more liberal remuneration, than can well be expected in America. The modesty of this artist is no less remarkable than his genius. He uniformly judges his own performances by the highest standard of criticism, and is far rather disposed to exaggerate than extenuate their defects. Such a character of mind holds out high hopes of future achievement. In truth, even now, he is deficient in nothing, but a certain softness and finish, which time and a little practice will undoubtedly supply.

The better society of Boston, I imagine, is somewhat more exclusive than that of New York. Both pride of family, and pride of knowledge, contribute to this, though there is no public or apparent assertion of either. It is the custom on every Sunday evening for the different branches of a family to assemble at the house of one or other of its members. This generally produces a very social and agreeable party, and though a stranger, I was sometimes hospitably permitted to join the circle. It certainly at first appeared rather singular, that the Bostonians, who are strict observers of the Sabbath, should select that day for any festive celebration, however innocent. I learned, however, that on the literal interpretation of the assertion in Genesis, that "the evening and the morning were the first day," the Sabbath is not observed, as with us, from midnight to midnight, but from sunset to sunset. In conformity with this doctrine, the shops are generally closed at twilight on Saturday evening, and all business is suspended. Of course, after sunset on the day following, they consider themselves discharged from further religious observance, and the evening is generally devoted to social intercourse.

Having passed nearly three weeks in Boston, it became necessary that I should direct my steps to the southward. I determined to return to New York by land, being anxious to see something of the country, and more than I had yet done of its inhabitants. The festivities of Christmas, therefore, were no sooner over, than I quitted Boston, with sentiments of deep gratitude for a kindness, which, from the hour of my arrival, to that of my departure, had continued unbroken.

I have already described an American stage-coach. The one in which I now travelled, though distinguished by the title of "mail-stage," could boast no peculiar attraction. It was old and rickety, and the stuffing of the cushions had become so conglomerated into hard and irregular masses, as to impress the passengers with the conviction of being seated on a bag of pebbles. Fortunately it was not crowded, and the road, though rough, was at least better than that on which I had been jolted on my journey from Providence. It was one o'clock before we got fairly under way, and it is scarcely possible, I imagine, for a journey to commence under gloomier auguries. The weather was most dismal. The wind roared loudly among the branches of the leafless trees, and beat occasionally against the carriage in gusts so violent, as to threaten its overthrow. At length the clouds opened, and down came a storm of snow, which, in a few minutes, had covered the whole surface of the country, as with a winding-sheet.

The first night we slept at Worcester, a town containing about 3000 inhabitants, which the guide-book declares to contain a bank, four printing-offices, a court-house, and a gaol, assertions which I can pretend neither to corroborate nor deny. Its appearance, however, as I observed on the following morning, was far from unprepossessing; the streets were clean, and round the town stood neat and pretty-looking villas, which might have been still prettier, had they displayed less gaudy and tasteless decoration.

As the county court,—or some other,—was then sitting, the inn was crowded with lawyers and their clients, at least fifty of whom already occupied the public *salon,* which was certainly not more than twenty feet square. The passengers were left to scramble out of the coach as they best could in the dark, and afterwards to explore their way without the smallest notice, beyond that of a broad stare from the master of the house. On entering the room, I stood for some time, in the hope that a party who engrossed the whole fire, would compassionate our half-frozen condition, and invite our approach. Nothing, however, was farther from their thoughts than such benevolence. "Friend, did you come by the stage?" asked a man immediately in my front, "I guess you found it tarnation cold." I assured him his conjecture was quite correct, but the reply had not the effect of inducing any relaxation of the blockade. I soon observed, however, that my fellow-travellers elbowed their way without ceremony, and by adopting Rodney's manœuvre of cutting the line, had already gained a comfortable position in rear of the *cordon.* I therefore did not hesitate to follow their example, and pushing resolutely forward, at length enjoyed the sight and warmth of the blazing embers.

In about half an hour, the ringing of a bell gave welcome signal of supper, and accompanying my fellow-passengers to the eating-room, we found a plentiful meal awaiting our appearance. On the score of fare there was certainly no cause of complaint. There were dishes of beef-steaks—which in this country are generally about half the size of a newspaper,—broiled fowl, ham, cold turkey, toast—not made in the English fashion, but boiled in melted butter,—a kind of crumpet called waffles, &c. &c. The tea and coffee were poured out and handed by a girl with long ringlets and ear-rings, not remarkable for neatness of apparel, and who remained seated, unless when actually engaged in the discharge of her functions. Nothing could exceed the gravity of her expression and deportment, and there was an air of cool indifference about her mode of ministering to the wants of the guests, which was certainly far from prepossessing. This New England Hebe, however, was good-looking, and with the addition of a smile would have been pleasing.

Having concluded the meal, I amused myself on our return to the public room, by making observations on the company. The clamour of Babel could not have been much worse than that which filled the apartment. I attempted to discriminate between lawyer and client, but the task was not easy. There was in both the same keen and callous expression of worldly anxiety; the same cold selfishness of look and manner. The scene altogether was not agreeable; many of the company were without shoes, others without a cravat, and compared with people of the same class in England, they were dirty both in habit and person. It is always unpleasant to mingle in a crowd, with the consciousness that you have no sympathy or fellow-feeling with the individuals that compose it. I therefore soon desisted from my task of observation, and having fully digested the contents of a Worcester newspaper, determined on retiring for the night.

The process in England in such circumstances, is

to ring for the chamber-maid, but in America there are no bells, and no chamber-maids. You therefore walk to the bar, and solicit the favour of being supplied with a candle, a request which is ultimately, though by no means immediately, complied with. You then explore the way to your apartment unassisted, and with about the same chance of success as the enterprising Parry in his hunt after the north-west passage. Your number is 63, but in what part of the mansion that number is to be found, you are of course without the means of probable conjecture. Let it be supposed, however, that you are more fortunate than Captain Parry, and at length discover the object of your search. If you are an Englishman, and too young to have roughed it under Wellington, you are probably, what in this country is called "mighty particular;" rejoice in a couple of comfortable pillows, to say nothing of a lurking prejudice in favour of multiplicity of blankets, especially with the thermometer some fifty degrees below the freezing point. Such luxuries, however, it is ten to one you will not find in the uncurtained crib in which you are destined to pass the night. Your first impulse, therefore, is to walk down stairs and make known your wants to the landlord. This is a mistake. Have nothing to say to him. You may rely on it, he is much too busy to have any time to throw away in humouring the whimsies of a foreigner; and should it happen, as it does sometimes in the New England States, that the establishment is composed of natives, your chance of a comfortable sleep for the night, is about as great as that of your gaining the Thirty Thousand pound prize in the lottery. But if there are black, and, still better, if there are Irish servants, your prospect of comfort is wonderfully improved. A douceur, judiciously administered, generally does the business, and when you at length recline after the fatigues of the day, you find your head has acquired at least six inches additional elevation, and the superincumbent weight of woollen has been largely augmented.

It was at Worcester that I received this most useful information. Being in want of the above-mentioned accommodations, I deputed my servant to make an humble representation of my necessities to the landlord. The flinty heart of Boniface, however, was not to be moved. The young lady with the ringlets and ear-rings was no less inexorable, but, luckily for me, a coloured waiter was not proof against the eloquence of a quarter dollar. In five minutes the articles were produced, and as sailors say, "I tumbled in" for the night, with a reasonable prospect of warmth and comfort.

After a good breakfast on the following morning, I felt again fortified for the perils and disagreeables of the mail-stage. Mr Harding, to whose merits as an artist I have already alluded, was fortunately a fellow-passenger, being on his way to join his family at Springfield. The only other passenger was a young lady, with an enormous band-box on her knee, to whom Mr Harding introduced me. There was something in this fair damsel and her band-box peculiarly interesting. She sat immediately opposite to me, but nothing of her face or person was visible, except a forehead, a few dark ringlets, and a pair of the most beautiful eyes in the world, which, like the sun just peeping above the horizon, sent the brightest flashes imaginable, along the upper level of this Brobdignag of a band-box.

The snow had continued to fall during the night, and the jolting of the "mail-stage" was certainly any thing but agreeable. When out of humour, however, by the united influence of the weather and the road, I had only to direct a single glance towards the beautiful orbs scintillating in my front, to be restored to equanimity. When any thing at all jocular was said, one could read a radiant laughter in this expressive feature, though her lips gave utterance to no sound of merriment. For about five hours the fair oculist continued our fellow-traveller, and I had at length come to think of her as some fantastic and preternatural creation; such a being as one sometimes reads of in a German romance, half band-box, and half eye.

At length she left the coach. When her band-box was about to be removed from its position, I remember averting my face, lest a view of her countenance might destroy the fanciful interest she had excited. She departed, therefore, unseen; but those eyes will live in my memory, long after all record of her fellow-traveller shall have faded from hers.

After her departure, Harding told me her story;

she was a young lady of respectable connexions, and with the consent of her family, had become engaged to a young man, who afterwards proved false to his vows, and married a wealthier bride. She had suffered severely under this disappointment, and was then going on a visit to her aunt at Northampton, in the hope that change of scene might contribute to the restoration of her tranquillity. That this result would follow I have no doubt. Those eyes were too laughing and brilliant, to belong permanently to a languishing and broken-hearted maiden.

We dined at a tolerable inn, and proceeded on our journey. The snow had ceased; there was a bright sun above, but I never remember to have felt cold so intense. It was late before we reached Springfield, where I had determined on making a day's halt. The inn was comfortable, and I succeeded in procuring private apartments. On the following morning I took a ramble over the village, which is by far the gayest I had yet seen in the course of my tour. It abounds with white framework villas, with green Venetian blinds, and porticoes of Corinthian or Ionic columns sadly out of proportion. It appears to me, however, that massive columns—and columns not *apparently* massive at least, must be absurd—are sadly out of place when attached to a wooden building. When such fragile materials are employed, *lightness* should be the chief object of the architect, but these transatlantic Palladios seem to despise the antiquated notions of fitness and proportion which prevail in other parts of the world. They heap tawdry ornament upon their gingerbread creations, and you enter a paltry clapboard cottage, through—what is at least meant for—a splendid colonnade.

In the country through which I passed, the houses are nearly all of the class which may be called comfortable. The general scenery at a more favourrable season I can easily conceive to be pretty. The chief defect is the utter flimsiness of the houses, and the glaring effect arising from the too profuse use of the paint-brush. They are evidently not calculated to last above fifteen or twenty years, and this extreme fragility renders more glaring the absurdity of that profusion of gewgaw decoration in which the richer inhabitants delight to indulge.

The country is too new for a landscape painter. With variety of surface, and abundance of wood and water, an artist will certainly find many scenes worthy of his pencil, but the worm fences, and the freshness and regularity of the houses, are sadly destructive of the picturesque. Had the buildings been of more enduring materials, time, the beautifier, would have gradually mellowed down their hardness of outline, and diminished the unpleasant contrast which is here so obtrusively apparent between the works of man and those of nature. But at present there is no chance of this. Each generation builds for itself, and even the human frame is less perishable than the rickety and flimsy structures erected for its comfort.

The advantages of a country, however, are not to be measured by the degree of gratification it may administer to the taste or imagination of a traveller. Where plenty is in the cottage, it matters but little what figure it may make on the canvass of the painter. I have travelled in many countries, but assuredly never in any, where the materials of happiness were so widely and plentifully diffused as in these New England States. And yet the people are not happy, or if they be, there is no faith in Lavater. Never have I seen countenances so furrowed by care as those of this favoured people. Both soul and body appear to have been withered up by the anxieties of life; and with all appliances of enjoyment within their reach, it seems as if some strange curse had gone forth against them, which said, "Ye shall *not* enjoy." One looks in vain here for the ruddy and jovial faces which in England meet us on every hand. The full, broad, and muscular frame; the bold serenity of aspect; the smile, the laugh, the song, the dance,—let not a traveller seek these, or any indications of a light heart and a contented spirit in the New England States.

Let me not, however, be misunderstood. The distinction I would draw is simply this. The Englishman has the inclination to be happy, though not always the means of happiness at command. The New Englander, with a thousand blessings, is deficient in what outvalues them all, the disposition to enjoyment. He is *inter opes inops*.

Something of this misfortune, I have no doubt, is

attributable to climate, but I cannot help believing it in a great degree hereditary. The pilgrim fathers were certainly not men of a very enviable temperament. Full of spiritual pride, needy, bigoted, superstitious, ignorant and despising knowledge, intolerant, fleeing from persecution in the Old World, and yet bringing it with them to the New; such were the men to whom this people may trace many of their peculiarities. That they were distinguished by some of these qualities, was their misfortune; that they were marked by others, was their crime. They and their descendants spread through the wilderness, and solitude had not the effect of softening the asperities of faith or feeling. The spirit of social dependence became broken; and as ages passed on, and the increase of population, and the pursuits of gain, induced them to collect in masses, the towns and villages became peopled with men of solitary habits, relying on their own resources, and associating only for the purposes of gain. Such, doubtless, the New Englanders were; and such they are now, to the observation of a stranger, who is conscious of no temptation to misrepresent them.

The character of the New Englanders is a subject on which I confess I feel tempted to be prolix. In truth, it seems to me so singular and anomalous, so compounded of what is valuable and what is vile, that I never feel certain of having succeeded in expressing the precise combination of feeling which it inspires. As a philanthropist, I should wish them to be less grasping and more contented with the blessings they enjoy, and would willingly barter a good deal of vanity, and a little substantial knavery, for an additional infusion of liberal sentiment, and generous feeling.

Springfield is the seat of one of the chief arsenals and manufactories of arms in the United States. An officer of artillery was good enough to conduct me over these. Every thing seemed well managed, and the machinery at all points very complete. About twelve or thirteen thousand muskets are produced annually. My conductor was a particularly well-informed and obliging person, who had lately returned from Europe, where he had been sent to receive instruction in regard to the recent improvements in gunnery.

The officers of the United States army are better paid than the English. A captain receives about L.400 a-year, or about L.100 more than a lieutenant-colonel in our service. But there is this difference between the British army and that of the United States; no one can enter the latter for pleasure, or to enjoy the enviable privilege of wearing an epaulet and an embroidered coat. The service is one of real and almost constant privation. The troops are scattered about in forts and garrisons in remote and unhealthy situations, and are never quartered, as with us, in the great cities. The principal stations are on the Canadian and Indian frontiers, and on the Mississippi, and I imagine the sort of life they lead there would not be greatly relished by his Majesty's Coldstream Guards or the Blues. I confess I was rather surprised at the smallness of the United States army. It amounts only to 6000 men including all arms, and I was certainly not less astonished at the enormous proportion of desertions, which are no less than 1000 annually, or one-sixth of the whole numbers. Desertions in the British army do not exceed one in a hundred.

On the following day the snow was so deep as to render the road impassable for coaches, so with the thermometer fifteen degrees below zero, I took a sleigh for Hartford, where, after a journey of five hours, we were deposited in safety. Hartford is a small and apparently a very busy town on the Connecticut river. It is rather remarkable as being the seat of the celebrated convention, which, during the late war with Britain, threatened the dissolution of the Union.

I slept at Hartford. The inn was dirty, but this disadvantage was more than counterbalanced by its possession of an Irish waiter, to whom nothing was impossible, and who bustled about in my behalf with an activity and good-will which fortunately it was not difficult to repay. The stage for Newhaven did not start till late on the following day, and I had all the morning on my hands. What to make of it I did not know; so I wandered about the town, saw the College and the New Exchange Buildings, and a church, and a gaol, and a school, and the Charter Oak, and peeped into all the shops, and then returned to the inn with the assured conviction that

Hartford is one of the stupidest places on the surface of the globe. I may as well, however, relate a circumstance which happened here, since it may perhaps throw some light on the New England character.

I had returned from my ramble, and was sitting near the stove in the public room, engaged in the dullest of all tasks, reading an American newspaper, when a woman and a girl, about ten years old, entered, cold and shivering, having just been discharged from a Boston stage-coach. The woman was respectable in appearance, rather good-looking, and evidently belonging to what may in this country be called the middling class of society. She immediately enquired at what hour the steam-boat set off for New York, and, on learning that owing to the river being frozen up, it started from Newhaven, some thirty miles lower, she was evidently much discomposed, and informed the landlord, that calculating on meeting the steam-boat that morning at Hartford, her pocket was quite unprepared for the expense of a further land journey, and the charges of different sorts necessarily occasioned by a day's delay on the road.

The landlord shrugged up his shoulders and walked off; the Irish waiter looked at her with something of a quizzical aspect, and an elderly gentleman, engaged like myself in reading a newspaper, raised his eyes for a moment, discharged his saliva on the carpet, and then resumed his occupation. Though evidently without a willing audience, the woman continued her complaints; informed us she had left her husband in Boston to visit her brother in New York; explained and re-explained the cause of her misfortune, and a dozen times at least concluded by an assurance,—of the truth of which the whole party were quite satisfied,—that she was sadly puzzled what to do.

In such circumstances, I know not whether it was benevolence, or a desire to put a stop to her detestable iteration, or a mingled motive compounded of both, that prompted me to offer to supply her with any money she might require. However, I did so, and the offer, though not absolutely refused, was certainly very ungraciously received. She stared at me expressed no thanks, and again commenced the detail of her grievances, of which, repetition had something staled the infinite variety. I therefore left the apartment. Shortly after the sleigh for Newhaven drove up, and I had entirely forgotten the amiable sufferer and her pecuniary affliction, when she came up, and said, without any expression of civility, " You offered me money, I'll take it." I asked how much she wished. She answered, sixteen dollars, which I immediately ordered my servant to give her. Being a Scotchman, however, he took the prudent precaution of requesting her address in New York, and received a promise that the amount of her debt should be transmitted to Bunker's on the following day.

A week passed after my arrival in New York, and I heard no more either of the dollars or my fellow-traveller, and being curious to know whether I had been cheated, I at length sent to demand repayment. My servant came back with the money. He had seen the woman, who expressed neither thanks nor gratitude; and on being asked why she had violated her promise to discharge the debt, answered that she could not be at the trouble of sending the money, for she supposed it was my business to ask for it. It should be added, that the house in which she resided, was that of her brother, a respectable shopkeeper in one of the best streets in New York, whose establishment certainly betrayed no indication of poverty.

The truth is, that the woman was very far from being a swindler. She was only a Yankee, and troubled with an indisposition—somewhat endemic in New England—to pay money. She thought, perhaps, that a man who had been so imprudent as to lend to a stranger, might be so negligent as to forget to demand repayment. The servant might have lost her address; in short, it was better to take the chances, however small, of ultimately keeping the money, than to restore it unasked. All this might be very sagacious, but it certainly was not very high-principled or very honest.

It was late before we reached Newhaven, and the greater part of the journey was performed in the dark. The inn was so crowded, that the landlord told me fairly he could not give me a bed. I then requested a sofa and a blanket, but with no greater success. However, he proved better than his word. I was shown to a sort of dog-hole without plaster, which I verily believe was the dormitory of the black waiter, who was displaced on my account. The smell of the bed was most offensive, the sheets were dirty, and the coverlid had the appearance of an old horse-cloth. The only other furniture in the apartment was a table and a wooden chair; no glass, no washing-stand, no towels. These articles were promised in the morning, but they never came, though most importunately demanded. The heat of the crowded sitting-room was intense; the temperature of the bed-room was in the opposite extreme. At length, driven from the former, I wrapped myself in my cloak, and sought slumber on the filthy mass of flock from which its usual sable occupant had been expelled.

Cold weather and strong odours are not favourable to sleep. In about two hours I arose, and exploring my way to the sitting-room, now untenanted, passed the rest of the night in a chair by the fire. The steam-boat was to start at five in the morning, and at half past four several coaches drove up to convey the passengers to the quay. I saw nothing of Newhaven, and its associations in my memory are certainly far from pleasant. It was with satisfaction I reached the steam-boat, and bade farewell to it for ever.

The night concluded, however, more fortunately than it commenced. I procured a berth in the steam-boat, and was only roused from a comfortable snoose by the announcement of breakfast, and the clatter of knives and plates which immediately succeeded it. Under such circumstances, I had experience enough to know that no time was to be lost. There is a tide in the affairs of steam-passengers in America, which must be taken at the flood in order to lead either to breakfast or dinner. A minute, therefore, was enough to find me seated at the table, and contributing my strenuous efforts to the work of destruction. Breakfast was succeeded by the still greater luxury of basin and towel, and when I went on deck, a few whiffs of a cigar, and the fine scenery of Long Island Sound, had the effect of obliterating all trace of the disagreeables of the night.

The voyage was pleasant and prosperous; the weather, though still cold, was clear, and before day closed, I again found myself at New York.

CHAPTER IX.

NEW YORK.

On the day after my arrival at New York, the city was thrown into a bustle by the intelligence that a packet from Liverpool had been telegraphed in the offing. Owing to the prevalence of contrary winds, an unusual period had elapsed without an arrival from Europe, and the whole population seemed agog for news. I dined that day with a friend; and as there was no party, and we were both anxious to receive the earliest intelligence, he proposed our walking to the News-room, and afterwards returning to wine and the dessert. On approaching the house, we found some thousands of people collected about the door, and in the window was exhibited a placard of the following import:—" Duke of Wellington and Ministry resigned; Lord Grey, Premier; Brougham, Lord Chancellor," &c.

It was impossible not to be struck with the extreme interest this intelligence excited. Here and there were groups of quidnuncs engaged in earnest discussion on the consequences of this portentous intelligence. Some anticipated immediate revolution; a sort of second edition of the Three Days of Paris. Others were disposed to think that Revolution, though inevitable, would be more gradual. A third party looked forward to the speedy restoration of the Duke of Wellington to power. But all partook of the pervading excitement, and the sensation produced by these changes in the government, could scarcely have been greater in Liverpool than in New York.

On the last night of the year there was a public assembly, to which I received the honour of an invitation. The ball-rooms were very tolerable, but the entrance detestable. It led close past the bar of the City Hotel, and the ladies, in ascending the stair, which, by the by, was offensively dirty, must have been drenched with tobacco smoke. Within, however, I found assembled a great deal of beauty. At seventeen, nothing can be prettier than a smiling damsel of New York. At twenty-two, the same damsel, metamorphosed into a matron, has lost a good deal of her attraction. I had never been in so large and miscellaneous a party before. I looked about for solecisms of deportment, but could detect none on the part of the ladies. There was, however, a sort of *Transatlanticism* about them; and even their numerous points of resemblance to my fair country-women, had the effect of marking out certain shadowy differences, to be felt rather than described.

There was certainly an entire absence of what the French call *l'air noble*,—of that look of mingled elegance and distinction which commands admiration rather than solicits it. Yet the New York ladies are not vulgar. Far from it. I mean only to say that they are not precisely European; and with the possession of so much that is amiable and attractive, they may safely plead guilty to want of absolute conformity to an arbitrary standard, the authority of which they are not bound to acknowledge.

But what shall be said of the gentlemen? Why,

simply that a party of the new police, furnished forth with the requisite *toggery*, would have played their part in the ball-room, with about as much grace. There is a certain uncontrollable rigidity of muscle about an American, and a want of sensibility to the lighter graces of deportment, which makes him perhaps the most unhopeful of all the votaries of Terpsichore. In this respect the advantage is altogether on the side of the ladies. Their motions are rarely inelegant, and never grotesque. I leave it to other travellers to extend this praise to the gentlemen.

An American dandy is a being *sui generis*. He has probably travelled in Europe, and brought back to his own country, a large stock of second-rate fopperies, rings, trinkets, and gold chains, which he displays, evidently with full confidence in their powers of captivation. For a season after his return he is all the fashion. He suggests new improvements in quadrille dancing, and every flourish of his toe becomes the object of sedulous imitation. Tailors wait on him to request the privilege of inspecting his wardrobe. His untravelled companions regard with envy his profusion of jewellery and waistcoats of figured velvet. He talks of "Dukes and Earls, and all their sweeping train; and garters, stars and coronets, appear" in his conversation, as if such things had been familiar to him from his infancy. In short, he reigns for a time the *Magnus Apollo* of his native town, and his decrees in all matters of taste are received as the oracles of the god.

But time passes on. The traveller has returned to the vulgar drudgery of the counting-house; his coats, like his affectations, become threadbare, and are replaced by the more humble productions of native artists; later tourists have been the heralds of newer fashions and fopperies; his opinions are no longer treated with deference; he sinks to the level of other men, and the vulgar dandy is gradually changed into a plain American citizen, content with the comforts of life, without concerning himself about its elegancies.

The ball was very pleasant, and one of its chief *agrémens* undoubtedly was an excellent supper. The oyster-soup, a favourite dish in this part of the world, was all that Dr Kitchiner could have desired.

Turkey, ham, terrapin—a sort of land crab, on which I have not ventured—jellies, creams, ices, fruit, hot punch, and cold lemonade, were in profusion. Having afterwards remained to witness some badly danced quadrilles, and the perpetration of the first gallopade ever attempted on the American continent, I returned to take "my pleasure in mine inn."

It is the custom in New York, on the first day of the year, for the gentlemen to visit all their acquaintances; and the omission of this observance in regard to any particular family, would be considered as a decided slight. The clergy, also, hold a levee on this day, which is attended by their congregation. For my own part, I confess, I found the custom rather inconvenient, there being about thirty families, whose attentions rendered such an acknowledgment indispensable. Determined, however, to fail in nothing which could mark my sense of the kindness of my friends, I ordered a coach, and set forth at rather an early hour on this task of visit-paying.

The first person on whom I waited was Dr Wainwright, the clergyman of Gracechurch, in whose society I had often experienced much pleasure. I found him attired in full canonicals, with a table displaying a profusion of wine and cake, and busied in conversing and shaking hands with his parishioners. Having paid my compliments, I proceeded on my progress, and in the course of about four hours had the satisfaction of believing that I had discharged my duty, though not,—as I afterwards remembered,—without some omissions, which I trust my friends were good enough to forgive.

The routine is as follows: The ladies of a family remain at home to receive visits; the gentlemen are abroad, actively engaged in paying them. You enter, shake hands, are seated, talk for a minute or two on the topics of the day, then hurry off as fast as you can. Wine and cake are on the table, of which each visitor is invited to partake. The custom is of Dutch origin, and, I believe, does not prevail in any other city of the Union. I am told its influence on the social intercourse of families, is very salutary. The first day of the year is considered a day of kindness and reconciliation, on which petty differences are forgotten, and trifling injuries forgiven. It sometimes happens, that between friends long connected, a misunderstanding takes place. Each is too proud to make concessions, alienation follows, and thus are two families, very probably, permanently estranged. But on this day of annual amnesty, each of the offended parties calls on the wife of the other, kind feelings are recalled, past grievances overlooked, and at their next meeting they take each other by the hand, and are again friends.

In company with a most intelligent and kind friend, who was lately mayor of the city, I visited the Navy yard at Brooklyn. Commodore Chauncey, the commander, is a fine specimen of an old sailor of the true breed. He has a good deal of the *Benbow* about him, and one can read in his open and weatherbeaten countenance, that it has long braved both the battle and the breeze. He took us over several men-of-war, and a frigate yet on the stocks, which appeared the most splendid vessel of her class I had ever seen. American men-of-war are built chiefly of live oak, the finest and most durable material in the world.

Every thing in these navy yards is conducted with admirable judgment, for the plain reason, as the

Americans themselves assure me, that the management of the navy is a department in which the mob, everywhere else triumphant, never venture to interfere. There is good sense in this abstinence. The principles of government, which are applicable to a civil community, would make sad work in a man-of-war. The moment a sailor is afloat, he must cast the slough of democracy, and both in word and action cease to be a free man. Every ship is necessarily a despotism, and the existence of any thing like a deliberative body, is utterly incompatible with safety. The necessity of blind obedience is imperious, though it is not easy to understand how those accustomed to liberty and equality on shore, can readily submit to the rigours of naval discipline.

In the same excellent company I made the round of the most interesting public institutions of the city —the House of Refuge for juvenile delinquents, the Deaf and Dumb Asylum, and the Asylum for Lunatics. All are conducted with exemplary judgment, and benevolence exerted with an ardent but enlightened zeal for the general interests of humanity. The first of these institutions is particularly laudable, both as respects its objects and management. It is an asylum for juvenile offenders of both sexes, who, by being thrown into the depraved society of a common gaol, would, in all probability, grow up into hardened and incorrigible criminals. In this institution, they are taught habits of regular industry; are instructed in the principles of religion, and when dismissed, they enter the world with ample means at command of earning an honest livelihood.

The girls are generally bred up as sempstresses or domestic servants; and on quitting the institution, are uniformly sent to a part of the country, where their previous history is unknown. By this judicious arrangement they again start fair, with the full advantage of an unblemished character. The establishment seemed a perfect hive of industry. The taste and talent of the boys is consulted in the choice of a trade. There were young carpenters and blacksmiths, and tailors and brushmakers, and Lilliputian artificers of various kinds, all busily engaged in their peculiar handicraft. Though looking at the details of the establishment with a critical eye, I could detect no fault in any department. There can be no doubt, I think, that the benevolence to which this institution is indebted for its origin and support, is of the most enlightened kind.

I have not yet spoken of the political parties in this country, and, in truth, the subject is so complicated with opinions continually varying, and interests peculiar to particular districts, and includes the consideration of so many topics, apparently unconnected with politics altogether, that I now enter on it with little expectation of making it completely intelligible to an English reader. Of course, all the world knows that the population of the Union is, or was, divided into two great parties, entitled Federalist and Republican. These terms, however, by no means accurately express the differences which divide them. Both parties are Federalist, and both Republican, but the former favour the policy of granting wider powers to the Federal legislature and executive; of asserting their control over the State governments; of guarding the Constitution against popular encroachment; in short, of strengthening the bonds of public union, and maintaining a presiding power of sufficient force and energy, to overawe turbulence at home, and protect the national honour and interests abroad.

The Democratic Republican, on the other hand, would enlarge to the utmost extent the political influence of the people. He is in favour of universal suffrage; a dependent judiciary; a strict and literal interpretation of the articles of the Constitution, and regards the Union simply as a voluntary league between sovereign and independent States, each of which possesses the inalienable right of deciding on the legality of the measures of the general government. The Federalist, in short, is disposed to regard the United States as one and indivisible, and the authority of the United government as paramount to every other jurisdiction. The Democrat considers the Union as a piece of mosaic, tesselated with stones of different colours, curiously put together, but possessing no other principle of cohesion than that of mutual convenience. The one regards the right of withdrawing from the national confederacy as indefeasible in each of its members; the other denies the existence of such right, and maintains the Federal government to be invested with the power of enforcing its decrees within the limits of the Union.

During the period succeeding the Revolution, New England, pre-eminent in wealth, population, and intelligence, gave her principles to the Union. The two first presidents were both Federalists, but their political opponents were rapidly increasing both in numbers and virulence, and even the services, the high name, and unsullied character of Washington, were not sufficient to protect him from the grossest and most slanderous attacks. Adams succeeded him, and certainly did something to merit the imputations which had been gratuitously cast on his predecessor. His sedition law was bad; the prosecutions under it still worse, and in the very first struggle he was driven from office, to return to it no more.*

It is evident that a constitution, however precisely defined, must differ in its practical operation, ac-

* Carey in the Olive Branch mentions a prosecution under this act, in which a New Jersey man was tried and punished for expressing a desire, that the wadding of a gun discharged on a festival day, "had singed or otherwise inflicted damage on" a certain inexpressible part of Mr Adams! After such a prosecution, one is only tempted to regret that the efficiency of the wish was not equal to its patriotism.

cording to the principles on which it is administered. From the period of Jefferson's accession to power, a change in this respect took place. The government was then administered on democratic principles; a silent revolution was going forward; the principles, opinions, and habits of the people, all tended towards the wider extension of political rights; and at the conclusion of the war with England, the Federalists became at length convinced, that the objects for which they had so long strenuously been contending, were utterly unattainable. Farther contention, therefore, was useless. The name of Federalist had become odious to the people; it was heard no more. No candidate for public favour ventured to come forward and declare his conviction, that a government, which looked for support to the prejudices of the populace, was necessarily less secure and beneficial than one which represented the deliberate convictions of the wealthier and more enlightened.

The result of all this was, an apparent harmony of political principle throughout the Union. Open differences of opinion were no longer expressed, as to the broad and fundamental doctrines of government.

The ascendency of numbers, in opposition to that of property and intelligence, had been firmly established; the people, in the widest sense of the term, had been recognised as the only source of power and of honour; and the government, instead of attempting to control and regulate the passions and prejudices of the multitude, were forced, by the necessity of their situation, to adopt them as the guide and standard of their policy. They were compelled, in short, to adopt the measures, and profess the principles most palatable to the people, instead of those which wider knowledge and keener sagacity might indicate as most for their advantage.

I remember one of my first impressions in the United States was that of surprise, at the harmony in regard to the great principles of government, which seemed to pervade all classes of the community. In every thing connected with men and measures, however, all was clamour and confusion. The patriot of one company was the scoundrel of the next, and to an uninterested observer, the praise and the abuse seemed both to rest on a foundation too narrow to afford support to such disproportionate superstructures. Parties there evidently were, but it was not easy to become master of the distinctions on which they rested. I asked for the Federalists, and was told, that like the mammoth and the megatherion, they had become extinct, and their principles delighted humanity no longer. I asked for the Democrats, and I was desired to look on the countenance of every man I met in the street. This puzzled me, for the principles of this exploded party, appeared, in my deliberate conviction, to be those most in accordance with political wisdom, and I had little faith in the efficacy of sudden conversions, either in politics or religion.

In such circumstances, instead of attempting to grope my way to a conclusion, by any dark and doubtful hypothesis, I determined to demand information from those best calculated to afford it. I therefore explained my difficulties to one of the most eminent individuals of the Union, whom I knew at least to have been formerly a Federalist. " How comes it," I asked, " that the party which you formerly adorned by your talents and eloquence, is no longer to be found? Is it, that the progress of events, increased experience, and more deliberate and enlightened views, have induced you to relinquish your former tenets; or, that still entertaining the same opinions, you are simply withheld by policy from expressing them?" His answer—in substance as follows—was too striking to be forgotten. "My opinions, and I believe those of the party to which I belonged, are unchanged; and the course of events in this country has been such, as to impress only a deeper and more thorough conviction of their wisdom. But, in the present state of public feeling, we *dare not* express them. An individual professing such opinions, would not only find himself excluded from every office of public trust, within the scope of his reasonable ambition, but he would be regarded by his neighbours and fellow-citizens with an evil eye. His words and actions would become the objects of jealous and malignant scrutiny, and he would have to sustain the unceasing attacks of a host of unscrupulous and ferocious assailants. And for what object is his life to be thus embittered, and he is to be cut off from the common objects of honourable ambition? Why, for the satisfaction of expressing his adherence to an obsolete creed, and his persuasion of the wisdom of certain doctrines of government, which his judgment assures him, are utterly impracticable in the present condition of society."

When the Americans do agree, therefore, their unanimity is really *not* very wonderful, seeing it proceeds from the observance of the good old rule, of punishing all difference of opinion. The consequence, however, has been, not the eradication of federal principles, but a discontinuance of their profession. The combatants fight under a new banner, but the battle is not less bitter on that account. There is no longer any question with regard to increase of power on the part of the general government; that has long since been decided; but the point of contention now is, whether it shall keep that authority with which it is at present understood to be invested. But even this substantial ground of difference is rarely brought prominently forward in debate. The struggle generally is with regard to particular measures, involving many collateral interests, but which are felt to have a tendency to one side or the other.

Thus one great subject of discussion relates to the

power of the government to expend a portion of the national funds in internal improvements. In 1830, a bill which had passed the legislature for the construction of a national road, was returned with the veto of the President. By the articles of the constitution, the federal legislature are invested with the power of "establishing post-offices and post-roads." The doubt is, whether the word *establish* gives the privilege to *construct*, or is to be understood as simply granting authority to convert into post-roads, thoroughfares already in existence. A principle of great importance is no doubt involved in this question, since by it must be decided whether the federal government have the power of adopting any general system of improvements, or of executing public works with a view to the national advantage. The existence of such a power would no doubt materially tend to strengthen its influence, and this, which is a recommendation with one party, constitutes the chief objection with the other. General Jackson is the leading champion on the one side; Mr Clay, his opponent for the Presidency, on the other. The latter is backed by the northern and a considerable portion of the Central States; the former by the Southern and Western.

There can be no doubt, I imagine, that the Federalists, in supporting the affirmative of this question, are influenced by the *tendency* of the opinions they advocate, to enlarge and strengthen the power of the executive, but the grounds on which they attempt to gain proselytes are entirely collateral. They urge the general expediency of such a power; the impossibility of inducing the legislatures of the different States to concur heartily in any one project for the benefit of the whole; the necessity of unity of execution, as well as unity of design; and the probability, that if such improvements are not undertaken by the federal government, they will never be executed at all.

Of course, such questions as the Tariff, and that of which I have just spoken, are not exclusively decided by political principle. Private interest steps in; many of the democratic party adopt the views of their opponents on some single question of policy, and where that is of great importance, range themselves under the same banner. Thus, a candidate for

Congress is often supported by men differing on many questions, and agreeing only in one. Commercial men are usually in favour of the system of internal improvements, because these must generally bring with them increased facilities for commerce. A new road may open a new market; the deepening of a harbour may change the whole aspect of a province; and those, who by their local position or pursuits are more immediately interested in these benefits, may be pardoned, if, on an occasion of such moment, they lay aside their principles, and act on the narrower and stronger motive of personal advantage.

In a country of such extraordinary extent as the United States, there are of course a vast number of local interests, which modify the application of theoretical principle. In the representative of each district, some peculiarity of creed is commonly necessary to secure the support of his constituents. Conformity on leading points of opinion is not enough; there is almost always some topic, however unconnected with politics, on which coincidence of sentiment is demanded. I may quote a striking instance of this in the State of New York.

Some years ago a man of the name of Morgan, who wrote a book revealing the secrets of Free-Masonry, was forcibly seized in his own dwelling-house, carried off, and murdered. Of the latter fact there is no direct proof, but it is impossible to account for the circumstances on any other supposition. He is known to have been conveyed to the neighbourhood of Niagara, and there is evidence of his having passed a night there; but from that period to the present, no traces of the unfortunate man have ever been discovered. Of course the vigilance of justice was aroused by this outrage. The public prosecutor was long unsuccessful in his attempts to bring the criminals to trial. At length, however, strong circumstantial evidence was obtained, which went to fix participation in the crime on two individuals. They were brought to trial. A majority of the jury had no doubt of their guilt, but the minority thought otherwise, and the men were acquitted.

The circumstance of the jurymen who procured the acquittal being Free-Masons, contributed to inflame the public indignation, already strongly excited by the original outrage. The principles of this secret society had not only caused crime to be committed, but justice to be denied. Unquestionably Free-Masonry had given rise to murder, and as unquestionably, in the opinion of many, its influence had secured impunity to the offenders. The question thus arose,—is a society which produces such consequences to be tolerated in a Christian community? A large portion of the people banded together in hostility to all secret and affiliated societies. They pronounced them dangerous and unconstitutional, and pledged themselves to exert their utmost efforts for their suppression.

The Masons, on the other hand, were a widely ramified and powerful body, embracing in their number nearly half the population of the State. Their constitution gave them the advantage of unity of purpose and of action. The keenness of contest, of course, excited the passions of both parties. The public press ranged itself on different sides; every candidate for office was compelled to make confession of his creed on this important subject, and to fight under the banner of one party or the other; and the distinction of Mason or Anti-Mason superseded, if it did not extinguish, those arising from differences more legitimately political. In the late elections the Masonic party were triumphant; but the struggle is still carried on with vigour, and there is no doubt that the votes in the next presidential election will be materially affected by it. Indeed the mania on this subject is daily spreading. It was at first exclusively confined to the State of New York; it is now becoming diffused over the New England States and Pennsylvania.

It is such collateral influences which puzzle an Englishman, when he attempts to become acquainted with the state of parties in this country. He looks for the broad distinction of political principle, and he finds men fighting about Masonry, or other matters which have no apparent bearing on the great doctrines of government. He finds general opinions modified by local interests, and seeks in vain to discover some single and definite question which may serve as a touchstone of party distinctions. It is only by acute and varied observation, and by conversation with enlightened men of all parties, that he is enabled to make due allowance for the variations of the political compass, and judge accurately of the course which the vessel is steering.

The Americans have a notion that they are a people not easily understood, and that to comprehend their character requires a long apprenticeship of philosophical observation, and more both of patience and liberality than are usually compatible with the temper and prejudices of foreign travellers. This is a mistake. The peculiarities of the Americans lie more on the surface than those of any people I have ever known. Their features are broad and marked; there exists little individual eccentricity of character, and it is in their political relations alone that they are difficult to be understood. One fact, however, is confessed by all parties, that the progress of democratic principles from the period of the Revolution has been very great. During my whole residence in the United States, I conversed with no enlightened American, who did not confess, that the constitution now, though the same in letter with that established in 1789, is essentially different in spirit. It was undoubtedly the wish of Washington and Hamilton to counterpoise, as much as circumstances would permit, the rashness of democracy by the caution and wisdom of an aristocracy of intelligence and wealth. There is now no attempt at counterpoise. The weight is all in one scale, and how low, by continued increase of pressure, it is yet to descend, would require a prophet of some sagacity to foretell. I shall state a few circumstances which may illustrate the progress and tendency of opinion among the people of New York.

In that city a separation is rapidly taking place between the different orders of society. The operative class have already formed themselves into a society, under the name of "*The Workies,*" in direct opposition to those who, more favoured by nature or fortune, enjoy the luxuries of life without the necessity of manual labour. These people make no secret of their demands, which to do them justice are few and emphatic. They are published in the newspapers, and may be read on half the walls of New York. Their first postulate is "EQUAL AND UNIVERSAL EDUCATION." It is false, they say, to maintain that there is at present no privileged order, no practical aristocracy, in a country where distinctions of education are permitted. That portion of the population whom the necessity of manual labour cuts off from the opportunity of enlarged acquirement, is in fact excluded from all the valuable offices of the State. As matters are now ordered in the United States, these are distributed exclusively among one small class of the community, while those who constitute the real strength of the country, have barely a voice in the distribution of those loaves and fishes, which they are not permitted to enjoy. There does exist then—they argue—an aristocracy of the most odious kind,—an aristocracy of knowledge, education, and refinement, which is inconsistent with the true democratic principle of absolute equality. They pledge themselves, therefore, to exert every effort, mental and physical, for the abolition of this flagrant injustice. They proclaim it to the world as a nuisance which must be abated, before the freedom of an American be something more than a mere empty boast. They solemnly declare that they will not rest satisfied, till every citizen in the United

States shall receive the same degree of education, and start fair in the competition for the honours and the offices of the state. As it is of course impossible —and these men know it to be so—to educate the labouring class to the standard of the richer, it is their professed object to reduce the latter to the same mental condition with the former; to prohibit all supererogatory knowledge; to have a maximum of acquirement beyond which it shall be punishable to go.

But those who limit their views to the mental degradation of their country, are in fact the MODERATES of the party. There are others who go still further, and boldly advocate the introduction of an AGRARIAN LAW, and a periodical division of property. These unquestionably constitute the *extrême gauche* of the Worky Parliament, but still they only follow out the principles of their less violent neighbours, and eloquently dilate on the justice and propriety of every individual being equally supplied with food and clothing; on the monstrous iniquity of one man riding in his carriage while another walks on foot, and after his drive discussing a bottle of

Champagne, while many of his neighbours are shamefully compelled to be content with the pure element. Only equalize property, they say, and neither would drink Champagne or water, but both would have brandy, a consummation worthy of centuries of struggle to attain.

All this is nonsense undoubtedly, nor do I say that this party, though strong in New York, is yet so numerous or so widely diffused as to create immediate alarm. In the elections, however, for the civic offices of the city, their influence is strongly felt; and there can be no doubt that as population becomes more dense, and the supply of labour shall equal, or exceed the demand for it, the strength of this party must be enormously augmented. Their ranks will always be recruited by the needy, the idle and the profligate, and like a rolling snowball it will gather strength and volume as it proceeds, until at length it comes down thundering with the force and desolation of an avalanche.

This event may be distant, but it is not the less certain on that account. It is nothing to say, that the immense extent of fertile territory yet to be occupied by an unborn population will delay the day of ruin. It will delay, but it cannot prevent it. The traveller, at the source of the Mississippi, in the very heart of the American Continent, may predict with perfect certainty, that however protracted the wanderings of the rivulet at his foot, it must reach the ocean at last. In proportion as the nearer lands are occupied, it is very evident that the region to which emigration will be directed must of necessity be more distant. The pressure of population therefore will continue to augment in the Atlantic States, and the motives to removal become gradually weaker. Indeed, at the present rate of extension, the circle of occupied territory must before many generations be so enormously enlarged, that emigration will be confined wholly to the Western States. Then, and not till then, will come the trial of the American constitution; and until that trial has been passed, it is mere nonsense to appeal to its stability.

Nor is this period of trial apparently very distant. At the present ratio of increase, the population of the United States doubles itself in about twenty-four years, so that in half a century it will amount to about fifty millions, of which ten millions will be slaves, or at all events a degraded caste, cut off from all the rights and privileges of citizenship. Before this period it is very certain that the pressure of the population, on the means of subsistence, especially in the Atlantic States, will be very great. The price of labour will have fallen, while that of the necessaries of life must be prodigiously enhanced. The poorer and more suffering class, will want the means of emigrating to a distant region of unoccupied territory. Poverty and misery will be abroad; the great majority of the people will be without property of any kind, except the thews and sinews with which God has endowed them; they will choose legislators under the immediate pressure of privation; and if in such circumstances, any man can anticipate security of property, his conclusion must be founded, I suspect, rather on the wishes of a sanguine temperament, than on any rational calculation of probabilities.

It is the present policy of the government to encourage and stimulate the premature growth of a manufacturing population. In this it will not be successful, but no man can contemplate the vast internal resources of the United States,—the varied productions of their soil,—the unparalleled extent of river communication,—the inexhaustible stores of coal and iron which are spread even on the surface,—and doubt that the Americans are destined to become a great manufacturing nation. Whenever increase of population shall have reduced the price of labour to a par with that in other countries, these advantages will come into full play; the United States will then meet England on fair terms in every market of the world, and in many branches of industry at least, will very probably attain an unquestioned superiority. Huge manufacturing cities will spring up in various quarters of the Union, the population will congregate in masses, and all the vices incident to such a condition of society will attain speedy maturity. Millions of men will depend for subsistence on the demand for a particular manufacture, and yet this demand will of necessity be liable to perpetual fluctuation. When the pendulum vibrates in one direction, there will be an influx of wealth and prosperity; when it vibrates in the other, misery, discontent, and turbulence will spread through the land. A change of fashion, a war, the glut of a foreign market, a thousand unforeseen and inevitable accidents are liable to produce this, and deprive multitudes of bread, who but a month before were enjoying all the comforts of life. Let it be remembered that in this suffering class will be practically deposited the whole political power of the state; that there can be no military force to maintain civil order, and protect property; and to what quarter, I should be glad to know, is the rich man to look for security, either of person or fortune?

There will be no occasion however for convulsion or violence. The *Worky* convention will only have to choose representatives of their own principles, in order to accomplish a general system of spoliation, in the most legal and constitutional manner. It is not even necessary that a majority of the federal legislature should concur in this. It is competent to the government of each state to dispose of the property within their own limits as they think proper, and whenever a *numerical* majority of the people shall be in favour of an Agrarian law, there exists no counteracting influence to prevent, or even to retard its adoption.

I have had the advantage of conversing with many of the most eminent Americans of the Union on the future prospects of their country, and I certainly remember none who did not admit that a period of trial, such as that I have ventured to describe, is according to all human calculation inevitable. Many of them reckoned much on education as a means of safety, and unquestionably in a country where the mere power of breathing carries with it the right of suffrage, the diffusion of sound knowledge is always essential to the public security. It unfortunately happens, however, that in proportion as poverty increases, not only the means but the desire of instruction are necessarily diminished. The man whose whole energies are required for the supply of his bodily wants, has neither time nor inclination to concern himself about his mental deficiencies, and the result of human experience does not warrant us in reckoning on the restraint of individual cupidity, where no obstacle exists to its gratification, by any deliberate calculation of its consequences on society. There can be no doubt, that if men could be made wise enough to act on an enlarged and enlightened view of their own interest, government might be dispensed with altogether; but what statesman would legislate on the probability of such a condition of society, or rely on it as a means of future safety?

The general answer, however, is, that the state of things which I have ventured to describe, is very distant. "It is enough," they say, "for each generation to look to itself, and we leave it to our descendants some centuries hence to take care of their interests as we do of ours. We enjoy all manner of freedom and security under our present constitution, and really feel very little concern about the evils which may afflict our posterity." I cannot help believing, however, that the period of trial is somewhat less distant than such reasoners comfort themselves by imagining; but if the question be conceded that democracy necessarily leads to anarchy and spoliation, it does not seem that the mere length of road to be travelled is a point of much importance. This, of course, would vary according to the peculiar circumstances of every country in which the experiment might be tried. In England the journey would be performed with railway velocity. In the United States, with the great advantages they possess, it may continue a generation or two longer, but the termination is the same. The doubt regards time, not destination.

At present the United States are perhaps more safe from revolutionary contention than any other country in the world. But this safety consists in one circumstance alone. *The great majority of the people are possessed of property*; have what is called a stake in the hedge; and are therefore, by interest, opposed to all measures which may tend to its insecurity. It is for such a condition of society that the present constitution was framed; and could this great bulwark of prudent government, be rendered as permanent as it is effective, there could be no assignable limit to the prosperity of a people so favoured. But the truth is undeniable, that as population increases, another state of things must necessarily arise, and one unfortunately never dreamt of in the philosophy of American legislators. The majority of the people will then consist of men without property of any kind, subject to the immediate pressure of want, and then will be decided the great struggle between property and numbers; on the one side hunger, rapacity, and physical power; reason, justice, and helplessness on the other. The weapons of this fearful contest are already forged; the hands will soon be born that are to wield them. At all events, let no man appeal to the stability of the American government as being established by experience, till this trial has been overpast. Forty years are no time to test the permanence, or, if I may so speak, the vitality of a constitution, the immediate advantages of which are strongly felt, and the evils latent and comparatively remote.

It may be well to explain, that what I have hitherto said has rather been directed to the pervading democracy of the institutions of the different States than to the federal government. Of the latter it is difficult to speak, because it is difficult to ascertain with any precision, the principles on which it is founded. I think it was a saying of Lord Eldon, that there was no act of Parliament so carefully worded that he could not drive a coach and six through it. The American lawyers have been at least equally successful with regard to their federal constitution. No man appears precisely to understand what it is, but all agree that it is something very wise. It is a sort of political gospel, in which every man finds a reflection of his own prejudices and opinions. Ask a New England statesman what is the constitution, and he will tell you something very different from a Georgian or South Carolinian. Even the halls of Congress yet echo with loud and bitter disputation as to the primary and fundamental principle on which it is based. Ask the President of the United States, what is the nature of the government he administers with so much honour to himself and advantage to his country, and General Jackson will tell you that it is a government of *consolidation*, possessing full power to enforce its decrees in every district of the Union. Ask the Vice-president, and he will assure you that the government is merely *confederative*, and depends for its authority on the free consent of the individual States. Ask Mr Clay or Mr Webster what are the powers of this apparently unintelligible constitution, and they will probably include in their number the privilege of taxing at discretion the commerce of the country, and expending the money so raised in projects of internal improvement. Put the same question to General Hayne or Mr Van Buren, and they will assert that such doctrine is of the most injurious tendency, and proceeds altogether on a false interpretation; and yet all will agree that the federal constitution is the highest, most perspicuous, and faultless achievement of human legislation! It may be so, but till this masterpiece of polity becomes something more definite and intelligible, a foreigner may perhaps be excused for holding his admiration in abeyance.

At all events, it is abundantly clear, that the seeds of discord are plentifully scattered throughout the Union. Men of different habits, different interests, different modes of thought; the inhabitants of different climates, and agreeing only in mutual antipathy, are united under a common government, whose powers are so indefinite as to afford matter for interminable and rancorous disputation. Does such a government bear the impress of permanence? Or does it not rather seem, in its very structure, to concentrate all the scattered elements of decay?

When we contemplate the political relations of this singular people, the question naturally arises whether unity of government be compatible with great diversities of interest in the governed. There may possibly be reasoners who are prepared to answer this question in the affirmative, and to these we may look for instruction as to the advantages such a government as that of the United States possesses over others of smaller extent, and therefore capable of closer adaptation to the peculiar wants and interests of a people. To me it certainly appears that there can be no firm adhesion without homogeneity in a population. Let men once feel that their interests are the same; that they are exposed to the same dangers; solicitous for the same objects, partaking of the same advantages, and connected by some reasonable degree of geographical propinquity, and in such a community there is no fear of separation or dismemberment. The population in such circumstances forms one uniform and firmly-concatenated whole, whereas a Union on other principles resembles that of a bag of sand, in which the separate particles, though held together for a time, retain their original and abstract individuality.

Let us look for a moment at this Union. In Florida and Louisiana they grow sugar; in Maine there is scarcely sun enough to ripen a crop of maize. The people of these States are no less different than the productions of their soil. They are animated by no sentiment of brotherhood and affinity. Nature has divided them by a distance of two thousand miles; the interests of one are neither understood nor cared for in the other. In short, they are connected by nothing but a clumsy and awkward piece of machinery most felicitously contrived to deprive both of the blessing of self-government. What is gained by this? A certain degree of strength, undoubtedly, but not more than might be produced by an alliance between independent States, unaccompanied by that jealousy and conflict of opposing interests, which is the present curse of the whole Union.

I remember, when at Washington, stating my impressions on this subject to a distinguished member of the House of Representatives, who admitted that the ends of good government would most probably be better and more easily attainable were the Union divided into several republics, firmly united for purposes of defence, but enjoying complete legislative independence. "And yet," he continued, "the scheme could not possibly succeed. The truth is, the Union is necessary to prevent us from cutting each other's throats." Nor is this to be considered as the singular opinion of some eccentric individual. I have often conversed on the subject with men of great intelligence in different parts of the Union, and found a perfect harmony of opinion as to the results of separation. The northern gentlemen, in particular, seemed to regard the federal government as the ark of their safety from civil war and bloodshed. In such circumstances it might charitably be wished, that their ark was a stronger seaboat, and better calculated to weather the storms to which it is likely to be exposed.

In truth, every year must increase the perils of this federal constitution. Like other bubbles, it is at any time liable to burst, and the world will then discover that its external glitter covered nothing but wind. It may split to-morrow on the Tariff question, or it may go on, till, like a dropsical patient, it dies of mere extension, when its remains will probably be denied even the decent honours of Christian burial. It was near giving up the ghost at the time of the Hartford Convention, and is now in a state of grievous suffering from the Carolina fever. It will probably survive this attack as it did the former, since the great majority of the States are at present in favour of its continuance. But, with the prevalence of the doctrine of nullification, it is impossible it can ever gain much strength or vigour. If each State is to have the privilege of sitting in judgment on the legality of its measures, the range of its legislation must necessarily be very confined. It will puzzle the ingenuity of American statesmen, to discover some policy which will prove palatable to the various members of the Union, and which all interpreters of the Constitution will confess to be within the narrow limits of its power.

Let us suppose in England that every county asserted the privilege of nullifying, when it thought proper, the acts of the British Parliament. Leicestershire would summon her population in convention to resist any reduction of the foreign wool-duty. Kent and Surry would nullify the hop-duty. Lay a rude finger on kelp, and a distant threat of separation would be heard from the Orkneys. Dorset and Wilts would insist on the continuance of the corn-laws, and woe to the Chancellor of the Exchequer who should venture to raise the Highland war-slogan by an impost on horned cattle! Yet in Great Britain there exist no provincial jealousies, and the interests of the whole kingdom are far more intimately amalgamated than can ever be the case in the United States.

Amid the multitude of events which threaten the dissolution of the Union, I may venture to specify one. The influence of each State in the election of the President is in the exact ratio of the amount of its population. In this respect the increase in some States is far greater than in others. The unrivalled advantages of New York have already given it the lead, and the same causes must necessarily still continue to augment its comparative superiority. Ohio—

a State also rich in natural advantages—has recently been advancing with astonishing rapidity, and the time is apparently not far distant when three States (New York, Pennsylvania, and Ohio) must possess a numerical majority of the whole population, and of course the power of electing the President, independently of the other twenty-one States. Will the States thus virtually excluded, tamely submit to this, or will they appeal to Congress for an amendment of the constitution? There can be no prospect of redress from this quarter. The same superiority of population which gave those three States the power of electing the President, has of course also given them the majority of the House of Representatives, and no amendment of the constitution can take place without the concurrence of two-thirds of both houses. Besides, the principle of election by numerical majority is fundamental throughout the Union, and could not be abrogated without a total violation of consistency. It does appear, therefore, that in no great distance of time the whole substantial influence of the federal government may be wielded by three States, and that whenever these choose to combine, it will be in their power to carry any measure, however obnoxious, to the rest of the Union. The Senate, it is true, which consists of delegates in equal number from each State, would be free from this influence, but in any struggle with the more popular house, it must of course prove the weaker party, and be compelled to yield.

Those know little of the character of the American people, who imagine that the great majority of the States would tolerate being reduced to the condition of political ciphers. Their jealousy of each other is very great, and there can be no doubt, that should the contingency here contemplated occur, it must occasion a total disruption of the bonds of union. I believe it is the probability of such an event, joined to the apprehension of some interference with the condition of the slave population, which makes the people of the Southern States so anxious to narrow the power of the general government. At all events, it will be singular indeed if the seeds of civil broil, disseminated in a soil so admirably fitted to bring them to maturity, should not eventually yield an abundant harvest of animosity and dissension.*

After much — I hope impartial and certainly patient—observation, it does appear to me, that universal suffrage is the rock on which American freedom is most likely to suffer shipwreck. The intrinsic evils of the system are very great, and its adoption in the United States was the more monstrous, because a qualification in property is there not only a test of intelligence, but of moral character. The man must either be idle or profligate, or more probably both, who does not, in a country where labour is so highly rewarded, obtain a qualification of some sort. He is evidently unworthy of the right of suffrage, and by every wise legislature will be debarred from

* The opinions I have ventured to express on this subject are by no means singular. They are those of a large portion of the American people. Chancellor Kent—the ablest constitutional lawyer of his country—says, in his Commentaries, " *If ever the tranquillity of this nation is to be disturbed, and its peace jeopardised by a struggle for power among themselves, it will be upon this very subject of the choice of a President. It is the question that is eventually to attest the goodness and try the strength of the constitution.*" And many other authorities might be adduced, were the subject one on which *mere* authority could have much weight.

its exercise. In densely peopled countries the test of property in reference to moral qualities is fallible, —perhaps too fallible to be relied on with much confidence. In the United States it is *unerring*, or at least the possible exceptions are so few, and must arise from circumstances so peculiar, that it is altogether unnecessary they should find any place in the calculations of a statesman. But American legislators have thought proper to cast away this inestimable advantage. Seeing no immediate danger in the utmost extent of suffrage, they were content to remain blind to the future. They took every precaution that the rights of the poor man should not be encroached on by the rich, but never seem to have contemplated the possibility that the rights of the latter might be violated by the former. American protection, like Irish reciprocity, was all on one side. It was withheld where most needed; it was profusely lavished where there was no risk of danger. They put a sword in the hand of one combatant, and took the shield from the arm of the other.

The leader who gave the first and most powerful

impulse to the democratic tendencies of the constitution was unquestionably Jefferson. His countrymen call him great, but in truth he was great only when compared with those by whom he was surrounded. In brilliance and activity of intellect he was inferior to Hamilton; but Hamilton in heart and mind was an aristocrat, and too honourable and too proud to shape his political course to catch the flitting gales of popular favour. Death, fortunately for Jefferson, removed the only rival, by whom his reputation coul dhave been eclipsed, or his political principles successfully opposed. Adams he encountered and overthrew. Federalism, never calculated to secure popular favour, dwindled on, till in the termination of the late war it received its death-blow, and the democratic party remained undisputed lords of the ascendant.

We seek in vain in the writings of Jefferson for indications of original or profound thought. When in France, he had been captivated by that shallow philosophy of which Diderot and Condorcet were the apostles, and he returned to America, the zealous partisan of opinions, which no subsequent experience could induce him to relinquish or modify. During by far the greater portion of his life, the intellect of Jefferson remained stationary. Time passed on; generations were gathered to their fathers; the dawn of liberty on the continent of Europe had terminated in a bloody sunset; but the shadow on the dial of his mind remained unmoved. In his correspondence we find him to the very last, complacently putting forth the stale and flimsy dogmas, which, when backed by the guillotine, had passed for unanswerable in the Jacobin coteries of the Revolution.

The mind of Jefferson was essentially unpoetical. In his whole works there is no trace discoverable of imaginative power. His benevolence was rather topical than expansive. It reached France, but never ventured across the channel. Had Napoleon invaded England, the heart and prayers of Jefferson would have followed him in the enterprise. He would have gloated over her fallen palaces, her conflagrated cities, her desolate fields. Her blood, her sufferings, her tears, the glorious memory of her past achievements, would in him have excited no feeling of compassionate regret. Jefferson had little enthusiasm of character. Nor was he rich in those warm charities and affections, in which great minds are rarely deficient. He has been truly called a good hater. His resentments were not vehement and fiery ebullitions, burning fiercely for a time, and then subsiding into indifference or dislike. They were cool, fiendlike, and ferocious; unsparing, undying, unappeaseable. The enmities of most men terminate with the death of their object. It was the delight of Jefferson to trample even on the graves of his political opponents. The manner in which he speaks of Hamilton in his correspondence, and the charges by which he vainly attempts to blast his reputation, will attach an indelible tarnish to his own memory. He never forgave the superior confidence which Washington reposed in the wisdom and integrity of Hamilton. The only amiable feature in the whole life of Jefferson was his reconciliation with Adams, and there the efficient link was community of hatred. Both detested Hamilton.

The moral character of Jefferson was repulsive. Continually puling about liberty, equality, and the degrading curse of slavery, he brought his own children to the hammer, and made money of his debaucheries. Even at his death, he did not manumit his numerous offspring, but left them, soul and body, to degradation, and the cart-whip. A daughter of Jefferson was sold some years ago, by public auction, at New Orleans, and purchased by a society of gentlemen, who wished to testify, by her liberation, their admiration of the statesman,

"Who dreamt of freedom in a slave's embrace."

This single line gives more insight to the character of the man, than whole volumes of panegyric. It will outlive his epitaph, write it who may.

Jefferson was succeeded by Madison, a mere reflex of his political opinions. If he wanted the harsher points of Jefferson's character, he wanted also its vigour. The system he pursued was indistinguishable from that of his predecessor, and during his Presidency the current of democracy flowed on with increased violence and velocity. Munroe came next, and becoming at length aware of the prevailing tendencies of the constitution, was anxious to steer a middle course. He organized a piebald cabinet, composed of men of different opinions, and the result of their conjunction was a sort of hybrid policy, half federalist and half democratic, which gave satisfaction to no party.

At the termination of Mr Munroe's second period of office, Mr John Quincy Adams became his successor, by a sort of electioneering juggle which occasioned a universal sentiment of disgust. What the principles of this statesman were, or are, seems a matter not very intelligible to his own countrymen, and of course is still less so to a foreigner. All that is necessary to be known is, that at the expiration of four years Mr Quincy Adams was turned out, to the great satisfaction of the whole Union, and that though he still continues in the healthy enjoyment of all corporeal and mental functions, there is assuredly no chance that he will ever again be promoted to any office of political trust and importance.

General Jackson, the present President, has always been an eminent member of the democratic party. His accession to office however, united to the experience of a long life, is understood to have induced a change in some of his opinions, and a modification of others. His policy is as moderate as the circumstances of the times will permit. On the Tariff question his opinions are not precisely known, but he decidedly opposes the application of the public money, under direction of the federal government, to projects of internal improvement.

General Jackson was certainly indebted for his present elevation, to the reputation he acquired in the successful defence of New Orleans. In truth, I believe his popularity is rather military than political, since even those—and they are many—who dislike him as a politician, extol him as the first general of the age, whose reputation beggars the fame of the most celebrated modern strategists.

It is excusable to smile at this, but scarcely fair to visit it with the severity of ridicule. New Orleans, —for want of a better,—is the American Waterloo; and while the loss to England occasioned by this disaster is a fixed quantity neither to be increased nor diminished, why should we object to the display of a little harmless vanity, or demand that our successful opponents should measure the extent of their achievement rather by our standard than by their own?

When talking of American statesmen, I may as well detail a few circumstances connected with one, who has certainly played a very conspicuous part in the politics of his country. I allude to the celebrated Colonel Burr, formerly Vice-President of the United States, and who, in 1800, was within a vote of becoming President in opposition to Jefferson and Adams. It is well known, that strong political differences with General Hamilton, embittered by a good deal of personal dislike, led to a duel, in which Hamilton lost his life. To this misfortune is attributable the entire ruin of Colonel Burr's prospects as a statesman. Hamilton was admired by all parties, and the voice of lamentation was heard from the whole Union on the premature extinction of the highest intellect of the country. There arose a general and powerful feeling of indignation against the author of this national calamity; but Burr was not a man to shrink from the pelting of any tempest, however vehement. He braved its violence, but at once knew that his popularity was gone for ever.

Subsequently he was concerned in some conspiracy to sieze on part of Mexico, of which he was to become sovereign, by the style and title—I suppose—of Aaron the First, King or Emperor of the Texas. Colonel Burr was likewise accused of treason to the commonwealth, in attempting to overthrow the constitution by force of arms. But a veil of mystery hangs around this portion of American history. I have certainly read a great deal about it, and left off nearly as wise as when I began. A conspiracy of some sort did undoubtedly exist. Preparations were in progress to collect an armament on the Ohio, and there was some rumour of its descending the Mississippi and seizing on New Orleans. Some of Burr's followers were tried, but—unless my memory deceives me—acquitted. At all events, materials could not be discovered for the conviction of the Great Catiline, whose projects, whether defensible or not, were original, and indicative of the fearless character of the man.

His acquittal, however, by two juries, was not sufficient to establish his innocence in the opinion of his countrymen. He was assailed by hatred and execration; his name was made a by-word for every thing that was odious in morals, and unprincipled in politics. It was under such circumstances that Burr became an exile from his country for several years. During that period he visited England, where he attracted the jealous observation of the ministry, and his correspondence with France being more frequent than was quite agreeable, and of a cast somewhat too political, he received a polite invitation to quit the country with the least possible delay. Colonel Burr now lives in New York, secluded from society, where his great talents and extensive professional knowledge, still gain him some employment as a consulting lawyer.

A friend of mine at New York enquired whether I should wish an interview with this distinguished person. I immediately answered in the affirmative, and a note was addressed to Colonel Burr, requesting permission to introduce me. The answer contained a polite assent, and indicated an hour when his avocations would permit his having sufficient leisure for the enjoyment of conversation. At the time appointed, my friend conveyed me to a house in one of the poorer streets of the city. The Colonel received us on the landing place, with the manners of a finished courtier, and led the way to his little library, which—judging from the appearance of the volumes—was principally furnished with works connected with the law.

In person, Colonel Burr is diminutive, and I was much struck with the resemblance he bears to the late Mr Percival. His physiognomy is expressive of strong sagacity. The eye keen, penetrating, and deeply set; the forehead broad and prominent; the mouth small, but disfigured by the ungraceful form of the lips; and the other features, though certainly not coarse, were irreconcilable with any theory of beauty. On the whole, I have rarely seen a more remarkable countenance. Its expression was highly intellectual, but I imagined I could detect the lines of strong passion mingled with those of deep thought. The manners of Colonel Burr are those of a highly bred gentleman. His powers of conversation are very great, and the opinions he expresses on many subjects marked by much shrewdness and originality.

When in England he had become acquainted with many of the Whig leaders, and I found him perfectly versed in every thing connected with our national politics.

It would be an unwarrantable breach of the confidence of private life, were I to publish any particulars of the very remarkable conversation I enjoyed with this eminent person. I shall, therefore, merely state, that having encroached perhaps too long, both on the time and patience of Colonel Burr, I bade him farewell, with sincere regret that a career of public life, which had opened so brilliantly, should not have led to a more fortunate termination.

CHAPTER X.

PHILADELPHIA.

On the 8th of January I again bade farewell to New York, and embarked on board of a New Brunswick steamer on my way to Philadelphia. Our course lay up the Raritan river, which has nothing interesting to display in point of scenery, and the morning being raw and gusty, the voyage was not particularly agreeable. It occupied about four hours, and on reaching Brunswick we found a cavalcade of nine stage-coaches, drawn up for the accommodation of the passengers. In these we were destined to cross the country between the Raritan and Delaware, which forms part of the State of New Jersey. In theory nothing could be easier than this journey. The distance was only twenty-seven miles;

and in a thoroughfare so much travelled as that between the two great cities of the Union, it was at least not probable that travellers would be subjected to much inconvenience.

But theory and experience were at variance in this case, as in many others. We changed coaches at every stage, and twice had the whole baggage of the party to be unpacked and reloaded. The road was detestable; the jolting even worse than what I had suffered on my journey from Providence to Boston. For at least half the distance the coach was axle-deep in mud, and once it fairly stuck in a rut, and might have continued sticking till doomsday, had the passengers not dismounted to lighten the vehicle. I enquired the reason of the disgraceful neglect of this important line of communication, and was answered, that as it was intended at some future period to have a railway, it would be mere folly to go to any expense in repairing it. Thus are this intelligent people content to sacrifice a great present benefit, to a mere speculative, and probably remote contingency.

The scenery through which our route lay was devoid of beauty, and the soil wretchedly poor. The whole country had evidently at one time been under cultivation, but in much of it the plough had long ceased from labour, and the forest had already resumed its ancient rights. The weather added to the bleakness of the landscape, and though the coach crept on with the velocity of a tortoise, it was not till long after dark that we reached Bristol. Here we took boat again, and our troubles were at an end. A plentiful dinner contributed to beguile the distance, and the city clocks were in the act of chiming ten as we landed on the quay of Philadelphia.

Having procured a coach, I drove to Head's hotel, which had been recommended to me as one of the best houses in the Union. Here I could only procure a small and nasty bedroom, lighted by a few panes of glass fixed in the wall, some eight or ten feet from the floor. On the following morning, therefore, I removed to the United States Hotel, where I found the accommodation excellent. My letters of introduction were then despatched, with the result which my experience of American kindness had led me to anticipate.

Philadelphia stands on an isthmus about two miles wide, between the Delaware and the Schuylkill. Below the city, both rivers are navigable for vessels of any class, but the severity of the winter climate generally causes an interruption to the communication with the sea, of considerable duration. As a great seat of commerce the advantage is altogether on the side of New York. Philadelphia has but trifling extent of river communication with the interior. The Delaware is navigable only for about thirty miles above the city, and the Schuylkill is too full of shoals and rapids to be practicable for any thing but small craft. To remedy this inconvenience there are several canals, and others are in progress, which must contribute largely to the prosperity of the State.

There is nothing striking in the appearance of Philadelphia when seen from the river. It stands on a flat surface, and presents no single object of beauty or grandeur to arrest the attention. Spires may be monsters in architecture, but they are beautiful monsters, and the eye feels a sad want of them, as it wanders over the unvaried extent of dull uniform building presented by Philadelphia. When one enters the city the scene is certainly improved, but not much. The streets are rather respectable than handsome, but there is everywhere so much appearance of real comfort, that the traveller is at first delighted with this Quaker paradise. He looks from the carriage windows prepared to see every thing *couleur de rose.* The vehicle rolls on; he praises the cleanness and neatness of the houses, and every street that presents itself seems an exact copy of those which he has left behind. In short, before he has got through half the city, he feels an unusual tendency to relaxation about the region of the mouth, which ultimately terminates in a silent but prolonged yawn.

Philadelphia is mediocrity personified in brick and mortar. It is a city laid down by square and rule, a sort of habitable problem,—a mathematical infringement on the rights of individual eccentricity,—a rigid and prosaic despotism of right angles and parallelograms. It may emphatically be called a *comfortable* city, that is, the houses average better than in any other with which I am acquainted. You here see no miserable and filthy streets, the refuge of squalid poverty, forming a contrast to the splendour of squares and crescents. No Dutch town can be cleaner, and the marble stairs and window sills of the better houses, give an agreeable relief to the red brick of which they are constructed.

The public buildings are certainly superior to any I have yet seen in America. Some of the churches are handsome, and the United States Bank, with its marble portico of Grecian Doric, gives evidence, I trust, of an improving taste. I confess, however, that my hopes on this matter are not very strong. Even persons of information are evidently unable to appreciate the true merit of the building or the architect, and connect ridicule with both by declaring the former to be "the finest building in the world!" Is a poor traveller in the United States, when continually beset by such temptation, to be held utterly inexcusable, if he sometimes venture to indulge in a sneer?

The Bank of Pennsylvania is another structure entitled to applause. Its front presents a flight of steps sustaining an Ionic portico of six columns, with an entablature and pediment. The banking-house of Mr Girard,—the Coutts of the Union,—is likewise handsome. Like the two buildings I have already mentioned its whole front is of marble, but in taste it is far less chaste, and presents more faults than I have time or inclination to enumerate. There are likewise two buildings of some pretension, in the Gothic style. Both are contemptible.

The State House, from which issued the declaration of American independence, is yet standing. It is built of brick, and consists of a centre and two wings, without ornament of any sort. There is something appropriate, and even imposing in its very plainness. Above is a small cupola with a clock, which at night is illuminated by gas.

The Philadelphians, however, pride themselves far more on their waterworks than on their State House. Their *Io Pæans* on account of the former, are loud and unceasing, and I must say, the annoyance which these occasion to a traveller, is very considerable. A dozen times a-day was I asked whether I had seen the waterworks, and on my answering in the negative, I was told that I positively must visit them; that they were unrivalled in the world; that no people but the Americans could have executed such works, and by implication, that no one but an Englishman, meanly jealous of American superiority, would omit an opportunity of admiring their unrivalled mechanism.

There is no accounting for the eccentricities of human character. I had not heard these circumstances repeated above fifty times, ere I began to run restive, and determined not to visit the waterworks at all. To this resolution I adhered, in spite of all annoyance, with a pertinacity worthy of a better cause. Of the waterworks of Philadelphia, therefore, I know nothing, and any reader, particularly solicitous to become acquainted with the principle of this remarkable piece of machinery, must consult the pages of other travellers.

I had the honour of being present at an annual celebration of the American Philosophical Society. About a hundred members sat down to a most excellent supper, and the wine and punch were equally unimpeachable. The President, Mr Du Ponceau, then made a speech, in which he gave a very interesting account of the rise and progress of the Society to its present flourishing condition. It was originally established by Franklin, and a few of his fellow-tradesmen, who met in some back-room of an obscure tavern, and having supped on bread and cheese, enjoyed the feast of reason over a pot of London Particular. The Society now includes in its members all that America can boast of eminence in literature or science.

On the following evening, I passed an hour or two very agreeably at one of a series of meetings, which are called "Wistar Parties," from the name of the gentleman at whose house they were first held. Their effect and influence on society must be very salutary. These parties bring together men of different classes and pursuits, and promote the free interchange of opinion, always useful for the correction of prejudice. Such intercourse, too, prevents the narrowness of thought, and exaggerated estimate of the value of our own peculiar acquirements, which devotion to one exclusive object is apt to engender in those who do not mix freely with the world.

These meetings are held by rotation at the houses of the different members. The conversation is generally literary or scientific, and as the party is usually very large, it can be varied at pleasure. Philosophers eat like other men, and the precaution of an excellent supper is by no means found to be superfluous. It acts too as a gentle emollient on the acrimony of debate. No man can say a harsh thing with his mouth full of turkey, and disputants forget their differences in unity of enjoyment.

At these parties I met several ingenious men of a class something below that of the ordinary members. When an operative mechanic attracts notice by his zeal for improvement in any branch of science, he is almost uniformly invited to the Wistar meetings. The advantage of this policy is obviously very great. A modest and deserving man is brought into notice. His errors are corrected, his ardour is stimulated, his taste improved. A healthy connexion is kept up between the different classes of society, and the feeling of mutual sympathy is duly cherished. During my stay in Philadelphia I was present at several of these Wistar meetings, and always returned from them with increased conviction of their beneficial tendency.

Most of the great American cities have a peculiar character,—a sort of civic idiosyncracy, which distinguishes their population even to the eye of an unpractised observer. There is no mistaking that of Philadelphia ; it is Quaker all over. All things, animate and inanimate, seem influenced by a spirit of quietism as pervading as the atmosphere. The manners of the higher orders are somewhat more reserved than in other parts of the Union, and I must say that all ranks are particularly free from the besetting sin of curiosity. Fortunately for travellers, it is not here considered essential that they should disclose every circumstance connected with their past life and opinions.

Philadelphia is *par excellence* a city of mediocrity. Its character is republican not democratic. One can read the polities of its inhabitants in the very aspect of the streets. A coarse and vulgar demagogue would have no chance among a people so palpably observant of the proprieties, both moral and political. The Philadelphians are no traffickers in extremes of any sort, and were I to form my opinion of a government, from the impression made by its policy on some particular district of the Union, I should certainly take this enlightened and respectable city as the guide and standard of my creed.

The chief defect of Philadelphia is want of variety. It is just such a city as a young lady would cut out of a thread paper,—

> Street answers street, each alley has a brother,
> And half the city just reflects the other.

Something is certainly wanted to relieve that unbroken uniformity, which tires the eye and stupifies the imagination. One would give the world for something to admire or to condemn, and would absolutely rejoice, for the mere sake of variety, to encounter a row of log huts, or to get immersed in a congress of dark and picturesque *closes*, such as delight all travellers—without noses—in the old town of Edinburgh.

The Utilitarian principle is observed, even in

the nomenclature of the streets. Those running in one direction are denoted by the name of some particular tree,—such as vine, cedar, chestnut, spruce, &c. The cross-streets are distinguished by numbers, so that a stranger has no difficulty in finding his way, since the name of the street indicates its situation. Market Street is the great thoroughfare of the city, and stretches from one river to the other, an extent of several miles. The streets are generally skirted by rows of Lombardy poplars, for what reason I know not. They certainly give no shade, and possess no beauty.

Notwithstanding the attractions of Philadelphia, it was not my intention to have remained there longer than a week, but while engaged in preparation for departure, a deep fall of snow came on, and the communications of the city were at once cut off. A week passed without intelligence from the northward, and even the southern mails were several days in arrear. The snow lay deep on the streets, and wheeled carriages were of necessity exchanged for sledges, or, as they are usually called, sleighs. Of course, it would have been absurd for a traveller, with no motive for expedition, to commence a journey under such circumstances, and I determined to prolong my stay until the roads should be reported in such condition as to threaten no risk of detention in my route to Baltimore.

During this interval I visited the Penitentiary. It stands about two miles from the city, but owing to the depth of snow, the sleigh could not approach within a considerable distance of the building, and the pedestrian part of the excursion presented much difficulty. A thin icy crust had formed over the surface of the snow, which often gave way beneath the foot, and more than once I was immersed to the shoulders.

I did, however, reach the Penitentiary at last. It is a square granite building of great extent, with a tower at each angle, and the walls enclose a space of ten acres. In the centre of the area stands an observatory, from which it is intended that seven corridors shall radiate, but three only have been yet completed. The cells are arranged on either side of these corridors, with which they communicate by a square aperture, which may be opened at pleasure from without. There is likewise a small eye-hole, commanding a complete view of the cell, and attached to each is a walled court, in which the prisoner may take exercise. The only entrance to the cells lies through these court-yards.

The system pursued in this institution is entirely different from that which, in a former part of this volume, I have had occasion to describe. No punishment is permitted within its walls but that of solitary confinement. Nothing is left to the discretion of the gaoler, or his assistants, and all risk of abuse is thus obviated. I cannot but consider this as an inestimable advantage. If discretionary power be confessedly dangerous when exercised by a judge in open court, under the strong check of public opinion, what are we to say of it when confided to a gaoler, and exercised without responsibility of any sort, amid the secrecy of his prisonhouse?

The warder of the establishment struck me as a person of much enthusiasm and benevolence. He evidently took pleasure in affording every information in regard to the practical operation of the system, though its introduction is too recent to afford room for any conclusive appeal to experience. The punishment originally contemplated in this prison was solitary confinement, unmitigated by labour. All experience is against the practicability of combining this system with the continuance of bodily health and mental sanity in the prisoners. It was therefore wisely given up, and of that adopted in its stead I shall now offer a few details.

A convict, on arriving at the prison, is blindfolded, and conveyed to a room, where his hair is cut, and after a complete personal ablution, he is led with the same precaution, to the cell destined for his reception. He is thus kept in ignorance of the localities of the prison, and the chances of escape are diminished. Each cell is provided with an iron bedstead, a comfortable mattrass, two blankets, and a pillow. There is likewise a water-cock and tin mug, so that the prisoner may supply himself *ad libitum* with the pure element. The cells are heated by pipes, and though I visited the prison in the very coldest weather, the temperature was very pleasant.

When a prisoner is first received, he is uniformly left to enjoy the full privilege of solitary idleness;

but in the course of a short time he generally makes application for work, and for a Bible. Each man is permitted to select his own trade, and those who understand none when they enter the prison are taught one. The allowance of food is good and plentiful, but those who refuse to work, are kept on a reduced allowance. Their number, however, is exceedingly small, and the great majority consider even the temporary withdrawal of work as a severe punishment.

Having taken up rather strong opinions with regard to the injurious influence of solitary confinement, I was rather anxious to have an opportunity of conversing with a few of the prisoners. To this no objection was made, and I was accordingly ushered into the cell of a black shoemaker, convicted of theft, whom I found very comfortably seated at his trade. I asked him many questions, which he answered with great cheerfulness. He had been confined—I think—for eighteen months, yet this long period of separation from his fellow-creatures had occasioned no derangement of his functions, bodily or mental. I likewise conversed with two other prisoners, and the result of my observations certainly was the conviction, that solitary confinement, when associated with labour, is by no means liable to the objections which I have often heard urged to its adoption as a punishment. I have likewise the assurance of the warder, that during his whole experience, he has not known a single instance of the discipline adopted being found prejudicial to health, either of mind or body.

There is undoubtedly much that is admirable in this Penitentiary, but I am not sure that either the plan or the practice of the establishment is so perfect as to admit of no improvement. In the first place, I cannot but think that the Panopticon principle is on the whole preferable. Facility of supervision is always important, and there is no point in the present prison from which the keeper can command a general and complete view, either of the cells or of the exercise yards. The central observatory commands only the corridors. In the second place, it strikes me as a defect that there should be no entrance to the cells from the corridors, by which a far more ready and convenient access would be obtained. There is also a defect in the construction of the exercise courts, in which it is quite possible for the adjoining prisoners to hold conversation.

There is no chapel attached to this establishment, and when divine service is performed, the clergyman takes his station at the head of the corridors; the apertures communicating with the cells are thrown open, and his voice I am assured, is distinctly audible, even by the most distant prisoner. Strange to say, however—and I confess that in a state so religious as Pennsylvania, the fact struck me with astonishment—morning and evening prayers are unknown in the Penitentiary. Surely, it is both wholesome and fitting that the days of these suffering criminals should be begun and ended by an appeal to the mercy of that Maker, whose laws they have offended. It is true, that divine service is performed once every Sunday, but this will scarcely be held sufficient, either by the moralist who simply regards the interest of society in the reformation of a criminal, or by him whose philanthropy is connected with the higher hopes and motives of religion.

On the whole, I am inclined to prefer the system

of solitary confinement to that adopted in the prisons at Auburn and Charleston. The former obviates all necessity for punishment of any kind, beyond that inflicted by the execution of the sentence. Whatever be his sufferings, the prisoner has the distinct knowledge that they are not arbitrary or extrajudicial. Even amidst the solitude of his cell, he feels that he is in one sense a *free man.* He undergoes the sentence of the law, but he is not dependent on the capricious discretion of those by whom he is surrounded. In Charleston each prisoner knows himself to be a slave. His punishment is in truth unlimited, for its only measure is the conscience of his gaoler, an unknown and indeterminate quantity.

There is nothing humiliating in solitary confinement. The interests of society are protected by the removal of the criminal, while the new circumstances in which he is placed are precisely the most favourable to moral improvement. It is the numerous temptations of the world, the scope which it affords for the gratification of strong passion, that overpower the better principles implanted in the heart of the most depraved of mankind. Remove these temptations, place the criminal in a situation where there are no warring influences to mislead his judgment; let him receive religious instruction, and be taught the nature and extent of his moral obligations, and when, after such preparation, he is left to reflection, and communion with his own conscience, all that human agency can effect, has probably been done for his reformation.

Solitary confinement contributes to all this. It throws the mind of the criminal back upon itself. It forces him to think who never thought before. It removes all objects which can stimulate the evil passions of his nature. It restores the prisoner to society, if not "a wiser and a better man," at least undegraded by a course of servile submission. His punishment has been that of a man, not of a brute. He has suffered privation, but not indignity. He has submitted to the law, and to the law alone, and whatever debasement may still attach to his character, is the offspring of his crime, not of its penalty.

The other system is far less favourable I should imagine to moral improvement. The gaoler must necessarily appear to the prisoners in the light of an arbitrary tyrant. He is an object of fear and hatred. His inflictions are accompanied by none of the solemnities of justice, and they are naturally followed by smothered rancour and desire of revenge. Even where there is no abuse of authority, it is impossible for those subjected to it, to appreciate the motives for its rigid exercise. They cannot be supposed to discriminate between severity and cruelty.

All this is unfortunate. The character of the prisoners is rendered callous to shame, while their evil passions are in a state of permanent excitement. They are taught obedience like spaniels, and by the same means. They are forced down to the very lowest point of human debasement. Never again shall these men know the dignity of self-respect; never again can they feel themselves on a level with their fellow-men. Human endurance can extend no further than they have carried it, and it were well that American legislators should remember, that it is easy to degrade the freeman, but impossible to elevate the slave.

One great advantage belongs to the Philadelphia

system. A prisoner on being discharged enters the world without danger of recognition, and thus enjoys the benefit of starting with a fair character. If his confinement has been long, disease and the gibbet have probably disposed of the great majority of his former companions in crime, and in a country like the United States, nothing but honest industry is wanting to the attainment of independence. But a convict discharged from a prison like those of Charleston and Auburn, must continue through life a marked man. His face is known to thousands, and go where he will—unless he fly altogether from the haunts of men—the story of his past life will follow him. Excluded from communion with the more respectable portion of the community, he will probably again seek his associates among the dissolute. His former course of crime will then be renewed, and all hope of reformation will be at an end for ever.

It is impossible, however, to praise too highly that active benevolence which in America takes so deep an interest in the reformation of the objects of punishment. In their ameliorations of prison discipline, the people of this country have unquestionably taken the lead of Europe. In old established communities the progress of improvement is necessarily slow, and there are difficulties to be overcome which are fortunately unknown on this side of the Atlantic. Let the Americans, therefore, continue as they have begun, to lead the way in this important department of practical philanthropy. By doing so, they will earn a distinction for their country more honourable than could result from the highest eminence in arts, or achievements in arms.

Of all the American colleges beyond the limits of New England, that of Pennsylvania is perhaps the most distinguished. Its medical school is decidedly so, and an Esculapian armed with a Philadelphia diploma, is held to commit slaughter on his fellow-creatures according to the most approved principles of modern science. Till within a few years, however, the scientific and literary departments of this institution had fallen into comparative neglect. But a revolution in an American college is an easier affair than the introduction of the most trifling change in such establishments as Oxford or Cambridge. The statutes were revised by a board of trustees appointed for the purpose. The system of education was corrected and enlarged, and men of competent talent and acquirements were invited to preside over the various departments of instruction. A new edifice was erected, and an extensive addition made to the former beggarly account of philosophical apparatus. The natural consequences followed. The number of students was considerably increased, and the benefits of the institution were augmented not only in magnitude, but in extent of diffusion.

In this establishment there is no discretion permitted in regard to the course of study to be followed by the student. Every one is compelled to travel in the same track, and to reach the same point, whatever may be his future destination in life. It is perhaps quite right that such portions of a university course should be considered imperative, as relate to the preparatory developement of the intellectual powers, but it does appear somewhat absurd to insist on cramming every boy with mathematics, chemistry, and natural philosophy. In America, the period devoted to education is so short, that there can be no folly greater than that of frittering it away in a variety of pursuits, which contribute little to the general elevation of the intellect. It is the certain result of attempting too much, that nothing will be accomplished. With such a system of education the standard of acquirement must of necessity be greatly lower than in other countries, where excellence in some one department constitutes the great object of individual ambition. The truth of this position is in perfect accordance with the state of knowledge in America. In illustration of it, I shall direct the attention of the reader to an extract from the report of the Board of Trustees of this very University of Pennsylvania. Alluding to the prescribed course of education, these gentlemen assure the public, that "Its object is to communicate *a profound* and *critical knowledge* of the *classics;* an *extensive acquaintance* with the *different branches of mathematical science*, *natural philosophy*, and *chemistry*, combined with *all the varieties of knowledge* comprehended within the sphere of *moral philosophy*, *logic*, *rhetoric*, *metaphysics*, and the *evidences of Christianity*. *This course of instruction will occupy* FOUR YEARS*!*"

Had the number of years to be devoted to the acquisition of this vast mass of knowledge been *forty* instead of *four*, the promise of the Board of Trustees might still have been objectionable on the score of hyperbole. In Europe no body of gentlemen connected with any public seminary durst have ventured on such a statement. Respect for their own character, and the certainty of ridicule, would have prevented it. But in America it is different. The standard of knowledge being there infinitely lower, the Trustees promised nothing more than they might reasonably hope to accomplish. On the Western shores of the Atlantic, a young man is believed to have "a profound and critical knowledge of the classics," when he can manage to construe a passage of Cæsar or Virgil, and—by the help of the lexicon—haply of Xenophon or Anacreon. And so with the other branches of acquirement. In mathematics, it is scarcely meant to be implied that the student shall have mastered the works of La Grange or La Place; nor in metaphysics, that he shall even understand the philosophy of Kant or Cousin, but simply that he shall have acquired enough to constitute, in the eyes of the American public, "an extensive acquaintance with the different branches of mathematical science, combined with all the varieties of knowledge comprehended within the sphere of moral philosophy, logic, rhetoric, and metaphysics."

It thus appears that what in one country would be nothing better than impudent quackery, becomes the language of sober truth in another. The same terms carry different meanings on different sides of the water, and the cause of the discrepancy is too obvious to be mistaken. Having alluded to this subject, I would willingly be permitted to offer a few observations on the interesting question, How far the condition of society in the United States, and the influence of its institutions are favourable, or otherwise, to the cultivation of philosophy and the higher literature ?

The termination of the Revolutionary war left the United States with a population graduating in civilisation from slaves to planters. The scale went low enough, but unfortunately not very high. The great mass of the white population, especially in the Northern States, were by no means deficient in such education as was suited to their circumstances. In a country to which abject poverty was happily a stranger, there existed few obstacles to the general diffusion of elementary instruction. But between the amount of acquirement of the richer and the poorer orders, little disparity existed. Where the necessity of labour was imposed on all, it was not probable that any demand should exist for learning not immediately connected with the business of life. To the grower of indigo or tobacco; to the feller of timber, or the retailer of cutlery and dry goods, the refinements of literature were necessarily unknown. In her whole population America did not number a single scholar, in the higher acceptation of the term, and had every book in her whole territory been contributed to form a national library, it would not have afforded the materials from which a scholar could be framed.

It is true, that in several of the States there existed colleges, but these were little better than schools without the necessary discipline; and had their pretensions been greater, it is very certain that such poor and distant establishments could offer no inducement to foreigners of high acquirement to exchange "the ampler ether, the diviner air," of their native universities, for the atmosphere of Yale or Harvard. At all events, the Americans had no desire to draw our men of letters from their learned retreats. In the condition of society I have described, it was impossible that learning should engross any portion of the public favour. Even to the present day, the value of education in the United States is estimated, not by its result on the mind of the student, in strengthening his faculties, purifying his taste, and enlarging and elevating the sphere of thought and consciousness, *but by the amount of available knowledge which it enables him to bring to the common business of life.*

The consequences of this error, when participated in by a whole nation, have been most pernicious. It has unquestionably contributed to perpetuate the very ignorance in which it originated. It has done its part, in connexion with other causes, in depriving the United States of the most enduring source of national greatness. Nor can we hope that the evil will be removed, until the vulgar and unworthy sophistry which has imposed on the judgment, even of the most intelligent Americans, shall cease to influence some wiser and unborn generation.

The education of the clergy differed in little from that of laymen. Of theological learning there was none, nor did there exist the means of acquiring it. It is probable, that within the limits of the United States, there was not to be found a single copy of the works of the Fathers. But this mattered not. Protestantism is never very amenable to authority, and least of all when combined with democracy. Neither the pastors nor their flocks were inclined to attach much value to primitive authority, and from the solid rock of the Scriptures, each man was pleased to hew out his own religion, in such form and proportions as were suited to the measure of his taste and knowledge. It was considered enough that the clergy could read the Bible in their vernacular tongue, and expound its doctrines to the satisfaction of a congregation, not more learned than themselves. To the present day, in one only of the colleges has any provision been made for clerical education. Many of the religious sects, however, have established theological academies, in which candidates for the Ministry may, doubtless, acquire such accomplishment as is deemed necessary for the satisfactory discharge of their high function.*

In short, the state of American society is such as to afford no leisure for any thing so unmarketable as abstract knowledge. For the pursuit of such studies, it is necessary that the proficient should "fit audience find though few." He must be able to calcu-

* The American Almanac for 1831 contains a list of all the theological establishments in the United States, with the number of students at each seminary, and of the volumes contained in its library. According to this document, the whole number of theological students is 657. The combined aggregate of volumes in possession of all the institutions is 43,450. The best furnished library in the list is that of the theological department of Yale College, which contains 8000 volumes. None of the others approach nearly to this amount. The institution of New Hampton possesses only 100 volumes, and is attended by fourteen students. Calculating each book to consist, on the average, of three volumes, the New Hampton library contains *thirty-three* works on theology. But this is not all. Seven of these establishments possess *no libraries at all,* so that the earning of the students must come by inspiration. Until the year 1808, no seminaries for religious instruction appear to have existed in the United States. One was founded in that year, another in 1812, but the great majority are of far more recent origin.

late on sympathy at least, if not encouragement, and assuredly he would find neither in the United States.

Whatever were the defects of Jefferson, he seems to have been impressed with a deep consciousness of the deficiencies of his countrymen. He saw that the elements of knowledge were diffused every where, but that all its higher fruits were wanting. He endeavoured, not only to rouse his countrymen to a sense of their intellectual condition, but to provide the means by which it might be improved. With this view he founded a university in his native State, and his last worldly anxieties were devoted to its advancement. Jefferson felt strongly, that while philosophy and literature were excluded from the fair objects of professional ambition, and the United States continued to be dependent for all advances in knowledge on importations from Europe, she was wanting in the noblest element of national greatness. Though the commerce of mind be regulated by loftier principles than more vulgar traffic, it should consist, unquestionably, of exchange of some kind. To receive, and not to give, is to subsist on charity ; to be a mute and changeling in the great family of nations.

The obstacles to success, however, were too great for the powers of Jefferson to overcome. In a community where the gradations of opulence constitute the great distinction between man and man, the pursuits which lead most readily to its attainment will certainly engross the whole volume of national talent. In England there are various coexistent aristocracies which act as mutual correctives, and by multiplying the objects of ambition, give amplitude and diffusion to its efforts. In America there exists but one, and the impulse it awakens is, of course, violent in proportion to its concentration. Jefferson, therefore, failed in this great object, towards the accomplishment of which his anxious efforts were directed. As a politician, he exercised a far greater influence over the national mind than any other statesman his country has produced. But in his endeavours to direct the intellectual impulses of his countrymen towards loftier objects, the very structure of society presented an insuperable barrier to success.

I am aware, it will be urged, that the state of things I have described is merely transient, and that when population shall become more dense, and increased competition shall render commerce and agriculture less lucrative, the pursuits of science and literature will engross their due portion of the national talent. I hope it may be so, but yet it cannot be disguised, that there hitherto has been no visible approximation towards such a condition of society. In the present generation of Americans, I can detect no symptom of improving taste, or increasing elevation of intellect. On the contrary, the fact has been irresistibly forced on my conviction, that they are altogether inferior to those, whose place, in the course of nature, they are soon destined to occupy. Compared with their fathers, I have no hesitation in pronouncing the younger portion of the richer classes to be less liberal, less enlightened, less observant of the proprieties of life, and certainly far less pleasing in manner and deportment.

In England every new generation starts forward into life with advantages far superior to its predecessor. Each successive crop—if I may so write—

of legislators, is marked by increase of knowledge and enlargement of thought. The standard of acquirement necessary to attain distinction in public life, is now confessedly higher than it was thirty years ago. The intellectual currency of the country, instead of being depreciated, has advanced in value, while the issue has been prodigiously enlarged. True, there are no giants in our days, but this may be in part at least accounted for, by a general increase of stature in the people. We have gained at least an inch upon our fathers, and have the gratifying prospect of appearing diminutive when compared with our children.

But if this be so in America, I confess my observation is at fault. I can discern no prospect of her soon becoming a mental benefactor to the world. Elementary instruction, it is true, has generally kept pace with the rapid progress of population; but while the steps of youth are studiously directed to the base of the mountain of knowledge, no facilities have been provided for scaling its summit. There is at this moment nothing in the United States worthy of the name of a library. Not only is there an entire absence of learning, in the higher sense of the term, but an absolute want of the material from which alone learning can be extracted. At present an American might study every book within the limits of the Union, and still be regarded in many parts of Europe—especially in Germany—as a man comparatively ignorant. And why does a great nation thus voluntarily continue in a state of intellectual destitution so anomalous and humiliating? There are libraries to be sold in Europe. Books might be imported in millions. Is it poverty, or is it ignorance of their value, that withholds America from the purchase?* I should be most happy to believe the former.

In one point of view at least, the strong—and I fear not to say, the insuperable prejudice against the

* The value of books imported from Europe during the year 1829-30 for public institutions, amounted only to 10,829 dollars! Even of this wretched sum, I am assured the greater part was expended in works strictly new. Of the old treasures of learning, America seems content to remain destitute.

In regard to science, it is a fact scarcely credible, that the second maritime power in the world does not at the present moment possess a single astronomical observatory, and is dependent on France and England for the calculations of an ephemeris by which her ships may be enabled in tolerable safety to navigate the ocean!

claims of primogeniture, is unfavourable to national advancement. It must continue to prevent any large accumulations of individual wealth, and the formation of a class which might afford encouragement to those branches of science and literature, which cannot be expected from their very nature to become generally popular. Nor is it likely that the impediments to which I have alluded, will be at all diminished by the character of the government, on which I shall hazard a few observations.

When we speak of a government being popular or otherwise, we mean that it is more or less influenced by the prevailing currents of opinion and feeling in those subjected to its action. A highly popular government, therefore, can neither be in advance of the average intelligence of a people, nor can it lag behind it. It is, and must be, the mere reflex of the public mind in all its strength and weakness; the representative not only of its higher qualities and virtues, but of all the errors, follies, passions, prejudices, and ignorances by which it is debased.

It is in vain, therefore, to expect from such a

government any separate and independent action. It cannot react upon, it is merely co-operative with, the people. It embodies no self-existent or countervailing influence. It is only when it ceases to be expressly representative, and stands on a firmer basis than mere popular favour, that a government can acquire a positive and determinate character, and be recognised as an influence distinct from that of national opinion.

Neither in the American legislative or executive, is there any thing of this latter character discernible. The institutions of the United States afford the purest specimen the world has yet seen, of a representative government; of an executive, whose duties are those of mere passive agency; of a legislative, which serves but as the vocal organ of the sole and real dictator, the people. Into whatever speculations, therefore, we may be induced to enter, either with regard to the present condition or further prospects of the United States, it would be mere folly to attribute influence of any kind to a government, which, in truth, is nothing more than a mere recipient of popular impulse.

To an American of talent, there exist no objects to stimulate political ambition, save the higher offices of the federal government, or of the individual States. The latter, indeed, are chiefly valued for the increased facilities they afford for the attainment of the former; but to either, the only passport is popular favour. Acquirements of any sort, therefore, which the great mass of the people do not value, or are incapable of appreciating, are of no practical advantage, for they bring with them neither fame, nor more substantial reward. But this is understating the case. Such knowledge, if displayed at all, would not merely be a dead letter in the qualifications of a candidate for political power, it would oppose a decided obstacle to his success. The sovereign people in America are given to be somewhat intolerant of acquirement, the immediate utility of which they cannot appreciate, but which they do feel has imparted something of mental superiority to its possessor. This is particularly the case with regard to literary accomplishment. The cry of the people is for "*equal and universal education;*" and attainments which circumstances have placed beyond their own reach, they would willingly discountenance in others.

It is true, indeed, that with regard to mere professional acquirements, a different feeling prevails. The people have no objection to a clever surgeon or a learned physician, because they profit by their skill. An ingenious mechanic they respect. There is a fair field for a chemist or engineer. But in regard to literature, they can discover no practical benefit of which it is productive. In their eyes it is a mere appanage of aristocracy, and whatever mental superiority it is felt to confer, is at the expense of the self-esteem of less educated men. I have myself heard in Congress the imputation of scholarship bandied as a reproach; and if the epithet of "literary gentleman" may be considered as malignant, as it did sometimes appear to be gratuitous, there assuredly existed ample apology for the indignant feeling it appeared to excite. The truth I believe is, that in their political representatives, the people demand just so much knowledge and accomplishment as they conceive to be practically available for the promotion of their own interests. This, in their opinion, is enough. More were but to gild refined gold, and paint the lily, operations which could add nothing to the value of the metal, or the fragrance of the flower.

The consequence of all this has been, that the standard of judgment, in regard to public men, is decidedly lower in the United States than in most countries of Europe. It is perhaps natural, that the demand for political accomplishment should not precede its necessity, and I am far from wishing to assert, that American statesmen have not been hitherto found adequate to all the wants of the commonwealth. But if it be the great object of enlightened institutions to encourage the development of the highest faculties, and, generally, to raise man in the scale of intellectual being; if knowledge be confessedly power, and freedom from prejudice a nobler enfranchisement than mere physical liberty, then I fear that, in reference to this great and ultimate function, those of the United States will be found wanting. I am far from arguing, that science and literature should be indebted for their promotion to a system of direct encouragement. Such policy is always dubious, and has rarely proved successful. But I certainly regard as one most important standard of excellence in a government, the degree in which, *by its very constitution*, it tends to call into action the higher powers and qualities of the human mind. It is a poor policy, which, in matters of intellect, looks not beyond the necessities of the present hour. There is no economy so shortsighted, as that which would limit the expenditure of mind, and assuredly the condition of society cannot be desirable, in which great qualities of every sort do not find efficient excitement and ample field for display.

How far the influences, which have hitherto prevented the intellectual advancement of the Americans, may hereafter be counteracted by others more favourable to the cultivation of learning, I presume not to predict. There is certainly no deficiency of talent in the United States; no deficiency of men, stored even to abundance with knowledge, practically applicable to the palpable and grosser wants of their countrymen. But of those higher branches of acquirement, which profess not to minister to mere vulgar necessities, or to enlarge the sphere of physical enjoyment, and of which the only result is the elevation of the intellect, I fear it must be acknowledged she has not yet been taught even to appreciate the value.

CHAPTER XI.

PHILADELPHIA.

THE United States' hotel, where I had taken up my abode, was a favourite resort of American naval officers. An opportunity was thus afforded me, of forming acquaintance with several, to whom I was indebted for many kind and most obliging attentions. It must be confessed, that these republicans have carried with them their full share of "Old Albion's spirit of the sea," for better sailors, in the best and highest acceptation of the term, I do not believe the world can produce. During the course of my tour, I had a good deal of intercourse with the members of this profession; and I must say, that in an officer of the United States' navy, I have uniformly found, not only a well-informed gentleman, but a person on whose kindness and good offices to a stranger, I might with confidence rely. They betray nothing of that silly spirit of bluster and bravado, so prevalent among other classes of their countrymen; and even in conversing on the events of the late war, they spoke of their successes in a tone of modesty which tended to raise even the high impression I had already received of their gallantry.

In company with one of these gentlemen I visited the Navy Yard, and went over a splendid line-of-battle ship, the Pennsylvania. She is destined to carry a hundred and forty-four guns; and is, I believe, the largest ship in the world. I likewise inspected a magnificent frigate called the Raritan. Both of these vessels are on the stocks, but I was assured that a couple of months would suffice at any time to make them ready for sea. They are completely covered in from the weather; and every aperture of the wood is carefully filled with sea-salt to prevent decay. Great faith is placed in the efficacy of this preservative.

Messrs Carey and Lea are the chief booksellers of Philadelphia, and, I believe, of the Union. Their establishment is very extensive, and they are evidently men of much sagacity and enterprise. The principal part of their business consists in issuing reprints of English works, which, either from their merit or their notoriety, may be expected to have a considerable circulation on this side of the water. Of original publications the number is comparatively small; though, I am told, of late years it has considerably increased.

The three great publishing cities of the Union are Boston, New York, and Philadelphia. From the first and last of these places I have seen some very respectable specimens of typography; but, in general, the reprints of English works are executed in the coarsest and most careless manner. It is quite a mistake to suppose that books are cheaper in the United States than in England. If there were no copyright, and the British public would be content to read books printed in the most wretched manner on whitey-brown paper, there can be no doubt that the English bibliopole would beat his American brother out of the field. A proof of this is, that the British editions of works of which the copyright has expired, are quite as cheap, and much superior in execution, to those produced in this country.

Copyright in the United States is not enjoyable by a foreigner, though an American can hold it in England. The consequence is, that an English author derives no benefit from the republication of his work in America, while every Englishman who purchases the work of an American, is taxed in order to put money in the pocket of the latter. There is no reciprocity in this; and it is really not easy to see why Mr Washington Irving or Mr Cooper should enjoy greater privileges in this country than are accorded to Mr Bulwer or Mr Theodore Hook in the United States. There is an old proverb, "What is good for the goose is good for the gander," which will be found quite as applicable to the policy of Parliament as the practice of the poultry-yard. It is to be hoped this homely apophthegm will not escape the notice of the Government, and that by an act of signal justice, (the abolition of American copyright in England,) it will compel the United States to adopt a wiser and more liberal system.

All novels, good, bad, and indifferent, which appear in England, seem to be reprinted in this country. Indeed, the American appetite in this respect is apparently quite as indiscriminate as our own. A good deal also of the more valuable British literature issues from the Philadelphia press, but in the most democratic form. I have been sometimes amused at observing the entire transmogrification undergone by one of Mr Murray's hot-pressed and broad-margined volumes under the hands of an American bookseller. It enters his shop a three guinea quarto; it comes out a four and twopenny duodecimo. The metamorphosis reminds one of a lord changing clothes with a beggar. The man is the same, but he certainly owes nothing to the toilet.

The Americans are as jealous on the subject of their literature as on other matters of national pretension. The continual importation of European books contributes to excite a consciousness of inferiority which is by no means pleasant. There are many projects afloat for getting rid of this mental bondage, and establishing intellectual independence. By one party it is proposed to exclude English works altogether, and forbid their republication under a high penalty. "Americans," say the advocates of this system, "will never write books, when they can be had so cheaply from England. Native talent is kept under; it wants protection against the competition of foreign genius. Give it the monopoly of the home market; deal with intellect as you do with calico and broad-cloth, and do not prematurely force our literary labourers into a contest with men enjoying the advantages of larger libraries, learning, and leisure." In short, what these gentlemen want is, that ignorance and barbarism should be established by legislative enactment, a policy which, till America has suffered more than she has yet done from the inroads of knowledge, will probably strike a foreigner as somewhat gratuitous.

If the American legislature, however, has not done this, it has certainly done what is something akin to it. A duty of thirty cents, or about fifteen pence a-pound, is charged on all imported books, which, in every point of view, is highly injudicious. In the first place, American books require no protection, because the expense of copyright, and of transport, is far more than enough to secure to native booksellers the undisturbed possession of their own market. When a book is of a character to lead to republication in the United States, of course the only effect of the duty is to force those, who might wish handsomer and better copies, to furnish their libraries with inferior material. The number of these however, would be found very small. In this country, when a book is once read, it is cast aside and thought of no more. In comparatively few instances, is it bound and consigned to the shelves of the bookcase, and therefore it is, that the purchasers of books almost uniformly prefer the very cheapest form. The injurious effect, however, of the duty on imported works, is felt with regard to those which, although valuable, are not of a character to repay the cost of republication. The duty in all such cases acts not as a protection—for when the book is not reprinted there is nothing to protect—but as *a tax upon knowledge*; or, in other words, a premium for the perpetuation of ignorance.

During my stay at Philadelphia, I frequently visited the courts of law. The proceedings I happened to witness were in nothing remarkable, and I have already described the externals of an American Court. It is not unusual among the lower orders in England, when any knotty point is proposed for discussion, to say it would "puzzle a Philadelphia lawyer." To do this, however, it must be knotty indeed, for I have never met a body of men more distinguished by acuteness and extensive professional information than the members of the Philadelphia bar.

In the American courts there is much tacit respect paid to English decisions, each volume of which is reprinted in this country as soon as it appears. Indeed, but for these, law in America would soon become an inextricable jumble. It is impossible to expect much harmony of decision from twenty-four independent tribunals, unless there exist some common land-marks to serve as guides to opinion. Even as it is, the most anomalous discrepancies occur between the decisions of the different State Courts; but without a constant influx of English authorities, the laws regarding property would be speedily overcast by such a mass of contradictory precedents as to be utterly irrevocable to any system.

The low salaries of the judges constitute matter of general complaint among the members of the bar, both at Philadelphia and New York. These are so inadequate, when compared with the income of a well-employed barrister, that the State is deprived of the advantage of having the highest legal talent on the bench. Men from the lower walks of the profession, therefore, are generally promoted to the office, and for the sake of a wretched saving of a few thousand dollars, the public are content to submit their lives and properties to the decision of men of inferior intelligence and learning.

In one respect, I am told the very excess of democracy defeats itself. In some States the judges are so inordinately underpaid, that no lawyer, who does not possess a considerable private fortune, can afford to accept the office. From this circumstance something of aristocratic distinction has become connected with it, and a seat on the bench is now more greedily coveted than it would be, were the salary more commensurate with the duties of the situation.

All lawyers with whom I have conversed agree, that the discrepancy between the laws of the different States is productive of much injury. The statutes of one State are often defeated in the tribunals of another, when not in accordance with the tone of public opinion in the latter. A laxity thus arises in the administration of municipal law incompatible with good government. The criminal codes are likewise highly discordant, and from the variety of jurisdictions, the probability of crime being followed by punishment is much diminished. When a man guilty of an offence in one State escapes into another, he can only be apprehended on the formal demand of the executive authority of the State having jurisdiction of the crime. Before the necessary machinery, however, can be set at work, he has generally time and opportunity for a second evasion, and it thus often happens that the ends of justice are entirely defeated.

There can be no doubt that the want of uniformity in the administration of justice, is injurious both to public morals and private security. But the evil is one naturally arising from the political subdivisions of the Union, and for which, with the jealousy which prevails of the jurisdiction of the federal government, it is perhaps impossible to devise a remedy. With so many co-existent and independent legislatures, uniformity of legislation is impossible, and we can only hope that in the growing political experience of American statesmen, the evil may be diminished, though there exist no prospect of its being entirely removed.

Philadelphia may be called the Bath of the United States, and many individuals who have amassed fortunes in other parts of the Union, select it as the place of their residence. Money-getting is not here the furious and absorbing pursuit of al ranks and conditions of men. On the contrary, every thing goes on quietly. The people seem to dabble in business, rather than follow it with that impetuous energy observable in other cities. The truth is, that a large portion of the capital of the Philadelphians is invested in New York, where there is ample field for its profitable employment. The extent of their own traffic is limited, and in this respect I should imagine it to be inferior even to Boston. But, in point of opulence, Philadelphia is undoubtedly first city of the Union. It is the great focus of American capital, the pecuniary reservoir which fills the various channels of profitable enterprise.

In Philadelphia it is the fashion to be scientific, and the young ladies occasionally display the *bas bleu*, in a degree, which in other cities would be considered rather alarming. I remember at a dinner party, being instructed as to the component parts of the atmosphere by a fair spinster, who anticipated the approach of a period when oxygen would supersede champagne, and young gentlemen and ladies would hob or nob in gas. The vulgar term *drunk* would then give place to *inflated*, certainly more euphonious to ears polite, and the coarser stimulants, such as alcohol and tobacco, in all their forms and uses, be regarded with contempt.

There is no American city in which the system of *exclusion* is so rigidly observed as in Philadelphia. The ascent of a *parvenu* into the aristocratic circle is slow and difficult. There is a sort of holy alliance between its members to forbid all unauthorized approach. Claims are canvassed, and pretensions weighed; manners, fortune, tastes, habits, and descent, undergo a rigid examination; and from the temper of the judges, the chances are, that the final oscillation of the scale, is unfavourable to the reception of the candidate. I remember being present at a party, of which the younger members expressed a strong desire to enliven the dulness of the city, by getting up a series of public balls. The practicability of this project became matter of general discussion, and it was at length given up, simply because there were many families confessedly so respectable as to afford no tangible ground for exclusion, and yet so unfashionable as to render their admission a nuisance of the first magnitude.

I have already alluded to the existence of this aristocratic feeling in New York, but it certainly is there far less prevalent than in Philadelphia. This may easily be accounted for. In the former city, the vicissitudes of trade, the growth and dissipation of opulence, are far more rapid. Rich men spring up like mushrooms. Fortunes are made and lost by a single speculation. A man may go to bed at night worth less than nothing, and pull off his nightcap in the morning with some hundred thousand dollars waiting his acceptance. There is comparatively no settled and permanent body of leading capitalists, and consequently less room for that sort of defensive league which naturally takes place among men of common interests and position in society.

In Philadelphia, on the other hand, the pursuits of commerce are confined within narrower limits. There is no field for speculation on a great scale, and the regular trade of the place is engrossed by old established houses, which enjoy a sort of prescriptive confidence, against which younger establishments, however respectable, find it in vain to contend. The keener, and more enterprising traders, therefore, generally remove to New York, and Philadelphia continues comparatively untroubled by those fluctuations of wealth, which impede any permanent and effective union among its aristocracy.

In society in Philadelphia, I had the good fortune to meet the Count de Survilliers, better known by the untitled name of Joseph Bonaparte. This personage has purchased an estate in the neighbourhood, and by his simplicity and benevolence of character, has succeeded in winning golden opinions from all classes of Americans. He often visits Philadelphia, and mingles a good deal in the society of the place. In the party where I first met him, a considerable time elapsed before I was aware of the presence of a person so remarkable. He was at length pointed out to my observation, with an offer of introduction which I thought proper to decline; being aware, that in a work with which he was probably unacquainted, I had spoken of him in a manner, which, whether just or otherwise, made it indelicate that I should be obtruded on his notice.

Joseph Bonaparte, in person, is about the middle height, but round and corpulent. In the form of his head and features there certainly exists a resemblance to Napoleon, but in the expression of the countenance there is none. I remember, at the Pergola theatre of Florence, discovering Louis Bonaparte from his likeness to the Emperor, which is very striking, but I am by no means confident that I should have been equally successful with Joseph. There is nothing about him indicative of high intellect. His eye is dull and heavy; his manner ungraceful and deficient in that ease and dignity which we vulgar people are apt to number among the necessary attributes of majesty. But Joseph was not bred to kingcraft, and seems to have been forced into it rather as a sort of political stop gap, than from any particular aptitude or inclination for the duties of sovereignty. I am told he converses without any appearance of reserve on the circumstances of his short and troubled reign—if reign, indeed, it can be called—in Spain. He attributes more than half his misfortunes, to the jealousies and intrigues of the unruly marshals, over whom he could exercise no authority. He admits the full extent of his unpopularity, but claims credit for a sincere desire to benefit the people.

One circumstance connected with his deportment I particularly remember. The apartment was warm, and the ex-king evidently felt it so; for taking out his pockethandkerchief, he deliberately mopped his bald " discrowned head," with a hand which one would certainly have guessed to have had more connexion with a spit than a sceptre.

I remained a fortnight waiting for a change of

weather, but it never came. The roads, however, had become quite practicable for travelling, and I at length determined on departure. At five o'clock in the morning I accordingly drove to Market Street, where I took possession of a place in a sleigh shaped like an omnibus, which contained accommodation for about as many passengers. The snow lay deep on the ground, and the weather was cold in the extreme. After some delay the vehicle got into motion, and when we reached the Schuylkill, which is crossed by a wooden bridge of very curious mechanism, I looked back on the Quaker city, yet glimmering in the distance, and bade farewell to it for ever.

END OF VOLUME ONE.

[THOMAS HAMILTON]

MEN AND MANNERS IN AMERICA

[1833]

With additions from the edition of 1843

Two Volumes in One

VOLUME II

REPRINTS OF ECONOMIC CLASSICS

AUGUSTUS M. KELLEY · PUBLISHERS
NEW YORK 1968

MEN AND MANNERS IN AMERICA.

BY THE AUTHOR OF CYRIL THORNTON, ETC.

IN TWO VOLUMES.

VOL. II.

Ἴδεν ἄστεα καὶ νόον ἔγνω.

WILLIAM BLACKWOOD, EDINBURGH; AND
T. CADELL, STRAND, LONDON.
M.D.CCC.XXXIII.

CONTENTS

OF VOLUME SECOND.

MEN AND MANNERS

IN AMERICA.

CHAPTER I.

JOURNEY—BALTIMORE—WASHINGTON.

THE mail sleigh in which I found myself a passenger, was one of the most wretched vehicles imaginable. The wind—a north-wester—penetrated the curtains of the machine, at a thousand crevices, and, charged with particles of snow so fine as to be almost impalpable, communicated to the faces of the passengers the sensation of suffering under a hurricane of needles. Our route lay through a country flat and uninteresting, which presented no object to arrest the attention of a traveller. We breakfasted at a wretched *cabaret*, and the pretensions of the dinner house were not much greater. The fare, however, though coarse, was abundant; and proceeding on our journey about six o'clock, we reached Lancaster, a town of some note, and famous for its manufacture of rifles. After an hour's halt, we again started in a sort of covered sledge-waggon, and the number of passengers being reduced to myself, my servant, and a Hungarian pedlar, we without ceremony ensconced ourselves among the straw in the bottom of the cart.

This part of the journey was comparatively comfortable. I had passed the night before leaving Philadelphia in writing, and "tired nature's kind restorer" now visited my eyelids very pleasantly. The rumbling of the waggon on the vast wooden bridge which crosses the Susquehanna at length broke my slumber. I rose to gaze on the scenery, which showed finely in the moonlight. There were rocks, and giant trees, and a frozen river, and the thought of Wyoming lent a charm to them all. In a few minutes, however, the Susquehanna was no longer visible, and resuming my former position, I again became as happy as an oblivion of all earthly cares could make me.

How long I enjoyed this happiness I know not, but it was at length effectually dissipated by a most unpleasant disturbance. The waggon had stopped, and the rascal of a pedlar, in scrambling out of the machine, chose to plant his great hobnailed foot on the pit of my stomach. My first confused impression was that I had been crushed to death by the wheel of the Newcastle waggon, or the great elephant in Exeter Change. But by degrees the truth dawned on my bewildered intellect, and though not, I trust, much given to swearing, I confess I did indulge in a profane objurgation at finding myself thus unceremoniously converted into the footstool of a Magyar pedlar.

Even to my own perceptions at the moment, however, there was something laughable in the whole affair. To be stretched alongside of my servant in straw on the bottom of a cart, and in such pickle to be trampled on by a common hawker of thimbles and pockethandkerchiefs! But travelling in America is like misery, for it occasionally brings a man acquainted with strange bedfellows.

I had already found, that in travelling, it was impossible to adhere to those conventional regulations in regard to servants which in England are held to be inviolable. It is the invariable custom in this country for *all* the passengers of a stage-coach to eat at the same table, and the time allowed for meals is so short, that unless John dines with his master, the chances are that he goes without dinner altogether. I had already learned that in the United States no man can put forward pretensions to superiority of any kind, without exciting unpleasant observation. A traveller, to get on comfortably, must take things as he finds them, assume nothing, and get rid as soon as possible of all superfluous refinement. He must often associate with men, whose companionship he cannot but feel carries with it something of degradation. Yet a person of true breeding will rarely be treated with disrespect. He will receive tribute without exacting it, and even in this democratic country, may safely leave it "to men's opinion, to tell the world he is a gentleman."

The day's journey terminated at York, where, after all its annoyances and fatigues, I found efficacious restoratives in an excellent supper and comfortable bed. In America, a traveller's sufferings are rarely connected with the table. Go where he may, he always finds abundance of good and wholesome food. To be sure, if the devil send cooks to any part of the world, it is to the United States, for in that country it is a rare thing to meet any dish dressed just as it ought to be. No attention is paid to the preserving of meat, which is generally transferred direct from the shambles to the spit. Then the national propensity for grease is inordinate. It enters largely into the composition of every dish, and constitutes the sole ingredient of many. The very bread is, generally, not only impregnated with some unctuous substance, but when sent up to the breakfast table, is seen to float in a menstruum of oleaginous matter. But with all this, a traveller—*not* a "very particular gentleman"—will have very little cause of complaint. At dinner he will always find ham, turkey, and a joint of some kind; and if with such materials he cannot contrive to make a tolerable meal, it is pretty evident that he has mistaken his vocation, and should limit his journeys to an annual migration between Pall-Mall and the Palais Royal.

In the morning we left York. Inured, as I had been, on the present journey, to what appeared the most wretched vehicles on earth, I soon discovered in the one in which I now embarked, an illustration of the adage, that in every depth there is a deeper still. Our sleigh was a machine apparently got-up for the nonce, and consisted merely of rough boards nailed together in the form of an oblong box, with a drapery and roof of common calico. There were narrow cross boards for seats, on which the passengers—six in number—were compelled to sit bolt upright without support of any kind. This was not comfortable, but the snow was smooth and firm, and we rattled on very fast and very smoothly, and soon after nightfall, I found myself in Baltimore.

Before leaving Philadelphia, I had written to a fellow-passenger to secure apartments for me in the Indian Queen, and on my arrival found every thing prepared. On the whole, I was, perhaps, more comfortable in this hotel than in any other during the whole course of my tour. The culinary arrangements of the establishment were excellent, and the assiduity of an old negro waiter in even anticipating my wants, left me only the apprehension, that, by excess of present comfort, I might become less patient under future privations.

I was now in a slave state, and the knowledge of being so, brought with it something of excitation. I had never even seen a slave, and my fancy had framed a sort of abstract impersonation of the whole class,—a being of strong passions and melancholy aspect, crushed by labour, degraded by ignorance, brutalized by the lash; in short, a monster like that of Frankenstein, human in form, but subject only to the influences which affect the animal part of our nature. I found the domestics in the hotel were all slaves, and there was a certain novelty of sensation, half pleasant and half painful, connected with their services. For the first time in my life, did I bless God for the whiteness of my skin.

It was not in the class of domestic servants, however, that I could reasonably expect to discover the marked peculiarities which my imagination had pictured as the badge of all the tribe. My idea of a slave had always been associated with field labour, a burning sun, and the splendid peculiarities of tropical scenery. In the hotel, I saw only decent-looking waiters and housemaids, observant of all external proprieties of demeanour, discharging their several duties with exactitude, and distinguishable from European servants by nothing but colour.

Of the secrets of the prison-house,—of the modes adopted to enforce obedience in those unhappy creatures, I know nothing from personal observation, and certainly those with whom I conversed made no complaints of their condition. My servant, however, was admitted rather more behind the scenes, and made some rather shocking reports of inflictions by broomsticks and cow-hides, which it had been his fortune to witness. In regard to one atrocity, I remember he was particularly eloquent. The master or mistress of the establishment, for reasons no doubt deemed satisfactory, judged it expedient to lay open the skull of poor Boots with the spit or poker, and in corroboration of the charge,

I can certainly testify having observed that functionary with his dexter organ of secretiveness covered by a plaster. But in gentlemen's families, of course, such disgraceful scenes do not occur, being utterly irreconcilable with that benevolent intelligence, by which the citizens of Baltimore are eminently distinguished.

It is indeed highly probable that Maryland will not long continue to be disgraced by the existence of slavery within its boundaries. The agricultural staples of the State are corn and tobacco, the climate is healthy and temperate, nor is there any possible reason why the system of slave labour might not be instantly abolished. The continuance of the curse —and a curse deeper and more deadly never was inflicted on any community—is entirely gratuitous, the consequence of long habit and deep-rooted prejudice, rather than any beneficial result which it can even be imagined to produce. In the more southern states it is different. The climate is less salubrious, and the cultivation of rice or sugar certainly could not be carried on without slave labour. The immediate interests of the proprietors, therefore, are decidedly opposed to emancipation. Whenever it shall take place, it is certain that vast tracts of country, at present highly productive, will be thrown out of cultivation. But in Maryland, and even in Virginia, such difficulties do not occur. There slave labour would instantly be replaced by that of freemen, to the infinite benefit of the landed proprietors, and the general advancement of morals in the whole community. In the adjoining state of Pennsylvania, the experiment has been already tried, with the most complete success. The introduction of free labour seemed to operate like a charm. A load was instantly removed which had impeded the natural energies of the population, and Pennsylvania has since continued to advance in intelligence and prosperity, with a vigour and rapidity, to which no parallel can be found among her slave-holding competitors.

Baltimore stands on the Patapsco, a small river which discharges its waters into the Chesapeake. Its general aspect very much resembles that of Boston, though the streets display somewhat more of regularity in their architecture. The trade of Baltimore is very considerable, yet there is less appearance of bustle and business than either in New York or Boston. It is, I believe, the greatest mart of flour in the world, and the amount of its exports of this article considerably exceed those of any other city of the Union. The prevalent religion is the Roman Catholic, and the Archiepiscopal Cathedral is perhaps the chief lion of the place. It is built in form of a cross, with a dome in the centre, by no means happily proportioned to the dimensions of the building. It contains a few inferior pictures, some of which were presented by the late King of France. The effect of the building is poor, though the interior might be greatly improved by the distribution of statues and altars along the walls, to get rid of the bareness, which at present is scarcely diminished by a few pilasters.

Baltimore has the honour, I believe, of being the first city which has raised an architectural memorial of its gratitude to Washington. It consists of a column of white marble rising from a quadrangular base. The shaft of the column is about a hundred and twenty feet high, and is surmounted by a colossal statue, which, from its throne, seems proudly to overlook the city. The design of this monument, which is yet unfinished, is simple and grand, and does honour to the taste of the city. Its gross height, including the statue and pedestal, is about a hundred and sixty feet.

In one of the squares of the city, there is what is called the Battle Monument, a sort of trophy column, erected to commemorate the repulse of the attack on the city during the late war, and the names of those who fell in its defence. This structure, which is about fifty feet in height, consists of a column representing the Roman fasces, symbolical of the Union, rising from a square pedestal, which tapers in the Egyptian style, with a griffin at each corner. Above, is the statue of Victory, with an eagle at her side. The effect of the whole is sadly injured by a most anomalous complexity of petty details. Indeed, so vicious is this monument in point of taste, that it is difficult to believe it the production of the same period which has adorned the city with the noble structure to Washington.

I remember being asked by a lady, in one of the first visits I paid in Baltimore, whether I had seen this monument. Having answered in the negative, she proceeded to inform me that it was very beautiful, but, as if struck by a sudden recollection, somewhat eagerly apologized for the introduction of the subject, on account of the painful feelings which this memorial of failure in his country's arms, could not fail to excite in an English spectator. In reply, I took the liberty to assure her that her regrets on this matter were entirely gratuitous; that I should have great pleasure in examining the monument, and really entertained no apprehension of suffering from any pungency of feeling on the occasion. It was easy to observe, however, that my disclaimers, like the inaugural *nolo episcopari* of the Bishops, went for nothing with my fair auditor. Her apologies for having wounded my feelings, became even more strenuous than before; and as it was evidently agreeable that I should appear in the light of a mortified man, I at length judged it better to desist from further disclamation. If I know any thing of John Bull, he is not quite so sensitive a person, as it pleases the good people on this side of the water to believe him; and the idea of an Englishman at the present day, being distressed by regret at the failure of the attack on Baltimore, is perhaps somewhat closely connected with the ludicrous.

Baltimore is celebrated for hospitality, and the beauty of its women, and I can bear testimony to the justice of its reputation for both. In no other city of the United States is the former so frequent and habitual, and in none are there so few of the sordid characteristics of traffic apparent to a stranger. There struck me as being at Baltimore, more effort than elsewhere, to combine the pleasures of social life with professional labour. The effect of this is generally felt in society. The tone of conversation is lighter and more agreeable, and topics of mere commercial interest are rarely obtruded at the dinner table.

In Baltimore there is not much pretension of any sort, and the average of literary accomplishment is perhaps lower than in Philadelphia or Boston. In such matters, however, a transient visitor can form at best but an uncertain and very fallible judgment; but I can with truth assert, that my recollections of Baltimore are of the most agreeable kind, and that I quitted it with a strong sentiment of regard for several of its inhabitants, which time has yet done nothing to diminish.

The ladies of Baltimore, I have already intimated, are remarkable for personal attraction; indeed, I am not aware that, in proportion to the numbers assembled, I have ever seen so much beauty as in the parties of Baltimore. The figure is perhaps deficient in height, but sylphlike and graceful; the features are generally regular and delicately modelled, and the fair Baltimoreans are less remarkable than American ladies usually are for the absence of a certain fulness and grace of proportion, to which, from its rarity, one is led perhaps to attach somewhat too much value as an ingredient of beauty.

The figure of an American lady, when past the first bloom of youth, presents an aggregate of straight lines and corners altogether ungraceful and inharmonious. There is an overweening proportion of bone, which occasionally protrudes in quarters where it certainly adds nothing to the general charms of the person. The result is, perhaps, a certain tendency to *scragginess*, which I have no doubt to the eye of a young poet would be exceedingly annoying. A middle-aged gentleman, however, looks on such objects through a medium more philosophical; and I imagine, that, were it possible to combine the scattered and impalpable elements of female attraction, and to form a fair estimate of their amount, the ladies of the United States would have no deficiency to lament in comparison with other nations.

The trade of Baltimore, I have been assured, has, within the last twenty years, been greatly on the decline. During the long war which agitated Europe, America enjoyed nearly the whole carrying trade of the world. While her flag had only to brave the breeze, and not the battle, it was to be seen waving in every sea and in every harbour of the world. Wealth flowed in on her from all quarters, and, like the lawyer in the fable, while each of the belligerents received a shell in the shape of victories and Extraordinary Gazettes, this prudent and sagacious people contrived to keep possession of the oyster. But the United States at length resigned the innumerable benefits of neutrality. Mr Madison's proclamation of war was the signal for the decay of Baltimore; and the termination of hostilities in Europe having left other nations at liberty to exert their natural advantages in the pursuits of commerce, the harbour is now comparatively deserted, and the quays are no longer thronged with a busy and bustling crowd, as in the good old times, when people in Europe cut each other's throats because they happened to live on different sides of the Pyrenees, or were divided by the Rhine.

The worthy citizens of Baltimore no doubt deplore with great sincerity the decrease of pugnacity among their European brethren. Indeed I have heard since my arrival in America the toast of "A bloody war in Europe" drank with enthusiasm. The general progress of intelligence is unquestionably adverse to the gratification of the humane aspirations of these republican philanthropists; but a still greater obstacle consists in a prevailing deficiency in what is emphatically called the sinews of war. If the people of the United States, for the sake of getting up a good desolating war, which may tend eventually to their advantage, will only pay the piper to set the thing fairly agoing, they may, no doubt, as matters at present stand in Europe, be indulged with hostilities to any profitable amount. A note, a word, from Metternich or Talleyrand, will do the business; and the Continent, from Moscow to Madrid, will witness a repetition of the same scenes with which it must already be tolerably familiar. Indeed, without any such exercise of liberality on Jonathan's part, it is only too probable that his wish may erelong be gratified; and certainly, if wealth is to flow from such a source, it could not have a better destination than the pockets of the good citizens of Baltimore, who would not fail to employ it liberally in acts of benevolence and hospitality.

Being anxious to witness some of the proceedings of the State Legislatures, it was my intention to proceed to Annapolis, the seat of government, where both houses were in session. To this project, however, I found my Baltimore friends exceedingly adverse. They assured me that I would meet with nothing at Annapolis to repay the trouble of the journey; that the inns were bad, the roads still worse, and their representatives very far from incarnations either of good breeding or absolute wisdom. I own that all this had rather the effect of stimulating my curiosity than repressing it; and, in spite of all obstacles, I should probably have visited Annapolis, had I not received a letter from a friend in Washington, informing me, that, unless I repaired immediately to the seat of the General Government, the opportunity of observing the proceedings of Congress in the discharge of their more interesting duties would be lost. I therefore determined on setting out for Washington without farther delay, and bade a temporary farewell to my friends in Baltimore, whom I rejoiced in the prospect of revisiting before proceeding in my route to the southward.

While at Baltimore, I enjoyed the honour of introduction to Mr Carrol, the last survivor of that band of brave men, who signed the declaration of their country's independence. Mr Carrol is in his ninety-fifth year, yet enjoys the full use of all his faculties, and takes pleasure in social intercourse, which he enlivens by a fund of valuable anecdote. It was with great interest that I heard this aged patriot speak of the companions of his youth, Jay, Adams, Jefferson, and Hamilton, and describe those scenes of stormy struggle, in which he had himself partaken with honorable distinction. Baltimore, which now contains nearly eighty thousand inhabitants, he remembers a pretty fishing hamlet of some half dozen houses. But the progress of change throughout the whole Union has been equally rapid. Little more than half a century ago, the Americans were a handful of poor colonists, drivers of slaves and smal traffic in lumber and tobacco, from whom it was the policy of the mother country to squeeze all she could, and give nothing in return which it might be at all profitable to keep. With a judicious economy of gibbets and jail room at home, she was so obliging as to accelerate the natural increase of population by the transmission of certain gentlemen and ladies, who, being found somewhat awkwardly deficient in the ethics of property in their own country, were despatched to improve their manners on the plantations of Maryland and Virginia. Then, in her motherly care, she fenced in their trade with all manner of restrictions, which could in any way contribute to the replenishing of her own parental exchequer, and, to crown her benefits, condescended to export a copious supply of Lord Johns and Lord Charleses, to fill their empty pockets, and keep the people in good humour, with fine speeches, strong prisons, and a round military force.

All this Mr Carrol remembers, but he has lived to see a state of matters somewhat different. The colonies have disappeared, and in their place has risen a powerful confederation of free states, spreading a population of twelve millions over a vast extent of fertile territory, and possessing a commerce and marine second only to those of that nation from whom they boast their descent. He beholds his countrymen as happy as the unfettered enjoyment of their great natural advantages, and institutions of the broadest democracy, can make them. He sees whole regions, formerly the savage haunts of the panther and the wild Indian, covered with the dwellings of civilized and Christian man. The mighty rivers, on which a few wretched *flats* used to make with difficulty an annual voyage, he now sees covered with steam-vessels of gigantic size, and loaded with valuable merchandize. He has seen lakes in the very heart of a great continent, formerly approachable only by some adventurous traveller, connected with the ocean by means of canals. In short, the lot of Mr Carrol has been cast in what must ever be the most eventful period of his country's history; and having witnessed changes so vast and extraordinary, and beheld the whole of his early companions, one by one, drop into the grave, this venerable patriot may well be content to follow them, happy till the last in the enjoyment of the attachment of his family, and the esteem and reverence of his fellow-citizens.*

For the last fortnight the weather had been very bad. Heavy falls of snow had been alternated with thaws, and considerable difficulty was anticipated in accomplishing the journey to Washington. The perils of travelling, however, are generally greater in expectation than experience, and we got over the distance, forty miles, with greater facility, and fewer moving accidents, than I should have been glad to

* Mr Carrol, since my return to England, has paid the debt of nature. When the intelligence of his death reached Washington, both houses immediately adjourned, in testimony of respect for this "*ultimus Romanorum.*"

have compounded for, before leaving Baltimore. I was looking from the window of the coach, in a sort of brown study, at fields covered with snow, when one of my fellow-passengers enquired how I liked Washington. "I will tell you when I see it," was my reply. "Why, you have been in Washington for the last quarter-of-an-hour," rejoined my fellow-traveller. And so it was; yet nothing could I discern but a miserable cottage or two occasionally skirting the road at wide intervals. Presently, however, we came on the Capitol, and winding round the eminence on which it stands, rattled gaily down Pennsylvania Avenue, the principal street of the city. Houses now began to appear at somewhat closer distances, and every here and there was what is called in the vernacular of the country "a block of building," or, in other words, a connected range of shops and dwelling-houses. The coach at length stopped at Gadsby's hotel, where—though with some difficulty—I succeeded in procuring apartments.

When I arrived it was little more than three o'clock, so, in order to pass the time till dinner, I sallied forth to view the lions. The Capitol stands on elevated ground, and it consists of a centre and wings. It is covered with whitewash, which the Americans say was necessary to hide the smoke of the conflagration in 1814. This is nonsense. The smoke-marks, instead of injuring, would probably have improved the effect of the building, and diminished that rawness of aspect, which is so strongly opposed to architectural beauty. The structure is certainly imposing, both from situation and magnitude, though full of faults. The greatest is want of simplicity and definite character. The different parts of the building are good, but I could not help feeling that there was a general deficiency of congruity and adaptation. Like a volume of the Elegant Extracts, it contains a great many fine things, without any assignable affinity to account for their collocation. In the principal front—the western—the façade is broken from the wings being thrown back. This is unfortunate, and the effect is still further injured by the basement of the centre being brought too prominently into view. The vestibule opens on a large circular hall, which occupies the centre of the building, and is lighted by the dome. This spacious apartment is adorned by four pictures by Colonel Trumbull, a gentleman distinguished both as a patriot and an artist. He bore, I believe, considerable part in the contest of the Revolution, and has since been employed by the General Government to commemorate, by his pencil, those triumphs to which he contributed with his sword. The subjects he has selected, are the surrender of Burgoyne, the Declaration of Independence, the surrender of York Town, and Washington's resignation of his command at the termination of the war. Regarding these pictures merely as works of art, it is impossible to compliment Colonel Trumbull on his success. The truth is, the subjects are unmanageable. In the Declaration of Independence, we have a respectable congregation of decent farmer-looking men, staring quite as vacantly, from under their periwigs, as the solemnity of the occasion could possibly demand. A few are seated or standing at the table, which displays a large scroll of parchment. The rest are seated on benches, waiting apparently with exemplary patience the completion of the important document. Out of such materials Titian himself could not have made a picture. The subject admits of no action, nor of strong emotion of any kind. Then the quantity of canvass which is devoted to coat, waistcoat, and breeches, and the rows of clumsy legs without one bit of drapery to conceal them!

The other pictures are better, though they too involved great difficulties of management. The artist has patriotically given to Burgoyne a certain craven look, which has at least the fault of being commonplace in conception. In the figure of Washington, however, Colonel Trumbull has been very successful. There is a calm and unobtrusive grandeur about him, which satisfies the imagination. We are content to believe that the soul of the hero animated such a form as that we gaze on in Colonel Trumbull's canvass, and our interest is heightened by the knowledge, that the artist has given us a faithful portrait of the great man with whom in early life he enjoyed the privilege of personal intercourse.

Having reached the Rotunda, I enquired the way

to the House of Representatives, and following the directions I received, found myself at the bottom of a narrow stair which led directly to the gallery appropriated for strangers. On ascending, I entered a splendid semicircular saloon, round the arc of which is a range of anomalous columns, composed of breccia, found in the neighbourhood, with a highly-decorated entablature of white marble. In the centre of the chord is the chair of the Speaker, from which radiate seven passages to the circumference, and the desks and seats of the members are ranged in concentric rows. Behind the chair is a sort of corridor or gallery, with a fireplace at either end, and furnished with seats and sofas, which serves as a lounging place for the members and strangers to whom the Speaker may think proper to grant the privilege of *entré*.

On my entrance I found the House in animated debate, and listened with much interest to the first specimens of American eloquence I had enjoyed the opportunity of hearing. At five o'clock the House adjourned, and I returned to the hotel.

In the evening I accompanied a member of Congress, whose family I had known in Baltimore, to a ball given by a lady of his acquaintance, to whom he obligingly assured me that my intrusion would be welcome. On arriving, I found a very large party crowded into narrow compass, the houses at Washington being generally on a smaller scale than in the other cities I had visited. During the evening I had to pass through a formidable array of introductions to distinguished individuals, and after four hours of almost unbroken conversation, much of which could not be carried on without considerable expenditure of thought, I confess I did feel somewhat tired, and about three in the morning rejoiced to find myself stretched in a comfortable bed at Gadsby's.

The capital of the Federal Union is situated on a point of land formed by a bifurcation of the Potomac, about a hundred and twenty miles from the sea. Attached to it is a territory ten miles square, called the district of Columbia, which, in order to secure the complete independence of the general government, is placed under the immediate control of Congress. It would have been inconsistent with the American character, had the original plan of the future metropolis not been framed on a scale of gigantic magnitude. A parallelogram, nearly five miles in length, and more than two in breadth, was at once parcelled out with pleasing regularity into streets, squares, and avenues, and preparations were fondly made for the rapid growth of a city, compared with which London would dwindle into a village. In short, nothing could be more splendid than Washington *on paper*, and nothing more entirely the reverse of splendid than the real city, when at wide intervals a few paltry houses were seen to arise amid the surrounding forest.

The founders of Washington imagined it would become the seat of a large foreign commerce. This expectation has been disappointed. Washington has no trade of any kind, and there is at present no prospect of its ever possessing any. Its only hopes are now founded on its advantages as the seat of government, which must secure to it the benefit arising from the expenditure of a large diplomatic body, and of those immediately connected with the executive government.

Many years have passed since the foundation of Washington, and it has at length begun to assume something of the appearance of a city. It is not easy, however, to detect in its present aspect any thing of that system and regularity so delightful in the scheme of its founders. Instead of commencing this gigantic undertaking at a central point, it was considered most judicious to begin at the extremities, and build inward from the circumference. The consequence has been, that there is perhaps no city in the world of the same population, in which the distances to be traversed in the ordinary intercourse of society are so large. The most glaring want in Washington is that of compactness and consistency. The houses are scattered in straggling groups, three in one quarter, and half a dozen in another; and ever and anon our compassion is excited by some disconsolate dwelling, the first and last born of a square or crescent yet *in nubibus*, suffering like an ancient maiden in the mournful solitude of single blessedness.

There is nothing sordid in Washington, but nothing, at the same time, which claims a higher praise than is implied in the epithet respectable. The chief street of the city is called Pennsylvania Avenue, and extends from the Capitol to the President's house, a distance, which I guessed in walking it to be about a mile and a half. Near to the latter of these buildings are the public offices, unadorned edifices of brick, with nothing about them which it would be very easy either to censure or admire. In this quarter also are the houses of the foreign ministers, and generally of the members of the Cabinet, so that its claims to being the *Court* end are undeniable.

On the morning after my arrival, having despatched my letters, I returned to the Capitol, where I passed the morning very agreeably in the Senate and the House of Representatives. The Speaker of the latter, and the Vice-President of the United States, who presides in the former,—to both of whom I had the honour to be the bearer of introductions,—were obliging enough to grant me the privilege of *entré* to the body of the house, so that during my stay in Washington I enjoyed the advantage of being able to listen to the debates without any of the jostling and inconvenience often unavoidable in the gallery.

I have already described the hall of the Representatives: I would now say something of the members. Their aspect as a body was certainly somewhat different from any idea I had formed of a legislative assembly. Many were well dressed, and of appearance sufficiently senatorial to satisfy the utmost demands even of a severer critic in such matters than I pretend to be. But a large proportion undoubtedly struck me as vulgar and uncouth, in a degree which nothing in my previous experience had prepared me to expect. It is impossible to look on these men without at once receiving the conviction, that they are not gentlemen by habit or education, and assuredly in no society in Europe could they be received as such.

Each member is furnished with a desk, and a considerable number are usually engaged during the progress of public business in writing letters, or reading newspapers. Generally speaking, great decorum prevails in debate. Neither cheering, nor interruption of any kind, is permitted, and it is rare that any strenuous exercise of the Speaker's authority is demanded for the preservation of order. There have been occasions, however, on which the violent passions excited by antagonism of opinion, combined with personal dislike, have led to scenes perhaps unprecedented in any other deliberative assembly in the world. But the course of debate, though often troubled and vehement, is rarely violent, and the moral sense of propriety entertained by the majority of the House, is practically found to operate as a sufficient restraint on the irritable passions of individuals.

The hall of the Senate is a good deal smaller than that of the Representatives, and is very elegantly fitted up. It is likewise in the form of a semicircle, with desks at convenient distances for the members who sit uncovered. The President's chair is in the centre, and the office of this functionary—so far at least as it is connected with the maintenance of order—I should imagine to be something of a sinecure. In the course of the many debates of the Senate at which I was present during my stay in Washington, I do not remember any instance in which it was found necessary for the President to interpose his authority. The appearance of the assembly is grave and dignified. The senators are generally men of eminence in their several States, who may be supposed to bring to the task of legislation the results of more mature judgment and varied experience. The tone of debate is therefore pitched higher than in the more popular House. Questions are discussed in a temper more philosophical and statesmanlike. The range of argument is widened, that of invective narrowed; and the members of the Senate are less given to indulge in those flights of vapid and puerile declamation, which prove nothing but deficiency of taste and judgment in the orator.

Washington is undoubtedly the gayest place in the Union, and must, I should imagine, be the very paradise of hackney-coachmen.* If these gentle-

* During the first week of my stay in Washington, I paid thirty dollars in coach hire. I then contracted with a man for twenty, to have a carriage at my disposal from five in the evening till daylight.

men do not get rich, it must be owing to some culpable extravagance, for their vehicles are in continual demand from the hour of dinner till five in the morning, and long distances and heavy charges are all in their favour. Washington, too, is the only place in the Union where people consider it necessary to be agreeable,—where pleasing, as in the Old World, becomes a sort of business, and the enjoyments of social intercourse enter into the habitual calculations of every one.

The reason of this is obvious enough. The duties of legislation bring together a large body of gentlemen from all quarters of the Union, whose time in the morning is generally passed in the Capitol, but who, without the *delassements* of dinner parties and balls, would find their evening hours a burden somewhat difficult to dispose of. Idle men are always pleasant; they feel the necessity of being so, and make

On the first night of the agreement, however, I happened to go to four parties, and Jehu drew back from his bargain, and insisted on five dollars more. I argued strenuously against this *Punica fides*, but, finding I could not do better, was forced to give in to his demand. The charge for being conveyed to and from a dinner party alone was three dollars.

it their occupation, when they have no other. Your lawyer or your merchant, on the other hand, is so engrossed by weightier matters, that he has no time to cultivate the graces of life, or those thousand arts of courtesy which contribute so materially to enhance the enjoyments of society. The experience of the world is in favour of the assertion, that it is impossible to excel both in pleasure and business. A man of talent may select the sphere of his ambition, the bar, the pulpit, the exchange, the senate, or the drawing-room; but to attempt the honours of a double triumph, is, in general, to secure but duplicity of failure.

In Washington all are idle enough to be as agreeable as they can. The business of Congress is no great burden on the shoulders of any of its members; and a trip to Washington is generally regarded as a sort of annual *lark*, which enables a man to pass the winter months more pleasantly than in the country. A considerable number of the members bring their families, with the view of obtaining introduction to better society than they can hope to meet elsewhere; but the majority leave such incumbrances at home, some, it may be presumed, from taste, and others from economy.

There are few families that make Washington their permanent residence, and the city, therefore, has rather the aspect of a watering-place than the metropolis of a great nation. The members of Congress generally live together in small boarding-houses, which, from all I saw of them, are shabby and uncomfortable. Gentlemen with families take lodgings, or occupy apartments in a hotel; and it is really marvellous, at the Washington parties, to see how many people are contrived to be stowed away in a drawing-room somewhat smaller than an ordinary-sized pigeon-house. On such occasions one does not suffer so much from heat as from suffocation; for not only does the whole atmosphere become tainted in quality, but there seems an absolute deficiency in quantity for the pulmonary demands of the company.

Within a few days of my arrival, I enjoyed an opportunity of seeing at one comprehensive view the whole society of Washington. The French minister, who had recently arrived from Europe, had determined to open his diplomatic career by a splendid ball, an event of no ordinary magnitude in a society like that of Washington. On my arrival, I found the house, though a large one, filled even to overflow, by one of the motliest crowds in which it had ever been my fortune to mingle. The members of the foreign legations were of course present; and the contrast between their appearance, and that of a considerable portion of the company, was more striking than will readily be considered credible in England. I presume the invitation to members of Congress had been indiscriminate, for the party was adorned by many members of that body who would not probably have been present on any principle of selection. Many of the gentlemen had evidently not thought it necessary to make any change in their morning habiliments, and their boots certainly displayed no indication of any recent intimacy with Day and Martin. Others were in worsted stockings, and their garments, made evidently by some tailor of the backwoods, were of a fashion which, when displayed amid a scene so brilliant, was somewhat provocative of a smile. I was informed that the gentlemen whose appearance I have attempted to describe, were chiefly members from the Western States, and they might be seen parading the apartments with ladies of aspect quite as unique, and sometimes even more grotesque than their own.

The majority of the company, however, were unobjectionable, and the scene altogether was very interesting to a traveller, whose object was to see every thing which could at all illustrate the general condition of manners and society in the United States. It afforded me the advantage of introduction to many persons of eminence with whose reputation I was already familiar; and, after partaking with partial success in the scramble for supper, I returned home, satisfied that my hours had been very far from unprofitably spent.

Mr Vaughan, the British minister, being indisposed, was good enough to request Mr Van Buren, the Secretary of State, to present me to the President. The hour appointed was two o'clock on the day following; and, having to deal with personages of such importance, I was of course punctual in my attendance. The President's house is rather a handsome building, with a portico in front of four columns, of what order I forget. It is built of stone, but the walls, like those of the Capitol, are coated with whitewash. The entrance hall is spacious, and we were received in a plainly furnished apartment, without ornament of any kind. The President was seated in an easy-chair, from which he arose on our entrance, and, on my name being announced, very cordially presented his hand, and requested me to occupy a chair beside him. Mr Van Buren then took his departure, and I enjoyed half an hour's very pleasant conversation with this distinguished person.

General Jackson is somewhat above the middle height, spare, and well formed. Though he has probably numbered more than the years specified by the Psalmist as forming the ordinary limit of human life, no symptom of decrepitude is visible in his air or motions. His hair, though nearly white, is abundant, and on the upper part of the head bristles up somewhat stiffly. The forehead is neither bold nor expansive, though by no means deficient in height. The head, like that of Sir Walter

Scott, is particularly narrow in the region of ideality. The countenance of General Jackson is prepossessing; the features are strongly defined, yet not coarse; and, even at his advanced age, the expression of the eye is keen andvivid. The manner of the President is very pleasing. He evidently feels the dignity of his high office, and supports it; but there is no exaction of external deference beyond that which in ordinary society one gentleman is entitled to claim from another. One sees nothing of courtly elegance, but, on the other hand, nothing which the most rigid critic could attribute to coarseness or vulgarity.

The conversation I had the honour of holding with this distinguished person related principally to European politics. The world was then occupied with Poland, her wrongs, her sufferings, her chances of success in the unequal contest with the vast power of Russia. This subject naturally led to the general prospects of Europe, the progress of intelligence, and the probable duration of peace. Of course these were matters which did not admit of much novelty either of thought or illustration, but the observations of General Jackson were always marked by sagacity, and a certain directness both of thought and expression for which European statesmen are rarely remarkable. On the whole, I retired from the interview with sentiments of very sincere respect both for the intellectual and moral qualities of the American President.

In the hotel there was a mission from one of the more distant Indian tribes—the Mnemonies, I believe,—who were entertained during their stay in Washington at the public expense. There were five or six men, not handsome, certainly, in the European sense of the term, but fine athletic weather-beaten-looking fellows, and quite as savage in appearance as the most ardent hunter of the picturesque could possibly desire. Their faces and foreheads were daubed with red paint, and my fair readers will probably agree that rouge, however becoming on the cheek, must lose much of its efficacy as a cosmetic, when exhibited on the forehead and the nose. The hair,—indeed, the whole person, was anointed with some unctuous substance, the odour of which was far from agreeable. The distinguishing, and almost invariable characteristics of the Indian countenance, are generally known. The head round and somewhat flat on the summit, the hair dark, the eye full but not protuberant, the bones of the cheek prominent, the nose short, low, and dilated, the mouth large, the lips full and rarely compressed, and the general form of the face a broad oval.

In person, those composing the deputation were below the middle height, and certainly owed nothing to the decoration of the toilet. Several of them wore only a blanket fastened in front by a skewer, and their hair was stuck over with feathers. There were two ladies attached to the mission, neither of whom were good-looking, being in person short and squab, and deficient in that expression of grave and dignified intelligence which distinguishes the males.

There were also several children, and I desired the waiter, if possible, to induce some of them to pay me a visit. One evening he brought in two, a boy and a girl. The girl seemed about eleven or twelve years old. Her costume consisted of a sort of printed bed gown without sleeves, fastened close up to the throat; trowsers, mocassins or leggins of deer skin, worn generally by the Indians, and the whole covered by a blanket, the drapery of which she really managed with a good deal of grace. In each ear she wore two large silver earrings. Fastened to the crown of the head, was a piece of blue ribbon which hung down not unbecomingly on one side of the face.

The boy was apparently younger by two or three years, and a fine manly little fellow. He also wore a blanket by way of Benjamin; but instead of a bed-gown, rejoiced in a long coat, the tails of which reached almost to his heels, and which being made for some one of form and dimensions very different, was not remarkable for felicity of adaptation. Neither could speak English, but the boy evidently was the leading person, the girl only following his example.

Having a bottle of claret on the table, I filled each of them a glass, but the flavour of the wine did not seem to meet their approbation. They ate almonds and raisins, but evidently without relish, and walnuts had no better success. I then gave them cigars, which they appeared to enjoy; indeed I never saw any one blow a cloud with greater zest than the young lady. The failure of the claret then induced me to try the effect of stronger potations, and I brought a bottle of Eau de Cologne from my dressing table, the contents of which they finished without difficulty, or apparent inconvenience from the strength of the spirit.

They remained with me about half an hour, during the whole of which time they supported the sober gravity of demeanour, which the Indians consider to be inseparable from true dignity. Nothing seemed to excite surprise, and the only symptom of animation they displayed, was on catching a view of their own countenances in a mirror, when they both laughed. During their whole visit, neither uttered a word, but when I gave the girl a dollar, explaining to her by signs that half of it was to be given to her brother, she readily understood me, and nodded her head in promise of compliance. At length the boy rose to take leave, followed by the young lady, and shaking hands with me, they strode out of the apartment with a sort of barbaric grace which well became these children of the wilderness.

Before quitting the subject of these Indians, whose wild appearance had excited in my imagination a thousand fantastic associations, I must mention one circumstance which I found sadly hostile to poetical interest. One morning, a few days before leaving Washington, I observed my diplomatic friends, lounging and walking about as usual in the gallery of the hotel, but, alas! how miserably transmogrified! Their "Great Father," the President, had, it appeared, preparatory to their departure, presented each person attached to the mission with a new coat, in shape something like that worn by a coachman, and of blue cloth, turned up at the collar and cuffs with scarlet. The women wore cloaks of the same colours and materials, and my two little friends, whose barbaric appearance had been so delightful, now exhibited like the footboy in green livery, whom Hazlitt describes as having contributed so much to the splendours of Barry Cornwall's tea parties. In short, instead of Indian chiefs, I saw before me a set of beings who reminded one of the servants' hall, certainly not the most pleasing or genial region for the fancy to wander in. The poor men, however, seemed so proud of their new finery, and to do them justice, strutted in it with so grand an air, that it almost became doubtful whether the effect of this anomalous conjunction was not rather to ennoble the livery, than to degrade brave men who never before had suffered degradation.

CHAPTER II.

AMERICAN CONSTITUTION.

In the observations I have already hazarded on the character of the federal government, it was my object simply to illustrate the fallacy of the leading and fundamental principles on which it is established. I would now willingly be permitted to direct the attention of the reader to those practical defects, arising from want of congruity and adaptation in its separate institutions, which have contributed materially to derange the whole action of the machine.

The colonies had no sooner achieved their independence, than they became desirous of establishing such an union between the different States, as might maintain tranquillity at home, and ensure unity in their relations to foreign powers. In 1787, a convention, over which Washington presided, was held in the city of Philadelphia. This convention consisted of delegates from all the States, with the exception of Rhode Island. After long deliberation, the plan of government, which forms the present federal constitution, was recommended and submitted for the separate consideration of the different States. In each of these a convention was assembled, and in 1789, the constitution, all the necessary formalities having been gone through, was duly organized and put in operation.

The legislative power conferred by this constitution is vested in Congress, which consists of two bodies—the House of Representatives and the Senate. The former of these is chosen biennially, in a proportion not exceeding one member for every thirty thousand inhabitants. The minimum only being specified, Congress possesses the power of extending the number of electors who are to enjoy the privilege of returning a member. No person is eligible to this assembly who is not twenty-five years old, who is not resident in the State in which he is chosen, or who has not enjoyed the privileges of citizenship for seven years. No qualification in property is required, and the right of suffrage is universal, or nearly so.

This system of representation, though simple enough, is connected with some anomalies. The slave-holding States enjoy the privilege of sending more representatives than the others. The total number of white persons, and three-fifths of the slave population, constitute the amount to which the right of representation has been accorded. Thus, suppose the States of Ohio and Virginia each to contain one million of white inhabitants, and the latter to possess half a million of slaves, while the former has none; Virginia will send representatives to Congress, on a population of 1,300,000, and of course will exercise the greater influence in the national councils.

The Senate is composed of two representatives from each State. They are elected by the State legislatures for a term of six years, one-third of the number going out by rotation every second year. The qualifications demanded for a senator are, that he shall be thirty years of age, a citizen of nine years standing, and an inhabitant of the state which he represents.

In addition to its legislative functions, the Senate is recognised as a branch of the executive. In this capacity it is invested with the privilege of ratifying or annulling the official appointments of the President. A treaty with any foreign power is not valid until a majority of two-thirds of the Senate shall have given it their sanction.

Some of the particulars stated in this brief outline seem to demand a few observations. In the course of the present work, I have already had occasion to express my convictions as to the results of universal suffrage in a country like the United States. But there are other minor points connected with the election and constitution of the legislative bodies, which appear calculated to derogate very materially from their usefulness. The regulation, that the members of both Houses should be *resident* in the particular State in which they are elected, I cannot but consider as particularly objectionable. In the first place, it narrows, very unnecessarily, the limits of choice in the electors. In the second, it tends to promote that sectional feeling, that exclusive devotion to the petty interests of some particular district, which is generally inconsistent with the adoption of an enlarged and statesmanlike policy. It places the representative in a state of absolute dependence on his immediate constituents, and prevents all appeal to other bodies of electors, by whom his talents and principles may be more justly appreciated. It prevents a state, in which there happens to be a dearth of talent, from availing itself of the superfluity in another. It contributes also to feed and keep alive those provincial jealousies, which often border so closely on hostility of feeling, and to render more prevalent in the different States that conviction of incompatibility in their various interests which threatens at no distant period to cause a total disruption of the Union.

In opposition to the injurious effects of this clause of the constitution, what are its good ones? I can discover none. As a precaution to secure the election of members sufficiently acquainted with the interests of the particular district they represent, it is utterly useless. Indeed, a more gratuitous piece of legislation can scarcely be conceived. An American cannot doubt either the will or the capacity of the electors to take care of their own interests, and to judge of the qualifications of the several candidates who may solicit their suffrages. Even without restriction, it will rarely occur that the inhabitants of a particular state or district will elect a stranger for their representative. There are a thousand feelings arising from neighbourhood and habitual intercourse in the common business of life, which in ordinary cases would prevent this. A candidate from a different State would always come into the field under great disadvantages. The current of local prejudice would be entirely in favour of his opponents, and if in spite of every obstacle he did succeed in securing his return, what would this prove but that he was manifestly the person best qualified to discharge the duties of their representative?

In Great Britain, notwithstanding the experience of centuries, no such legislative absurdity ever was contemplated. A man from the Land's End may sit for Caithness or the Orkneys. A burgess of Berwick-upon-Tweed may be elected at Cork or Limerick. In short, a member, without once changing his domicile, often sits in different Parliaments, for different places; nor has it ever entered the imagination of any one, that this freedom of choice has been productive either of injury or inconvenience. Its advantages, however, are manifold. An English member of Parliament is not necessarily dependent on the judgment of his immediate constituents. He advocates the particular policy which appears to him best calculated to promote the interest of his country, and, whatever his opinions may be, he is not afraid to express them emphatically and openly. It is no doubt possible that this may prevent his re-election for some borough or county, but the whole country is open to him; he does not feel himself to be meanly subservient to the inhabitants of one particular district; and his opinions must be strange indeed, if he cannot find some body of constituents with whose notions of policy his own are in accordance.

But in America all this is different. There no man can be elected except for the particular district in which he chances to reside. If his opinions differ from those which happen to prevail in his own petty circle, he is excluded from public life altogether.

There is no alternative, but that of giving up all hope of political distinction, or of speaking and acting in a manner basely subservient to the prejudices and caprices of his constituents. Let a member of Congress attempt to follow a bold, manly, and independent course, and he is instantly sent back into private life, with his feelings injured, and his future chances of success materially diminished by the reputation of public failure.

The absurdity of the amount of representation of the different States being at all influenced by the number of slaves, is too gross to require elaborate exposure. Yet without this, the Union could not have been effected, owing to the extreme jealousy of the Southern States. It is the fashion in America to dilate on the anomalies of the British constitution, but even the Scottish Highland proprietors, though by no means a body celebrated either for wisdom or disinterestedness, have not yet ventured to petition that the black cattle, which, like slaves in Virginia, are sent annually in droves to the south, should be taken into the census of population, with a view to add to their political influence.

There can be no doubt, that the division of the legislature into two bodies, acting separately, and with co-ordinate powers, is founded in wisdom. It may be doubted, however, whether in times of excitement the American Senate would practically be found to have any efficient influence in preventing violent and hasty legislation. Unlike the British House of Peers, the Senate is not composed of members having a direct and personal interest in maintaining the privileges of their branch of the legislature. They are men taken for a temporary purpose from the common walks of life, to which, at the expiration of their political service, they immediately return. They are subject to all the impulses which can affect the deliberations of the more popular House. In no point of view do they present themselves under the aspect of an independent body. They are the creatures of popular favour, and in that, like the representatives, they live, move, and have their being. The interests, the habits, the modes of thought, of both bodies are the same.

It is in vain, therefore, to look to the American Senate as affording any check on the tendency towards democracy, which is discernible in all the workings of the constitution. It was the wish of Hamilton, that the Senators should be elected for life, and that a considerable qualification of property should be attached to the office. Had Washington publicly supported him in these views, it is probable that a scheme of government, combining greater vigour and durability, might have been adopted. But Washington, though bold in the field, was timid in the cabinet. The opportunity was suffered to pass, and from the period of the adoption of the present constitution, all hopes of organizing a government on a broader and more permanent basis, were for ever at an end.

The President of the United States is elected for four years. On entering office, he takes an oath to preserve, protect, and defend the constitution of the United States. He is Commander-in-Chief of the army and navy, and of the militia of the different States, when called into actual service by the general government. He has the power of negotiating treaties, but not of ratifying them, until sanctioned by a majority of two-thirds of the Senate. He nominates all officers, civil and military, but the assent of the Senate is necessary to the validity of the appointment. He receives foreign ambassadors. He may grant pardons and reprieves, except in cases of treason and impeachment. Should the two Houses of Congress disagree as to the period of adjournment, he may adjourn them to such time as he may think proper. He fills offices *ad interim* when the Senate are not sitting; but, on their reassembling, that body may annul the appointments.

Under the control of the President are three executive departments, the heads of which constitute what is called the Cabinet. The Secretary of State discharges all the duties of the foreign department. Through this officer the President expresses his opinions in all diplomatic intercourse. The other members of the Cabinet, are the Secretaries of the Treasury, of War, and of Naval Affairs.

Of such materials is the American executive composed, and it is impossible to observe the restrictions with which every exercise of its authority has been clogged, without at once perceiving that it was from this quarter alone, that danger to the Constitution was expected to proceed. The idea of a perpetual Dictator was the bugbear which frightened American statesmen from their propriety, and rendered them indifferent to all perils which assumed another and less alarming aspect. Even at the present day, after forty years experience of their Constitution, there are many individuals, otherwise distinguished for talent and good sense, whose imagination is still haunted by "chimeras dire" of military tyranny, organised by a quadrennial President with a salary of five thousand a-year, an army of six thousand men, and without independent and unshackled patronage of any sort! One might be content to smile at such nonsense if it carried with it no serious consequences; but when we see the destinies of a great nation materially affected by it, we cannot but lament the extent and influence of the delusion. In truth, the manifest and pervading defect of the American government is the very want of that independent energy which her statesmen regard with so much futile apprehension. The President is a kind of King Log, whom it has been thought prudent to deprive of members altogether, in order to prevent the possibility of his doing mischief. It might have been very judicious, no doubt, to extract the teeth and pare the claws of so ferocious an animal, but certainly not to carry the mutilation so far as to destroy the whole bodily functions, if these could be rendered useful to the community.

It is to be lamented that a government of greater vigour and efficiency was not originally adopted, since the very newness of political institutions is of itself a source of weakness. It is only by slow degrees that the intellect and habits of a people become accommodated to the operation of a government, that their prejudices are enlisted in its favour, and a sort of prescriptive respect is obtained which adds materially to the benefit it is capable of conferring. Until the American institutions should have gained this vantage-ground, it was above all things desirable, that they should be established on broad and permanent principles, with enough of independent energy to resist the inroads of mere wanton innovation. Had the federal government been so framed as to rest for support, not on the precarious favour of the multitude, but on the deliberate intelligence of the property and talent of the country, there could have been no assignable limit to the prosperity and intellectual advancement of this fortunate people. At present it only contrives to drag on a feeble existence, by adapting its whole policy to the prejudices and passions of the most ignorant part of the community, which it is the bounden duty of every government to restrain and regulate.

Since we have seen that both the legislative bodies are absolutely and necessarily subservient to the popular feeling, it might have been expected, at least, that the highest executive office of the Republic would have been rendered inaccessible to such influence. It was natural to imagine that the President of the United States would be placed above temptation of every sort, and be assailed by no inducement to swerve from the policy which he might consider best calculated to promote the interests of his country.

Such a presumption, however, would be entirely unwarranted. The President is elected for a period of four years, but the custom has generally been to re-elect him for a second term of equal duration.

From the time of his first inauguration, therefore, the policy of every President is naturally directed to secure this re-election. He takes especial care that the opinions expressed in every State document bearing his sanction, shall be in accordance with the passions or prejudices of the numerical majority of the people. Being without the means of leading opinion, he is content to follow it. He stands in circumstances too precarious to admit of his boldly adopting measures of enlarged and liberal policy, or attempting to stem the tide of ignorance and prejudice. In short, during his first period of office at least, the American President is any thing but independent, and when he has succeeded in extending the duration of his power, he stands so committed, so trammelled by pledges of all sorts, so identified with particular opinions, and some particular policy, that it is impossible to retrace his steps without loss both of consistency and character.

The appointment of the great officers of State rests with the President, subject to the approval of the Senate; and since he bears the whole responsibility of the Cabinet, it seems only fair that he should possess the privilege of selecting the individuals of whom it shall be composed. But even here, independently of the check of the Senate, his choice is not practically free, nor can he always select the men best qualified for the duties to be performed. With a view to his own re-election, the greater and more influential States must be conciliated by the advancement of one of their citizens to a seat in the Cabinet. If the Secretary of State be a native of New York, a citizen of Pennsylvania will probably be appointed to the Treasury, so that the very construction of the Cabinet is materially influenced by the dependence of the President, and the consequent necessity he feels of truckling to local and sectional interests, instead of following the upright and unbending policy, which his own principles and judgment would probably have dictated.

All this is bad, but laying it entirely out of view, the mere shortness of the period during which any President or any Cabinet can hope to continue in office, appears a circumstance directly injurious to the national interests. It prevents the adoption of any permanent and far-sighted policy, tending progressively to augment the public wealth and prosperity. One man will not plant, that another may reap the harvest of his labours; he will not patiently lay the foundation of a structure, the plan of which is continually liable to be changed by his successors, and on whom, if completed, the whole honours must ultimately devolve. In short, it is an inherent and monstrous evil, that American statesmen must legislate for the *present*, not for the *future;* that they are forced, by the necessity of their situation, to follow the policy most in accordance with the immediate prejudices of the people, rather than that which is calculated to promote the highest and best interests of the community. Immediate and temporary expediency is, and must be, the moving and efficient impulse of American legislation. The political institutions of the United States are consistent neither with stability of purpose in the legislative, nor vigour in the executive departments. Let us look where we will, all is feeble and vacillating. There is no confidence reposed in public men; no appeal to the higher and more generous motives which influence conduct; no scope for the display of lofty and independent character; no principle from the operation of which we can rationally expect any higher developement of the national mind.

The exclusion of the ministers from even a deliberative voice in either branch of the legislature, is another curious feature in the American constitution. It proceeds, no doubt, from that extreme jealousy of the executive to which I have alluded, and is necessarily productive of much delay and inconvenience. No communication can take place between the legislative bodies and the heads of departments otherwise than by writing, and the consequence is, that long and inconclusive debates are constantly taking place, which a little information from an official functionary might have prevented. Under the present arrangement, a minister of state never appears at all in the eyes of the public. He has to brave no enemy, and repel no attack. He can be cited before no tribunal, and cannot be called upon to stand forth and vindicate his conduct in the face of his country. He remains securely sheltered under the cloak of the President, on whose shoulders rests the whole political responsibility of the cabinet.

It is somewhat strange that the American constitution, which evidently presumes that every man in office is a scoundrel, should have removed, in this instance, one of the strongest and most efficient securities for public virtue. In England, for one half the year at least, ministers are brought into immediate contact with their political opponents. They are compelled to give public explanations of their conduct. They are kept in continual remembrance of their official responsibility. They are subjected to a test, which it requires not only upright policy, but high talents, to encounter successfully. A British minister cannot skulk in Downing Street, when the Commons of England are discussing the wisdom of his measures, or the purity of his motives. He stands forward in the eye of the world; he challenges enquiry; he meets his accusers face to face; he answers publicly a public accusation, and according to the verdict given he stands or falls.

No man can believe, I should imagine, that such habitual and inexorable scrutiny, anticipated by every public officer, is not productive of the most beneficial consequences. But from any thing like this the high functionaries in the United States are scrupulously protected. The oracles of an American minister are issued only from the shrine of his bureau. He is too delicate a flower for the rough handling of a public assembly, and of course may disregard attack, where the constitution has so wisely precluded the possibility of defence.

It is no answer to all this to say, that every public officer in the United States is liable to impeachment, in case of individual malversation in office. No doubt he is so; but violation of trust in a minister of state, so flagrant as to warrant impeachment, is an offence of rare occurrence, and one for which the disgrace of public exposure is generally a sufficient punishment. What is chiefly to be guarded against are the jobs, the trickeries, the petty impurities of office, which the necessity of braving personal examination in a public assembly would probably prevent. The Americans, therefore, in excluding their executive officers from all place in their representative bodies, have gratuitously discarded a powerful and efficient security for the honest and upright administration of their affairs.

The knowledge that every political measure will be subjected to a rigid and unsparing scrutiny, and must be defended to the satisfaction of honourable men in open discussion, is perhaps the most powerful safeguard devised by human ingenuity to secure the integrity of public men.

When we look, however, somewhat more minutely into the details of this republican government, it is soon perceived that the members of the cabinet are, in truth, nothing better than superintending clerks in the departments over which they nominally preside. At the commencement of every Congress, the practice is to appoint standing committees, who, in fact, manage the whole business of the executive departments. The process is as follows :—The President, in his message, invites the attention of Congress to such subjects as may appear of national importance. Permanent committees are appointed by both Houses, and to these the consideration of the various interests of the country is referred. Thus, whatever relates to finance falls within the department of the "committee of ways and means," while that on foreign affairs assumes cognizance of every thing connected with the external relations of the government. These committees have separate apartments, in which the real business of the country is carried on, and from which the heads of the executive departments are rigidly excluded. The whole power of the government is thus absolutely and literally absorbed by the people, for no bill connected with any branch of public affairs could be brought into Congress with the smallest prospect of success, which had not previously received the initiative approbation of these committees.

It should be remembered that the power thus assumed by the people is wholly unknown to the Constitution. It is one of those important, but silent encroachments which are progressively affecting the forms, as they have long done the spirit of the government. It is still, however, the fashion to say, if not to believe, that the C nstitution remains unchanged, and it is scarcely worth while to argue the point, with men who are evidently deficient either in sincerity or penetration. But if any man of sense and sagacity, who can be considered unbiassed by the prejudices of habit and education, will declare, after a deliberate examination of the working of this government, that its whole important functions are not practically engrossed by the House of Representatives, I shall be ready to give up those opinions which I now offer to the world, as embodying the result of my own observations in the United States.

CHAPTER III.

WASHINGTON.

THOUGH the soil of the United States may be considered ungenial for the growth of philosophy and literature, it would certainly appear to be very happily adapted for the cultivation of eloquence. It is one effect of free institutions, that in multiplying the depositories of political power, they render the faculty of persuasion a necessary element on which successful ambition must rest for support. Under a despotic government there is "ample room and verge enough" for no eloquence but that of the pulpit. There exists little community of sentiment between the governors and the governed, and habits of passive obedience are incompatible with that buoyancy of thought and feeling with which true eloquence is inseparably connected. But in a republic the whole interests of man, individually and collectively, become matter of unrestricted discussion, and afford vantage-ground for the orator. Earth, air, ocean, and the living myriads that inhabit them, and that wider world of thought and consciousness existing in the human breast, are all comprised within the limits of his dominion, and obey the impulse of his genius.

In America the power of persuasion constitutes the only lever of political advancement. In England, though the field for the exercise of this talent be very great, yet rank, wealth, family connexions, hereditary claims, and a thousand other influences must be taken into account, in reckoning the ordinary elements of successful ambition. How powerful —whether for good or evil I shall not enquire— many of these are, is well known, but none of them exist in the United States. There, rank is unknown; there are no great accumulations of property; and competition for the higher offices of the commonwealth, has long been rather the struggle of men, or more properly, perhaps, of sectional interests, than of principles. The candidates, however, for every situation of emolument, are, beyond all example, in this country, numerous; and, as each individual is naturally anxious to establish some trifling point of superiority in reference to his opponents, the consequence is, that political opinion is dissected with a degree of nicety which the most accomplished metaphysician would find it difficult to surpass. But all enter the contest armed with the same weapons, displaying the same banner, appealing to the same umpire, and contending for the same reward. Patronage of every kind is virtually in the hands of the people. They are the fountain of fame and of honour, the ultimate tribunal by which all appeals must be heard and decided.

In the United States, oral eloquence, and the newspaper press, constitute the only instruments really available in acquiring influence over this many-headed and irresponsible arbiter of merit and measures. There exists, indeed, no other channel through which there is any possibility of attaining political distinction. The influence and circulation of newspapers is great beyond any thing ever known in

Europe. In truth, nine-tenths of the population read nothing else, and are, consequently, mentally inaccessible by any other avenue. Every village, nay, almost every hamlet, has its press, which issues secondhand news, and serves as an arena in which the political gladiators of the neighbourhood may exercise their powers of argument and abuse. The conductors of these journals are generally shrewd but uneducated men, extravagant in praise or censure, clear in their judgment of every thing connected with their own interests, and exceedingly indifferent to all matters which have no discernible relation to their own pockets or privileges.

The power exercised by this class of writers over the public mind is very great. Books circulate with difficulty in a thinly-peopled country, and are not objects on which the solitary denizen of the forest would be likely to expend any portion of the produce of his labour. But newspapers penetrate to every crevice of the Union. There is no settlement so remote as to be cut off from this channel of intercourse with their fellow-men. It is thus that the clamour of the busy world is heard even in the wilderness, and the most remote invader of distant wilds is kept alive in his solitude to the common ties of brotherhood and country.

Newspapers have a character and influence, distinct from that of all other literature. They are emphatically *present* existences; the links between the past and the future. Forming part, as it were, of the very business of life, they are never alien to the minds of those who participate in its interests. They are read; laid aside; forgotten at night, to be again remembered in the morning. In truth, it is this incessant recreation which constitutes their power. The opinions of men are yielded willingly to their influence. It is constant dropping, as the old proverb hath it, which wears the stone.

But the newspaper press is perhaps better adapted for the advocation and diffusion of the principles of a party, than for the attainment of the immediate objects of individual ambition. The influence of a public journal can scarcely be considered a thing personal to its conductor. It circulates in a thousand places where his name and existence are entirely unknown. Indeed, to the great mass of his readers he is not a man of thews and sinews, broad cloth and corduroys, eating, drinking, spitting, and tobacco-chewing like themselves, but a sort of airy and invisible being, "a voice, a mystery," which it requires an effort of abstraction to impersonate.

In America, therefore, the influence of the pen, though admitting of vast extension, is only secondary, as an instrument of political ambition, to that of the tongue. A writer may enforce the peculiar tenets of his party with the utmost skill, and support them with great logical acuteness, and yet be very scantily endowed with the powers of a debater. Such powers, however, are indispensable, or, at least, in the estimation of the electors, are practically found to outweigh every other accomplishment. A convincing proof of this almost uniform preference may be found in the fact, that of the whole federal legislature *nineteen-twentieths* are lawyers, men professionally accustomed to public speaking. The merchants—the great capitalists of New York, Boston, and Philadelphia, and the other Atlantic cities, constituting, I fear not to say, the most enlightened body of citizens in the Union—are almost as effectually excluded from political power, by deficiency in oratorical accomplishment, as they could be by express legal enactment.

The acquisition of a faculty so important, therefore, is necessarily one of the primary objects of Transatlantic education. Teachers of elocution, and of all the petty trickeries of delivery, to which inferior men find it necessary to resort, abound everywhere. An American boy, from the very first year of his going to school, is accustomed to spout. At college he makes public orations. On emerging into life he frequents debating societies, numerous everywhere, and his qualifications thus become known to the electors, whose suffrages on some future occasion he is anxious to obtain. He then commences practice as a lawyer, and in that capacity reaps some advantage from his previous notoriety. The road to political distinction then opens. He is probably elected a member of the legislature of his native State. Should he acquit himself in his new capacity with credit, in a few years he becomes a delegate to Congress, and enters on a higher sphere of legislative duty. At no period of his progress, however, is his tenure of the favour of his constituents secure. There is a sectional jealousy prevalent throughout the United States; a restless anxiety in the inhabitants of each district, that their local, and perhaps exclusive interests, however insignificant, should be resolutely obtruded on the attention of the legislature. They consider also that their own consequence is intimately affected by the figure made by their representative in Congress, and would feel it to be a dereliction, on his part, of their just claims, were he to suffer any interesting question to pass without engrossing some portion of the attention of the Assembly.

Verily, the yoke of such constituents is not easy, nor is their burden light. The public prints must bear frequent record of the loquacity of their representative, or they are not satisfied. The consequence is, that in the American Congress there is more of what may be called *speaking against time*, than in any other deliberative assembly ever known. Each member is aware that he must either assume a certain prominence, or give up all hope of future re-election, and it is needless to say which alternative is usually preferred. A universal tolerance of long speeches is thus generated, and no attempt is ever made to restrict the range of argument or declamation, within the limits even of remote connexion with the subject of debate. One continually reads in the public papers such announcements as the following:—

"In the House of Representatives, yesterday, Mr Tompkins occupied the whole day with the continuation of his brilliant speech on the Indian question, and is in possession of the floor to-morrow. He is expected to conclude on Friday; but, from the press of other business, it will probably be Tuesday next before Mr Jefferson X. Bagg will commence his reply, which is expected to occupy the whole remainder of the week."

In fact, an oration of eighteen or twenty hours is no uncommon occurrence in the American Congress. After this vast expenditure of breath, the next step of the orator is to circulate his speech in the form of a closely-printed pamphlet of some hundred and fifty pages. A plentiful supply of copies is despatched for the use of his constituents, who swallow the bait; and at the conclusion of the session, the member returns to his native town, where he is lauded, feasted, and toasted, and—what he values, I doubt not, still more—re-elected.

The Americans enjoy the reputation in Europe of being *par excellence* a sensible people. I fear their character in this respect must suffer some depreciation in the opinion of those who have enjoyed the advantage of observing the proceedings of their legislative assemblies. The mode in which the discussion of public business is carried on in Congress, certainly struck me as being not only unstatesmanlike, but in flagrant violation of the plainest dictates of common sense. The style of speaking is loose, rambling, and inconclusive; and adherence to the real subject of discussion evidently forms no part, either of the intention of the orator, or the expectation of his audience. A large proportion of the speakers seem to take part in a debate with no other view than that of individual display, and it sometimes happens that the topic immediately pressing on the attention of the assembly, by some strange perversity, is almost the only one on which nothing is said.

It is evident that such a style of discussion—if

discussion it can be called—could only become prevalent in an assembly with abundance of leisure for the enactment of these oratorical interludes. In a body like the British Parliament, compelled by the pressure of business to be economical of time, it could not possibly be tolerated. The clamorous interests of a great nation are matters too serious to be trifled with, and time is felt to be too valuable for expenditure on speeches better fitted for a spouting club, than a grave deliberative assembly.

The truth, I believe, is, that the American Congress have really very little to do. All the multiplied details of local and municipal legislation fall within the province of the State governments, and the regulation of commerce and foreign intercourse practically includes all the important questions which they are called on to decide. Nor are the members generally very anxious so to abbreviate the proceedings of Congress, as to ensure a speedy return to their provinces. They are well paid for every hour lavished on the public business; and being once at Washington, and enjoying the pleasures of its society, few are probably solicitous for the termination of functions which combine the advantage of real emolument, with the opportunities of acquiring distinction in the eyes of their constituents. The farce, therefore, by common consent, continues to be played on. Speeches apparently interminable are tolerated, though not listened to; and every manœuvre by which the discharge of public business can be protracted is resorted to, with the most perfect success.

Of course I state this merely as the readiest hypothesis by which the facts already mentioned can be explained; but, in truth, there are many other causes at work. Though in either House there is no deficiency of party spirit, and political hostilities are waged with great vigour, yet both in attack and defence there is evidently an entire want both of discipline and organization. There is no concert, no division of duties, no compromise of opinion; but the movements of party are executed without regularity or premeditation. Thus, instead of the systematic and combined attack of an organized body, deliberately concerted on principles which will unite the greatest number of auxiliaries, government have in general to sustain only the assaults of single and desultory combatants, who mix up so much of individual peculiarity of opinion, with what is common to their party, that any general system of effective co-operation is impossible. It is evident enough, in whatever business the House may be engaged, that each individual acts for himself, and is eager to make or to discover some opportunity of lavishing all his crudities of thought or fancy on his brother legislators.

The consequence of all this is, that no one can guess, with any approach to probability, the course of discussion on any given subject: A speech, an argument, an insinuation, an allusion, is at any time sufficient to turn the whole current of debate into some new and unforeseen channel; and I have often found it absolutely impossible to gather from the course of argument, even the nature of the question on which the House were divided in opinion. In England, it is at least pretty certain that a motion on criminal law will not lead to a discussion on foreign policy, including the improvement of turnpike roads, the expenses of Plymouth breakwater, the renewal of the East India Company's charter, and the prospects of Swan River settlement. But in America, a debate in Congress is a sort of steeple-chase, in which no one knows any thing of the country to be crossed, and it often happens that the object of pursuit is altogether lost sight of by the whole party.

One effect—I do not know that it is a bad one—of this excursive style of discussion is, that every member finds it necessary to be on the *qui vive*. Something may at any moment be said, to which it is necessary that the representative for a particular state or district should immediately reply. Whatever may be the subject of debate, no member—especially in the Lower House—can be absent a single hour with safety, when an orator of the hostile party, according to American phrase, is "in possession of the floor." I have often, in coming to the Capitol, enquired at members of the House of Representatives whether it was probable that any interesting discussion would take place in the course of the day. The answer uniformly was, that it was impossible to foresee; for though the topic then occupying the attention of the House might be of the most commonplace kind, the debate on it was liable at any moment to diverge, and bring on the most unexpected results. But on this matter, as I have already perhaps dealt too much in "wise saws," I shall take the liberty of adducing a few modern instances.

One of the first debates at which I was present, related to a pecuniary claim of the late President Monroe on the United States, amounting, if I remember rightly, to sixty thousand dollars. This claim had long been urged, and been repeatedly referred to committees of the House of Representatives, who, after a careful investigation of the subject, had uniformly reported in favour of its justice.

The question at length came on for discussion, "Is the debt claimed by Mr Monroe from the United States a just debt, or not?" Nothing could possibly be more simple. Here was a plain matter of debtor and creditor; a problem of figures, the solution of which must rest on a patient examination of accounts, and charges, and balances. It was a question after the heart of Joseph Hume,—a bone, of which that most useful legislator understands so well how to get at the marrow.

Well, how was this dry question treated in the House of Representatives? Why, as follows. Little or nothing was said as to the intrinsic justice or validity of the claim. Committees of the House had repeatedly reported in its favour, and I heard no attempt, by fact or inference, to prove the fallacy of their decision. But a great deal was said about the political character of Mr Monroe some dozen years before, and a great deal about Virginia, and its Presidents and its members, and its attempts to govern the Union, an its selfish policy. A vehement discussion took place as to whether Mr Monroe or Chancellor Livingstone had been the efficient agent in procuring the cession of Louisiana. Members waxed warm in attack and recrimination, and a fiery gentleman from Virginia was repeatedly called to order by the Speaker. One member declared, that, disapproving *toto cœlo* of the former policy of Mr Monroe's Cabinet, he should certainly now oppose his demand for payment of a debt, the justice of which was not attempted to be disproved. Another thought Mr Monroe would be very well off if he got half of what he claimed, and moved an amendment to that effect, which being considered a kind of compromise, I believe, was at length carried, after repeated adjournments and much clamorous debate.

Another instance of discussion somewhat similar struck me very forcibly, and will afford, I imagine, sufficient illustration of the mode of doing business in the House of Representatives. It took place on a claim put forward by the widow of Commodore Decatur, for prize money due to him and his ship's crew for something done in the Mediterranean. The particulars I forget, but they are of no consequence. The Commodore having no family, had bequeathed the whole of his property, real and personal, to his wife, whom circumstances had since reduced to poverty. When I entered, the debate had already commenced, and the House seemed almost unanimous in the admission of the claim. This was dull enough, and as the subject itself had little to engage the attention of a stranger, I determined to try whether any thing of more interest was going forward in the Senate. While I was conversing with a member of the House, however, some symptoms of difference of opinion began to manifest themselves.

One member proposed, that as the money was to be granted principally with a view to benefit the widow of Commodore Decatur, the ordinary rules of prize division should not be adhered to, and that a larger share than usual should be allotted to the commander of the armament. This proposition, however, was evidently adverse to the wishes of the majority, and the amendment met with little support. This matter being settled, the discussion for some time went on smoothly enough, and there seemed every prospect of its reaching a speedy and amicable termination.

At length, however, a member rose, and argued that the circumstance of the Commodore having bequeathed his whole property to his wife, when he imagined he had very little property to leave, afforded no ground for the conclusion, that had he known of this large addition, it might not have been differently applied. He, therefore, expressed his firm determination to oppose its exclusive appropriation to the widow. The widow, however, was not without able and zealous advocates to set forth her claims, and urge their admission. These pronounced her to be one of the most amiable and excellent of her sex, and maintained that, as the House had no possible access to know how the Commodore would have acted under circumstances merely hypothetical, there was no course to be pursued but to appropriate the money according to the desire actually expressed in his last will and testament.

While the House were, for the nonce, divided into *widowites* and *anti-widowites*, the discussion became still further embroiled. New matter of debate arose. Admitting that Mrs Decatur was entitled to the usufruct of the money during her life, was it fitting that she should have the power of alienating it at her death from the relatives of her husband? This was very warmly debated. At length, a gentleman, in a very vehement and pathetic speech, set forth the attractions, both mental and personal, of two young ladies, daughters of a sister of Captain Decatur, whose necessities unfortunately were equal to their merits. He had the honour, he said, of being their neighbour in the country; they were elegant and accomplished, and often did his family the honour to accept such hospitality as they could offer. He should certainly oppose the grant altogether, if these young ladies were not to come in for a share.

This speech had evidently great effect, and the party of the young ladies—comprising, of course, all the bachelors of the House—was evidently a strong one. A grave elderly member, however, took up the cudgels on the other side. He informed the House, that the brother of Commodore Decatur had been his intimate friend, and unfortunately had left a family very scantily provided for. What claims could any young ladies, however accomplished, who were daughters only of a sister, possess equal to those of this brother's children? The latter were evidently the proper objects to be benefited by the present grant. He should oppose it on any other terms.

The number of amendments had now become very great, and the accumulation of obstacles was increasing with every speech. I was assured,—and from the tenor of the debate, I have no doubt it was so,—that a majority was decidedly in favour of the original claim, but minor discrepancies of opinion were found to be irreconcilable. Some insisted on the widow receiving the whole amount of the grant, others that it should go to the brother's family, others that the young ladies should be enriched by it, and others still were for a general division, while a considerable party advocated the propriety of voting the grant untrammelled by condition of any sort. The result was, that, after a most unprofitable waste of many hours, no money was granted at all, and the matter left for farther debate in another Congress, when the farce I have just described will be re-enacted, no doubt, with all its original spirit.

During my attendances at the Capitol, I have been sometimes amused by observing the process by which a question, originally simple, becomes, in the progress of discussion, so complicated and mixed up with irrelevant matter, and loses so completely all logical form, that it might puzzle the most expert dialectician to form any judgment on it at all. I have often attempted, on entering the House during a debate, to discover from the speeches something of the nature of the topic which occupied the attention of the assembly. In this I was generally unsuccessful, and my conjectures were sometimes almost ludicrously wide of the mark. Indeed, it was no uncommon occurrence for the mass of amendments to become so great, that even the members were bewildered, and were compelled to apply to the Speaker to explain their bearing on each other and the original question; and certainly nothing gave me a higher opinion of the powers of that gentleman, than the clear and skilful manner in which he managed to recall the attention to the real point at issue, and prevent the House from becoming absolutely stultified by its own proceedings.

In looking back to the earlier days of the republic, it would be scarcely fair to try the specimens of oratory that have come down to us by the standard of very rigid criticism. The appropriate eloquence of the time was that of *action*, not of words. While the struggle for liberty was undecided, the men who dwelt in camps, and spoke with swords in their hands, had no leisure to think of tropes and figures, and their addresses to their countrymen were distinguished by a manly earnestness worthy of the great cause in which they had embarked, and which more than compensated for unavoidable deficiencies of taste.

But with the achievement of the national independence a different state of things arose. Oratory, which on great and critical occasions, when mighty interests are at stake, and men give strong utterance to irrepressible convictions, is less an art than an impulse, became in more peaceful times a mere branch of professional accomplishment, which it was considered necessary for political aspirants to acquire. The succeeding generation of Americans were not content as their fathers had been with the simple expression of their feelings and opinions, without rhetorical embellishment, or studied artifices of speech. They attempted higher flights, but their ambition was more remarkable for its daring than its success. The recorded specimens of this period of the republic indicate a sad deficiency of taste, originality, and imaginative power. Starting, like another Adam, into sudden political existence, speaking the language, preserving the laws, and dependent on the literature of England, America found it more difficult to cast off the trammels of mental allegiance, than to burst asunder the bonds of physical enthralment. Strong arms and brave hearts had proved adequate to the one, but a higher intellectual advancement than they had yet attained was necessary for the other.

Thus it was, that from the very dawn of their independence, the Americans became an imitative people. Having no examples of native excellence to appeal to, they at once adopted the models of another nation, without reflecting that these, however excellent, might be ill adapted for imitation in a state of manners and society altogether different. Surrounded by all the elements of originality in the world of untried images and associations with which they were familiar, they renounced them all, to become the imitators of a people who to this hour have denied them even the praise of skilful imitation.

The world affords no instance of a people, among whom an eloquence, merely imitative, ever was successful. It is indeed quite evident, that eloquence, to be effective, must be expressly accommodated, not only to the general condition of society, but to the habits, intelligence, sympathies, prejudices, and peculiarities of the audience. The images which appeal most forcibly to the feelings of one people, will fail utterly of effect when addressed to another, living under a different climate, accustomed to a different aspect of external nature, and of habits and partialities generated under a different modification of social intercourse.

The first great objection, therefore, to American eloquence, is, that it is *not* American. When a traveller visits the United States, and sees the form and pressure of society; a population thinly scattered through regions of interminable forest; appearances of nature widely varying from those of European countries; the entire absence of luxury; the prevailing plainness of manner and expression; the general deficiency of literary acquirement; the thousand visible consequences of democratic institutions; he is naturally led to expect that the eloquence of such a people would be marked at least by images and associations peculiar to their own circumstances and condition. This anticipation would no doubt be strengthened by the first aspect of Congress. He would find in the Capitol of Washington two assemblies of plain farmers and attorneys; men who exhibited in their whole deportment an evident aversion from the graces and elegancies of polished society ; of coarse appetites, and coarser manners; and betraying a practical contempt for all knowledge not palpably convertible to the purposes of pecuniary profit. The impression might not be pleasing, but he would congratulate himself on having at least escaped from the dull regions of commonplace, and calculate on being spared the penalty of listening to the monotonous iteration of hackneyed metaphor, and the *crambe recocta* of British oratory, hashed up for purposes of public benefit or private vanity, by a Washington *cuisinier*.

In all this he would be most wretchedly deceived. He might patiently sit out speeches of a week's duration, without detecting even the vestige of originality, either of thought or illustration. But he would be dosed *ad nauseam* with trite quotations from Latin authors, apparently extracted for the nonce from the schoolbooks of some neighbouring academy for young gentlemen. He would hear abundance of truisms, both moral and political, emphatically asserted and most illogically proved ; he would learn the opinions of each successive orator on all matters of national policy, foreign and domestic. He would be gorged to the very throat with the most extravagant praises of the American government, and the character and intelligence of the people. He would listen to the interminable drivellings of an insatiable vanity, which, like the sisters of the horseleech, is for ever crying, " Give, give." He would follow the orator into the seventh heaven of bombast, and descend with him into the lowest regions of the bathos. Still in all this he would detect nothing but a miserably executed parody—a sort of bungling plagiarism—an imitation of inapplicable models—a mimicry like that of the clown in a pantomime, all ridicule and burlesque. In American oratory, in short, he will find nothing vernacular but the vulgarities, and the entire disregard of those proprieties, on the scrupulous observance of which the effect even of the highest eloquence must necessarily depend.

In Congress, the number of men who have received —what even in the United States is called—a classical education, is extremely small, and of these the proportion who still retain sufficient scholarship to find pleasure in allusion to the words of the great writers of antiquity, is yet smaller. The great majority are utterly and recklessly ignorant of the learned languages, and the whole literature embodied in them; and it is evident that, with such an audience, any appeal to classical authority is mere waste of breath in the one party, and of patience in the other. It may appear strange, under such circumstances, but I have no doubt of the fact, that in the course of a session, more Latin—such as it is—is quoted in the House of Representatives, than in both Houses of the British Parliament. Indeed it is ludicrous enough to observe the solicitude of men, evidently illiterate, to trick out their speeches with such hackneyed extracts from classical authors, as they may have picked up in the course of a superficial reading. Thus, if a member be attacked, he will probably assure the House, not in plain English, that the charge of his opponent is weak, and without foundation, but in Latin, that it is "*telum imbelle et sine ictu.*" Should he find occasion to profess philanthropy, the chances are that the words of Terence, "*Homo sum, humani nihil,*" &c. will be mispronounced in a pathetic accent, with the right hand pressed gracefully on the breast. In short, members were always ready with some petty scrap of threadbare trumpery, which, like the Cosmogonist in the Vicar of Wakefield, they kept cut and dry for the frequent occasions of oratorical emergency.

During my stay in Washington, I had the good fortune to be present at one debate in the House of Representatives which excited much public interest. It related to the appointment of Mr Randolph as Minister to the Court of Russia. The circumstances were as follow. Early in 1830, it was judged right by the Cabinet of Washington to have a resident minister at the Court of Russia. The individual selected for this high appointment was Mr John Randolph, a gentleman of much eccentricity, high talents, and confessedly gifted with extraordinary powers as a debater. Though this gentleman has never held any political office, yet he has uniformly engrossed a very large share of the public attention, and has had the art or the misfortune in his own country to attract an unexampled portion of sincere admiration and vehement dislike. No man in America ever brought to debate an equal power of biting sarcasm, and few men perhaps, if so gifted, would have used it so unsparingly. With the qualities of a statesman, Mr Randolph is not considered by his countrymen to be largely endowed. His true element is opposition. He has attacked every successive administration for the last thirty years, with what vigour and effect those who have writhed under the torture of his withering invectives can alone adequately describe. There is indeed something almost fearfully ingenious in his employment of epithets, which cut, as it were, to the very core, the objects of his wrath. In habit and feeling, no man can be more aristocratic than Mr Randolph, yet he has always been the stanch advocate of democratic principles. In one respect, he is the very converse of Jefferson. He detests French literature and French society, praises England and her government perhaps more than they deserve, and among his strange and multifarious acquirements must be included an accurate acquaintance with the genealogies of the whole British Peerage!

When the situation of Minister to the Court of St

Petersburg was offered to this remarkable individual, he candidly informed the President that the state of his health was such, as to render him incapable of braving the severities of a Russian climate, and that, unless permitted to pass the winter months in London or Paris, he should feel compelled to decline the appointment. The permission was granted, and Mr Randolph departed on his mission. He left, however, many enemies behind him, men who had suffered under the lash of his eloquence, and were naturally anxious to seize every opportunity of retorting punishment on so formidable an opponent.

A few days before my arrival in Washington, the subject of this appointment had been fairly brought into debate, and a Mr Tristram Burgess, from Rhode Island, had made a vehement attack, both on Mr Randolph, and on the Government. This called up Mr Cambreleng, one of the members for New York, a gentleman of great talent, and decidedly the first political economist of the Union, who entered warmly on the defence of Ministers. There is no doubt that Mr Cambreleng, under the influence of temporary excitement, in some degree, exceeded the legitimate limits of legislative discussion. Mr Tristram Burgess happened to be an elderly gentleman, with a hooked nose, a head bald on the summit, but the sides of which displayed hair somewhat blanched by time. In allusion to these personal peculiarities, Mr Cambreleng certainly said something about the fires of Etna glowing beneath the snows of Caucasus, and also, rather unpleasantly, compared his opponent to a bald-headed vulture. There can be no doubt of the bad taste of all this; and I know Mr Cambreleng well enough to entertain the perfect conviction, that had any opportunity of subsequent explanation been afforded him, he would have been most ready to disclaim any hasty expression that could be considered personally offensive to his opponent. It appeared, however, that explanation was neither demanded nor expected. The House adjourned, and nearly three weeks elapsed before the subject again came on for discussion.

I had no sooner reached Washington than I learned that great expectations were excited by the anticipated reply of Mr Burgess, who was one of the crack orators of the House. Poor Mr Cambreleng was evidently regarded as a doomed man; his fate was sealed; he could have no chance in a war of words with an intellectual giant like Mr Tristram Burgess! I received congratulations on all hands on my good fortune in enjoying at least one opportunity of hearing a first-rate specimen of American eloquence. In short, the cry was still "he comes;" and when, on the appointed day, he did come, it was bearing such a mass of written papers, as gave promise of a prepared and voluminous speech.

The promise was not belied. Mr Burgess's talent for diffusion was of the first order, and the speech was Shandean. Being, however, what is vulgarly called *a slow coach*, he did not get over the ground so rapidly as might have been desired, considering the vast distance he was determined to travel. I know at least that he was three days on the road, and the point to which he at last conducted his passengers appeared to my vision very similar to that from which he started.

Though my curiosity had been a good deal excited, the first three sentences were enough to calm it. Mr Burgess was evidently a man of some cl everness with a tolerable command of words, and a good deal of worldly sagacity. He occasionally made a good hit, and once or twice showed considerable adroitness in parrying attack; but he was utterly wanting in taste and imagination; there were no felicities either of thought or expression; nor could I detect a trace of any single quality which could be ranked among the higher gifts of an orator. A three days' speech from such a man was certainly a very serious affair; and though, as a matter of duty, on so great an occasion, I did bring myself to sit out the whole of it, it was done with the resolute determination to endure no second penance of a similar description.

Were it possible to give any tolerable report of a speech, which, of itself, would fill a volume, I would willingly appeal to it as exemplifying the justice of every blunder, both of taste and judgment, which I have attributed to American eloquence. There were scraps of Latin and of Shakspeare; there were words without meaning, and meanings not worth the trouble of embodying in words; there were bad jokes, and bad logic, and arguments without logic of any kind; there was abundance of exotic graces, and home-bred vulgarities,—of elaborate illustration of acknowledged truths,—of vehement invective and prosy declamation,—of conclusions without premises, and premises that led to no conclusion; and yet this very speech was the subject of an eight days' wonder to the whole Union! The amount of praise bestowed on it in the public journals, would have been condemned as hyperbolical if applied to an oration of Demosthenes. Mr Burgess, at the termination of the session, was fêted at New York; and Rhode Island exulted in the verbal prowess of the most gifted of her sons!

There can be no doubt, therefore, that the speech of Mr Burgess was an excellent speech of the kind; and in order to give the reader some more definite notion of what that kind was, I shall enter on a few details. Be it known, then, that a large portion of the first day's oration related to the personal allusions of Mr Cambreleng, who, as the reader is aware, had said something about the snows of Caucasus, and bald-headed vultures. Such an affair in the British Parliament would probably have been settled at the moment by the good feeling of the House. If not, a short and pithy retort was certainly allowable, and good sense would have prevented more.

But the House of Representatives and Mr Burgess manage these affairs differently. The orator commenced upon grey hair, and logically drew the conclusion, that as such discolouration was the natural consequence of advanced years, any disrespectful allusion to the effect, implied contempt for the cause. Now, among every people in the world, Mahometan or Christian, civilized or barbarous, old age was treated with reverence. Even on the authority of Scripture we are entitled to assert, that the grey head should be regarded as a crown of honour. All men must become old, unless they die young; and every member of this House must reckon on submitting to the common fate of humanity, &c. &c. &c., and so on for about a quarter-of-an-hour.

Having said all that human ingenuity could devise about grey hair, next came bald heads; and here the orator, with laudable candour, proceeded to admit that baldness might in one sense be considered a defect. Nature had apparently intended that the human cranium should be covered with hair, and there was no denying that the integument was both useful and ornamental. I am not sure whether, at this stage of the argument, Mr Burgess took advantage of the opportunity of impressing the House with a due sense of the virtues of bear's grease and macassar oil. I certainly remember anticipating an episode on nightcaps and Welsh wigs, but on these the orator was unaccountably silent. He duly informed the House, however, that many of the greatest heroes and philosophers could boast little covering on their upper region. Aristotle was bald, and so was Julius Cæsar, &c. &c. &c.

It was not till the subject of baldness had become as stale and flat, as it certainly was unprofitable, that the audience were introduced to the vulture, who was kept so long hovering over the head of Mr Burgess's opponent, that one only felt anxious that he should make his pounce and have done with it. Altogether, to give the vulture—like the devil—his due, he was a very quiet bird, and more formidable from the offensive nature of his droppings, than any danger to be apprehended from his beak or claws. In truth, he did seem to be somewhat scurvily treated by the orator, who, after keeping him fluttering about the hall for some three hours, at last rather unceremoniously disclaimed all connexion with him, and announced that he—Mr Burgess—was "an eagle soaring in his pride of place, and, therefore, not by a moping owl, to be hawked at, and killed!" This was too much for gravity, but luckily the day's oration had reached its termination, and the House broke up in a state of greater exhilaration, than could reasonably have been anticipated from the nature and extent of the infliction.

Having dealt, perhaps somewhat too largely, in censure, it is only fair that I should now advert to a few items which are entitled to a place on the *per contra* side of the account. In Congress, there is certainly no deficiency of talent, nor of that homely and practical sagacity, which, without approaching the dignity of philosophy, is perhaps even a safer guide in the administration of a government like that of the United States. American legislators talk nonsensically, but they act prudently; and their character is the very reverse of that attributed by Rochester to the second Charles—

"Who never said a foolish thing,
And never did a wise one."

It is not right that these men should be judged exclusively by their words; their actions also must be taken into account in forming a fair estimate of their character, moral and political. Were the condition of society to continue unchanged, they might commit blunders without end, but there would be no danger that the interests of the community would suffer from pertinacious adherence to them. In this country, measures are judged less by their speculative tendencies, and more remote consequences, than by their direct and immediate results on the pockets or privileges of the people. In Congress there is much clearness of vision, but little enlargement of view; considerable perspicacity in discerning effects, but none of that higher faculty which connects them with their causes, and traces the chain of consequences beyond the range of actual experience. In short, it strikes me that American legislators are more remarkable for acuteness than foresight; for those qualities of intellect which lead men to profit by experience, than those which enable them to direct it.

I have already said that the speaking in the Senate is very superior to that in the other House; an opinion which I early took up, and subsequently felt no temptation to change. Yet the faults of both bodies differ rather in degree than in character. There is the same loose, desultory, and inconclusive mode of discussion in both; but in the Senate there is less talking for the mere purpose of display, and less of that tawdry emptiness and vehement imbecility which prevails in the Representatives. Though the members of the Senate be absolutely and entirely dependent on the people, they are dependent in a larger sense; dependent not on the petty clubs and coteries of a particular neighbourhood, but on great masses and numbers of men, embracing every interest and pursuit, and covering a wide extent of country. Then, from the comparative paucity of their numbers, there is less jostling and scrambling in debate, more statesmanlike argument, and less schoolboy declamation; in short, considerably less outcry, and a great deal more wool.

The Senate contains men who would do honour to any legislative assembly in the world. Those who left the most vivid impression on my memory are Mr Livingstone, now Secretary of State, and Mr Webster, whose powers, both as a lawyer and a debater, are without rival in the United States. Of these eminent individuals, and others, whose intercourse I enjoyed during my stay in Washington, I shall hereafter have occasion to speak. There were other members of the Senate, however, to whose speeches I always listened with pleasure. Among these were General Hayne, from South Carolina,—who, as Governor of that State, has since put the Union in imminent peril of mutilation,—and Mr Tazewell, of Virginia, a speaker of great logical acuteness, clear, forcible, and direct in his arguments. General Smith, of Maryland, and Mr Forsyth, of Georgia, both struck me as being particularly free from the sins that do most easily beset their countrymen. When either of these gentlemen addressed the House, I always felt secure, not only that they had something to say, but that they had something worth saying; an assurance of which they only who have gone through a course of Congressional debates can appreciate the full value.

But whatever advantages the speeches of the Senate may possess over those of the Representatives, certainly brevity is not of the number. Every subject is overlaid; there is a continual sparring about trifles, and, it struck me, even a stronger display of sectional jealousies than in the other House. This latter quality probably arises from the senators being the representatives of an entire community, with separate laws, interests, and prejudices, and constituting one of the sovereign members of the confederation. When a member declares his opinions on any question, he is understood to speak the sentiments of a State, and he is naturally jealous of the degree of respect with which so important a revelation may be received. Then there are state antipathies, and state affinities, a predisposition to offence in one quarter, and to lend support in another; and there is the *odium in longum jaciens* between the Northern and Southern States, shedding its venom in every debate, and influencing the whole tenor of legislation.

One of the great evils arising, in truth, out of the very nature of the Union, is the sectional spirit apparent in all the proceedings of Congress. A representative from one State by no means considers himself bound to watch over the interests of another; and each being desirous to secure such local objects as may be conducive to the advantage of his own district, every species of trickery and cabal is put in requisition by which these objects may be obtained. There can be no doubt that the prevalence of such feelings is quite inconsistent with sound and wholesome legislation. Measures are estimated, not by their own merits, and their tendency to benefit the whole Union, but by the degree in which they can be made to subserve particular interests. One portion of the States is banded against another; there is no feeling of community of interests; jealousies deepen into hostilities; the mine is laid, a spark at length falls, and the grand federal Constitution is blown into a thousand fragments.

Many evils arise from the circumstance of the Government, both in its executive and legislative branches, being purely elective. The members of the latter, being abjectly dependent on the people, are compelled to adopt both the principles and the policy dictated by their constituents. To attempt to stem the torrent of popular passion and clamour, by a policy at once firm and enlightened, must belong to representatives somewhat more firmly seated than any which are to be found in Congress. Public men in other countries *may* be the parasites of the people, but in America they are necessarily so. Independence is impossible. They are slaves, and feel themselves to be so. They must act, speak, and vote according to the will of their master. Let these men hide their chains as they will, still they are on their limbs, galling their flesh, and impeding their motions; and it is, perhaps, the worst and most demoralizing result of this detestable system, that every man, ambitious of popular favour,—and in America who is not so?—is compelled to adopt a system of reservation. He keeps a set of exoteric dogmas, which may be changed or modified to suit the taste or fashion of the moment. But there are esoteric opinions, very different from any thing to be found in State documents, or speeches in Congress, or 4th of July orations, which embody the convictions of the man, and which are not to be surrendered up at the bidding of a mob.

I speak now of minds of the higher order. The majority of Congress are fitted for nothing better than what they are. God meant them to be tools, and they are so. But there are men among them qualified to shine in a higher sphere ; who stand prominently out among the meaner spirits by whom they are surrounded, and would be distinguished in any country by vigour, activity, and comprehension of thought. These men must feel, that to devote their great powers to support and illustrate the prejudices of the ignorant and vulgar, is to divert their application from those lofty purposes for which they were intended. It cannot be without a sense of degradation that they are habitually compelled to bear part in the petty squabbles of Congress; to enter keenly into the miserable contests for candles-ends and cheeseparings; to become the cats' paws of sectional cupidity; to dole out prescribed opinions; to dazzle with false glitter, and convince with false reasoning; to flatter the ignorant, and truckle to the base; to have no object of ambition but the offices of a powerless executive; to find no field for the exercise of their higher faculties; to know they are distrusted, and, judging from the men with whom they mingle, to feel they ought to be so.

It is to be wished that the writings of Burke were better known and appreciated in America. Of all modern statesmen, Burke brought to the practical duties of legislation the most gifted and philosophical mind. In an age prolific in great men, he stood confessedly the greatest; and while the efforts and the eloquence of his contemporaries were directed to overcome mere temporary emergencies, Burke contemplated the nobler achievement of vindicating unanswerably the true principles of enlightened government, and bequeathing to posterity the knowledge by which future errors might be avoided, and future difficulties overcome.

It is this loftiness of purpose which constitutes the leading distinction of Burke, when compared with contemporary or succeeding statesmen. They spoke for the present; he for all times, present and future. Their wisdom was directed to meet the immediate perils and exigencies of the state; his to establish great and memorable principles, by which all perils and all difficulties might be successfully encountered. The consequence has been, that while their words have passed away, his endure, and exert a permanent and increasing influence on the intellect of mankind. Who now resorts for lessons in political wisdom to the speeches of North, or Chatham, or Pitt, or Fox? but where is the statesman who would venture to profess himself unread in those of Burke?

That the opinions of this great political philosopher were sometimes erroneous may be admitted, yet it may truly be said that they were never founded on mere narrow views of temporary expediency, and that his errors were uniformly those of a grand and glorious intellect, scarcely less splendid in failure than in triumph.

The nature of the connexion which ought to exist between the representative and his constituents, and the duties it imposes, are finely illustrated in the final address of Burke to the electors of Bristol. It were well if the people, both of England and America, would read, mark, learn, and inwardly digest the following noble passages, not more remarkable for their wisdom and eloquence, than for their tone of dignified independence.

"It is the duty of the representative," says this memorable man, "to sacrifice his repose, his pleasures, his satisfactions, to his constituents. *But his unbiassed opinion, his mature judgment, his enlightened conscience, he ought not to sacrifice to you, to any man, or any set of men living. They are a trust from Providence, for the abuse of which he is deeply answerable. Your representative owes you, not his industry only, but his judgment, and* HE BETRAYS INSTEAD OF SERVING YOU *if he sacrifice it to your opinion.*"

Again.

"If government were a matter of will upon any side, yours, without question, ought to be superior. But government and legislation are matters of reason and judgment, not of inclination. And *what sort of reason is that, in which the determination precedes the discussion; in which one set of men deliberate and another decide; and where those who form the conclusion are perhaps three hundred miles distant from those who hear the arguments?*"

Once more.

"*Authoritative instructions, mandates, which the member is bound blindly and implicitly to obey; these are things unknown to the laws of this land, and which arise from* A FUNDAMENTAL MISTAKE OF THE WHOLE ORDER AND TENOR OF OUR CONSTITUTION. *Parliament is not a Congress of Ambassadors from different states, and with hostile interests, which interests each must maintain as an agent against other agents; but Parliament is a deliberative assembly of* ONE *nation, with* ONE *interest, and that of the whole.* You choose a member, indeed; but when you have chosen him, he is *not* member for Bristol, but he is a member of Parliament."

There is another evil connected with the practical working of the constitution, to which I feel it necessary briefly to advert. The election of the President affects so many interests and partialities, and appeals so strongly to the passions of the people, that it is uniformly attended with a very injurious disturbance of the public tranquillity. The session of Congress immediately preceding the election, is chiefly occupied by the manœuvres of both parties to gain some advantage for their favourite candidate. The quantity of invective expended on men and measures is enormously increased. The ordinary business of the country is neglected. Motions are made, and enquiries gone into, in the mere hope that something may be discovered which party zeal may convert into a weapon of attack or defence. In short, the legislature of a great nation is resolved into electioneering committees of rival candidates for the Presidency.

Without doors, the contest is no less keen. From one extremity of the Union to the other, the political war slogan is sounded. No quarter is given on either side. Every printing press in the United States is engaged in the conflict. Reason, justice, charity, the claims of age and of past services, of high talents and unspotted integrity, are forgotten. No lie is too malignant to be employed in this unhallowed contest, if it can but serve the purpose of deluding even for a moment the most ignorant of mankind. No insinuation is too base, no equivocation too mean, no artifice too paltry. The world affords no parallel to the scene of political depravity exhibited periodically in this free country.

In England I know it will be believed that this

picture is overcharged, that it is utterly impossible that any Christian community can be disgraced by scenes of such appalling atrocity. It may be supposed too, that in getting up materials for the charge, I have been compelled to go back to the earlier period of the constitution, to the days of Adams and Jefferson, when the struggle of men was the struggle of great principles, and the people were yet young and unpractised in the enjoyment of that liberty which they had so bravely earned.

Of either hypothesis I regret to say that it is more charitable than true. I speak not of the United States as they were, but *as they are.* Let the moral character of the past generation of Americans rest with them undisturbed in their graves. Our business at present is with living men, and it is these who are now charged, not by *me*, but by *writers of their own age and country*, with the offences I have ventured to describe.

"*Party spirit*," says the late Governor Clinton, in his annual message to the legislature in 1828, quoted by Captain Hall, "*has entered the recesses of retirement, violated the sanctity of female character, invaded the tranquillity of private life, and visited with severe inflictions the peace of families. Neither elevation nor humility has been spared, nor the charities of life, nor distinguished public services, nor the fireside, nor the altar, been left free from attack; but a licentious and destroying spirit has gone forth, regardless of every thing, but the gratification of malignant feelings, and unworthy aspirations.* The causes of this portentous mischief must be found, in a great measure, in the incompetent and injudicious provisions relative to the office of chief magistrate of the Union."

In the American Annual Register, published at New York, for the years 1828 and 1829, a work of great merit and impartiality, the editor, in narrating the circumstances of the last Presidential election, thus writes:—

"Topics were introduced tending still more to inflame the public mind, and to prevent it from forming an unbiassed judgment upon continuing the existing policy of the country. In the excited state of popular feeling, the character and services of both candidates were overlooked; and even Congress, in more instances than one, by a party vote, manifested that it had forgotten that some respect was due to the high and honourable station held by one of the candidates.

"The example thus given by men from whose character and station better things might have been expected, was not without its effect upon the community. *In conducting the political discussions which followed the adjournment of Congress, both truth and propriety were set at defiance. The decencies of private life were disregarded; conversations and correspondence which should have been confidential were brought before the public eye; the ruthless warfare was carried into the bosom of domestic life; neither age nor sex was spared; the daily press teemed with ribaldry and falsehood; and even the tomb was not held sacred from the rancorous hostility which distinguished the presidential election of* 1828."

I shall certainly not endeavour, by any observations of my own, to heighten the sentiment of disgust which such extraordinary revelations are calculated to excite. If I know my own motives, I allude to them at all, not with the contemptible and unworthy object of lowering the character of the

American people in the eyes of my countrymen; not to afford a paltry triumph to those in whose eyes freedom is a crime, and despotism a virtue; but because it is due to truth and justice, and nearly concerns the political welfare of other nations, that the practical results of the Constitution of the United States should be known.

In all previous experience, an elective chief magistracy—it matters not whether the object of contention be the throne of a King, or the chair of a President—has been found incompatible with the peace and welfare of a community. The object is too high and spirit-stirring; it appeals too strongly to the hopes and passions of men; it affects too many interests, not to lead to the employment of every available instrument for its attainment. In some circumstances the contest is decided by physical force; in others, by falsehood, calumny, and those artifices by which cunning can impose upon ignorance. Blood flows in the one case, and the land is desolated by civil war; character, moral dignity, and the holiest charities of life, are sacrificed in the other.

One thing is certain. In the United States the experiment of an elective executive has been tried under the most favourable circumstances. The population is diffused over a vast extent of surface, and therefore less subject to be influenced by those delusions and impulses by which masses of men are liable to be misled. There exists in America no great and absorbing question of principle or policy, by which the feelings or the prejudices of men are violently excited. On the contrary, the general character of public measures has long ceased to furnish any broad or distinct grounds of dispute; and the contest, however vehement, has been that of rival politicians, rather than of contending principles. Moreover, in the United States, a class of men condemned by uncontrollable causes to the sufferings of abject poverty, is unknown. The means of subsistence are profusely spread everywhere, and the temptations to crime comparatively small. Let it be remembered, therefore, that it is under such circumstances, and among a people so situated, that the experiment of periodically electing the chief officer of the commonwealth has been tried and failed.

It is true indeed, that while confessing the grossness of the failure, many Americans would willingly attribute it to the injudicious provisions for the collection of the national suffrage. But the evil lies deeper. However the electoral body may be formed, an abundant field must always be left for the exercise of trickery and intrigue. The passions and prejudices of men must always be too deeply interested in the distribution of this high patronage for the continuance of public tranquillity. Slander, calumny, and the thousand atrocities which have hitherto disgraced the presidential elections, will continue to burst their floodgates, and spread contamination through the land; and should a period of strong political excitement arrive, when men shall be arrayed, not in demonstration of mere personal partialities, but in support of conflicting principles connected with their immediate interests, I confess, that I, at least, can find nothing in the American Constitution, on which to rest a hope for its permanence.

CHAPTER IV.

WASHINGTON

In the basement story of one of the wings of the Capitol is the hall of the Supreme Court of the United States. It is by no means a large or handsome apartment; and the lowness of the ceiling, and the circumstance of its being under ground, give it a certain cellar-like aspect, which is not pleasant. This is perhaps unfortunate, because it tends to create in the spectator the impression of justice being done in a corner; and, that while the business of legislation is carried on with all the pride, pomp, and circumstance of glorious debate, in halls adorned with all the skill of the architect, the administration of men's rights is considered an affair of secondary importance.

Though the American law courts are no longer contaminated by wigs, yet the partiality for robes would appear not yet to be wholly extinct. The judges of the Supreme Court wear black Geneva gowns; and the proceedings of this tribunal are conducted with a degree of propriety, both judicial and forensic, which leaves nothing to be desired. I certainly witnessed none of those violations of public decency, which in the State Courts are matters of ordinary occurrence. There was no lounging either at the bar or on the bench; nor was it, apparently, considered necessary to sink the gentleman in the lawyer, and assume a deportment in the discharge of professional duty which would not be tolerated in private society.

The Supreme Court consists of seven judges, removable only by impeachment, and possesses a federal jurisdiction over the whole Union. It sits annually in Washington for about two months, and is alone competent to decide on questions connected with the constitution or laws of the United States. Though possessing original jurisdiction in a few cases, its chief duties consist in the exercise of an appellate jurisdiction from the Circuit Courts, which are held twice a-year in the different States.

It would be tedious to enumerate the various cases in which the Federal Courts, in their three gradations of Supreme, Circuit, and District, exercise an exclusive or concurrent jurisdiction. It is enough that it should be generally understood that the Supreme Court is the sole expounder of the written constitution; and when we consider how open this important instrument has been proved to diversity of interpretation, what opposite meanings have been put upon its simplest clauses, and, in short, that the Constitution is precisely whatever four judges of this court may choose to make it, it will be seen how vitally important is the power with which it has been intrusted, and how difficult must be its exercise.

But the difficulties of the Supreme Court do not end here. Its jurisdiction extends not over a homogeneous population, but a variety of distinct communities, born under different laws, and adopting different forms in their administration.

Causes before the State Courts, in which the laws of the United States are even collaterally involved, are removable by writ of error to the Supreme Federal Court, and the decision of the State Court may be affirmed or reversed. In the latter case, a mandate is issued directing the State Court to conform its judgment to that of the Supreme Court. But the State tribunal is at perfect liberty to disregard the mandate, should it think proper; for the principle is established, that no one court can command another, but in virtue of an authority resting on express stipulation, and it is the duty of each judicature to decide how far this authority has been constitutionally exercised.

Then the legislatures of different States have found it occasionally convenient to pass laws for the purpose of defrauding their foreign creditors, while, in the case of Great Britain at least, the federal government is bound by express treaty that no lawful impediment shall be interposed to the recovery of the debts due by American citizens to British subjects. Under such circumstances, the Federal Court, backed by the whole honest portion of the people, certainly succeeded in putting a stop to the organized system of State swindling adopted by

Kentucky after the late war; but awkward circumstances occurred, and the question may yet be considered practically undecided, whether the State legislatures possess a controlling power over the execution of a judgment of the Supreme Court.

Should a case occur, as is far from improbable, in which the federal legislature and judiciary are at variance, it would, no doubt, be the duty of the latter to declare every unconstitutional act of the former null and void. But under any circumstances, the Court has no power of enforcing its decrees. For instance, let us take the Indian question, and suppose, that in defiance of treaties, Georgia should persist in declaring the Creek and Cherokee Indians subject to the State laws, in order to force them to migrate beyond the Mississippi. The Indians appeal to the Supreme Court, and demand protection from unprincipled violence. The Court recognises their rights, and issues its mandate, which is just so much waste paper, unless the Government choose to send a military force along with it, which neither the present Congress nor executive would be inclined to do.

With all its sources of weakness, however, the United States Court is a wise institution. It is truly the sheet-anchor of the Union; and the degree of respect in which its decrees are held, may be considered as an exact index of the moral strength of the compact by which the discordant elements of the federal commonwealth are held together.

The most distinguished lawyers of the Union practise in the Supreme Court, and I had there an opportunity of hearing many of the more eminent members of Congress. During my stay there was no Jury trial, and the proceedings of the Court consisted chiefly in delivering judgments, and in listening to legal arguments from the bar. The tone of the speeches was certainly very different from any thing I had heard in Congress. The lawyers seemed to keep their declamation for the House of Representatives, and in the Supreme Court spoke clearly, logically, and to the point. Indeed, I was more than once astonished to hear men whose speeches in Congress were rambling and desultory, in an extreme degree, display, in their forensic addresses, great legal acuteness, and resources of argument and illustration of the first order. In addressing the bench, they seemed to cast the slough of their vicious peculiarities, and spoke, not like schoolboys contending for a prize, but like men of high intellectual powers, solicitous not to dazzle but to convince.

A few days after the interview already mentioned, I received the honour of an invitation to dine with the President. It unfortunately happened, that on the day indicated, I was already engaged to a party at Mr Van Buren's; and on enquiring the etiquette on such occasions, I was informed that an invitation from the President was not held to authorize any breach of engagement to the leading member of the Cabinet. The President, however, having politely intimated that he received company every evening, I ventured, along with a distinguished member of the House of Representatives, to present myself, on one occasion, at the "White House."*

We found the President had retired with a headache, but in a few minutes he appeared, though, from the heaviness of his eye, evidently in a state of

* The President's house is very generally so designated in Washington.

considerable pain. This, however, had no influence on his conversation, which was spirited, and full of vivacity. He informed us that he had been unwell for several days, and having the fatigues of a levee to encounter on the following evening, he had retired early in order to recruit for an occasion which required the presence of all his bodily powers. When this subject was dismissed, the conversation turned on native politics, the Indian question, the powers of the Supreme Court, and a recent debate in the Senate, which had excited considerable attention.

Of the opinions expressed by this distinguished person, it would be unpardonable were I to say any thing; but I heard them with deep interest, and certainly considered them to be marked by that union of boldness and sagacity, which is generally supposed to form a prominent feature of his character. General Jackson spoke like a man so thoroughly convinced of the justice of his views, that he announced them unhesitatingly and without reserve. This openness might be increased, perhaps, by the knowledge of my companion being a decided supporter of his government; but sincerity is so legible both in his countenance and manner, that I feel convinced that nothing but the strongest motives of state policy could make him hesitate, under any circumstances, to express boldly what he felt strongly.

On the following evening I attended the levee. The apartments were already full before I arrived, and the crowd extended even into the hall. Three —I am not sure that there were not four—large saloons were thrown open on the occasion, and were literally crammed with the most singular and miscellaneous assemblage I had ever seen.

The numerical majority of the company seemed of the class of tradesmen or farmers, respectable men fresh from the plough or the counter, who, accompanied by their wives and daughters, came forth to greet their President, and enjoy the splendours of the gala. There were also generals and commodores, and public officers of every description, and foreign ministers and members of Congress, and ladies of all ages and degrees of beauty, from the fair and laughing girl of fifteen, to the haggard dowager of seventy. There were majors in broad cloth and corduroys, redolent of gin and tobacco, and majors' ladies in chintz or russet, with huge Paris ear-rings, and tawny necks, profusely decorated with beads of coloured glass. There were tailors from the board, and judges from the bench; lawyers who opened their mouths at one bar, and the tapster who closed them at another;—in short, every trade, craft, calling, and profession, appeared to have sent its delegates to this extraordinary convention.

For myself, I had seen too much of the United States to expect any thing very different, and certainly anticipated that the mixture would contain all the ingredients I have ventured to describe. Yet after all, I was taken by surprise. There were present at this levee, men begrimed with all the sweat and filth accumulated in their day's—perhaps their week's—labour. There were sooty artificers, evidently fresh from the forge or the workshop; and one individual, I remember—either a miller or a baker—who, wherever he passed, left marks of contact on the garments of the company. The most prominent group, however, in the assemblage, was a party of Irish labourers, employed on some neighbouring canal, who had evidently been apt scholars in the doctrine of liberty and equality, and were determined, on the present occasion, to assert the full privileges of "the great unwashed." I remarked these men pushing aside the more respectable portion of the company with a certain jocular audacity, which put one in mind of the humours of Donnybrook.

A party, composed of the materials I have described, could possess but few attractions. The heat of the apartment was very great, and the odours—certainly not Sabæan—which occasionally affected the nostrils, were more pungent than agreeable. I therefore pushed on in search of the President, in order that, having paid my respects in acknowledgment of a kindness for which I really felt grateful, I might be at liberty to depart. My progress, however, was slow, for the company in the exterior saloons were wedged together in a dense mass, penetrable only at occasional intervals. I looked everywhere for the President as I passed, but without success; but at length a friend, against whom I happened to be jostled, informed me that I should find him at the extremity of the most distant apartment.

The information was correct. There stood the President, whose looks still indicated indisposition, paying one of the severest penalties of greatness; compelled to talk when he had nothing to say, and shake hands with men whose very appearance suggested the precaution of a glove. I must say, however, that under these unpleasant circumstances, he bore himself well and gracefully. His countenance expressed perfect good-humour; and his manner to the ladies was so full of well-bred gallantry, that having, as I make no doubt, the great majority of the fair sex on his side, the chance of his being unseated at the next election must be very small.

I did not, however, remain long a spectator of the scene. Having gone through the ordinary ceremonial, I scrambled out of the crowd the best way I could, and bade farewell to the most extraordinary scene it had ever been my fortune to witness. It is only fair to state, however, that during my stay in Washington, I never heard the President's levee mentioned in company without an expression of indignant feeling on the part of the ladies, at the circumstances I have narrated. To the better order of Americans, indeed, it cannot but be painful that their wives and daughters should thus be compelled to mingle with the very lowest of the people. Yet the evil, whatever may be its extent, is in truth the necessary result of a form of government essentially democratic. Wherever universal suffrage prevails, the people are, and must be, the sole depository of political power. The American President well knows that his only chance of continuance in office, consists in his conciliating the favour of the lowest—and therefore most numerous—order of his constituents. The rich and intelligent are a small minority, and their opinion he may despise. The poor, the uneducated, are, in every country, *the people.* It is to them alone that a public man in America can look for the gratification of his ambition. They are the ladder by which he must mount, or be content to stand on a level with his fellow-men.

Under such circumstances, it is impossible there should be any exclusion of the real governors of the country wherever they may think proper to intrude. General Jackson is quite aware, that the smallest demonstration of disrespect even to the meanest mechanic, might incur the loss of his popularity in a whole neighbourhood. It is evident, too, that the class in actual possession of the political patronage of a community, is in effect, whatever be their designation, the *first* class in the state. In America, this influence belongs to the poorest and least educated. Wealth and intelligence are compelled to bend to poverty and ignorance, to adopt their prejudices, to copy their manners, to submit to their government. In short, the order of reason and common sense is precisely inverted; and while the roots of the political tree are waving in the air, its branches are buried in the ground.

During the time I was engaged at the levee, my servant remained in the hall through which lay the entrance to the apartments occupied by the company, and on the day following he gave me a few details of a scene somewhat extraordinary, but sufficiently characteristic to merit record. It appeared that the refreshments intended for the company, consisting of punch and lemonade, were brought by the servants, with the intention of reaching the interior saloon. No sooner, however, were these ministers of Bacchus descried to be approaching by a portion of the company, than a rush was made from within, the whole contents of the trays were seized *in transitu*, by a sort of *coup-de-main;* and the bearers having thus rapidly achieved the distribution of their refreshments, had nothing for it but to return for a fresh supply. This was brought, and quite as compendiously despatched, and it at length became apparent, that without resorting to some extraordinary measures, it would be impossible to accomplish the intended voyage, and the more respectable portion of the company would be suffered to depart with dry palates, and in utter ignorance of the extent of the hospitality to which they were indebted.

The butler, however, was an Irishman, and in order to baffle further attempts at intercepting the supplies, had recourse to an expedient marked by all the ingenuity of his countrymen. He procured an escort, armed them with sticks, and on his next advance these men kept flourishing their *shillelahs* around the trays, with such alarming vehemence, that the predatory horde, who anticipated a repetition of their plunder, were scared from their prey, and, amid a scene of execrations and laughter, the refreshments, thus guarded, accomplished their journey to the saloon in safety!

Washington, the seat of government of a free people, is disgraced by slavery. The waiters in the hotels, the servants in private families, and many of the lower class of artisans, are slaves. While the orators in Congress are rounding periods about liberty in one part of the city, proclaiming, *alto voce*, that all men are equal, and that "resistance to tyrants is obedience to God," the auctioneer is exposing human flesh to sale in another! I remember a gifted gentleman in the Representatives, who, in speaking of the Senate, pronounced it to be "the most enlightened, the most august, and most imposing body in the world!" In regard to the extent of imposition, I shall not speak; but it so happened that the day was one of rain, and the effect of the eulogium was a good deal injured by recollecting that, an hour or two before, the members of this enlightened and august body were driven to the Capitol by slave coachmen, who were at that very moment waiting to convey them back, when the *rights of man* had been sufficiently disserted on for the day.

I trust I do not write on this painful subject in an insulting spirit. That slavery should exist in the United States is far less the fault than the misfortune of the people. The present generation were born with the curse upon them; they are the involuntary inheritors of a patrimony of guilt and misery, and are condemned to pay the penalty of that original sin, which has left a deep tarnish on the memory of our common ancestors. But that slavery should exist in the district of Columbia, that even the footprint of a slave should be suffered to contaminate the soil peculiarly consecrated to Freedom, that the very shrine of the Goddess should be polluted by the presence of chains and fetters, is perhaps the most extraordinary and monstrous anomaly to which human inconsistency—a prolific mother—has given birth.

The man who would study the contradictions of individual and national character, and learn by how wide an interval, profession may be divided from performance, should come to Washington. He will there read a new page in the volume of human nature;

he will observe how compatible is the extreme of physical liberty, with bondage of the understanding. He will hear the words of freedom, and he will see the practice of slavery. Men who sell their fellow-creatures will discourse to him of indefeasible rights; the legislators, who truckle to a mob, will stun him with professions of independence; he will be taught the affinity between the democrat and the tyrant; he will look for charters, and find manacles; expect liberality, and be met by bigotry and prejudice;—in short, he will probably return home a wiser, if not a better man,—more patient of inevitable evils, —more grateful for the blessings he enjoys,—better satisfied with his own country and government,—and less disposed to sacrifice the present *good* for a contingent *better*.

In Washington, there is little to be done in the way of sight-seeing. There is a theatre, which I was too much occupied to visit. The churches have nothing about them to attract observation. The patent office contains models of all the mechanical inventions of this ingenious people, and their number is more remarkable than their value. In a thinly peopled country, men are thrown upon their individual resources. Where labour cannot be commanded, it is natural they should endeavour to strike out contrivances by which it may be economized. The misfortune is, that each man being ignorant of what has been effected by others, finds it necessary to begin *de novo.* He invents, takes out a patent, and then probably discovers that the same thing had been better done before.

In the Secretary of State's office, is an apartment containing portraits of all the Indian chiefs who have visited Washington. The portraits are ill executed, but full of character; and the collection is interesting, as exhibiting the last and only memorial of men, great in their generation, but without poet or historian to perpetuate the memory of their greatness. Many of the countenances are full of noble expression, and bear the impress of a wild but tranquil grandeur. Others are of dark, savage, and ferocious aspect, with an eye full of cunning, and a stern inflexibility of muscle, which seems to say, "I slay, and spare not." A few are expressive of mildness and benevolence; and when I remembered the melancholy history of this fated race, and the hopeless contest they are compelled to wage with civilized rapacity, I felt it impossible to gaze on these records of their lineaments without pain.

My visit to Washington brought with it the advantage of forming acquaintance with many distinguished individuals, of some of whom I would now willingly be permitted to record my impressions. First in rank is Mr Calhoun, the Vice-President of the United States. This gentleman was formerly a candidate for the Presidency, but resigned his pretensions in favour of General Jackson. Subsequent differences, however, with that eminent person, have produced a separation of their interests, and it is not generally supposed that he has much chance of succeeding at the next election. Mr Calhoun is about the middle height, spare, and somewhat slouching in person. His countenance, though not handsome, is expressive, and enlivened by a certain vivacity of eye which might redeem plainer features. His head is large, and somewhat disfigured by a quantity of stiff bristly hair, which rises very high above his forehead. In conversation he is pleasant, and remarkably free from that dogmatism which constitutes not the least of the *social* sins of Americans. Mr Calhoun evidently disregards all graces of expression, and whatever be the subject of discussion, comes directly to the point. His manner and mode of speaking indicate rapidity of thought, and it struck me, that, with full confidence in his own high talents, Mr Calhoun would probably find it more agreeable to carry truth by a *coup de main*, than to await the slower process of patient induction. It is evident, indeed, at the first glance, that the Vice-President is no ordinary person. His mind is bold and acute; his talent for business confessedly of the first order; and enjoying the esteem of his countrymen, there can be little doubt that he is yet destined to play a conspicuous part in the politics of the Union.

Mr Edward Livingstone, then Senator for Louisiana, shortly after my departure from Washington, became Secretary of State. Bred to the New York bar, he early took his station in the very first line of his profession. As a philosophical lawyer, he stands not only unrivalled, but unapproached. His experience in public life has been very great; and his high talents, extensive knowledge, and amiable character, have deservedly acquired for him the admiration and esteem of a people not prompt in the payment of such tribute.

Mr Livingstone's fame, however, is not American, but European. The criminal code which he has framed for Louisiana, is confessedly a magnificent specimen of philosophical legislation, and places the reputation of its author on a secure and permanent foundation. From this code the punishment of death is excluded, and Mr Livingstone is a warm advocate for its removal from the statute-books of the other States.

The labours of Mr Livingstone in the compilation of his code were, for many years, unwearied and assiduous. Men of more limited knowledge, and inferior powers, would have been unfit for such a task. Men of less enthusiasm would have shrunk from it in dismay. Mr Livingstone, fortunately for himself and his country, braved all difficulties, devoted to it the whole energies of his mind, and brought it to a happy completion.

Animated by the zeal of a philanthropist, he made

himself acquainted with the laws of all nations, and the contents of every treatise on crime and punishment which could be discovered in Europe. He maintained an extensive correspondence with the most eminent political philosophers of the age, and among others, with Bentham, by whose enlightened advice he professes to have largely profited.

One incident in the life of Mr Livingstone is worthy of record, as affording a fine illustration of the character of the man. His labours connected with the code were already far advanced, when his whole papers were destroyed by fire. This happened at ten o'clock at night, and at seven on the following morning, with unbroken spirit, he began his task afresh! Few men are endowed with such buoyancy of spirit, or such indomitable perseverance.

In person, Mr Livingstone is rather above the middle height. His countenance, though without elegance of feature, is peculiarly pleasing, from the benevolence of its expression, and a certain enthusiasm, unusual at his years, which lights up his eye when he discourses on any interesting subject. His manners are those of a finished gentleman, yet rather,

I should imagine, the spontaneous result of an innate and natural delicacy of thought and feeling, than of intercourse with polished society. To the courtesy and kindness of this eminent individual I feel deeply indebted. It is with pleasure that I now give public expression to those sentiments of admiration and respect, which I shall ever entertain for his character and talents.

The person, however, who has succeeded in riveting most strongly the attention of the whole Union, is undoubtedly Mr Webster. From the Gulf of St Lawrence to that of Mexico, from Cape Sable to Lake Superior, his name has become, as it were, a household word. Many disapprove his politics, but none deny his great talents, his unrivalled fertility of argument, or his power, even still more remarkable, of rapid and comprehensive induction. In short, it is universally believed by his countrymen that Mr Webster is a great man; and in this matter I certainly make no pretension to singularity of creed. Mr Webster *is* a man of whom any country might well be proud. His knowledge is at once extensive and minute, his intellectual resources very great; and whatever may be the subject of discussion, he is sure to shed on it the light of an active, acute, and powerful mind.

I confess, however, I did meet Mr Webster under the influence of some prejudice. From the very day of my arrival in the United States, I had been made involuntarily familiar with his name and pretensions. Gentlemen sent me his speeches to read. When I talked of visiting Boston, the observation uniformly followed, "Ah! there you will see Mr Webster." When I reached Boston, I encountered condolence on all hands. "You are very unfortunate," said my friends, "Mr Webster set out yesterday for Washington." Whenever, at Philadelphia and Baltimore, it became known that I had visited Boston, the question, "Did you see Mr Webster?" was a sequence as constant and unvarying as that of the seasons.

The result of all this was, that the name of Webster became invested in my ear with an adventitious cacophony. It is not pleasant to admire upon compulsion, and the very preeminence of this gentleman had been converted into something of a bore. To

Washington, however, I came, armed with letters to the unconscious source of my annoyance. The first night of my arrival I met him at a ball. A dozen people pointed him out to my observation, and the first glance riveted my attention. I had never seen any countenance more expressive of intellectual power.

The forehead of Mr Webster is high, broad, and advancing. The cavity beneath the eyebrow is remarkably large. The eye is deeply set, but full, dark, and penetrating in the highest degree; the nose prominent, and well defined; the mouth marked by that rigid compression of the lips by which the New Englanders are distinguished. When Mr Webster's countenance is in repose, its expression struck me as cold and forbidding, but in conversation it lightens up; and when he smiles, the whole impression it communicates is at once changed. His voice is clear, sharp, and firm, without much variety of modulation; but when animated, it rings on the ear like a clarion.

As an orator, I should imagine Mr Webster's forte to lie in the department of pure reason. I cannot conceive his even attempting an appeal to the feelings. It could not be successful; and he has too much knowledge of his own powers to encounter failure. In debate his very countenance must tell. Few men would hazard a voluntary sophism under the glance of that eye, so cold, so keen, so penetrating, so expressive of intellectual power. A single look would be enough to wither up a whole volume of bad logic.

In the Senate I had unfortunately no opportunity of hearing Mr Webster display his great powers as a debater. During my stay the subjects on which he happened to speak were altogether of inferior interest. In the Supreme Court he delivered several legal arguments which certainly struck me as admirable, both in regard to matter and manner. The latter was neither vehement nor subdued. It was the manner of conscious power, tranquil and self-possessed.

Mr Webster may be at once acquitted of all participation in the besetting sins of the orators of his age and country. I even doubt whether in any single instance he can be fairly charged with having uttered a sentence of mere declamation. His speeches have nothing about them of gaudiness and glitter. Words with him are instruments, not ends; the vehicles, not of sound merely, but of sense and reason. He utters no periods full of noise and fury, like the voice of an idiot, signifying—nothing; and it certainly exhibits proof that the taste of the Americans is not yet irretrievably depraved, when an orator like Mr Webster, who despises all the stale and petty trickery of his art, is called by acclamation to the first place.

In conversation, Mr Webster is particularly agreeable. It seems to delight him, when he mingles with his friends, to cast off the trammels of weighty cogitation, and merge the lawyer and the statesman in the companion;—a more pleasant and instructive one I have rarely known in any country. As a politician, the opinions of Mr Webster are remarkably free from intolerance. His knowledge is both accurate and extensive. He is one of the few men in America who understand the British Constitution, not as a mere abstract system of laws and institutions, but in its true form and pressure, as it works and acts upon the people, modified by a thousand influences, of which his countrymen in general know nothing.

Mr Van Buren, then Secretary of State, and now Vice-President, possesses perhaps more of the manner which in England would be called that of the world, than any other of the distinguished individuals whom I met in Washington. He is evidently a clever man, with a perfect knowledge of character, and the springs of human action. Neither his conversation nor his manner are marked by any thing of official reserve. Indeed, where the whole business of the government is conducted by committees of the Senate and Representatives, an American Secretary of State can have few secrets, and those not of much value. The opponents of the ministry, however, accuse Mr Van Buren of being a manœuvrer in politics—a charge, I presume, to which he is obnoxious only in common with his brother statesmen, of whatever party; for where independence is impossible, finesse is necessary. But on the details of party politics I say nothing; I only know that the Secretary of State is a gentleman of talent and information, of agreeable manners, and in conversation full of anecdote and vivacity.

After a sojourn of three weeks, I began to think of departure, but a farewell ball, given by the British Minister, preparatory to his quitting Washington, induced me to prolong my stay. Mr Vaughan had won golden opinions from all parties and conditions of Americans. No minister had ever been more highly esteemed, and the knowledge that the precarious state of his health rendered it necessary that he should return to England, contributed to cast something of gloom over the festivity. The scene, however, was very brilliant; and the company, though numerous, certainly more select than the party at the French Minister's. There were at least no dirty boots,—a blessing which the Washington ladies, I have no doubt, estimated at its full value.

On the day following I took my departure.

CHAPTER IV.

JOURNEY TO NEW ORLEANS.

FROM Washington I returned to Baltimore, where I experienced a renewal of that kindness and hospitality, to which on my former visit I had been so largely indebted. As the best mode of proceeding to the South, I had been recommended to cross from Baltimore to Wheeling, on the Ohio, and there to take steam for New Orleans, so soon as the navigation of the river should be reported open. For this intelligence, however, it was necessary to wait in Baltimore, and certainly a more agreeable place of confinement could not have been selected.

Fortune favoured me. In a few days the newspapers announced that the ice had broken up, and the Ohio was again navigable. Having had the good fortune to encounter one of my English fellow-passengers by the New York, likewise bound for New Orleans, we agreed to travel together, and on the morning of the 6th of March, before daylight, stepped into the railway carriage which was to convey us ten miles on our journey.

The vehicle was of a description somewhat novel. It was, in fact, a wooden house or chamber, somewhat like those used by itinerant showmen in England, and was drawn by a horse at the rate of about four miles an hour. Our progress, therefore, was not rapid, and we were nearly three hours in reaching a place called Ellicot Mills, where we found a wretched breakfast awaiting our arrival.

Having done honour to the meal in a measure rather proportioned to our appetites than to the quality of the viands, we embarked in what was called the "Accommodation Stage,"—so designated, probably, from the absence of every accommodation which travellers usually expect in such a vehicle. The country through which we passed was partially covered with snow. The appearance both of the dwelling-houses and the inhabitants gave indication of poverty, which was confirmed by the rough and stony aspect of the soil wherever it was visible. The coach stopped to dinner at a considerable village called Frederickstown, where the appearance of the entertainment was so forbidding that I found it impossible to eat. My appetite, therefore, was somewhat overweening, when we reached Hagarstown, a place of some magnitude, where we halted for the night, having accomplished a distance of eighty miles.

At three o'clock on the following morning we again started on our journey. The roads were much worse than we had found them on the preceding day, the country was buried deeper in snow, and our progress was in consequence slower. The appearance of poverty seemed to increase as we advanced. Here and there a ragged negro slave was seen at work near the wretched log hovel of his master; and the number of deserted dwellings which skirted the road, and of fields suffered to relapse into a state of nature, showed that their former occupants had gone forth in search of a more grateful soil.

We breakfasted at Clearspring, a trifling village,

and then commenced mounting the eastern ridge of the Alleghanies, called Sideling Mountain. To one who has trodden the passes of the Alps and Apennines, the Alleghany Mountains present nothing very striking. Indeed, the general character of American mountains is by no means picturesque. They are round and corpulent protuberances, and rarely rise into forms of wild and savage grandeur. But some of the scenes presented by the Alleghanies are very fine. Nature, when undisturbed by man, is never without a beauty of her own. But even in these remote mountain recesses the marks of wanton havoc are too often visible. Numbers of the trees by the road were scorched and mutilated, with no intelligible object but that of destruction. Objects the most sublime or beautiful have no sanctity in the eyes of an American. He is not content with the full power of enjoyment, he must exert the privilege to deface.

Our day's journey terminated at Flintstown, a solitary inn, near which is a mineral spring, whereof the passengers drank each about a gallon, without experiencing, as they unanimously declared, effect of any sort. I own I did not regret the inefficiency of the waters.

With the morning of the third day our difficulties commenced. We now approached the loftier ridges of the Alleghanies; the roads became worse, and our progress slower. The scenery was similar in character to that we had already passed. The mountains from base to summit were covered with wood, interspersed with great quantities of kalmias, rhododendrons, and other flowering shrubs.

On the day following our route lay over a ridge called the Savage Mountain. The snow lay deeper every mile of our advance, and at length, on reaching a miserable inn, the landlord informed us, that no carriage *on wheels* had been able to traverse the mountain for six weeks. On enquiring for a sleigh, it then appeared that none was to be had, and the natives all assured us that proceeding with our present carriage was impossible. The landlord dilated on the depth of snow, the dangers of the mountain, the darkness of the nights, and strongly urged our taking advantage of his hospitality till the following day. But the passengers were all anxious to push forward, and, as one of them happened to be a proprietor of the coach, the driver very unwillingly determined on making the attempt. We accordingly set forth, but had not gone above a mile when the coach stuck fast in a snow-drift, which actually buried the horses. In this predicament the whole men and horses of the little village were summoned to our assistance, and, after about two hours' delay, the vehicle was again set free.

We reached the next stage in a hollow of the mountain, without further accident, and the report as to the state of the roads yet to be travelled was very unpromising. The majority of the passengers, however, having fortified their courage with copious infusions of brandy, determined not to be delayed by peril of any sort. On we went, therefore; the night was pitchy dark; heavy rain came on, and the wind howled loudly amid the bare and bony arms of the surrounding forest. The road lay along a succession of precipitous descents, down which, by a single blunder of the driver, who was quite drunk, we might at any moment be precipitated. Dangerous as, under these circumstances, our progress unquestionably was, the journey was accomplished in safety; and halting for the night at a petty village, situated between the ridge we had crossed, and another which yet remained to be surmounted, the passengers exchanged congratulations on the good fortune which had hitherto attended them.

Before sunrise we were again on the road, and commenced the ascent of Laurel Mountain, which occupied several hours. The view from the summit was fine and extensive, though perhaps deficient in variety. We had now surmounted the last ridge of the Alleghanies, and calculated on making the rest of our way in comparative ease and comfort. This was a mistake. Though we found little snow to the westward of the mountains, the road was most execrable, and the jolting exceeded any thing I had yet experienced. The day's journey terminated at Washington, a town of considerable population, with a tavern somewhat more comfortable than the wretched and dirty dogholes to which, for some days, we had been condemned.

During our last day's journey we passed through

a richer country, but experienced no improvement in the road, which is what is called a *national* one, or, in other words, constructed at the expense of the general government. If intended by Congress to act as an instrument of punishment on their sovereign constituents, it is no doubt very happily adapted for the purpose. In its formation all the ordinary principles of road-making are reversed; and that grateful travellers may be instructed to whom they are indebted for their fractures and contusions, a column has been erected to Mr Clay, on which his claims to the honours of *artifex maximus*, are duly emblazoned.

The tedium of the journey, however, was enlivened by the presence of a very pretty and communicative young lady, returning from a visit in the neighbourhood, to Alexandria, the place of her residence. From her I gathered every information with regard to the state of polite society in these tramontane regions. This fair damsel evidently made conquest of a Virginian doctor, who had been our fellow-traveller for some days, and was peculiarly disgusting from an inordinate addiction to the vernacular vices of dram-drinking and tobacco-chewing. Being generally drunk, he spat right and left in the coach, and especially after dark, discharged volleys of saliva, utterly reckless of consequences. One night I was wakened from a sound sleep by the outcries of a Quaker, into whose eye he had squirted a whole mouthful of tobacco juice. The pain caused by this offensive application to so delicate an organ was very great. Broadbrim forgot for the nonce all the equanimity of his cloth; cursed the doctor for a drunken vagabond; and, on reaching our resting-place for the night, I certainly observed that his eye had suffered considerable damage. For myself, being a tolerably old traveller, I no sooner discovered the doctor's propensity, than I contrived to gain possession of the seat immediately behind him, and thus fortunately escaped all annoyance, except that arising from the filthiness of his person, and the brutality of his conversation.

About mid-day we reached Brownsville, a manufacturing town of considerable size, situated on the Monangahela, which, by its junction with the Alleghany, near Pittsburg, forms the Ohio. The appearance of Brownsville is black and disgusting; its streets are dirty, and unpaved; and the houses present none of the externals of opulence. The river is a fine one, about the size of the Thames at Westminster; and having crossed it, our route lay for some miles through a pretty and undulating country. At night we reached Wheeling, after a day's journey of only thirty miles, accomplished with more difficulty and inconvenience than we had before experienced.

Being anxious to gain a view of the Ohio, I took possession, during the last stage, of a seat beside the driver, on the box. Night was closing as we gained the summit of the hill, which overhangs the town of Wheeling. The river was just visible, with its noble volume of waters flowing onward in quiet and tranquil grandeur. Before we reached the town, it was dark; the sky was moonless, and I was therefore obliged to defer the gratification of my curiosity till the following morning.

I was abroad betimes. Immediately opposite to Wheeling, the stream of the Ohio is divided by an island of considerable size. Above and below, it is about the breadth of the Rhine at Mayence. The scenery, though very pleasing, could scarcely be termed beautiful Steam-boats, of all sizes, were ranged along the quays; and the loud hissing of the engines gave notice of numerous preparations for departure.

The town of Wheeling, dirty and smoke-begrimed, could boast of no attraction; and my English fellow-traveller having engaged berths in a steamer, about to sail in a few hours for Louisville, our baggage was immediately despatched on board. In order to pass the time, I then crossed over to the island, and spent an hour in examining its scenery. The proprietor informed me it contained about a hundred acres. Some of the timber was magnificent, but cultivation had made sad havoc in the natural beauties of the spot.

About two o'clock we started on our voyage. Our steamer was not a first-rate one, but the accommodation was good, and her progress, with the stream in her favour, very rapid. For several hours I remained on deck, gazing on a character of scenery to which I had seen nothing similar in Europe. The river is bounded by a succession of wooded eminences, sometimes rising from the very margin; sometimes receding to a short distance, and leaving a narrow plain of fertile land, on which here and there a stray settler had established himself. The dwellings of such settlers were of the very rudest construction, being generally log huts, about equal in comfort, I should imagine, to the cabin of an Irish peasant.

The great defect of the scenery of the Ohio is want of variety. During the first day I was delighted, but, on the second, something of the charm was gone; and at length its monotony became almost tedious. A thousand miles of any scenery, with one definite and unchanging character, will generally be found too much.

In two days we reached Cincinnati, a town of nearly thirty thousand inhabitants, finely situated, on a slope ascending from the river. The streets and buildings are handsome, and certainly far superior to what might be expected in a situation six hundred miles from the sea, and standing on ground which, till lately, was considered the extreme limit of civilisation. It is apparently a place of considerable trade. The quay was covered with articles of traffic; and there are a thousand indications of activity and business, which strike the senses of a traveller, but which he would find it difficult to describe. Having nothing better to do, I took a stroll about the town, and its first favourable impression was not diminished by closer inspection. Many of the streets and churches would have been considered handsome in New York or Philadelphia; and in the private dwellings considerable attention had been paid to external decoration.

The most remarkable object in Cincinnati, however, is a large Græco-Moresco-Gothic-Chinese looking building,—an architectural compilation of prettinesses of all sorts, the effect of which is eminently grotesque. Our attention was immediately arrested by this extraordinary apparition, which could scarcely have been more out of place had it been tossed on the earth by some volcano in the moon. While we stood opposite to the edifice, contemplating the gorgeousness of its effect, and speculating "what aspect bore the man" to whom the inhabitants of these central regions could have been indebted for so brilliant and fantastic an outrage on all acknowledged principles of taste, a very pretty and pleasant-looking girl, came out, and invited us to enter. We accordingly did so, and found every thing in the interior of the building had been finished on a scale quite in harmony with its external magnificence. Below, was a saloon of very spacious dimensions, which our fair conductress informed us had been intended for a bazaar. Above, were ball and supper apartments, with retiring rooms for the ladies, duly supplied with mirrors and toilet tables. Nothing, in short, was wanting, which could in any way contribute to splendour, elegance, or comfort.

All this excited our curiosity, for in truth it seemed as if the projector of this singular edifice had intended by its erection to contribute rather to the speculative and contingent wants of some future generation, than to minister to the present necessities of the prudent and hard-working Cincinnatians. We found our guide as communicative as could be desired. She informed us that the building had been erected by an English lady of the name of Trollope, who, induced by pleasure or business, had some years before taken up her residence in Cincinnati; that the experiment of a bazaar had been tried and failed; that the lower saloon was now altogether unoccupied, except on the 4th of July, when it witnessed the usual scene of festive celebration; that the sober Cincinnatians had always been content with two balls in the year, and would by no means consent to increase their annual modicum of dancing; in short, that the whole speculation had turned out a decided failure, and it was in contemplation of the fair proprietrix to convert it into a church.

I had then never heard of Mrs Trollope; but at New York I had afterwards the pleasure of becoming acquainted with her, and can bear testimony to her conversation being imbued with all that grace, spirit, and vivacity, which have since delighted the world in her writings. How far Mrs Trollope's volumes present a just picture of American society it is not for me to decide, though I can offer willing testimony to the general fidelity of her descriptions. But her claims to the gratitude of the Cincinnatians are undoubtedly very great. Her architectural talent has beautified their city; her literary powers have given it celebrity. For nearly thirty years Cincinnati had gradually been increasing in opulence, and enjoying a vulgar and obscure prosperity. Corn had grown, and hogs had fattened; men had built houses, and women borne children; but in all the higher senses of urbane existence, Cincinnati was a nonentity. It was "unknown, unhonoured, and unsung." Ears polite had never heard of it. There was not the glimmering of a chance that it would be mentioned twice in a twelvemonth, even on the Liverpool Exchange. But Mrs Trollope came, and a zone of light has ever since encircled Cincinnati. Its inhabitants are no longer a race unknown to fame. Their manners, habits, virtues, tastes, vices, and pursuits, are familiar to all the world; but, strange to say, the market-place of Cincinnati is yet unadorned by the statue of the great benefactress of the city! Has gratitude utterly departed from the earth?

These western regions are undoubtedly the chosen abode of plenty. Provisions are so cheap that no one ever seems to dream of economy. Three times a-day was the table in the steam-boat literally covered with dishes, wedged together as closely as a battalion of infantry in solid square. Though the passengers were only about twenty in number, there was always dinner enough for a hundred. Joints, turkeys, hams, chops, and steaks, lay spread before us in most admired confusion. Brandy bottles were *located* at judicious intervals; and porter was to be had on paying for it. I had asked for wine, but in vain; so, being at the luxurious city of Cincinnati, and tolerably tired of the poison called brandy, I sent for a bottle of Champagne from the inn. The bottle came, but on being opened, the contents were much more like sour cider than Champagne. In short, the stuff was decidedly too bad for drinking, and was accordingly pushed aside. But the appearance of this anomalous-looking flask evidently caused some commotion among the passengers. The wine was probably one which few of them had tasted, and many were evidently determined to seize the earliest opportunity of enlarging their experience. "I should like a glass of your wine, sir, if you have no objections," said my old enemy the Virginian doctor. I immediately pushed the bottle to him, and he filled his tumbler to the brim. Observing this, the persons about him, without ceremony of any kind, seized the bottle, and its contents incontinently disappeared.

In regard to the passengers, truth compels me to say, that any thing so disgusting in human shape I had never seen. Their morals and their manners were alike detestable. A cold and callous selfishness, a disregard of all the decencies of society, were so apparent in feature, word, and action, that I found it impossible not to wish that their catalogue of sins had been enlarged by one more—hypocrisy Of hypocrisy, however, they were not guilty. The conversation in the cabin was interlarded with the vilest blasphemy, not uttered in a state of mental excitement, but with a coolness and deliberation truly fiend-like. There was a Baptist clergyman on board, but his presence did not seem to operate as a restraint. The scene of drinking and gambling had no intermission. It continued day and night. The captain of the vessel, so far from discouraging either vice, was one of the most flagrant offenders in both. He was decidedly the greatest gambler on board; and was often so drunk as to be utterly incapable of taking command of the vessel. There were a few female passengers, but with their presence we were only honoured at meals. At all other times, they prudently confined themselves to their own cabin.

One circumstance may be mentioned, which is tolerably illustrative of the general habits of the people. In every steam-boat there is a *public* comb and hair-brush suspended by a string from the ceiling of the cabin. These utensils are used by the whole body of the passengers, and their condition, the pen of Swift could alone adequately describe. There is no tooth-brush, simply, I believe, because the article is entirely unknown to the American toilet. A common towel, however, passes from hand to hand, and suffices for the perfunctory ablutions of the whole party on board. It was often with great difficulty that I procured the exclusive usufruct of one, and it was evident that the demand was not only unusual but disagreeable.

One day at dinner, my English fellow-traveller,

who had resided many years in the United States, enquired whether I observed an ivory hilt protruded from beneath the waistcoat of a gentleman opposite. I answered in the affirmative, and he then informed me that the whole population of the Southern and Western States are uniformly armed with daggers. On my expressing some doubt of this singular fact, he pointed to a number of sticks collected in one corner of the cabin, and offered a wager that every one of these contained either a dagger or a sword. I took the bet, and lost it; and my subsequent observations confirmed the truth of his assertion in every particular. Even in travelling in the State of New York, I afterwards observed that a great number of the passengers in stage-coaches and canal boats were armed with this unmanly and assassin-like weapon.

It is the fashion in the United States to ask a foreigner whether he does not admire the extraordinary respect and deference which the people pay to the law. It is pretty evident, however, from the circumstances I have mentioned, that whatever respect each individual may pay to the law in his own person, he has no great confidence in a similar demonstration on the part of his neighbour.

We left Cincinnati about two o'clock, and betimes on the following morning were at Louisville, in Kentucky. The scenery of the river continued unchanged. I was particularly struck with the vast masses of drift-wood carried down by the stream. Trees, of the most gigantic dimensions, seemed to have been uprooted by the floods from the spot in which they had stood for centuries. The great quantity of this driftwood occasions some danger; for the paddles, by striking it, are apt to break, and there is always a man on the look-out to report any apparent risk of contact.

At Louisville, the vessel terminated her voyage. It is a place of greater trade, I believe, than Cincinnati, though with scarcely half the population. Being tired of steam-boat living, we breakfasted at the inn. We were at first ushered into the bar, already crowded with about a hundred people, all assembled with the same object as ourselves. At length the bell sounded, and the crowd rushed up stairs to the breakfast-room as if famine-stricken. The meal was coarse and bad. The bread was made with grease, and a sight of the dressed dishes was enough. Immediately opposite was a cold fowl, to which I requested a gentleman to help me. He deliberately cut out the whole body for himself, and then handed across the dish with the drumsticks.

After breakfast, we went over all the New Orleans vessels, but could find none about to sail, sooner than the following day at noon. My companion and myself accordingly took places in the Huntress, and, for fifty dollars, I had the good fortune to secure a separate cabin for myself and servant. This was of some consequence; because, in these regions, no white man can appear without disgrace in the capacity of servant to another. I was therefore obliged, at Wheeling, to desire mine to designate himself as my clerk or secretary; and in cleaning my clothes, he generally ensconced himself behind a curtain. On the present occasion, with the promise of this accommodation, I was content to put up with a very inferior vessel to many others then at Louisville.

Within forty miles of Louisville, is the residence of Mr Clay, and I had entered Kentucky with the intention of visiting that eminent person, who is considered equally remarkable for his powers as a statesman and a companion. I learned, however, at Louisville, that Mr Clay was then at New Orleans, but expected to leave that city in the course of the following week. As I was particularly anxious to become acquainted with the great rival of the present President, I determined on giving up all idea of a tour in Kentucky, and pushing on to New Orleans with the least possible delay. This decision was unfortunate, for it prevented my becoming acquainted with a very interesting State, and availing myself of several hospitable invitations I had received in New York and Washington. I found, too, on my arrival at New Orleans, that Mr Clay had taken his departure, so that the only effect of my arrangements was a double disappointment.

The Kentuckians may be called the Irish of America. They have all that levity of character, that subjection of the moral to the convivial, that buoyancy of spirit, that jocular ferocity, that ardour, both of attachment and of hatred, which distinguish the natives of the Emerald Isle. The Kentuckians are the only Americans who can understand a joke. There is a kind of native humour about them which is very pleasant; and, I must say, that several Kentucky gentlemen were among the most agreeable companions, with whom I had the good fortune to become acquainted during my tour.

About a mile below Louisville are the falls, or rather rapids, of the Ohio, which, when the river is low, offer a formidable obstruction to the navigation. In order to avoid them, a canal has been constructed near a place called Shipping-port. The work was one of some difficulty, and has been executed in the most expensive manner. Owing to the quantities of sediment which the river carries into it when in flood, I was sorry to learn that this fine work is considered likely to prove a failure. As the canal is only to be used, however, when the river is low, and consequently free from impurity, I cannot but think that, by the addition of floodgates, the evil might be easily remedied.

The New Orleans steam-boats are a very different description of vessels to any I had yet seen. They are of great size, and the object being to carry as large a cargo as possible, the whole vessel, properly so called, is devoted to this purpose, and the cabins for the passengers are raised in successive tiers above the main deck. The lower of these cabins is appropriated to the gentlemen. It is generally spacious, and very handsomely fitted up. Three of its sides are surrounded by a gallery and veranda. Over this is the ladies' cabin, equally handsome, though smaller. On the roof of the ladies' cabin is a deck on which the passengers may amuse themselves as they think proper. Near the forecastle, at the same elevation, is the place for the steerage passengers. These vessels have very much the appearance of three-deckers, and many of them are upwards of 500 tons burden. Their engines are generally constructed on the high pressure principle, and one or two generally blow up every season, sending a score or two of parboiled passengers to an inconvenient altitude in the atmosphere.

On the day following we commenced our voyage, of 1500 miles, to New Orleans. The weather was delightful, and I now enjoyed the privilege of reading and writing undisturbed in my cabin. The passengers, though coarse as heart could desire, were at least less openly and obtrusively profligate than those I have already described. There was the same scene of gambling and drinking, but I was now able to remove from the din and the blasphemy.

After leaving Louisville, we were nearly three days in reaching the point of junction between the Mississippi and Ohio. The latter river receives the waters of several large tributaries, the Tenessee, the Cumberland, the Wabash, &c., by which its magnitude is prodigiously increased. We skirted the new and flourishing states of Indiana and Illinois, which I did not visit. With their facilities, agricultural and commercial, their advantages and disadvantages, their soil, their climate, their productions, the public have already been made familiar by writers far better qualified to afford instruction on such matters than I pretend to be.

To a traveller, whose leading objects are connected with the structure of society, there is little in a scantily peopled territory to excite speculation. He that has seen one settler in the backwoods has seen a thousand. Those whom the love of lucre, and consciousness of independence, have induced to seek the recesses of the forest, who gaze daily on the same aspect of nature, who endure the same privations, encounter the same difficulties, and struggle by the same means, for the same ultimate reward, can present but one aspect of human character, and that far from the most interesting. With individuals so situated, indeed, I was necessarily, in different portions of my journey, brought into frequent contact. But I never voluntarily sought them, for I was chiefly anxious to contemplate men in their social and more extended relations, and to observe the influences, moral and political, by which the national character had been formed or modified. My steps, therefore, were directed to the city, not to the solitary *shantee;* to the haunts of large masses of men, rather than to those of isolated adventurers, who have yet to dispute the dominion of the forest with the bear and the panther.

On the second morning after our departure from Louisville, a change in the general character of the river seemed to indicate that we were rapidly approaching the Mississippi. For about fifty miles before the point of union, the surrounding scenery is flat, and the breadth of the Ohio is more than doubled, as if, from a feeling of rivalry, the river god had expanded his waters to the utmost. On the present occasion, the Ohio had the advantage of being very full from the melting of the snows along the whole line of its course, while the Mississippi, descending from higher latitudes, had experienced no such augmentation.

For hours I was on the tiptoe of expectation to catch the first glimpse of "the father of rivers," and with this view, had taken up a station on the highest pinnacle of the forecastle. At length, when yet about five miles distant, the Mississippi, sailing along in dark and solemn grandeur, became distinctly visible. Both rivers were about two miles broad, but the expanse of the Ohio struck me as being somewhat larger than that of its more powerful rival. I do not remember any occasion on which my imagination was more excited. I felt, in parting with the Ohio, as if I had done injustice to its attractions. True, it presents but one phasis of beauty, but that is of the noblest character. For a distance of nine hundred miles I had beheld it roll its clear waters, smoothly and peacefully, and I now, almost with a feeling of regret, bade it farewell.

The Huntress kept on her way rejoicing. We passed the small settlement of Cairo, standing on an isthmus between the two rivers, and in a few minutes beheld ourselves borne on the most majestic tribute of waters which Earth pays to Ocean.

It certainly appears strange that the Mississippi, after absorbing the Ohio, presents no visible augmentation of its volume. Below the point of junction, the river is not broader than the Ohio alone. Though flowing in the same channel, the streams are not mingled. For many miles there is a distinct line of demarcation between the waters of the two rivers. Those of the Ohio are clear, while the stream of the Mississippi is ever dark and turbid. When the Mississippi is in flood, it almost dams up the Ohio, and suffers it to occupy but a small portion of the common channel. But in other circumstances the case is different, and the Ohio constitutes, in parliamentary phrase, a very respectable minority.

After quitting *la belle rivière*, as the French first designated the Ohio, one feels as if he had made an exchange for the worse. The scenery of the Mississippi is even less varied than that of the Ohio. It is almost uniformly flat, though in the course of twelve hundred miles a few bluffs and eminences do certainly occur. The wood grows down to the very margin of the river, and the timber, for some hundred miles, is by no means remarkable for size. As the river descends to the southward, however, it is of finer growth; and about latitude 36°, vegetation becomes marked by a degree of rankness and luxuriance which I have never seen equalled anywhere else.

The American forests are generally remarkable for the entire absence of underwood, so that they are easily penetrable by a foot traveller, and generally even by a mounted one. But in the neighbourhood of the Mississippi there is almost uniformly a thick undergrowth of cane, varying in height from four or five to about twenty feet, according to the richness of the soil. Through this thicket of cane I should think it quite impossible to penetrate, yet I have been assured the Indians do so for leagues together, though by what means they contrive to guide their course, where vision is manifestly impossible, it is not easy to understand.

The steam-boats stop twice a-day to take in a supply of wood for the engine. These vessels have become so numerous that a considerable number of settlers make it their business to supply them, and thus turn their labour to better account than would be found in the cultivation of the soil. But the climate is deadly and pestilential; they are worn and sallow; and those with whom I spoke seemed to regard fevers as things of course. Medicine they have none; and when one's eyes rested on the miserable and pallid children, and their haggard mother, it was impossible not to feel compassion for these forlorn outcasts.

Outcasts they literally are. Many have fled for crimes, to a region where the arm of the law cannot reach them. Others are men of broken characters, hopes, and fortunes, who fly not from justice, but contempt. One man told me it was so. He had known better days. Men blamed him when he became poor. He withdrew his poverty from their sight, and came to labour amid the untrodden forests of the Mississippi. The man had been handsome, and still bore about him something of dignity. His manners were remarkably pleasing; but my fellow-passengers assured me that he was one who could stab while he smiled. I certainly should not much have fancied encroaching on the hospitality of his solitary shantee.

These settlers are called Squatters. They *locate* where they please, without troubling themselves about any title to the land they occupy. Should a rival in the business of wood-cutting choose to take up his residence inconveniently near, the rifle settles the dispute. One or other becomes food for the vultures, and the market continues uninjured by competition.

During the whole course of the voyage, we daily passed numbers of large arks or rafts, consisting of rough timbers, nailed together in the shape of a square box, in which the poorer proprietors of the upper country send down the produce of their land to New Orleans. These vessels were often without sails of any kind, and the only skill necessary in the navigation was to keep in the middle of the stream. Time was, and that not far distant, when these rafts constituted almost the only vehicles for conveying produce to the place of embarkation. In those days, a voyage to Louisville and back occupied about nine months, and by means of steam it can now be performed in little more than a fortnight. The application of steam navigation to the purposes of commerce has indeed given a mighty impulse to the prosperity of the central States. In the niches next to Mrs Trollope, the Cincinnatians should place statues of Fulton and James Watt. To the first they owe celebrity; to the two last, a market for their bacon and flour.

Time passed on board of the steam-boat, if not pleasantly, at least tranquilly. True, there was gambling and drinking, and wrangling and swearing; true, there was an utter disregard of all the decent courtesies of society: but to these things I had gradually become accustomed; for as they hourly and almost minutely "overcame us like a summer's cloud," they were no longer regarded with "special wonder." But there were some things to which I had not become accustomed, and one of these was slavery ; and another, eating and drinking and holding communion with a slave-dealer.

Unfortunately, the man generally occupied the place next to me at dinner; and, strange to say, with the soul of a brute, I remarked that he performed all the functions of an ordinary American. He ate, he drank, he voided profusion of tobacco juice, he swallowed brandy every half hour of the day, and passed three-fourths, both of day and night, in gambling. His poor gang of slaves were above stairs, the men loaded with heavy chains, and the women with scarcely rags enough to serve the purposes of decency. I spoke occasionally to both, and the women were certainly the more intelligent. They seemed to take pride in the largeness of the prices they had formerly brought in the market; and one, with a look of dignity, told me her master had refused three hundred dollars for her. Who, after this, shall presume to say, that vanity is not an inherent attribute of woman?

The men were in a state at once wretched and

disgusting. Their chains prevented their performing the ordinary functions of cleanliness, and their skin had become covered with a sort of scaly eruption. But I will not enlarge on a subject so revolting. I remember, however, that no one on board talked about freedom so loudly or so long as this slave-dealer. He at length left us, and the sky seemed brighter, and the earth greener, after his departure.

It has been the fashion with travellers to talk of the scenery of the Mississippi as wanting grandeur and beauty. Most certainly it has neither. But there is no scenery on earth more striking. The dreary and pestilential solitudes, untrodden save by the foot of the Indian; the absence of all living objects, save the huge alligators which float past, apparently asleep, on the drift-wood; and an occasional vulture, attracted by its impure prey on the surface of the waters; the trees, with a long and hideous drapery of pendent moss, fluttering in the wind; and the giant river rolling onward the vast volume of its dark and turbid waters through the wilderness, form the features of one of the most dismal and impressive landscapes on which the eye of man ever rested.

If any man think proper to believe that such objects are not, in themselves, sufficient, I beg only to say that I differ with him in point of taste. Rocks and mountains are fine things undoubtedly, but they could add nothing of sublimity to the Mississippi. Pelion might be piled on Ossa, Alps on Andes, and still, to the heart and perceptions of the spectator, the Mississippi would be *alone*. It can brook no rival, and it finds none. No river in the world drains so large a portion of the earth's surface. It is the traveller of five thousand miles, more than two-thirds of the diameter of the globe. The imagination asks, whence come its waters, and whither tend they? They come from the distant regions of a vast continent, where the foot of civilized man has never yet been planted. They flow into an ocean yet vaster, the whole body of which acknowledges their influence. Through what varieties of climate have they passed? On what scenes of lonely and sublime magnificence have they gazed? Have they penetrated

> "The hoary forests, still the Bison's screen,
> Where stalked the *Mammoth* to his shaggy lair,

> Through paths and alleys, roof'd with sombre green,
> Thousands of years before the silent air
> Was pierc'd by whizzing shaft of hunter keen ?"

In short, when the traveller has asked and answered these questions, and a thousand others, it will be time enough to consider how far the scenery of the Mississippi would be improved by the presence of rocks and mountains. He may then be led to doubt whether any *great* effect can be produced by a combination of objects of discordant character, however grand in themselves. The imagination is perhaps susceptible but of a single powerful impression at a time. Sublimity is uniformly connected with unity of object. Beauty may be produced by the happy adaptation of a multitude of harmonious details; but the highest sublimity of effect can proceed but from one glorious and paramount object, which impresses its own character on every thing around.

The prevailing character of the Mississippi is that of solemn gloom. I have trodden the passes of Alp and Appenine, yet never felt how awful a thing is nature, till I was borne on its waters, through regions desolate and uninhabitable. Day after day, and night after night, we continued driving right downward to the south; our vessel, like some huge demon of the wilderness, bearing fire in her bosom, and canopying the eternal forest with the smoke of her nostrils. How looked the hoary river-god I know not; nor what thought the alligators, when awakened from their slumber by a vision so astounding. But the effect on my own spirits was such as I have never experienced before or since. Conversation became odious, and I passed my time in a sort of dreamy contemplation. At night, I ascended to the highest deck, and lay for hours gazing listlessly on the sky, the forest, and the waters, amid silence only broken by the clanging of the engine. All this was very pleasant; yet till I reached New Orleans, I could scarcely have smiled at the best joke in the world; and as for raising a laugh—it would have been quite as easy to quadrate the circle.

The navigation of the Mississippi is not unaccompanied by danger. I do not now speak of the risk of explosion, which is very considerable, but of a peril arising from what are called *planters* and *sawyers.* These are trees firmly fixed in the bottom of the river, by which vessels are in danger of being impaled. The distinction is, that the former stand upright in the water, the latter lie with their points directed down the stream. We had the bad luck to sustain some damage from a planter, whose head being submersed was of course invisible.

The bends or flexures of the Mississippi are regular in a degree unknown in any other river; indeed, so much is this the case, that I should conceive it quite practicable for a hydrographer to make a tolerably accurate sketch of its course without actual survey. The action of running water, in a vast alluvial plain like that of the basin of the Mississippi, without obstruction from rock or mountain, may be calculated with the utmost precision. Whenever the course of a river diverges in any degree from a right line, it is evident that the current can no longer act with equal force on both its banks. On one side the impulse is diminished, on the other increased. The tendency in these sinuosities, therefore, is manifestly to increase, and the stream which hollows out a portion of one bank being rejected to the other, the process of curvature is still continued, till its channel presents an almost unvarying succession of salient and retiring angles.

In the Mississippi the flexures are so extremely great, that it often happens that the isthmus which divides different portions of the river gives way. A few months before my visit to the south a remarkable case of this kind had happened, by which forty miles of navigation had been saved. The opening thus formed was called the *new cut;* and it was matter of debate between the Captain and pilot whether we should not pass through it.

Even the annual changes which take place in the bed of the Mississippi are very remarkable. Islands spring up and disappear; shoals suddenly present themselves where pilots have been accustomed to deep water; in many places whole acres are swept away from one bank and added to the other; and the pilot assured me, that in every voyage he could perceive fresh changes.

Many circumstances contribute to render these

changes more rapid in the Mississippi than in any other river. Among these, perhaps, the greatest is the vast volume of its waters, acting on alluvial matter, peculiarly penetrable. The river, when in flood, spreads over the neighbouring country, in which it has formed channels, called *bayous*. The banks thus become so saturated with water that they can oppose little resistance to the action of the current, which frequently sweeps off large portions of the forest.

The immense quantity of drift-wood is another cause of change. Floating logs encounter some obstacle in the river, and become stationary. The mass gradually accumulates; the water, saturated with mud, deposits a sediment, and thus an island is formed, which soon becomes covered with vegetation. About ten years ago the Mississippi was surveyed by order of the Government; and its islands, from the confluence of the Missouri to the sea, were numbered. I remember asking the pilot the name of a very beautiful island, and the answer was, five hundred-and-seventy-three, the number assigned to it in the hydrographical survey, and the only name by which it was known. But in the course of these ten years, a vast variety of changes have taken place, and a more accurate chart has become highly desirable.

A traveller on the Mississippi has little to record in the way of incident. For a week we continued our course, stopping only to take in wood, and on one occasion to take in cargo, at an inconsiderable place called Memphis, which stands on one of the few bluffs we encountered in our progress. At length we reached Natchez, a town of some importance in the State of Mississippi. We only halted there for an hour, and the upper town, which stands on a height at some distance, I did not see. But the place was described by the passengers as being the scene of the most open and undisguised profligacy. All I observed in the lower town, certainly gave me no reason to doubt the accuracy of the description. Taverns full of men and women of the most abandoned habits, dancing, drinking, and uttering the most obscene language, were open to the street. I was advised not to walk to any distance from the landing place, for the risk of being robbed was considerable. I did however attempt to reach the upper town, about a mile off, but the bell announcing preparation for departure arrested my progress.

One of the most striking circumstances connected with this river voyage, was the rapid change of climate. Barely ten days had elapsed since I was traversing mountains almost impassable from snow. Even the level country was partially covered with it, and the approach of spring had not been heralded by any symptom of vegetation. Yet, in little more than a week, I found myself in the region of the sugar cane!

The progress of this transition was remarkable. During the first two days of the voyage, nothing like a blossom or a green leaf was to be seen. On the third, slight signs of vegetation were visible on a few of the hardier trees. These gradually became more general as we approached the Mississippi; but then, though our course lay almost due south, little change was apparent for a day or two. But after passing Memphis, in latitude 35°, all nature became alive. The trees which grew on any little eminence, or which did not spring immediately from the swamp, were covered with foliage; and at our wooding times, when I rambled through the woods, there were a thousand shrubs already bursting into flower. On reaching the lower regions of the Mississippi, all was brightness and verdure. Summer had already begun, and the heat was even disagreeably intense.

Shortly after entering Louisiana, the whole wildness of the Mississippi disappears. The banks are all cultivated, and nothing was to be seen but plantations of sugar, cotton, and rice, with the houses of their owners, and the little adjoining hamlets inhabited by the slaves. Here and there were orchards of orange-trees, but these occurred too seldom to have much influence on the landscape.

At Baton Rouge, a fort of some strength, which commands the navigation of the river, we discharged a major and a few private soldiers of the United States army, and on the following evening I found myself at New Orleans.

CHAPTER V.

NEW ORLEANS.

I LANDED at New Orleans on the 22d of March. The day had been one of heavy rain, and the appearance of the city was by no means prepossessing. The streets, being generally unpaved, were full of mud, and a dense canopy of mist shed a gloom on every thing.

We had some difficulty in finding accommodation. The principal hotel is that of Madame Herries, but the house was already full. We tried three others with no better success, and the streets of New Orleans are perhaps the last in the world in which a gentleman would choose to take up his night's lodging. At length the keeper of a boarding-house took compassion on our forlorn condition. There was an uninhabited house, she said, in an adjoining street, in which she thought she could prevail on the proprietor to furnish us with apartments, and at meals we might join the party in her establishment.

And so it was arranged. The rooms were bad, and wretchedly furnished, but they were quiet, and we had an old and ugly female slave to wait on us. This woman was in character something like the withered hags who are so finely introduced in the Bride of Lammermoor. During my stay, I tried every means to extract a smile from her, but without success. I gave her money, but that would not do; and wine, of which on one occasion she drank two tumblers, with no better effect. By way of recommending the lodgings, she told me three gentlemen had died in them during the last autumn of yellow fever. "Two were Englishmen," she added, "and she herself had laid out their corpses on that very table!" In short, though she did not often choose to converse, whenever the fit was on her, she displayed great tact and discrimination in the selection of topics.

The morning after my arrival was bright and beautiful, and I sallied forth to

> ——" view the manners of the town,
> Peruse the traders, gaze upon the buildings,
> And wander up and down to view the city."

It would be absurd to call New Orleans a handsome city. It is not so. The streets are generally narrow, and always filthy; and with the exception of the cathedral, there are no public buildings of any magnitude. But in comparison with such cities as those to which I had been accustomed in the United States, the general aspect of New Orleans may be called picturesque. The architecture of the older sections of the city is Spanish, and when Louisiana came into possession of France, the original taste in building seems still to have predominated. The houses are generally of one story, and the principal apartment opens at once on the street. They are built of wood, but here and there edifices of greater pretension, covered with stucco, and adorned with verandas, give something of pleasing variety.

In this quarter of the city reside the French and Spanish portion of the population; that occupied by the Anglo-Americans, has no attraction of any kind. The streets are wider, but unpaved; the houses larger, but bare and unseemly, and their internal superiority of comfort has been gained at the expense of external effect.

The condition of the streets in the greater part of New Orleans, is indeed an absolute nuisance. There are brick *trottoirs*, but the carriage-way is left in a state of nature. The consequence is, that after rain —and the climate is particularly humid—the centre of the street is at least a foot thick of mud, through which, foot-passengers, when desirous of crossing, must either wade up to their knees, or set off on a wild-goose chase after stepping-stones perhaps a mile distant, which may enable them—if they can jump like a kangaroo—to get over dry-shod.

In other respects, I must say, New Orleans is not an uncomfortable place. The American hotels are bad, but there is an admirable French restaurateur, whose establishment is conducted in a style far superior to any thing I had seen in the United States. When not otherwise engaged, I generally dined there, either alone, or with a companion, instead of scrambling at the public table of the boarding-house.

There is an old proverb, " give a dog a bad name and hang him." The proverb is as applicable to cities as to dogs, and unfortunately New Orleans has got a bad name. I have nothing to say which can make it any worse, and perhaps not much which would induce a very rigid moralist to delay execution. But I can bear witness that New Orleans contains a very well-bred and hospitable circle, where a traveller will meet more easy politeness than in most cities of the Union.

Both the language and manners are French. Few of the Creole ladies can speak English, and still fewer of the slaves. The latter jabber a sort of *patois* unlike any thing I ever heard in France, though my intercourse with the French peasantry has been tolerably extensive.

The situation of New Orleans is admirably adapted for commerce. It is and must be the great port of the south, as New York is of the north and centre of the Union. The Western States enjoy a ready communication with both; with the former, by the

Ohio and Mississippi; with the latter, by means of canals which now connect the Ohio with Lake Erie, and Lake Erie with the Hudson. The city stands on a bed of alluvium on the eastern bank of the Mississippi, about a hundred and twenty miles from the sea. Its population is about fifty thousand, and the number of slaves is very great.

I fear the standard of morals in New Orleans cannot be rated very high. Yet in no city are the externals of decorum more rigidly maintained. The eye is never shocked by any public display of indecency; and the coloured women, whatever may be their laxity of principle, are careful to maintain at least the outward semblance of virtue. I had heard a great deal of the beauty of these persons, but cannot profess having been at all smitten with their charms. One often meets a fine figure among them, but rarely a fine countenance. The skin is dingy, and the features are coarse. Something of the negro always remains—the long heel—the woolly hair—the flat nose—the thick lips—or the peculiar form of the head.

The Creole ladies, on the other hand, certainly

struck me as handsome. They too are dark, but their complexion is clear not clouded, like that of the Quadroons. Their figure is light and graceful, and with fine teeth, and an eye, large, dark, and bright, they must be admitted to possess quite as much attraction as the New Orleans gentlemen deserve. The effects of this enervating climate however are visible enough. The Creole ladies speak with a sort of languid drawl; their motions want energy and briskness, and the efficacy of their charms might perhaps be increased by a little more animation.

During my stay at New Orleans the legislature was in session, and I occasionally visited both houses. The mode of proceeding struck me as curious. The Creoles speak French, and the Americans English, neither understanding the language of the other. Whenever a speech is concluded, an interpreter gives as perfect a version of it as his memory can command. The time thus lost is enormous under any circumstances, but when the debate becomes personal, it has at least the advantage of giving members time to cool.

On one occasion, however, the discussion was conducted with a good deal of acrimony, and the scene became ludicrous enough. A French gentleman, when I entered the house, was delivering an energetic oration, impugning both the conduct and motives of an American. The latter during the whole time remained apparently in happy ignorance, both of the nature and extent of the punishment of which he was the object.

At length the honourable gentleman sat down, and the chief heads of his speech and arguments were detailed in English by the interpreter. The American then became, as they say in Scotland, "neither to hold nor to bind." He instantly commenced not only a vehement defence of himself, but an attack on his opponent, in a language of which the latter seemed to understand precisely as much as he did of Sanscrit. In short, I know of no body to whom the gift of tongues could be so useful as the legislature of Louisiana.

There is a French and an English theatre in New Orleans. The former is tenanted by a very tolerable set of comedians, who play musical pieces and

Vaudevilles with a great deal of spirit. The company of the English theatre was altogether wretched. I saw Damon and Pythias represented to a full house. Damon was so drunk that he could scarcely stand, and Pythias displayed his friendship in assisting him off the stage.

As in most Catholic countries, Sunday is the great day for amusements of every kind. The shops are open; the market displays unusual attractions, and the sounds of merriment and music are heard in every street. In the morning, three-fourths of the population run to hear mass, and the cathedral is crowded by people of all colours, in their best and gayest attire. In a European city the cathedral would probably pass without notice. In New Orleans it is a prominent object. As a building, it is full of inconsistencies, and the interior presents nothing to arrest the attention. The decorations of the altars are gewgaw enough, and there is no sculpture.

Both Catholic and Protestant agree in the tenet that all men are equal in the sight of God, but the former alone gives practical exemplification of his creed. In a Catholic church the prince and the peasant, the slave and his master, kneel before the same altar, in temporary oblivion of all worldly distinctions. They come there but in one character, that of sinners; and no rank is felt or acknowledged but that connected with the offices of religion. Within these sacred precincts the vanity of the rich man receives no incense; the proud are not flattered, the humble are not abashed. The stamp of degradation is obliterated from the forehead of the slave, when he beholds himself admitted to community of worship with the highest and noblest in the land.

But in Protestant churches a different rule prevails. People of colour are either excluded altogether, or are mewed up in some remote corner, separated by barriers from the body of the church. It is impossible to forget their degraded condition even for a moment. It is brought home to their feelings in a thousand ways. No white Protestant would kneel at the same altar with a black one. He asserts his superiority everywhere, and the very hue of his religion is affected by the colour of his skin.

From the hands of the Catholic priest, the poor slave receives all the consolations of religion. He is visited in sickness, and consoled in affliction; his dying lips receive the consecrated wafer; and in the very death-agony, the last voice that meets his ear is that of his priest uttering the sublime words, "Depart, Christian soul." Can it be wondered, therefore, that the slaves in Louisiana are all Catholics; that while the congregation of the Protestant church consists of a few ladies, arranged in well-cushioned pews, the whole floor of the extensive cathedral should be crowded with worshippers of all colours and classes?

From all I could learn, the zeal of the Catholic priests is highly exemplary. They never forget that the most degraded of human forms is animated by a soul, as precious in the eye of religion, as that of the sovereign Pontiff. The arms of the church are never closed against the meanest outcast of society. Divesting themselves of all pride of caste, they mingle with the slaves, and certainly understand their character far better than any other body of religious teachers. I am not a Catholic, but I cannot suffer prejudice of any sort to prevent my doing justice to a body of Christian ministers, whose zeal can be animated by no hope of worldly reward, and whose humble lives are passed in diffusing the influence of divine truth, and communicating to the meanest and most despised of mankind the blessed comforts of religion. These men publish no periodical enumeration of their converts. The amount, and the success of their silent labours, is not illustrated in the blazon of missionary societies, nor are they rhetorically set forth in the annual speeches of Lord Roden or Lord Bexley. And yet we may surely assert, that not the least of these labours is forgotten. Their record is, where their reward will be.

New Orleans and yellow fever are as inseparably connected as ham and chicken, and the writer who records his impressions of the one, is expected to say something of the other. I believe at no season of the year is New Orleans a healthy place of residence. The exhalations from the Mississippi, and the vast swamps by which it is surrounded, taint the atmosphere continually, and the variation at different seasons is only in degree. Even in March the air of New Orleans is manifestly unhealthy. It is sometimes so thick and impregnated with vapour, that the lungs play with difficulty, and the effect of such weather on the animal economy is very perceptible. The skin is clammy even in repose, and the slightest exertion brings on profuse perspiration. For myself, I could not walk a quarter of a mile without feeling a degree of lassitude to which I had never been accustomed. The resource under such circumstances is generous diet and a sofa, but the only absolute cure is a brisk north-wester, which, by clearing off the impurities of the atmosphere, at once restores the patient to his natural functions.

It is not, however, till the heats of summer are considerably advanced, that the yellow fever appears in its terrors. It comes in silence, and steals, as it were, unawares into the city. The sky is bright, and the weather beautiful. The city is reported healthy, and business and pleasure proceed with accelerated impulse. In such circumstances, a report probably spreads, that a sailor on board of one of the vessels at the river, has been stricken with this fearful malady. On the following day, the rumour of fresh cases becomes prevalent, but the inhabitants comfort themselves that these have been exclusively confined to the shipping. Even of this consolation, however, they are shortly deprived. The disease appears simultaneously in various quarters of the city, through which it stalks like a destroying angel, spreading havoc and desolation.

The Creoles are entirely exempt from its ravages. The chief victims are Europeans, and natives of the Northern States. Of these, not one in twenty escapes attack ; and of those attacked, not above two-thirds survive. The latter are then considered to be what is called "acclimated," and are not liable to a recurrence of the disease, unless their constitution be again changed by a residence in a colder climate.

One of the curiosities which all strangers should see—and which too many of them visit without seeing—is the public burying-ground, about half-a-mile from the city. It is simply a portion of the surrounding swamp, and, though very extensive, is not found too large for the wants of the population. There are always some twenty or thirty graves, of different sizes, kept open on speculation, so that there is no doubt of any gentleman, who chooses to die in a hurry, finding accommodation at the shortest notice. One acquires from habit a sort of lurking prejudice in favour of being buried in dry ground, which is called into full action by a sight of this New Orleans cemetery. The spade cannot penetrate even a few inches below the surface, without finding water, and considerable difficulty is experienced in sinking the coffins, since the whole neighbourhood could not furnish a stone the size of an orange.

Such a disposal of the dead may more properly be termed *inundation* than *interment*, and there is something so offensive to the imagination in the whole process, and in the idea of being devoured by the crawfish, which burrow in myriads, that the richer people generally prefer being kept above the level, both of ground and water, in little buildings like ovens, composed of brick and plaster, without ornament of any sort. Altogether, those who are content to live in New Orleans, may be content to be buried there when they die. I confess my own inclination prompted me to neither, and I quitted the cemetery with the firm resolution of never eating another crawfish, with whatever attractions the skill of the cook may have invested it.

There are slave auctions almost every day in the New Orleans Exchange. I was frequently present at these, and the man who wants an excuse for misanthropy, will nowhere discover better reason for hating and despising his species. The usual process differs in nothing from that of selling a horse. The poor object of traffic is mounted on a table; intending purchasers examine his points, and put questions as to his age, health, &c. The auctioneer dilates on his value, enumerates his accomplishments, and when the hammer at length falls, protests, in the usual phrase, that poor Sambo has been absolutely thrown away. When a woman is sold, he usually puts his audience in good humour by a few indecent jokes.

One of the first human beings whom I happened to see thus sold was a poor woman, apparently dying of a consumption. She was emaciated, her voice was husky and feeble, and her proper place was evidently the hospital. It was with difficulty she was raised upon the table. "Now, gentlemen, here is Mary!"

said the auctioneer; "a clever house-servant and an excellent cook. Bid me something for this valuable lot. She has only one fault, gentlemen, and that is shamming sick. She pretends to be ill, but there is nothing more the matter with her than there is with me at this moment. Put her up, gentlemen,—shall I say a hundred dollars to begin with? Will nobody say a hundred dollars for Mary, a clever servant and excellent cook? Thank you, sir, fifty—well, fifty dollars is bid for her." Here the auctioneer stopped for a minute or two, while several men began feeling the poor woman's ribs, and putting questions as to her health.

"Are you well?" asked one man.

"Oh, no, I am very ill."

"What is the matter with you?"

"I have a bad cough and pain in my side."

"How long have you had it?"

"Three months and more."

Here the auctioneer finding such interrogatories did not tend to enhance the value of the lot, again went on. "Never mind what she says, gentlemen,

I told you she was a shammer. Her health is good enough. Damn her humbug. Give her a touch or two of the cow-hide, and I'll warrant she'll do your work. Speak, gentlemen, before I knock her down. Seventy dollars only bid,—going, going, going, gone!" The sale concluded amid sundry jests, at the expense of the purchaser. "A bloody good lot of skin and bone," said one. "I guess that 'ere woman will soon be food for the land-crabs," said another; and amid such atrocious merriment the poor dying creature was led off.

If such scenes are acted in a Christian country, it is the duty of every traveller to take care at least, that they shall not be done in a corner, that they shall be proclaimed loudly to the world, and that those who perpetrate the enormities shall receive their due meed of indignation and contempt.

The time is past when it was necessary to write whole volumes, in illustration of the evils and injustice of slavery. These are now admitted and confessed by every one. They are so great as to admit of no exaggeration by eloquence, nor of palliation or concealment by sophistry. Public opinion in England requires no stimulus.

I feel anxious, that writing on this subject I should be clearly understood. It may not be a crime—it probably ought not to be charged as one—in the American people, that slavery still exists in by far the larger portion of the territory of the Union. But now when the United States have enjoyed upwards of half a century of almost unbroken prosperity, when their people, as they themselves declare, are the most moral, the most benevolent, the most enlightened in the world, we are surely entitled to demand, what have this people done for the mitigation of slavery? what have they done to elevate the slave in the scale of moral and intellectual being, and to prepare him for the enjoyment of those privileges to which, sooner or later, the coloured population *must* be admitted?

The answer to these questions unfortunately may be comprised in one word—NOTHING. Nothing during all this period has been done to raise the slave to the dignity of a rational and responsible being, or to mitigate the horrors of his servitude; nothing for the subversion of ignorant and degrading prejudice; nothing to remove from themselves and their posterity the reproach of a system which withers up all the better sympathies of our nature. The voice of justice and humanity has been raised in vain; and it may safely be predicted, that while the progress of intelligence is confessedly incompatible with slavery, its last stronghold will be found, not in Portugal—not in Turkey or Algiers—but in the United States.

It is true, indeed, that slavery has been abolished in many States of the Union, and that in others recently established it has never existed. Let the merit —whatever be its amount—of an enlightened appreciation of their own interests, be at once freely conceded to these States. Still it cannot be denied, that slavery has only ceased in those portions of the Union, in which it was practically found to be a burden on the industry and resources of the country. *Wherever it was found profitable, there it has remained;* there it is to be found at the present day, in all its pristine and unmitigated ferocity. Where its abolition involved no sacrifice, slavery has disappeared; but wherever justice was to be done at the expense of the pocket, the nuisance, so far from being abated, has gone on increasing, and has become rooted more widely and more deeply in the passions and prejudices of the people.

I have said that the abolition of slavery in the Northern, and some of the Central States, has involved no sacrifice. Let me explain this. When Pennsylvania, for instance, abolished slavery, she passed an act, that after a certain number of years all the slaves within her territory should be manumitted. What was the consequence? Why, that the great body of the slaves belonging to Pennsylvanian proprietors were in the meantime exported and sold in other States, and when the day of liberation came, those who actually profited by it, were something like the patients who visited the pool of Bethesda,—the blind, the halt, the maimed, the decrepid, whom it really required no great exercise of generosity to turn about their business, with an injunction to provide thereafter for their own maintenance.

I admit that the question of the abolition of slavery in the United States, is involved in peculiar difficulties, nor do I pretend to suggest any project by which it may be safely, and even remotely effected. But there are some crying evils on which immediate legislation is imperiously demanded. The first of these is undoubtedly the *slave trade.*

When I speak of the slave trade, I do not allude to the importation of slaves from abroad, but to the internal traffic which is carried on between the different States. Some of these, in which the climate is healthy, and the cultivation of the soil easy, are slave-breeders, not for their own consumption only, but for that of others, in which the climate is deadly and the labour severe. The cultivation of sugar in Louisiana, for instance, is carried on at an enormous expense of human life. Planters must buy to keep up their stock, and this supply principally comes from Maryland, Virginia, and North Carolina. On my return from New Orleans by the coast, I met a whole drove of these miserable creatures, chained together like felons, and driven on like brute beasts by the lash. In God's name let this unhallowed traffic be put a stop to. Let not men's eyes be shocked by sights so atrocious. Let not one State furnish materials for the cruelties of another, and by a system of wise legislation let humanity be made the interest, as it is the duty, of *all.*

It would be difficult to decide whether slavery is most to be lamented for the injustice perpetrated towards those who are its victims, or for its depraving influence on the class by whom that injustice is inflicted. The question must be decided by nicer casuists than I pretend to be. But sure I am that the evils of this detestable system cannot be exaggerated by the most fervid imagination. It will scarcely be believed, that in the United States it is common for fathers to sell their children, for sons to sell their brothers and their sisters; and that atrocities so heinous are unvisited by public indignation or contempt. And yet it is so. The smallest infusion of negro blood is held to abrogate not only the charities of life, but the ties of nature. I will not enlarge on this subject. It is too hateful and too odious. But in the name of consistency and common sense, either let such enormities cease to be perpetrated in the United States, or let the word *mo-*

rality be at once erased from the American vocabulary.

I did intend to have made some observations on the savage character of the slave codes of the different States, but I write for the British public, and the task has become unnecessary. Still I would earnestly call on every Englishman who has partaken in the delusion that the abolition, or even the mitigation of slavery, may be safely trusted to the humanity of those whose immediate interests are connected with its continuance, to look to the condition of the slaves in the United States. I again repeat that I do not charge it as a reproach on the inhabitants that slavery should still exist in their territory, but I own I do consider it as involving national disgrace, that during half a century no steps have been taken, I will not say for its abolition, but even for its mitigation. At the present hour slavery is seen in the United States decked out in every horrible attribute with which the imagination of man ever invested it. And, after all, it is perhaps better for the ultimate interests of humanity that it should be so. It is better that the front of the image should be of brass, while its feet are of clay. To suppose that slavery can long continue in this country when other nations shall have freed themselves from the foulest stain which has ever polluted their humanity, is to contemplate a period when the United States will become a nuisance upon earth, and an object of hatred and derision to the whole world.

It is only fair to state that during the whole course of my tour, I never conversed with any American on the subject of slavery without his at once admitting the magnitude of the evil. The planters uniformly speak of it as a noxious exhalation by which their whole atmosphere is poisoned. "Yet what is to be done?" they ask. "You express yourself shocked by the existence of slavery; have you formed any plan for its abolition? Can you see even a glimmering of light through the darkness by which this awful subject is surrounded? At all events, do not suppose that we maintain slavery in our territory from choice. Far from it. We regard those States where this curse is unknown with envy. We would gladly become as they are, but *cannot*. We are slave-holders by compulsion alone. As such, let us be treated with candour and fairness. If you can suggest any remedy, we shall be glad to hear it; if you cannot, cease to inveigh against an inevitable evil, for which the collective wisdom of mankind has yet discovered no cure."

There is much that is reasonable in all this, mixed up with a little misrepresentation, and as few men travel about with a plan for the abolition of American slavery, cut and dry in their pocket, it no doubt acts in conversation as a convenient stopper on a great deal of froth which might otherwise be discharged on so tempting a subject. But though it be unquestionably true that the slave-holders are in favour of abolition, it is abolition of a peculiar kind, which must be at once cheap and profitable; which shall peril no interest, and offend no prejudice; and which, in liberating the slave, shall enrich his master. It is needless to say, that the dream of Alnaschar, in the Arabian Nights, pictured nothing more visionary than such an abolition. Let slavery be abolished when it will, and how it will, by slow degrees, or by one sweeping and decisive measure of emancipation, the immediate interests of the planters must be injuriously affected. By no process can the injustice of centuries be repaired without sacrifice; and the longer this reparation is delayed, the sacrifice demanded will be greater.

The cessation of slavery must put a stop to the cultivation both of sugar and rice in the United States, and the compulsion of which the planters speak is the compulsion of money. Large tracts of the Southern States will be thrown out of cultivation. Two-thirds of their population will probably migrate to the West, since the cultivation of cotton, the great staple, must of course be limited by the demands of the market, which can only receive considerable increase from improvements in the process of manufacture.

That the United States, as a nation, would be prodigiously benefited by the abolition of slavery, there can be no doubt; but that the pecuniary interests of the planters is decidedly opposed to it, is at least equally clear. How long these men can hold out against nature, religion, and the common sympathies of mankind, it is impossible to foresee.

My own conviction is, that slavery in this country can only be eradicated by some great and terrible convulsion. The sword is evidently suspended; it will fall at last.

From New Orleans I made a pleasant excursion to a sugar plantation about eight or ten miles distant. The road lay along the margin of the river, which is prevented from inundating the country by embankment. Through this barrier, however, it often forces its way, by what are called *crevasses*, or small fissures, generally occasioned, I believe, by the burrowing of crawfish or water-rats. These fissures, by the pressure of the water, soon become formidable outlets; and the whole country, for miles, is sometimes overflowed to a depth of several feet. The Mississippi, too, occasionally overflows its banks though not often, I believe, to such extent as to occasion serious damage to the neighbouring plantations.

The country is in general cultivated to the distance of about half a mile from the river, and on these rich alluvial bottoms are the sugar plantations. That which I visited, though not one of the largest, was extensive. The family were of French origin, and few of its members could speak English. The proprietor took me over the sugar works, and I looked in to the huts of his negroes who were then in the field. He gave me full details of the whole process of sugar cultivation, which he confessed was only carried on at an appalling sacrifice of life. At the season when the canes are cut and the boilers at work, the slaves are compelled to undergo incessant labour for about six weeks. The fatigue is so great that nothing but the severest application of the lash can stimulate the human frame to endure it, and the sugar season is uniformly followed by a great increase of mortality among the slaves.

The climate of Louisiana is not happily adapted for sugar cultivation. It is too variable, and frosts often come on in November which destroy the whole saccharine matter of the canes. This had happened the season before my visit, and I saw the canes of nearly half the estate rotting on the ground. The crop in Louisiana is never considered safe till it is in the mill, and the consequence is, that when cutting once begins, the slaves are taxed beyond their strength, and are goaded to labour until nature absolutely sinks under the effort.

The poverty of the planters, too, generally prevents there being a sufficient stock of slaves on the estates; and where a plantation which requires two hundred and fifty slaves, is cultivated only by two hundred, it is very evident that the necessary work will not only be done worse, but that it will be done at a greatly increased expenditure of human life. Thus the tendency of the slave population in Louisiana is to diminish, and, but for importations from the northern slave States, would, under the present system, become extinct.

I passed a day and night with my hospitable entertainers, to whose kindness I felt much indebted. It is the fashion in this country to appoint a servant to attend upon the guests. When I retired for the night, I observed a very nice-looking black boy, who, after setting down my candle and adjusting the pillows of the bed, still remained standing right opposite to me when I began to undress. I bade him good-night, but he still showed no inclination to move. I then asked why he remained, and gathered from his reply that it is by no means usual in this country for a white person to perform any office for himself which can be performed by deputy. The boy said he thought I should like some one to assist me to undress, but I assured him I had no occasion for his services in any capacity except that of brushing my clothes in the morning. He then took leave, though evidently not without some surprise that a white gentleman should, under any circumstances, condescend to pull off his own stockings, and put on his nightcap. It must certainly be ranked among the minor evils of slavery, that it destroys all personal independence, and attaches something of disgrace to the discharge of the most ordinary functions.

Before quitting New Orleans I made a trip to visit the Delta of the Mississippi, in one of the steamers employed in towing vessels to and from the mouth of the river. Though with three large vessels attached, our bark made good way under the co-operative influences of steam and stream. About seven miles below the city is the field of battle. It is a plain about half a mile in breadth, bounded by the Mississippi on one side, and the forest on the other. Below is a bend of the river, which, from what reason I know not, is called "The English Turn." Plantations continue at intervals for about forty miles, when cultivation entirely ceases.

Below this, nature is to be seen only in her dreariest and most desolate aspect. At first there are forests springing in rank luxuriance from swamps, impassable even by the foot of the Indian hunter. But these soon pass, and nothing but interminable cane brakes are to be seen on either side. From the shrouds of the steam-boat, though the range of vision probably extended for many leagues, no other objects were discernible but the broad muddy river, with its vast masses of drift wood, and the wilderness of gigantic bulrushes shaking in the wind.

There are four passes or outlets by which the Mississippi discharges its mighty burden into the Gulf of Mexico. Two of these are navigable, but changes are ever taking place, and the passage formerly preferred by the pilots, is now rarely attempted even by vessels of the smallest class. On approaching the Gulf, verdure appears only at intervals, and the eye rests on tracts of mere mud, formed by the deposit of the river on the drift wood which some obstacle has arrested in its passage to the ocean. It is by this process that land is formed, and it may be traced in every step of its progress, from the island resting on a few logs, up to the huge tract in whose bosom are embedded many millions. Encountering no obstacle, the river sends out arms in every direction, which, after winding through the half-formed region in a thousand fantastic flexures, are again united to the main branches.

It would be difficult to convey an idea by words, of the effect which this most dismal scene produces on the heart and imagination of the spectator. It seems as if the process of creation were incomplete, and the earth yet undivided from the waters, for he beholds only an indeterminate mass which admits of being absolutely assigned to neither element. He feels that he has forsaken the regions of the habitable world. Above, beneath, around, there is nothing to excite his sympathies, and probably for the first time in his life he becomes conscious of the full sublimity of *desolation.*

The steamer having towed her burden safely across the bar, took up several inward bound vessels, and commenced her voyage back to the city. I felt it absolutely a relief when my eye again rested on the deep shadows of the forest. Then came the dwellings of man. Never had the smoke, which rose in spiral wreaths above the masses of foliage, appeared so beautiful. Even New Orleans seemed to have lost something of its dinginess, when, after a three days' voyage, I found myself comfortably seated at the French restaurateur's, and saw the waiter enter with a most tempting dish of beccaficas, or some bird very much like them, and very nearly as good.

CHAPTER VI.

JOURNEY TO CHARLESTON.

On the evening of the 10th of April, I bade farewell to New Orleans, and embarked on the canal which connects the city with the Bayou St John. These bayous are sluggish creeks which alternately supply nourishment to the Mississippi, and ease it of its load. When the river is in flood, the bayous which intersect the whole country, act as safety-valves, and prevent a general inundation. When it is low, they restore a portion of their waters, and thus contribute to equalize the volume of the river at different seasons.

The Bayou St John has all the appearance of a canal. Its course leads through a swamp covered with cedars, and other trees which delight in exuberant moisture. It was dark when we reached Lake Pontchartrain, and the steamer lay at anchor at some distance from the shore. As it did not sail till the following morning, I should probably have slept at the inn had its appearance been at all inviting. But there was a large party carousing at the bar, and its pretensions were simply those of a pot-house. I therefore determined to embark immediately, though the night was dark, and the wind unusually high.

It may appear ridiculous to talk of a storm on a lake some forty or fifty miles long, and not more than two or three in breadth. But the *tempestas in matula*—if so it must be called—was exceedingly disagreeable, and before we reached the vessel, our boat was nearly full of water. Both the constitution and equanimity of a traveller should be robust enough to stand an occasional drenching without injury or disturbance; but to have your whole baggage saturated with water,—your books, papers, and other perishable valuables, seriously damaged, if not entirely destroyed, is apt to produce an elongation of visage in a more philosophical tourist than myself.

At all events it was in such pickle that I reached the steam-boat. The more immediate and personal consequences of the misfortune were obviated by the exhibition of a cigar, and a glass of the truly American catholicon, brandy and water; and on the following morning my whole chattels were spread out to dry on the deck, apparently to the great satisfaction of several curious passengers who not only subjected the state of my wardrobe to a rigid inspection, but attempted to read my papers, a compliment which I begged leave to decline.

From Lake Pontchartrain we passed into Lake Borgne, a basin of similar character, and equally devoid of beauty. Both are surrounded by vast marshes, and the view on every side is dreary and monotonous. On a projection at the narrow pass by which these lakes are united, is a fort garrisoned by a company of the United States army. A more wretched place it is impossible to conceive. The climate is among the most villainous in the world; and an officer who happened to be a passenger, and had once for three years enjoyed the pleasures of this charming station, assured me that the mosquitoes are so numerous that it is absolutely necessary to live nine months of the year under gauze.

It was pitch-dark when we reached a place called Passamagoula, where our voyage terminated. It here became necessary to cross the lake, about half a mile broad, on a narrow and rickety bridge of planks. The exploit was achieved without accident, but it was really one of peril. To see was impossible, and to grope equally so, for the railing in many places had given way. At one point of our progress it was necessary to jump, and I remember plunging forward into the abyss with the delightful incertitude of whether, in the course of a second, I was not to find myself in the middle of Lake Borgne. The betting, I believe, would have been pretty equal between plank and water, but luckily the former carried it, and in a few minutes I was safely housed in a dirty log tavern.

The landlord was particularly anxious that some of the party should remain till the following day to proceed by another coach, but having already secured places at New Orleans, I would by no means listen to the suggestion, and, accordingly, about one o'clock in the morning, I had the satisfaction of finding myself in the mail stage, moving slowly onward towards Mobile. Our road was what is expressively called a *natural* one, and lay through a continued pine forest. In the whole distance I observed only two houses, one of which was a tavern, where we stopped to sup about four in the morning. Our fare was cold venison and bacon, for which the charge was so enormous as to excite the indignation of the passengers, who said not a word until we drove off, when they united in declaring that their pockets had been picked.

This forest drive is imprinted on my memory by association with a scene of peculiar beauty. The wind had fallen, and the night was warm and misty. After leaving the tavern, the forest suddenly became illumined with myriads of fire-flies. The dark foliage of the pines shone resplendently in the multitude of tiny corruscations. But in an hour day dawned, and the "ineffectual fires" of these beautiful insects were soon extinguished in its radiance.

About nine in the morning of the 12th of April we reached Mobile, a town, as every Liverpool merchant well knows, of considerable importance. It was burned down some years ago, but few traces of the conflagration are now discernible. On enquiry, I found the steam-boat for Montgomery did not start for three days, and, therefore, I judged it advisable to take advantage of my letters. These were not less efficacious in procuring kindness at Mobile, than I had found them in other places.

My observations during this three days' residence afforded little to record. Mobile is a place of trade, and of nothing else. It is the great port of the cotton-growing State of Alabama. The quays were crowded with shipping, and in amount of exports it is inferior only to New Orleans. The wealth of the Mobile merchants must accumulate rapidly, for they certainly do not dissipate it in expenditure. There are no smart houses or equipages, nor indeed any demonstration of opulence, except huge warehouses and a crowded harbour. Of amusements of any kind I heard nothing.

My mornings were passed in wandering about the

neighbouring forest, which is full of Indians. These men had evidently been debased by their intercourse with Europeans. It is only in the remote wilderness that they appear in their native dignity and independence. And yet something of their original grace and spirit seemed still to cling to them. They are poor, yet patient under suffering, and though subdued, are nobly submissive. During my walks I often attempted to converse with them, but their taciturnity was not to be overcome. I gave them money, but they received it rather with surprise than thankfulness. They were without experience in gratitude, and too manly to express that which they did not feel.

I was strongly recommended to lay in a store of cogniac and biscuits at Mobile, being assured that in the country I was about to traverse, there would be found neither bread nor brandy. Though not particularly apprehensive of suffering by privation of either, I adopted the advice of my friends, and visited a Scotch baker, whom I directed to pack for me a small box of biscuits. My countrymen are accused of cherishing a certain indestructible sentiment of affinity. Whether this moved the baker and myself I know not, but we had a good deal of conversation on the subject of emigration. My compatriot was a native of Hamilton, and had courted fortune there without success. Regardless of Malthus and his precepts, he had married, and unluckily his family increased quite as rapidly as his hope of supporting it diminished. Under these circumstances he turned his little moveables into money, and trusting his progeny for a season to God and their own industry, set off for America. On arriving at New York, he worked for some months as a journeyman, but learning from a friend that kneaders of dough were in greater request at Mobile, he there pitched his tabernacle and heated his oven. His family had since joined him, and he was now, he assured me, in the enjoyment of every comfort which the most prosperous baker could desire.

In conversation the man's mind seemed to be alternately influenced by attachment to his native land, and satisfaction in the enjoyment of those advantages which had resulted from his quitting it. At first he would talk of nothing but the beauties of the

Clyde. "Oh, sir," said he, "are not the banks of the Clyde beautiful? Did you ever see a river like it? Does not the road from Hamilton to Lanark pass through a perfect paradise? I am sure the whole world has nothing equal to it."

I agreed in all his praises of the Clyde, and enquired whether he had not found, in the solid comforts of the New World, a sufficient compensation for the loss of those beauties which it delighted his imagination to recall. This question seemed to have the effect of diverting the whole current of the baker's ideas. He dilated on his present comforts told me he lived like a duke,—the man was redolent of broth,—had two slaves, could pay his debts any day in the week, and had lately been able, without inconvenience, to send a hundred dollars to his poor mother. In regard to emigration he expressed his opinions at great length. "In Scotland, sir," said this sagacious master of the rolls, "there is so much competition in every trade that a great many must be unsuccessful. Take my own case as an example: when I set up a shop in Hamilton, I was honest and industrious enough, and understood my business quite as well as any baker in the county; still I could get little custom. The trade was already full, and those only who had considerable capital could afford to wait till business came in by slow degrees. This would not do for me, whose whole stock in trade consisted only of fifty pounds, borrowed from my wife's uncle. I was obliged to sell my bread to pay for my flour, and finding that impossible, soon got into the Gazette. My story is that of thousands more; and surely these men had better come to this country, than continue struggling for a precarious subsistence at home. They may not get rich here, but they will be sure, if they are sober, industrious, and do not suffer from the climate, to escape from poverty. But it is not actual want of the necessaries of life, sir, which occasions the chief suffering of the poor tradesman in the old country. It is the cares and anxieties that continually press on him, that deprive his bread of its nourishment, and disturb his sleep by horrible dreams; it is these things that wear out both soul and body, and make him an old man before his time. In America a man may look to the future without more apprehension than what naturally arises from the common accidents to which we are liable in all countries. He need have no fears about his family, for he has plenty to give them in the meantime; and if they live, they will soon be able to provide for themselves.

"Still I would not advise any one who is in a steady way of business at home, however small, and who can make both ends meet by strict economy, to think of emigrating. It is a sore trial, sir; and if I had been a single man, with no one to provide for but myself, I never would have left bonny Scotland. Oh, sir, the rivers here are not to be compared to the Clyde; and had the worst come to the worst, I would still have continued to get both bite and sup; and I often think now that a mouthful in that country would do me more good than a whole bellyful in this. The man that comes here, sir, only exchanges one set of evils for another: he is obliged to mingle with a most profane and godless set. He cannot hear the gospel preached, as he has been accustomed to, and the profanation of the Sabbath is most awful. He cannot give his children a religious education, and bring them up in the fear of the Lord; and it is shocking to think of the sights of depravity to which they must become accustomed from their very infancy. I am not sure, sir, that poverty is not a slight evil when compared to this.

"Then there is slavery, sir; men are treated in this country far worse than brute beasts in Scotland, and surely this is dreadful. There is no getting any thing done here without slaves, for all white men think it a disgrace to labour. I was obliged to buy a slave with the first money I could spare, and I have now two, but I treat them just like free servants, and teach my children that, in the eye of God, they are as good as themselves. After all, it is a sore trial of patience, for the creatures are dirty, and have no sense or gumption. Then, the ways of the people here are not pleasant to one from the old country: they are not social and neighbourly, and are so keen about money, that I believe they would skin a flea for lucre of the hide and tallow. There is a great deal, sir, that should be well-weighed and considered before a man decides on leaving the land of his birth. I have never advised a friend of mine to do so, and when applied to, though I give all the information in my power, I advise nothing but *caution.*"

So far as my memory would permit, I have embodied the oration of the baker in his own words. It struck me as being marked by an unusual degree of good sense, and may possibly be found useful. At all events his biscuits were excellent, and during my eight days' residence in the Creek country, I often thought of him with gratitude.

On the 15th of April I embarked on board of the steam-boat Isabella, bound up the Alabama river for Montgomery. As there were no ladies on board, my English friend and myself succeeded in getting possession of the cabin usually appropriated for their accommodation. Our apartment was immediately above that occupied by the gentlemen, and being surrounded by a balcony, it was impossible to desire any thing more agreeable. The party below seemed to consist almost exclusively of farmers, who, though exceedingly offensive both in habits and deportment, are yet a shade better than the inhabitants of towns. There is nothing *rustic*, however, about any American; nothing of that simplicity which distinguishes the peasantry of other countries. The eye is almost uniformly expressive of care and cunning; and often, as I looked on the furrowed and haggard countenances which surrounded the dinner table, have I asked myself, "Is it possible that these men make pretension to happiness?"

In my progress down the western waters, I had become accustomed to a table, loaded even to excess with provisions of all sorts. In the Southern States there is no such profusion. Our dinners on board the Isabella were scanty in quantity, and far from laudable on the score of quality. Plates, dishes, knives and forks, tablecloths, all were dirty and disgusting. But bating these disagreeables, our voyage was pleasant and prosperous. The Alabama is a river apparently about the size of the Hudson; and the scenery through which it led us, was very pleasing, though deficient in variety. Either bank presented a splendid mass of luxuriant foliage, and some of the noblest timber I had ever seen. Among the forest trees I remarked the plane, the cotton-tree, dogwood, oak of several varieties, magnolia grandiflora, maple, gum-tree, hackberry, &c. At night I was peculiarly struck with the beauty of the stars reflected in the pure waters of the river. The whole sky was mirrored with a vividness which exceeded every thing of the kind I have ever witnessed before or since.

In the evening we passed Claiborne, a petty village on a height, a short distance from the river. In a State so thinly peopled as Alabama, however, it is talked of as a considerable place; but from all I saw or heard of it, Claiborne is not increasing, nor is it likely to increase. On the morning following, we came to Portland, a miserable place, consisting of a store and a few wretched houses. This is what is called, in American phrase, "a great improvement." We called at every house in the place in search of milk, but could get none.

Our next stoppage was at Cahawba, which, a year or two back, was the seat of government of the State. It is a very poor collection of very poor houses, not, I should imagine, above twenty in number. The Court-house happening to be open, I entered, and found the Court engaged in the discharge of business. On an elevated platform, composed of rough unpainted boards, sat his honour, the judge, not better dressed, and apparently somewhat filthier in habits, than an English ploughman. The case concerned the payment of a doctor's bill: the counsel for defendant, a gentleman in a fustian jacket, was in the act of addressing the Court. He read an act of the legislature, enacting, that no practitioner of the healing art should recover for medical attendance, without having been previously licensed by a Board of Doctors, and called on the plaintiff, as a necessary preliminary, to produce his certificate.

This was evidently inconvenient, and the plaintiff's counsel, whose appearance seemed to indicate a combination of the trade of blacksmith with that of barrister, was somewhat taken aback by the demand. The learned gentleman, however, attempted with all his ingenuity, to get out of the scrape, and at the conclusion of every sentence, hitched up his corduroy breeches, which seemed in danger of dropping about his heels, with a grace peculiarly his own. Unfortunately I had not time to wait for the peroration of the speech. The steam-boat bell sounded, and no time was to be lost in getting on board.

Shortly after dark we reached Selma, the most considerable settlement on the Alabama, between Mobile and Montgomery. There was no quay, and a good deal of the cargo was rolled out upon the bank without any one to receive it. I did not see Selma, for the night was cloudy and moonless, and the village stands at a short distance from the river.

On the fourth day, our voyage terminated. Montgomery is what is called "a considerable place," though its population does not exceed a few hundreds, and these exclusively of the poorer order. There is not one tolerable house, and nothing could be worse than the inn. In the way of dormitory, nothing was to be had but a room with three beds in it, all of which were destined to be occupied. What was still worse, the beds were full of vermin, and the mosquitoes more annoying than I had yet found them.

In such circumstances I was up with the lark, and set out on a long ramble through the neighbouring country. The soil is poor and light, but presents a prettily undulating surface. From one height I enjoyed a fine view of the river, which is truly, even at this distance from the sea, a noble object. After a walk of three hours I returned to the inn, having fortunately succeeded in throwing off by exercise, the fever and fatigue of a restless night.

In the Southern States, there is little of that stirring spirit of improvement so apparent in the regions of the West. The towns and villages are without appearance of business, and the number of dilapidated—if the word may be applied to structures of wood—houses, indicates a decreasing, rather than an augmenting population. In Montgomery, many houses had been deserted, and the Court-house seemed fast falling into decay.

At four o'clock P. M., we started in the mail stage for Fort Mitchell. There were unfavourable reports abroad of the state of the rivers, which were asserted to be impassable; but I had so often experienced that difficulties, formidable at a distance, become insignificant on nearer approach, that I determined to push on at all hazards. In the present case, my determination was unlucky, for it involved both my companion and myself in some little danger, and occasioned considerable detention.

We accomplished the first stage without difficulty of any kind, but with the second commenced the tug of war. Our first obstacle was a bayou of such depth, that in crossing it, the water was ankle-deep in the bottom of the carriage. Night had set in before we reached Lime Creek, which, though generally a slow and sluggish stream, was now swelled into a very formidable torrent. It requires experience to understand the full danger of crossing such a river, and, perhaps fortunately, I did not possess it. But both the passengers and coachman were under considerable alarm, and one of the former, a Louisianian planter, in broken English threatened the black ferryman with instant death in case of negligence or blunder. This caused some merriment; but Sambo, who was evidently under no alarm, took the matter very coolly. The coach was run into the ferry-boat, and by means of a hawser stretched across the river, we soon found ourselves in safety on the opposite bank.

We were now in the territory of the Creek Indians, and in consequence of the darkness, it was soon found impossible to proceed without torches. We tried in vain to procure them at several of the Indian encampments, but were at last fortunate enough to discover an axe in the coach, with which abundance were soon cut from the neighbouring pines. I have had occasion to say a great deal about roads in these volumes, but I pronounce that along which our route lay on the present occasion, to be positively, comparatively, and superlatively, the *very worst* I have ever travelled in the whole course of my peregrinations. The ruts were axle-deep, and huge crevices occasionally occurred, in which, but for great strategy on the part of the coachman, the vehicle must have been engulfed.

In such circumstances none of the passengers seemed ambitious of the dangerous distinction of keeping his seat. We all walked, each armed with a pine torch, and the party, to a spectator, must have had very much the aspect of a funeral procession. Nothing, however, could be more beautiful than the scene presented by the forest. The glare of our torches, as we continued slowly advancing amid the darkness; the fires of the Indian encampments seen at a distance through the trees, and the wild figures by which they were surrounded; the multitude of fire-flies which flickered everywhere among the foliage,—formed a combination of objects which more than compensated in picturesque beauty, for all the difficulties we had yet encountered.

We had to pass two swamps on a sort of pavement formed of logs of trees, or what is called in America, a "corduroy road." The operation, though one of some difficulty, was effected without accident. The country, as we advanced, presented greater inequalities of surface. Stumps of trees often came in contact with the wheels, and brought the whole machine to a standstill; trees which had been blown over by the wind sometimes lay directly across the road, and it was with difficulty that the united exertions of the passengers succeeded in removing them.

In spite of all obstacles, however, we reached an Indian tavern, where we changed horses and had supper. We were now beyond the region of bread, and our fare consisted of eggs, broiled venison, and cakes of Indian corn fried in some kind of oleaginous matter. The venison was tolerable, and with the biscuits of my friend, the Mobile baker, I bade defiance to fate in the way of eating.

On returning to the coach, we found the night had become one of rain. The clouds began discharging their contents in no very alarming profusion, but this soon changed, and the rain absolutely descended in torrents. The pine torches refused to burn; the wind roared loudly among the trees; streams came rushing down the gullies, and inundated the road, and in spite of greatcoats and waterproof cloaks, in less than an hour I found myself fairly drenched to the skin.

At length the horses, on getting half way up a hill, became fairly exhausted, and no application of the lash could induce them to proceed. The passengers all pushed most lustily, but the horses were obstinate, and gave us no assistance. In short, we were evidently hard and fast for the night, and resigning all hope of immediate extrication, the driver was despatched on one of the leaders to the next stage for assistance, while in doleful mood, and absolutely saturated with water, we reseated ourselves in the coach to await his reappearance.

It would not, in truth, be easy to conceive a set of men in more miserable pickle. The storm, instead of abating, continued to increase. The peals of thunder were tremendous. The lightning split a huge pine-tree within a few yards of us, and one of the passengers declared he was struck blind, and did not recover his sight for an hour or two. The rain beat in through the sides and covering of the carriage, as if in wantonness of triumph to drench men who, sooth to say, were quite wet enough already. In short,

> " Such sheets of fire, such bursts of horrid thunder,
> Such groans of roaring wind and rain, I never
> Remember to have heard."

From one o'clock in the morning until seven did we continue in this comfortless condition, when we were somewhat cheered by the appearance of the driver, who, we afterwards discovered, had been sleeping very comfortably in an Indian cottage in the neighbourhood. He brought with him a couple of Negroes, but no additional horses, and of course it was quite preposterous to suppose that the poor animals, who had been standing all night without food, and exposed to the storm, could now perform a task to which they had formerly proved unequal. The attempt was made, however; and to lighten the coach, our baggage was tossed out upon the road. Neither the Negroes, horses, nor passengers, could move the coach one inch from its position. There it was, and there it was destined to remain. Our last hope of extrication had now failed us, and it became necessary to find shelter and hospitality as best we could.

Luckily an Indian cottage was discovered at no great distance, where, by the help of a blazing fire, we succeeded in drying our drenched garments. In the course of the day a bullock waggon was despatched for the mail-bags and luggage, and there was evidently nothing for it but roughing it with a good grace.

On the part of those on whose privacy we had intruded, our welcome was tranquil, but apparently sincere. Our host—one of the handsomest Indians I have ever seen—spread before us his whole store of eggs, venison, and Indian corn, with the air of a forest gentleman. His two wives, with greater advantages of toilet, would probably have been good-looking, but being unfortunately rather dirty, and clad only in a blanket and blue petticoat, the sum of their attractions was by no means overpowering. The children were nearly naked, yet graceful in all their motions. Their chief amusement seemed to consist in the exercise of the crossbow.

One of the passengers produced a musical snuff-box, which occasioned great excitement in the women and children. The men were too dignified or phlegmatic to betray either pleasure or astonishment. Our host, however, was evidently delighted with an air-gun with which several birds were killed for his amusement. He then asked permission to take a shot, and hit a dollar with great accuracy at about thirty yards.

It somewhat lowered the ideas of romance connected with these Indians, to find that they are many of them slave-owners. But slavery among this simple people assumes a very different aspect from any under which I had yet beheld it. The negroes speak English and generally act as *dragomen* in any intercourse with the whites. They struck me as being far handsomer than any I had yet seen, partly perhaps from being unhabituated to severe labour, and partly from some slight admixture of Indian blood. I conversed with several, who described their bondage as light, and spoke of their master and his family with affection. To the lash they are altogether unaccustomed, and when married, live in houses of their own, round which they cultivate a patch of ground. The Negro and Indian children are brought up together on a footing of perfect equality, and the government of the family seemed entirely patriarchal.

The weather had become fine, and the day passed more pleasantly than the night. The Indian territory being beyond the reach of American law, is sought as a place of refuge by criminals, and those to whom the restraints of civilized society are habitually irksome. These men intermarry with the natives, among whom they contribute to spread guilt and demoralization. In truth, the majority are ruffians, whose proneness to crime is here alike unchecked by principle, religion, public opinion, or dread of punishment.

Towards evening two of this class came in, and chose to pass the night in drinking. Nothing more offensive than their manners and conversation can readily be conceived. After bearing patiently with this annoyance for an hour or two, it at length became intolerable, and, in order to escape, I spread my cloak in a corner of the cabin and endeavoured to sleep. But this was impossible. The noise, the demands for liquor, the blasphemy, the wrangling, were unceasing. At length one of the men drew his dirk, and attempted to assassinate his opponent, who succeeded, however, in seizing him by the throat, and both rolled upon the floor. I immediately jumped up, and the alarm roused our host, who, with the assistance of a slave, barely succeeded in saving the life of one of the combatants. He was at first insensible. His mouth was wide open; his face and lips were livid; his eyes seemed bursting from their sockets, and on being raised, his head hung down upon his shoulder. His lungs, however, made a convulsive effort to regain their action. There was a loud and sudden gurgle, and he became better. The other man was prevailed on to depart; and towards four in the morning, silence, broken only by the snoring of some of its inmates, reigned in the cottage.

Sleep, however, was impossible, under the incessant attacks of a multitude of blood-suckers, which, flea for man, would have outnumbered the army of Xerxes. But morning came, and fortunately with it a coach intended to convey us on our journey. Our host could not be prevailed on to make any charge for our entertainment, but one of his wives received all we chose to offer, and appeared satisfied with its amount. Not an article of the baggage was found missing, and on departing I shook hands with the whole establishment—Negroes included—to the great scandal of the American passengers.

Even by daylight our way was beset by difficulties. First came Kilbeedy Creek, which we crossed by as awkward and rickety a bridge as can well be imagined. Then came Pessimmon's swamp which presented a delightful corduroy road, some parts of which had been entirely absorbed by the morass. At length we reached the inn kept by an American polygamist with three Indian wives. The breakfast was no better than might be expected in such an establishment. It consisted of bad coffee, rancid venison and corn cakes, no eggs, no milk, no butter. Our host apparently had no great taste in regard to wives. One was round as a hogshead; another skin and bone; of the third I saw, or at least remember, nothing.

The meal concluded, we again set forward. Our route lay through one continued pine forest. In the course of the day we passed many Indian wigwams, and a few houses of a better order, surrounded by small enclosures. The road by no means improved, and, in order to relieve the horses, we were compelled to walk. At one place it was completely obstructed by a huge fallen tree, which delayed our progress for at least two hours. About three o'clock we dined at the house of a half-caste Indian, on the usual fare, venison and Indian corn.

In the course of the evening we passed several heights which afforded extensive, if not fine, views of the neighbouring country. The road too became somewhat better, and being composed of sand without stones, though heavy for the horses, was not uncomfortable for the passengers. For myself, I never experienced greater fatigue. During the two preceding nights, I had never closed an eye, and when, at four in the morning, we reached a small tavern, where—owing to the desertion of the moon—it was found necessary to wait till daylight, I cast myself on the floor, and in a moment was asleep.

Daylight soon came, and I was again roused from my slumbers. We were yet fourteen miles from Fort Mitchell, and for the greater part of the distance were compelled to make progress on foot. The sun rose beautifully above the dark tops of the pine-trees, but he was never gazed on by more languid eyes. At ten o'clock we reached Fort Mitchell, having in twenty-four hours accomplished a distance of only ninety miles.

Fort Mitchell is garrisoned by a detachment of the United States army, in order to prevent aggression on the Georgian frontier by the Indians. Beyond the limits of the fort there are,—if I remember rightly,—only three houses, one of which is a tavern. Its accommodations were far from comfortable, but the landlord was civil, and evidently disposed to do his best in our behalf. Under such circumstances we made no complaint, though—judging from the scantiness of our meals—his larder must have rivalled in opulence the shop of the apothecary in Romeo and Juliet.

My first effort was to procure a place in the coach to Augusta, but in this I was disappointed. Fort Mitchell seemed a sort of *trou de rat* which it was difficult to get into, and still more difficult to get out of. I was detained there for nearly a week, and never did time pass more slowly. Had my sojourn been voluntary, I should probably have found a great deal to interest and amuse, but an enforced residence is never pleasant, and but for the privilege of grumbling, would be intolerable.

The officers of the garrison lived in the hotel, and took pleasure in showing kindness to a stranger. I rode with them through the neighbouring forest, and was indebted to them for much valuable information relative to the Indians. During my stay, there was a Ball Play, in which two neighbouring tribes contended for superiority. One of these was the Creeks, the other the Ewitches, a very small tribe which occupy a district in the Creek territory, and still retain all their peculiarities of language and custom.

On the appointed morning we repaired to the scene of action, where a considerable number of spectators—chiefly Indians—had already assembled. The players on each side soon appeared, and retired to the neighbouring thickets to adjust their toilet for the game. While thus engaged, either party endeavoured to daunt their opponents by loud and discordant cries. At length they emerged with their bodies entirely naked except the waist, which was encircled by a girdle. Their skin was besmeared with oil, and painted fantastically with different colours. Some wore tails, others necklaces made of the teeth of animals, and the object evidently was to look as ferocious as possible.

After a good deal of preliminary ceremony, the game began. The object of either party was to send the ball as far as possible into their adversary's ground, and then to make it pass between two poles, erected for the purpose of demarcation. I certainly never saw a finer display of agile movement. In figure the Creek Indians are tall and graceful. There is less volume of muscle than in Englishmen, but more activity and freedom of motion. Many of the players were handsome men, and one in particular might have stood as the model of an Apollo. His form and motions displayed more of the *idéal* than I had ever seen actually realized in a human figure. The Ewitches were by no means so good-looking as their competitors.

The game is accompanied with some danger, both to those engaged in it and to the spectators. It is quite necessary for the latter to keep clear of the *mêlée*, for in following the ball, the whole body of the players sweep on like a hurricane, and a gouty or pursy gentleman could be safe only when perched on the boughs of a tree. At length the Creeks were victorious, and the air rang with savage shouts of triumph. The poor Ewitches, chop-fallen, quitted the field, declaring, however, that none but their worst players had taken part in the game. The victors danced about in all the madness of inordinate elation, and the evening terminated in a profuse jollification, to which I had the honour of contributing.

During my stay at Fort Mitchell I saw a good deal of the United States troops. The discipline is very lax, and being always separated in small detachments, they have no opportunity of being exercised in field movements. On Sunday there was a dress parade, which I attended. Little was done, but that little in the most slovenly manner. It is only justice to the officers to state, that they are quite aware of the deficiencies of the service to which they belong. "You will laugh," they said, "at our want of method and discipline, but the fault is not ours; we cannot help it. The service is unpopular, we receive no support from the government, and we have no means of maintaining proper subordination." A non-commissioned officer, who had formerly been in our service, and therefore understood what soldiers should be, in answering some questions, treated the whole affair as a joke. He entered the American service, he said, because there was easy work, and little trouble of any sort. He had no intention of remaining long in it, for he could do better in other ways. There was no steady and effective command kept over the soldiers, and yet there was a great deal of punishment. Even from the small detachment at Fort Mitchell desertions happened every week. Whenever a man became tired of his duty, off he went, bag and baggage, and pursuit was hopeless.

The truth is, that men accustomed to democracy can never be brought to submit patiently to the rigours of military discipline. The nation take pride in their navy, but none in their army. The latter service is neglected; there is no encouragement for the display of zeal in the officers, and the stations are so remote as to remove the troops entirely from public observation. The people care nothing for a set of invisible beings mewed up in some petty forts on the vast frontier, who have no enemy to contend with, and are required to brave nothing but fever and mosquitoes. Then, whena case connected with the enforcement of discipline comes before the civil courts, the whole feeling is in favour of the prosecutor. I remember a curious instance of this, which was related to me by an officer of distinction in the United Service army. A soldier found guilty, by a court-martial, of repeated desertions, was sentenced to a certain period of imprisonment, and loss of pay. The man underwent the allotted punishment, and on being liberated, immediately brought actions against all the members of the court-martial. The ground taken up was this:—The articles of war state, that whoever is guilty of desertion, shall "suffer death, or such other punishment as, by a general court-martial, shall be awarded." It was maintained, that, by this clause, the court were empowered to inflict only one punishment, and that in passing sentence of imprisonment and stoppage of pay, they had inflicted *two*. The jury gave a verdict and high damages against the members of the court, who received no assistance nor protection of any kind from the government.

On leaving Fort Mitchell we crossed the Chatahouchy—a very considerable river, of which I had never heard—and entered the State of Georgia. Our road still continued to lie through an almost unbroken pine forest, and the roads were mere sand, in which the wheels sank half up to the axles. The heat was very great. We travelled all night, and on the evening of the following day reached Macon, the most considerable place I had seen since leaving Mobile. We dined there, and again set forward. About ten at night we reached Milledgeville, where I was obliged to remain through illness, though still nearly two days' journey from Augusta, to which I had secured places.

I passed a restless and uncomfortable night, and finding the fever still increase, sent for a doctor. I asked him whether he apprehended my complaint to be fever? He answered, he certainly feared that I was suffering under the commencement of a fever of some sort, but with regard to its character or probable termination, could pronounce no opinion. In spite of the doctor's medicines, I continued to get worse. The weather was intensely hot, and I began to calculate that Milledgeville would prove the termination of my travels. But during the third night, a profuse perspiration came on, and in the morning I had the satisfaction to find that the fever was gone.

Unfortunately my strength was gone with it. I

could only walk with the greatest difficulty, and required assistance to reach the veranda. Luckily, there was a good-natured black cook, who sent me up a boiled chicken, the first food I tasted since leaving Macon. This acted as a restorative. On the day following, I could creep about the city, of which, being the metropolis of a State, it may be well to say a few words.

Milledgeville has seen better days, and presents the appearance, not of a decayed gentleman, but of a starving mechanic. Many houses have already gone to decay, and others are fast following. It stands on the Oconee river, which, unfortunately, is every year becoming shallower, to the great injury both of trade and agriculture. The country round Milledgeville is undulating, and has been tolerably cleared. At first the soil was considered excellent, but wherever the forest has disappeared, the rains and torrents from the hills have swept off the earth from the declivities, and left nothing but gravel. It is chiefly to these causes, I believe, that the decline of population and prosperity may be attributed.

The Georgian Legislature was not sitting, but

I visited the State House. It is a brick building, which some blockhead of an architect has recently thought proper to *Gothicize.* The accommodation within is plain, but sufficient. There is a portrait of General Oglethorpe, who first received a grant of the settlement from the British Crown. He is a fine-looking old martinet, with a countenance full of talent, and an air of high breeding. I was invited to visit the State prison, but felt not the smallest curiosity.

The second night after my recovery, I left Milledgeville, in the mail stage. My friend, the doctor, was a worthy and kind hearted man, who forgave me for having disappointed his prognosis. We had had a good deal of conversation during his visits, and when he came to see me off in the coach, showed more feeling on the occasion than I deserved. He squeezed me heartily by the hand, and said, "Sir, I shall never see you again, but you have my very best wishes that health and happiness may attend you." To meet with kindness unexpectedly is always pleasant, and should these pages ever meet the eye of the worthy son of Galen—whose name, unfortunately, has escaped my memory—I beg him to receive this public and grateful acknowledgment of his warm-hearted attentions to a stranger.

A journey through Georgia presents little to record. The inhabitants bear a bad character in other parts of the Union. They are, perhaps, a little savage and ferocious; and, in regard to morals, one is tempted occasionally to regret that the gibbet is not abroad in Georgia as well as the schoolmaster. From Fort Mitchell I travelled with three attorneys, two store-keepers, two cotton-planters, and a slave-dealer. My notions of the sort of conversation prevalent in Newgate may not be very accurate, but I much doubt whether it would be found to indicate such utter debasement, both of thought and principle, as that to which I was condemned to listen during this journey.

Georgia receives large accessions of population in the offscourings of other slave States. The restraints of law are little felt, and it is the only State in the Union in which I heard it publicly asserted that justice is *not* purely administered. A Georgian, with whom I conversed a great deal about his native

State, declared, that, with plenty of money, he could, with facility, escape punishment for any offence, however heinous. I enquired the mode by which so tempting an impunity was to be realized. He would, first, he said, have a touch at the sheriff, bribe the prosecutor's counsel to keep back evidence, or leave some flaw by which the proceedings might be vitiated; then, the jury—it would be odd indeed if he could not gain over some of them; but even should all fail, there was the gaoler—a sure card. In Georgia, he assured me, there was really no danger to be apprehended from law by a gentleman with heavy pockets, who carried his wits about with him.

A great part of the journey to Augusta was performed in the night. I saw enough, however, to convince me that there was no change in the general character of the scenery which I have so often described. Our supper-house was in a village called Sparta, but the landlord had gone to bed, and nothing was to be had except brandy. On the following evening we reached Augusta.

Soon after our arrival, I took a walk through the

town. It stands on the Savannah river, and is the great depôt for the cotton grown in the surrounding country, which is there shipped for Savannah or Charleston. The main street is broad, and of considerable length. There is a handsome bridge across the river, and the place altogether formed a pleasing contrast to those I had seen since the commencement of my voyage up the Alabama.

My illness at Milledgeville had left a good deal of debility, and I determined on resting a day or two at Augusta. I had brought several letters, which I despatched, and was rather surprised to find that one of them was addressed to the landlord of the tavern in which I had taken up my abode. The best introduction to people of this class is generally a well-filled pocket; but it is only fair to state, that my letter did for me, what money most probably would not. Mine host was in the highest degree civil, placed me at dinner on his right hand, was particularly attentive to the condition of my plate, and when I ordered wine, gave me, I do believe, one of the very best bottles in his cellar. He likewise conveyed me in his carriage to visit a military station in the neighbourhood, and from the respect paid him by the officers, I concluded that he of the Red Lion was a topping man in the place.

From Augusta, I should have gone down the river to Savannah, but the steamer was not to sail for five days, and I determined on proceeding by coach direct to Charleston. We had not advanced above a few miles, when a dreadful storm came on. The thunder was very loud, and the rain very heavy, but in the course of an hour or two the sky was again clear, and we at least enjoyed the benefit of travelling without dust. Our route lay through a succession of swamps and pine forests. Here and there was a rice or cotton plantation, which scarcely contributed to diminish the dreariness of the prospect.

We travelled all night, and at two o'clock on the following day reached the Ashley river, within sight of Charleston. Unfortunately, the wind was too high for crossing, and till nine at night we were forced to remain in the ferry-house, where seventeen of us were crammed together in one miserable apartment. What we should do for the night became matter of puzzle, but luckily the wind lulled, and the appearance of the ferry-boat put an end to our perplexities.

Every Englishman who visits Charleston will, if he be wise, direct his baggage to be conveyed to Jones's hotel. It is a small house, but every thing is well managed, and the apartments are good. Our party at dinner did not exceed ten, and there was no bolting or scrambling. Jones is a black man, and must have prospered in the world, for I learned he was laid up with gout,—the disease of a gentleman.

The pleasure of getting into such a house,—of revisiting the glimpses of clean tablecloths and silver forks,—of exchanging salt pork and greasy corn cakes, for a table furnished with luxuries of all sorts,—was very great. For a day or two, I experienced a certain impulse to voracity, by no means philosophical; and, sooth to say, after the privations of a journey from New Orleans, the luxury of Jones's iced claret might have converted even Diogenes into a *gourmet.*

Except New Orleans, Charleston is the only place I saw in the Southern States, which at all realizes our English ideas of a *city*. It was quite a relief, after the miserable towns I had lately passed through, to get into one bearing the impress of what—in the United States at least—may be called respectable antiquity. The public buildings are very good; and though the streets, separately taken, had nothing handsome about them, the city presents an appearance of bustle and animation which tends to redeem minor defects. The greater part of the houses are of brick, and there are many buildings of pretensions equal to any in the Union. A considerable number of the better houses are decorated by gardens, stocked with orange-trees, the pride of India, and a variety of flowering shrubs.

The city stands on an isthmus formed by two rivers, the Ashley and the Cooper. The interior abounds in pestilential marshes, which are found to be happily adapted for the cultivation of rice, and the soil, in drier situations, produces excellent cotton. These articles constitute the staples of South Carolina, and the expenditure of human life in their cultivation is very great. The miasma generated by the rice grounds is peculiarly fatal. The slaves are forced to brave it, but at the expense of health and strength. They die—fortunately, perhaps—before their time, and yet " so slowly that the world cannot call it murder."

In point of climate, I believe Charleston is fully worse than New Orleans. In the latter, creoles are entirely exempt from the ravages of the prevailing endemic. But in Charleston, there is no impunity for any class. Even native Carolinians die of fever as well as their neighbours. The chances are that if a person from the country, however acclimated, sleeps in Charleston even for a night, at a certain season of the year, he catches the fever. Should a person living in the city pass a day with his friend in the country, there is not a doctor in the place, who, on his return, would not consider him in a state of peril. In short, the people of Charleston pass their lives in endeavouring to escape from a pursuer who is sure to overtake the fugitive at last. At one season, the town is unhealthy; and all who can afford it, fly to their estates. At another, the country is unhealthy, and they take up their abode in the pine barrens. From the pine barrens, they venture back into the town, from which, in a short time, they are again expelled.

In New Orleans, a man runs a certain risk, and has done with it. If he live, he continues to eat crawfish in a variety of savoury preparations. If he die, the crawfish eat him without cookery of any sort. He has no fear of dining with his friend in the country at any season of the year. But in Charleston, a man must be continually on the alert; for, go where he may, there is fever at his heels. This continual dodging with death strikes me as very disagreeable; and if compelled to fix my residence in either city, I should certainly choose New Orleans in preference. This, however, is mere matter of taste.

I was unfortunate in the time of my visit to Charleston. On the day after my arrival, I sent round a considerable number of letters, but found almost every body out of town. Of the society of Charleston, therefore, I can say little from personal observation. But I have been assured from various quarters that it is very agreeable, and have no reason to doubt the accuracy of the statement.

Finding Charleston in this deserted state, I at once determined on returning to New York. It had been my intention to perform the journey by land, but I was assured there was no object which would repay the inconveniences of the journey. The scenery was precisely similar to that of which I had already seen so much; the people not materially different; and I confess I had become sick to the very soul, of stage-coach travelling in the south.

My plans, however, were yet undecided, when, walking along one of the quays, I saw the blue Peter flying from the topmast head of a New York packet. The temptation was irresistible. I went on board, secured berths, and in less than an hour bade farewell to Charleston from the deck of the Saluda.

During my hurried progress through the Southern States, I was rarely brought into contact with men of opulence and intelligence. Indeed I much question whether Alabama and Georgia possess any considerable class of gentlemen, in the sense in which that term is applicable to the better order of the inhabitants of the northern cities. But in South Carolina it is otherwise. There is a large body of landed proprietors, who are men of education and comparative refinement; and who, though publicly advocating the broadest principles of democracy, are in private life aristocratic and exclusive. Like the Virginians, they are of blood purely English, and disposed to relinquish no claim, which a descent from several generations of respectable ancestors can be understood to confer.

The poles are not more diametrically opposed, than a native of the States south of the Potomac, and a New-Englander. They differ in every thing of thought, feeling, and opinion. The latter is a man of regular and decorous habits, shrewd, intelligent, and persevering; phlegmatic in temperament, devoted to the pursuits of gain, and envious of those who are more successful than himself. The former—I speak of the opulent and educated—is distinguished by a high-mindedness, generosity, and hospitality, by no means predicable of his more eastern neighbours. He values money only for the enjoyments it can procure, is fond of gaiety, given to social pleasures, somewhat touchy and choleric, and as eager to avenge an insult as to show a kindness. To fight a duel in the New England States would, under almost any circumstances, be disgraceful. To refuse a challenge, to tolerate even an insinuation derogatory from personal honour, would be considered equally so in the South.

In point of manner, the Southern gentlemen are decidedly superior to all others of the Union. Being more dependent on social intercourse, they are at greater pains perhaps to render it agreeable. There is more spirit and vivacity about them, and far less of that prudent caution, which, however advantageous on the exchange, is by no means prepossessing at the dinner-table, or in the drawing-room. When at Washington, I was a good deal thrown into the society of members from the South, and left it armed, by their kindness, with a multitude of letters, of which I regret that my hurried progress did not permit me to avail myself. Many of them were men of much accomplishment, and I think it probable that Englishmen unconnected with business would generally prefer the society of gentlemen of this portion of the Union to any other which the country affords.

In passing the bar, the Saluda unfortunately ran aground, but was soon floated by the returning tide. No other accident occurred. Our voyage was prosperous, and the pleasure of inhaling the pure sea-breeze, instead of an atmosphere poisoned by marsh exhalations, very great. In six days, I had the satisfaction of again finding myself at New York.

CHAPTER VII.

JOURNEY TO NIAGARA—THE FALLS.

In one respect New York was somewhat different from what I remembered it. The gay season had passed. There were no routs, no balls, few parties of any sort; all was gravity and family seclusion. Some families had removed to the country; others were preparing for a trip to Canada or Boston. Still I had the good fortune to encounter many of my former friends, with whom I enjoyed the pleasure of renewing my intercourse.

I believe this pleasure, unsupported by reasons of greater cogency, made me imagine a fortnight's breathing-time to be necessary, between the journey just accomplished, and that which I yet meditated to Niagara and Quebec. Nothing of any consequence, however, occurred during this interval; and as I always found the flight of time to be unusually rapid at New York, the period fixed for departure soon came.

On the 30th of May I ran up the Hudson to West Point, about fifty miles from New York. The scenery, now clad in all the verdure of summer, certainly transcended every thing I had ever seen on a scale so extensive. What struck me as chiefly admirable, was the fine proportion of the different features of the landscape. Taken separately, they were not much. Every one has seen finer rocks and loftier mountains, and greater magnificence of forest scenery, but the charm lay in the combination, in that exquisite harmony of detail which produces—if I may so write—a synthetic beauty of the highest order.

> " 'Tis not a lip or cheek, we beauty call,
> *But the joint force, and full result of all.*"

The Hudson, in truth, is one of nature's felicities. Every thing is in its proper place, and of the dimensions most proper to contribute to the general effect. Add elevation to the mountains, and the consequence of the river would be diminished. Increase the expanse of the river, and you impair the grandeur of the mountains. As it is, there is perfect subordination of parts, and the result is something on which the eye loves to gaze, and the heart to meditate, which tinges our dreams with beauty, and often in distant lands will recur, unbidden, to the imagination.

At West Point is a national establishment for the education of young men destined for the army. I had letters to Colonel Thayer, the commandant, a clever and intelligent officer, who has made it his pleasure, as well as his business, to acquire an intimate knowledge of tactic in all its branches. By him, I was conducted over the establishment, and in the system of discipline and education found much to approve. The cadets wear uniform, and are habitually inured to the disagreeables—so I remember I used to think them—of garrison duty. In the evening the young gentlemen displayed their proficiency in practical gunnery, and with some light pieces made several good shots at a target across the river. The distance, I believe, was about eight hundred yards. The guns, however, were not served in a military manner, nor with that speed and regularity which are essential to the practical efficiency of the arm.

I may also observe, that the carriage of the cadets was less soldierlike than might be wished. In most of them, I remarked a certain slouch about the shoulders, which demanded the judicious application of back boards and dumb bells. But, in truth, the remark is applicable to the whole population. Colonel Thayer himself is almost the only man whom I chanced to encounter in my travels, who appeared to me to possess any thing of the true military bearing. In him it was perfect. I believe he might brave the criticism of a Sergeant-Major of the Guards.

Having passed a pleasant day at West Point, I proceeded to Dr Hosack's, about thirty miles distant. I had before visited Hyde Park in the depth of winter, I now beheld its fine scenery adorned by the richest luxuriance of verdure. Poet or painter could desire nothing more beautiful. There are several villas in the neighbourhood tenanted by very agreeable families, and had it been necessary to eat lotus in the United States, I should certainly have selected Hyde Park as the scene of my repast. But I had determined on returning to England in the course of the summer, and was therefore anxious to proceed on my journey. On the third day, I bade farewell to my kind friends—for so I trust they will permit me to call them—and again embarked on the Hudson.

The scenery above Hyde Park assumes a new character. The river leads through a gently undulating country, and its banks present a succession of agreeable villas. I passed the Catskill mountains with regret. Their aspect is fine and commanding, and I was assured the views from the summit are very splendid. I was yet undecided whether I should visit them, when a summons to dinner occasioned an adjournment of the debate. When I returned to the deck, we had passed the Catskill landing-place, and I continued my route to Albany.

Albany is the capital of the State of New York. It is finely situated on the brow of a hill which rises from the margin of the river. On the summit stands the State-house, grandiloquently called the

Capitol, a building of some extent but no beauty. None of the public buildings present any thing remarkable, but the town has an antique appearance, rare in this country, and contains some of the primitive and picturesque buildings erected by the Dutch settlers. The streets struck me as being particularly clean, and the general aspect of the place is pleasing.

I had heard much of a Shaker village in the neighbourhood, and the day following being Sunday, I drove to it with the view of seeing their form of worship. The name of this peaceful settlement is Niskayuma, and its inhabitants possess a valuable estate of about two thousand acres, which their labour has brought into high cultivation. These simple enthusiasts hold every thing in common, and their tenets, so far as I could understand them, are curious enough.

Anne Lee, a woman who came to America many years ago, and brought with her the gift of tongues and of prophecy, is the object of peculiar veneration. With such evidences of inspiration, she of course became the founder of a sect. Though herself the wife of an honest blacksmith, Mrs Lee inculcated the indispensable necessity of absolute and entire celibacy, which, on spiritual grounds, she maintained to be essential to salvation. Sensual enjoyment of every kind was expressly forbidden, and though such tenets were little calculated to allure the fair or the young, Mother Anne contrived to gather about her a society of disappointed maidens and withered bachelors,—of all, in short, who, having survived the age of passion, were content to make a merit of resigning pleasures in which they could no longer participate. The number of her followers was increased by the accession of a few less antiquated enthusiasts, and an occasional accouchement among the fair sisterhood affords matter of jest to the profane. Mother Anne has long gone the way of all flesh, but her memory is yet "green in the souls" of her followers, who speak of her as a pure incarnation of the Divine Spirit.

When I arrived, public worship had already commenced, and the congregation were engaged in singing. The music was monotonous, and the words nonsense, or something nearly approaching it. The men were drawn up on one side of the chapel and the women on the other. The latter were the veriest scarecrows I had ever seen in the female form. They were old and cadaverous, with the exception of one bright-eyed girl, whose expression bespoke a temperament little fitted for the ascetic abstinence of her sect. The men were poor-looking creatures enough, but their appearance, on the whole, was a little better than that of the women.

Both, however, were critically clean. The men were without coats, but rejoiced in snuff-coloured waistcoats and unimaginables, and white neckcloths. The charms of the women were displayed in grey gowns, and white muslin handkerchiefs, and caps nicely plaited.

The singing concluded, we had something like a sermon. One of the brethren advanced to the centre of the room or chapel, and commenced in a calm deliberate tone, as follows:—

"We can do nothing of ourselves. Every thing good in us is the gift of God. Yet man is very fond of relying on himself and his own efforts, and almost all those who have been distinguished by spiritual gifts, through all the ages of the world, have had this grand defect in their character. But the truth is, my brethren, we are all helpless without the gift of grace, and if we, who have separated ourselves from the world, retiring from its temptations, and renouncing its pomps and vices, find ground for spiritual pride in this devotion of ourselves to the service of God, we are guilty of a very great sin, and a sin more unpardonable in us than others, because our light is greater. I would impress this on you, therefore, not to be vainglorious on account of the favour you have found in the sight of God, but to go on steadily, humbly, gratefully, and submissively, looking neither to the right hand nor the left, remembering always that your kingdom is not of this world, but of another and a better. Thank God for all his mercies, my brethren, but be not therefore puffed up."

After this we had another song, quite as nonsensical as the former, which was followed by a second discourse. The preacher on this occasion was a fat jolly-looking man, whose comfortable plight formed something of a contrast with the mummy-like aspect of his brethren. The only remarkable portion of the discourse was the peroration, in which he addressed himself particularly to those, who, like myself, had visited the meeting from motives of mere curiosity.

"Strangers, I would address myself to you. What motives brought you to this place of worship, I know not. Some may have come to join in our devotions, but the greater part of you, I fear, have come only to see the peculiarities of our worship. To this we do not object. We court no concealment in any thing we do, but we demand of you in return, that you offer no indecent interruption to our religious solemnities. I beseech you to remember that we are Christians like yourselves—that we are engaged in offering adoration to the great God who fashioned us all as we are. If you do not respect us, respect yourselves; and however ridiculous our forms may appear to you, we entreat that you will at least not interrupt our devotional exercises by any demonstration of contempt."

After such an appeal it became impossible for the most graceless spectator to offer any thing like insult to these simple fanatics. During the dance which followed, however, I confess I had a good deal of difficulty in maintaining due composure. On a given signal the whole congregation began singing and dancing with all their vigour. I observed that the more youthful and active introduced a few supererogatory gyrations, which were not attempted by the senior members; and one boy in particular signalized himself by a series of spirited saltations, not very dissimilar to the Highland fling. My attention, too, was attracted by the two preachers, who, though somewhat fallen into "the sere, the yellow leaf," kept capering about with the lightness and grace of cart-horses, till the very end of the performance.

The dance lasted for about a quarter of an hour, and I could not help sympathizing with the suffering performers. The weather was intensely hot, and the whole *corps de ballet* were thrown by their movements into a state of the most profuse perspiration. This circumstance produced a change in the condition of the atmosphere by no means pleasant, and, without waiting the conclusion of the service, I took my departure.

From the Shaker settlement I drove to the Cohoes Falls, about five miles distant. The Mohawk, a river about as large as the Severn, comes foaming down, throws itself over a precipice of about seventy feet with great majesty, and then flows calmly onward to its confluence with the Hudson. The sight was very noble, and after enjoying it about half an hour, I set out on my return to Albany.

The junction of the Champlain and Erie canals, near Troy, is considered a sight to which the admiration of travellers is justly due. Why, I know not. To my ignorant vision there seemed nothing remarkable. The canals are united, and there is an end of it. Of the amount of difficulties overcome I do not pretend to be qualified to judge.

A little above Troy I observed a crowd collected on the river, and found they were attracted by the ceremony of baptism, which two Baptist clergymen were performing on sundry proselytes. The first subject of immersion was an old lady, whose cold and shivering appearance excited my compassion. She was led in by one of the clergymen till the water reached her middle, when they both—somewhat rudely, I thought—seized the dowager by the shoulders, and throwing her back with a sudden jerk, soused her over head and ears in the water before she seemed aware of their intentions. Luckily, the poor woman escaped absolute suffocation, and with an aspect something like that of a drowned rat, was supported to the shore. Her sufferings, however, did not terminate here. The word *snuff* was written on the nose of one of the clergymen so legibly, that he who ran might read. I observed that immediately after employing his pocket-handkerchief in its most appropriate function, he applied it to the eyes of the patient matron! This was even worse than the ducking

At Albany a traveller has the choice of proceeding by stage-coach or canal I preferred the former, and accordingly secured places for Utica. The coach was full, and the heat so excessive, that till we reached Schenectady, I do not know that I ever experienced greater suffering. There, however, our fellow-travellers embarked on the canal, and the rest of the journey was performed in comparative comfort. The road—one of the roughest I ever travelled—winds along the banks of the Mohawk, through a country which presents many noble features. In point of cultivation, however, it appeared very inferior to what might be expected in so populous a district. The greater part of the journey was performed by night, yet not in darkness, for we had the light of a brilliant moon, which softened without obscuring the landscape.

About eleven o'clock on the following morning, we reached Utica, a handsome and flourishing town, which exhibits every external mark of prosperity. After dinner I engaged what is called an "extra exclusive" to convey me to Trenton Falls, a distance of fifteen miles. We did not reach Trenton till after nightfall, and I was obliged to delay the gratification of my curiosity till the following morning. The inn, however, was very comfortable, and after the jolting of the previous night, the attractions of clean sheets and a well-stuffed mattrass were by no means inconsiderable. After breakfast on the following morning, I sallied forth to visit the falls. They are formed by the West Canada creek in its passage through a glen or ravine about two miles in length, in the course of which it descends about three hundred feet. As may be supposed in such circumstances, the stream rushes onward with great violence. There are several falls, none of which are without beauty, and the whole scenery struck me as bearing strong resemblance to that of Roslin glen, to which, except in romantic associations, it is in nothing inferior.

The fall which pleased me most is one in which the torrent takes a double leap, the last of which is about forty feet. The surrounding rocks are grand and precipitous, and their crevices afford nourishment to trees which are writhed into a thousand fantastic forms. There is one sad drawback, however. At precisely the most beautiful point of the scene there has been erected—what, good reader? —but you will never guess—a *dram shop!*

How utterly so wild and beautiful a scene is degraded by the presence of a drinking shop may readily be conceived; and the outrage on taste; and even decency, is the more gratuitous, since the spot on which the building is erected is not above a mile from the hotel.

On such occasions one is betrayed unawares into

writing strongly. But *cui bono?* A writer may appeal to a moral sense, but he cannot create one; and assuredly the man whose imagination turns to the brandy bottle, even when gazing on the noble scenery of Trenton, will think of it in the death-agony.

Being still sore from the jolting of the stage-coach, I determined to proceed by the canal, and at two o'clock on the following day went on board the passage-boat. There were about forty passengers; the heat of the cabin was intolerable. Driven from within, I took a seat on deck, but without diminution of suffering. I found myself exposed to the full fervour of the sun, and the boards were literally burning to the feet. Add to this the nuisance of the numerous bridges, the arches of which are barely high enough to admit the passage of the boat, and leave to the passengers only the option of descending every time they approach one, or of being swept off by a more summary process.

The country through which we passed consisted chiefly of marshy forest, such as I had traversed for many a weary league in the south. Every here and there a town had sprung up in the wilderness, but with nothing to interest the spectator, who sees everywhere but one process and one result. He looks for the picturesque, and finds the profitable, and wishes from the bottom of his heart they had been found compatible.

The Americans are dilettanti in nomenclature. In following the course of the Erie Canal, a traveller will pass through Troy, Amsterdam, Frankfort, Manlius, Syracuse, Canton, Jordan, Port Byron, Montezuma, Rome, Smith's, Dumkin's, Carthage, Salina, Rochester, Ogden, Geddes, and Palmyra. The Eternal City here dwindles into "a half-shire town, which contains a court-house and gaol, and is pleasantly situated on the old canal!" So says the guide-book. Amsterdam is more fortunate, for it boasts "a post-office, a church, and about fifty houses or stores." Palmyra is charmingly located on Mud Creek. Carthage derived its consequence from a bridge which "fell under the pressure of its own weight." The maxim, *delenda est Carthago*, therefore, is likely to be realized in the new world as well as in the old.

Such absurdities are fair game, for they have their

origin in vanity. To adorn their cities by monuments of art is an expensive indulgence, from which Americans are content to abstain. But pretension of name costs nothing, and is found everywhere.

During the day the number of passengers increased to about sixty, including twenty ladies; and where this large party were to be stowed for the night, it was not easy to anticipate. In the cabin there was no appearance of sleeping berths by day, but at night ranges of shelves were put up, and the chairs, benches, and tables, were all converted into beds. The portion of the cabin destined for the use of the ladies was obscured from observation by a curtain. In order to prevent partiality, there was a sort of lottery, in which each person drew forth a number which determined his position for the night. Fortune fixed me on the table, and there I lay with the knee of one man thrust directly into my stomach, and with my feet resting upon the head of another. The sheets were offensively dirty, and the blankets not much better.

The Americans dread the circulation of pure air; and those in the vicinity of a window insisted on its being closed. Under these circumstances, the atmosphere became not only hot, but poisonous, and the act of inhalation was performed with disgust. Then there were legions of mosquitoes, whose carnival, from the use they made of it, seemed to have been preceded by a lent; and to crown all, at least a dozen noses were snoring bass to an unmelodious treble which proceeded from the ladies' division of the cabin.

One night of this kind was enough; and so, at Montezuma, being anxious to see something of the smaller lakes, of whose beauty I had heard a great deal, I removed into another packet-boat, and diverging into a branch canal which communicates with the Seneca lake, at night found myself in Geneva. The town makes a handsome display on an eminence near the northern extremity of the lake. It contains some three or four thousand inhabitants, several churches, and a school dignified by the name of a college. Near to the lake are a few pretty villas, and in the town a considerable number of respectable houses, built of brick or stone. Geneva is the depôt of the produce of the neighbouring country. It comes by the lake, and is then embarked on the canal for New York.

Seneca is a fine sheet of water undoubtedly, but its scenery—so far as I saw it—presents nothing of remarkable beauty. It is about forty miles long, with a mean breadth of three or four. It is navigated by a steam-boat, in which, had the weather been cooler, I should probably have made a trip. As it was, the temptations of an arm-chair and a cool veranda were irresistible.

The banks of the Seneca, like those of the Gareloch, have been the chosen seat of miracles. Some years ago, a woman called Jemima Wilson, announced herself as the Saviour of the world, and attracted a few followers somewhat more mad than herself. While her miraculous endowments were displayed only in the jabbering of unknown tongues, and unintelligible predictions, she stood on safe ground, but unluckily her ambition pointed to the honour of more palpable miracles. " Near Rapelyeas ferry," says the Northern Tourist, " the frame is still standing which Jemima constructed to try the faith of her followers. Having approached within a few hundred yards of the shore, she alighted from an elegant carriage, and the road being strewed by her followers with white handkerchiefs, she walked to the platform, and having announced her intention of walking across the lake on the water, she stepped ankle-deep into the clear element, when suddenly pausing, she addressed the multitude, enquiring whether they had faith that she could pass over, for if otherwise, she could not; and on receiving an affirmative answer, returned to her carriage, declaring, that as they believed in her power, it was unnecessary to display it." Miss Campbell, I believe, with similar pretensions, has been equally prudent in putting them to the proof.

On the night following, I left Geneva, by the Rochester stage. By day-dawn, we reached Canandaigua, which stands at the northern extremity of a beautiful lake, of which I caught a few glimpses in the moonshine. Canandaigua is a pretty village, and certainly the situation has a good deal of charm. More attention seems to have been paid here than elsewhere, to external decoration. The better houses are surrounded by ornamental trees, and the number of these is so considerable as to give a character to the place. In general, however, I have not been struck with, what in this country are called, "beautiful villages." These consist almost uniformly of rows of white framework houses, with green blinds and shutters; but they are flimsy in point of material, and the colours are too glaring to harmonize with the surrounding scenery.

We reached Rochester under the influence of a burning sun. The hotel was excellent, and the luxury of cold baths, and the civility of the landlord, induced me to delay progress till the following day. In the cool of the evening, I strolled out to see the falls of the Genesee. The height of the uppermost is considerable, being about ninety feet, and the water rushes over it gracefully enough, but the vicinity of sundry saw and corn mills has destroyed the romantic interest which invested it in the days when "the cataract blew his trumpet from the steep," amid the stillness of the surrounding forest.

The old proverb *de gustibus, &c.* receives illustration in every country. An eccentric man, called Sam Patch, having an aversion to honest industry, made it his profession to jump over all the waterfalls in the country. Niagara was too much for him, but he sprang from a lofty rock, some distance below the Horse-shoe fall, with impunity. His last jump was at the fall I have just described of the Genesee, in the autumn of 1829. From a scaffold elevated twenty-five feet above the table rock, making a descent altogether of a hundred and twenty-five feet, he fearlessly plunged into the boiling cauldron beneath. From the moment of his immersion, he was seen no more. His body was not discovered for many months, and was at length found at the mouth of the river, six miles below.

Rochester is a place worth seeing. Twenty years ago there was not a house in the neighbourhood, and now there is a town, containing thirteen thousand good Americans and true, with churches, banks, theatres, and all other oppidan appurtenances to match. Such growth is more like forcing in a hot-bed, than the natural progress of human vegetation. For a great deal of its prosperity, Rochester is indebted to the Erie canal, which brought its advantageous proximity to Lake Ontario into full play.

The canal runs through the centre of the town, and crosses the Genesee by an aqueduct which, according to the Northern Tourist, " cost rising of 80,000 dollars," whatever sum that may amount to. There are several streets in Rochester which might be backed at reasonable odds against any in Hull or Newcastle, to say nothing of Cork, Falmouth, or Berwick-upon-Tweed. The appearance of the shops indicates the prevalence of respectable opulence. Those of the jewellers display a stock of Paris trinkets and silver snuff-boxes. There are silks and Leghorn bonnets for the seduction of the ladies, and the windows of the tailors are adorned by coloured prints of gentlemen in tight fitting, swallow tails, with the epigraph, " New York fashions for May."

After passing a comfortable day and night in the Eagle tavern, which I strongly recommend to all future travellers, I took my departure from Rochester in the Lockport stage. We travelled by the " ridge road," which is composed of hard sand, and extends along what has evidently in former times been the embankment of Ontario. This ridge road, therefore, is entirely of nature's making, and I shall die in the belief that it is the very best in the United States. The coach rolled on as smoothly as it could have done between London and St Albans, and I began to think of reading, to have attempted which, in other portions of my peregrination, would have been strongly indicative of insanity.

I am aware of little which merits record in the journey to Lockport, except the unwonted luxury in which it was performed. Towards evening, we passed a camp meeting, to which several of the passengers directed their steps, and which, under other circumstances, I should have been glad to visit. We passed also several parties of what were called Mormonites, going to join a settlement established by their founder, in Ohio. Relative to this sect, of which I had never before heard, I gleaned the following particulars from one of the passengers. A bankrupt store-keeper, whose name I think was Smith, had an extraordinary dream. It directed him to go alone to a particular spot, distinctly indicated, where he was to dig to a certain depth. This dream was of course treated as a mere delusion, and, as is usual in such cases, was thrice repeated, with denunciation of heavy punishment in case of disobedience.

In this emergency, Smith judged it more prudent to shoulder his spade, than by further obstinacy to excite the vengeance of some unearthly intelligence. Having dug to the requisite depth in the place commanded, he found a book with golden clasps and cover, and a pair of elegantly mounted spectacles, somewhat old-fashioned to be sure, but astonishing magnifiers, and possessing qualities which it might puzzle Sir David Brewster to explain on optical principles.

Smith had some difficulty in undoing the clasps of this precious volume, but on opening it, though his eyes were good, it appeared to contain nothing but blank paper. It then occurred to him to fit on his spectacles, when, lo! the whole volume was filled with certain figures and pot-hooks to him unintelligible. Delighted with his good fortune, Smith trudged home with the volume in his pocket and the spectacles on his nose, happy as bibliomaniac who has been lucky enough to purchase some rare *Editio Princeps* "dog cheap" from the ignorant proprietor of an obscure bookstall. On reaching his own house, his first care was to secure his miraculous treasures from profane observation; his second, to copy out a page or two of the characters, and look about for an interpreter. His search was long fruitless, but at length he hit on precisely the two individuals who were qualified conjointly for the office. One of these gentlemen possessed the faculty of reading the hieroglyphics, and the other of interpreting them. It then appeared that the volume in question was entitled the book of Mormon, a converted Rabbi, who flourished in the days of our Saviour, or shortly after, and who, by the aid of divine inspiration, wrote the treatise in question in elucidation of all the dark points of religion which, to the present day, continue to puzzle theologians.

Smith's worldly prospects now brightened. With this invaluable treatise in his strong box, he commenced business afresh, under the firm of Mormon, Smith, and Co , and appears to possess an unlimited credit on the credulity of his followers. He has set up an establishment something similar to that of Mr

Owen, and already boasts a considerable number of opulent believers.

We slept at Lockport, in a dirty and uncomfortable tavern. In the morning we were again in motion. At Lewiston, a village on the frontier, I quitted the stage, and despatched a messenger across the river to secure an *extra exclusive* for Niagara. The delay occasioned by breakfast to an impatient traveller is generally not great, and entering the ferry-boat, I soon found myself once more on British ground. At Queenston, judging from their accent, the majority of the inhabitants are Scotch; and certainly to my ear the Doric of my country never sounded so musical before. About a mile from the landing place, are the heights of Queenston, which, during the late war, were gallantly and successfully defended by a small body of British, under Sir Isaac Brock, against an American force nearly ten times their number. The latter, however, consisted chiefly of militia; and had the achievement not unfortunately been rendered memorable by the death of the British leader, it would probably, like most other events of the war, have been forgotten. Its memory, however, has been perpetuated by the erection of a trophy column on the summit of the height. It is composed of freestone, and about a hundred-and-twenty feet high. I am not sure that in point of architecture it is quite faultless. The shaft struck me as wanting height in proportion to its diameter, and the general outline somewhat resembles that of an apothecary's phial. Were it surmounted by a statue, the effect would undoubtedly be improved.

The Niagara at Queenston is about a quarter of a mile broad; the current is rapid, and the depth very great,—not less, I believe, than two hundred feet. The colour of the water is a nondescript and very beautiful shade between azure and green. The banks for several miles are high and precipitous, and covered with the primeval forest.

Having reached Queenston, horses were immediately harnessed to a light open carriage, and we rattled off. The distance is about seven miles, and the road very tolerable. As we advanced, both eye and ear were awake to detect indication of our increasing proximity to the Falls. At length a cloud of white vapour, rising high above the foliage of the distant forest, announced the situation of the great cataract. Shortly after, I could detect a hollow rumbling sound like that of thunder; but though the distance was every instant diminishing, it did not proportionately increase in loudness or intensity.

About twelve o'clock I found myself in Forsyth's hotel, a large and not uncomfortable house, about half-a-mile distant from the Great Horse-shoe Fall. It stands upon a high level of table land, and from the upper balcony the Falls are distinctly visible. To a stranger visiting Niagara for the first time, I do not know that this circumstance is very desirable, and I confess the view did in my own case carry with it something of disappointment. The truth is, that from Forsyth's you see the upper portion of the Fall; but at least one half of the descent, the boiling cauldron below, and the impenetrable mass of vapour with which it is sublimely and mysteriously encanopied, you do not see.

No sooner had I reached the hotel, than the morning, which had been louring with dark and threatening clouds, set in with an absolute tempest of wind and rain. It was impossible to rest, however, before gazing on the great wonder which I had travelled so far to behold; so throwing on my cloak, I sallied forth, bidding defiance to the elements. The banks which descend to the bed of the river were very steep, and so slippery, that I encountered more than one tumble in my progress. But this was nothing; and most amply was I repaid for all the troubles of my journey, when in a few minutes I found myself standing on the very brink of this tremendous yet most beautiful cataract.

The spot from which I first beheld it was the Table rock, and of the effect produced by the overwhelming sublimity of the spectacle, it is not possible to embody in words any adequate description. The spectator at first feels as if stricken with catalepsy. His blood ceases to flow, or rather is sent back in overpowering pressure on the heart. He gasps, " like a drowning man," to catch a mouthful of breath. " All elements of soul and sense " are absorbed in the magnitude and glory of one single object. The past and future are obliterated, and he stands mute and powerless, in the presence of that scene of awful splendour on which his gaze is riveted.

In attempting to convey to those who have never visited the Falls, any notion of the impression which they produce, I believe it impossible to escape the charge of exaggeration. The penalty is one which I am prepared to pay. But the objects presented by Niagara are undoubtedly among those which exercise a permanent influence on the imagination of the spectator. The day—the hour—the minute—when his eye first rested on the Great Horse-shoe Fall, is an epoch in the life of any man. He gazes on a scene of splendour and sublimity far greater than the unaided fancy of poet or painter ever pictured. He has received an impression which time cannot diminish, and death only can efface. The results of that single moment will extend through a lifetime, enlarge the sphere of thought, and influence the whole tissue of his moral being.

I remained on the Table rock till drenched to the skin, and still lingered in the hope that some flash of the lightning—which had become very vivid—might disclose the secrets of the cloudy and mysterious cauldron, into which the eye vainly endeavoured to penetrate. But I was disappointed. Far overhead the fearful revelry of the elements still continued; but the lightning seemed to shun all approach to an object of sublimity equal to its own.

My window in the hotel commanded a view of the Falls, and their deep and hollow roar was at all times distinctly audible. I mention this, because, during the whole period of my stay, the circumstance was accompanied by serious annoyance. At night it was impossible to enjoy any thing which could be called sleep. Whenever I closed my eyes, there was a torrent foaming before them. Amid the darkness of midnight I was still gazing on the Horse-shoe, and the noise of the cataract, mingling with these visions of a perturbed imagination, contributed to keep up the delusion. My dreams were of rapids and waterfalls, and the exhaustion produced by this state of continual fever became so great, that by day I often wandered to the quiet recesses of the forest, where, undisturbed by the din of waters, I might enjoy a comfortable nap.

On the day after my arrival, the weather having

fortunately become fine, my hours were devoted to the Horse-shoe, which I viewed from every favourable point. About half a mile below, there is a shantee or log tavern, where brandy is attainable by gentlemen of sluggish temperament, who, surrounded by such objects, still require the stimulus of alcohol. From this tavern there is a circular wooden stair which leads down into the bed of the river, and on descending, I found myself at once immersed in a region of eternal moisture. By dint of scrambling along the *debris* of the overhanging rocks, I contrived to approach within a short distance of the Fall; and so powerful is the impression here produced, that a considerable time elapses before the spectator can command his faculties in a sufficient degree to examine its details. He stands amid a whirlwind of spray, and the gloom of the abyss, the dark firmament of rock which threatens destruction to the intruder, the terrors of the descending torrent, the deep thunder of its roar, and the fearful convulsion of the waters into which it falls, constitute the features of a scene, the sublimity of which undoubtedly extends to the very verge of horror.

The epithet of "the Horse-shoe" is no longer applicable to the greater Fall. In the progress of those changes which are continually taking place from the attrition of the cataract, it has assumed a form which I should describe as that of a semi-hexagon. The vast body of water in the centre of this figure, descends in one unbroken sheet of vivid green, and contrasts finely with the awful perturbation of the cauldron. But towards either extremity it is different. The water there, at the very commencement of its descent, is shivered into particles inconceivably minute, and assumes a thousand beautiful forms of spires and pinnacles, radiant with prismatic colours.

In the vast receptacle beneath, the water is so comminuted, and blended with air carried down by the cascade—probably to the depth of many hundred feet—that none but substances of the greatest buoyancy could possibly float on it. The appearance of the surface is very remarkable. It is that of finely triturated silver, in which, though the particles are in close proximity, there is no amalgamation. The whole mass is in convulsive and furious agitation, and continues so until, having receded to a considerable distance, the commotion gradually diminishes, and the water reassumes its ordinary appearance.

It is possible to advance to a considerable distance behind the cascade, and I determined to accomplish the achievement. Having marshalled my energies for the undertaking, I continued to advance, but the tempest of dense spray became suddenly so violent as apparently to preclude the possibility of further progress. I was driven back several yards, half suffocated and entirely blinded. But the guide encouraged me to proceed, and accordingly, *Teucro duce*, I made another and more successful effort. Having penetrated behind the Fall, the only footing was a ledge of rock about two feet broad, which was occasionally narrowed by projections in the face of the cliff. But even under these circumstances the undertaking is one of difficulty, rather than of danger. A great portion of the air carried down by the cataract is immediately disengaged, and the consequence is, that an intruder has to encounter a strong breeze which blows upwards from the cauldron, and sometimes even dashes him with unpleasant violence against the rock along which he is scrambling. As a practical illustration of this, our conductor plunged fearlessly down the precipitous rock to the very edge of the gulf, and was immediately blown back, with little effort of his own, to our narrow pathway.

At length, having advanced about fifty yards, the guide informed me that further progress was impossible. I had certainly no objection to retrace my steps, for my lungs played with extreme difficulty, and the hurricane of wind and spray seemed to threaten utter extinction of sight. It was impossible, however, to depart without gazing on the wonder I had visited. Far overhead was a canopy of rock; behind the perpendicular cliff. In front, the cascade—a glorious curtain—seemed to hang between us and the world. One's feelings were those of a prisoner. But never, surely, was there so magnificent a dungeon!

The noise of the great cataract is certainly far less than might be expected. Even at its very brink, conversation may be carried on without any considerable elevation of the voice. The sound is that of thunder in its greatest intensity, deep, unbroken, and unchanging. There is no hissing nor splashing; nothing which breaks sharply on the ear; nothing which comes in any degree into collision with the sounds of earth or air. Nothing extrinsic can either add to, or diminish its volume. It mingles with no other voice, and it absorbs none. It would be heard amid the roaring of a volcano, and yet does not drown the chirping of a sparrow.

Visitors generally wish, however, for a greater crash on the tympanum, for something to stun and stupify, and return home complaining that Niagara is less noisy than Trenton or the Cohoes. This is a mistake. The volume of sound produced by the Horse-shoe Fall, is far greater than they ever heard before, or probably will ever hear again. When the atmosphere is in a condition favourable to act as a conductor of sound, it may be heard at a distance of fifteen, and even twenty miles. A passenger in the coach, who lived six miles beyond Lewiston, assured me, that in particular states of the barometer, the noise was there distinctly perceptible. But it should be remembered that the great body of sound is generated in a cavern far below the level of the surrounding country, and fenced in on three sides by walls of perpendicular rock. The noise vibrates from side to side of this sunless cavity, and only a small portion escapes into the upper air, through the dense canopy of spray and vapour by which it is overhung. As an experiment, I employed a man to fire a musket below, while I stood on the Table rock. The report was certainly audible, but scarcely louder than that of a popgun.

Having devoted three days to the Horse-shoe, I rode up the river to survey its course above the Falls. Shortly after issuing from Lake Erie, the Niagara is divided by a huge island about seven miles in length. Lower is another island, of smaller dimensions, and having passed these, the river is about two miles in breadth, and tranquil as a lake. At Chippewa, about three miles above the Falls, navigation terminates. A short distance below, the stream evidently begins to accelerate its motion. There are no waves, however, nor is there any violent agitation of the current; nothing, in short, which seems to presage the scene of terrific agitation so soon to ensue. Further down is Goat Island, which divides the river into two branches, and forms the separation between the Falls. It is at the higher extremity of this island, that the rapids commence.

The grandeur of these rapids is worthy of the cataracts in which they terminate. In the greater branch, the river comes foaming down with prodigious impetuosity, and presents a surface of agitated billows, dashing wildly through the rocks and islands. This scene of commotion continues till within about thirty yards of the Fall. There the great body of the stream resumes its tranquillity, and in solemn grandeur descends into the cloudy and unfathomable abyss. Never was there a nobler prelude to a sublime catastrophe!

I at length crossed to the American side. If there were no Horse-shoe Fall, the American would be the wonder of the world. Seen from below it is very noble. The whole body of water is at once shattered into foam, and comes down in a thousand feathery and fantastic shapes, which, in a bright sunshine—as I beheld them—were resplendently beautiful.

But the form of the American fall is unfortunate. A straight line is never favourable to beauty, and the cataract descends, *not* into a dark abyss of convulsed and fathomless waters, but amid fragments of rock, from which it again rushes onward to the main bed of the river. In short, a traveller from the Canadian side has very little disposable admiration to lavish on this splendid object, and generally regards it with a cold and negligent eye.

In order to reach Goat Island, it is necessary to cross two bridges. One of these certainly is a very remarkable work. It leads across a rapid of tremendous velocity, and does honour to the engineer by whom it was constructed. Goat Island is covered with wood, and by the public spirit of its proprietor, General Porter, has been intersected with walks, trending to the different points from which the finest views may be commanded. From this island, a bridge—or rather pier—has been erected, which leads the spectator to a point where the frail structure on which he stands is directly over the great abyss of the Horse-shoe. As a trial of nerve, this is very well. The man, assuredly, has strong ones, who, from the extremity of this platform, can look beneath without quivering in every muscle. The prevailing feeling is that of horror, and a spectator partial to inordinate excitement, may here get enough of it. But his eye can rest only on a small portion of the Fall, and the position is decidedly unfavourable for pictorial effect.

The bridge is but a fragile structure, and vibrates with every motion, especially at the extremity where it is necessarily without support. I stood there for about a quarter of an hour, and should probably have remained longer, but the near approach of a gentleman, whose dimensions indicated a weight of twenty stone, induced me to retrace my steps with all convenient speed.

In the neighbourhood of the Falls, one can think of nothing else. They affect all thoughts and impulses, the waking reverie, and the midnight dream. Every day of my stay it was the same. Scarcely was breakfast concluded, when, putting a book in my pocket, I sallied down to the river, to lose and neglect the creeping hours of time, in the neighbourhood of the Horse-shoe. About a quarter of a mile above, the stream had deposited a number of huge trees, and I employed several men to launch them successively into the stream, while I stood on the extreme point of the Table rock to observe their descent. One by one, the vast masses—each fit for the mast of "some high ammiral"—came floating down, sometimes engulfed in the foaming eddies, sometimes driven with fury against the rocks, and then rushing onward with increased velocity, till, reaching the smooth water, the forest giants were floated slowly onward to the brink of the precipice, when they were seen no more.

Nothing which enters the awful cauldron of the Fall, is ever seen to emerge from it. Of three gun-boats which, some years after the termination of the war, were sent over the Falls, one fragment only, about a foot in length, ever was discovered. It was found near Kingston, about a month after the descent of the vessels.*

* Before quitting the subject of the Falls, I would willingly say something which may be of use to future visitors. It is usual with these persons to take up their abode at Manchester, and give the first day or two to the American Fall, and Goat Island. This strikes me as bad policy. The American Fall is just fine enough to impair the subsequent impres-

The country around Niagara is picturesque, and in a fine state of cultivation. English habits of agriculture evidently prevail. There is a greater appearance of neatness than I have seen anywhere in the United States. The fences are in excellent order,

sion of the Horse-shoe. By adhering to this routine, visitors come to the latter with an appetite partially sated, and the effect of the first burst of this sublime object is diminished. I would advise all travellers, therefore, to proceed first to Forsyth's, but by no means to indulge in any preliminary view of the Falls from the windows or balcony. Let the visitor repair at once to the Table rock, and there receive his first impression of the cataract. I would recommend him next to proceed lower down on the Canadian side, where there are many points from which he may become master of the general grouping of the landscape. His attention may then be directed to the rapids; and to see them to advantage, he should walk as far as Chippewa, and return—with a little scrambling and wading it is very possible—by the margin of the river. On the day following, let him descend to the bed of the river, and gaze on the cataract from below. Having done this, he may cross to the American side, and from midway on the river, he will see the only view of the Falls which I think it possible for the painter to give with any thing like adequate effect. Nothing, in truth, can be more splendid than the amphitheatre of cataracts by which he there seems almost surrounded.

With regard to the time which a traveller should give to the Falls, it is impossible to fix on any definite period. The imagination requires some time to expand itself, in order to take in the vastness of the objects. At first, the agitation of nerve is too great. A spectator can only *gaze*—he cannot *contemplate.* For some days the impression of their glory and magnitude will increase; and so long as this is the case, let him remain. His time could not be better spent. He is hoarding up a store and the fields are not disfigured by stumps of decaying timber. The farms are in general large; many contain two hundred acres of cleared land, and their owners are reputed wealthy. I dined with one of these gentlemen, and found comfort combined with hospitality. But of the lower orders in the Upper Province, it is impossible to speak favourably. They have all the disagreeable qualities of the Americans, with none of that energy, and spirit of enterprise, which often convert a bad man into a useful citizen. They are sluggish, obstinate, ignorant, offensive in manner, and depraved in morals, without loyalty and without religion. Of course, in a country to which the tide of emigration sets in so strongly, and

of sublime memories for his whole future life. But intimacy—such is our nature—soon degenerates into familiarity. He will at length begin to gaze on the scene around him with a listless eye. His imagination, in short, is palled with excess of excitement. Let him watch for this crisis, and whenever he perceives it, pack up his portmanteau and depart. Niagara can do nothing more for him, and it should be his object to bear with him the deepest and most intense impression of its glories. Let him dream of these, but return to them no more. A second visit could only tend to unsettle and efface the impression of the first. Were I within a mile of Niagara, I should turn my steps in the *opposite* direction. Every passing year diminishes our susceptibility, and who would voluntarily bring to such objects a cold heart, and faded imagination?

a mass of imported principle and intelligence is annually mingled with that of native growth, such observations must necessarily be limited in their application. I would be understood, therefore, as speaking chiefly of the older settlers, who consisted in a great measure of the refuse of disbanded regiments, and of adventurers who brought with them neither capital nor character. Of late years Canada has been enriched by the addition of a number of naval and military officers, whom these piping times of peace have left without professional employment. Men of property and enterprise have likewise embarked large sums in the improvement of this fertile region; the expenditure of the British government has enriched the province with works of great splendour and utility; industry is unfettered, taxation almost unknown; and with such elements of prosperity, Canada may now safely be trusted to her own resources.

CHAPTER VIII.

JOURNEY TO QUEBEC.

Having passed a week at Niagara, and seen the Falls under every aspect, in cloud and sunshine, in storm and calm, by star and moonlight, I took my departure. About four miles below is a very remarkable whirlpool, which I visited on my way to Fort George. This whirlpool is caused by the protrusion of a bed of rock across the rectilinear course of the river. The stream comes down with great impetuosity, and, when driven back by this obstacle, the current whirls round the basin with prodigious violence, and at length escapes in a direction nearly at right angles with its former course. The water has the appearance of molten lead, and the people in the neighbourhood declare that from the eddies of this vortex nothing living can escape. Even boats have been absorbed by them, and, when this happens, there is no possibility of help from the shore. The boat upsets, and the men are drowned; or if not, the boat is kept whirling round with the stream for perhaps a fortnight together, and the men are starved. Such were stated to be the horns of the dilemma.

Fort George is a military station at the mouth of the river, and the works, originally built of turf, have been suffered to go to decay. It is better it should be so, for it would be easy at any time to throw up others, and all immediate expense is avoided. On the opposite side is the American Fort Niagara, which, though built of stone, does not present an aspect much more formidable than its British rival. The latter was garrisoned by a party of the 79th regiment, and I own the pleasure with which I saw, in this remote district, our national flag and uniform, was very great. I no longer felt as a stranger in the land, and caught myself almost unconsciously doing the honours to a very pleasant party of Americans whom I accompanied in a ramble through the ruinous entrenchments and dismantled works.

A steam-boat starts daily from Fort George, for York, the capital of Upper Canada. I certainly never made a trip in a more comfortable vessel. It was commanded by a half-pay officer of the navy, and in point of cleanliness and nicety of arrangement, formed a strong contrast to the larger and more splendid vessels of the United States. Our steamer started about twelve o'clock. In five hours we had crossed the extremity of Lake Ontario, and were safely landed in York. In a body of water so extensive, one does not see a great deal of the scenery on shore. I saw enough, however, to convince me that the shores of Ontario are flat and devoid of beauty.

York has few objects to interest a traveller. It stands in a level and marshy country, and contains about five thousand inhabitants. It was once—I believe twice—taken by the Americans during the war, and is in truth a place scarcely capable of defence. There is no commanding point for the erection of a fort or battery; and the only one at present existing, could afford very inadequate protection in case of attack. The place, however, is prosperous, and the price of building ground struck me as very high. The Government house is of wood—rather a singular circumstance, since brick is a common building material in the town.

There is a college at York, which seems to be conducted on judicious principles. The public buildings are just what they ought to be, plain and substantial. In passing through the streets, I was rather surprised to observe an *affiche* intimating that ice creams were to be had within. The weather being hot, I entered, and found the master of the establishment to be an Italian. I never eat better ice at Grange's.

Having passed a day at York, I sailed in a very noble steamer, called the Great Britain, to Prescott, at the northern extremity of the lake. Our day's voyage presented nothing remarkable, but at night it came on to blow very hard, and our vessel, though one of the largest class, kept pitching very disagreeably. In the morning no land was visible, the waves were very high, and Ontario—not unsuccessfully—seemed to ape the Atlantic. Towards the middle of the lake the water is of a deep blue colour.

We stopped for an hour at Kingston, a place of considerable population, and certainly far better adapted than York to become the capital of the province. Its situation is so strong, as to afford complete security from a *coup de main*, and there is a fort which completely commands both town and harbour. In the dockyard there are two seventy-fours on the stocks, the building of which was arrested by the peace.

During the war, Kingston, from its fine harbour, and other natural advantages, was a place of much consequence. Sacketts harbour, the rival American port, is altogether inferior. The manner in which the lake warfare was conducted, affords a fine specimen of the folly and ignorance of a British Government. Frigates were sent out in frame to a country covered with the finest timber, and the mere expense of conveying these from Montreal to Kingston, was far greater than similar vessels could have been built for on the spot. The Navy Board were particularly careful that the armaments should not suffer from a deficiency of water-casks, though it was only necessary to drop a bucket to procure water of the finest quality from the lake; and to crown the absurdity, an apparatus for distilling sea water was supplied for each vessel!

Having passed Kingston, we were fairly in the St Lawrence, and the scenery became very striking. Towards evening we passed through that portion of the river called the Lake of the Thousand Isles. Nothing could be more beautiful, when seen in the light of a brilliant sunset. The islands are of all sizes—some only a few yards in extent, others upwards of a mile. One could fancy many of them to be—what they are not—the retreat of innocence and peace. Their number has never been correctly ascertained, but is generally estimated to be near two thousand.

The voyage terminated at a miserable village called Prescott, where we supped, slept, and breakfasted. I had been fortunate in meeting a detachment of the 71st regiment on board the Great Britain, who were about to descend the St Lawrence in batteaux to Montreal. The officers obligingly invited me to join their party—an arrangement too agreeable to be declined. The detachment consisted of about fifty men and three officers, and four boats were provided for their accommodation. One of these, intended for the officers, was fitted up with an awning, and by a judicious arrangement of the cloaks and portmanteaus, the whole party were comfortably provided with seats.

About ten o'clock we started. The boatmen were all natives of the Lower province, and spoke English with difficulty. A merrier set of beings it is scarcely possible to imagine. The buoyancy of their spirits was continally finding vent in song or laughter, unless when we approached a rapid, or our commander, tired of the incessant noise, thought proper to enjoin silence.

The rapids of the St Lawrence rank in the first order of sublimities They are caused by a great contraction and sudden descent in the bed of the river, and are generally accompanied by numerous islands and rocks in the middle of the stream.

The river, thus pent up and obstructed, is thrown into violent perturbation, and rushes onward with tremendous fury, roaring, dashing, and foaming in a manner truly formidable to weak nerves. When one looks at the turbulence of the waters, and the terrific eddies and whirlpools into which they are thrown by the conflict of opposing currents, it at first seems impossible that a boat can escape being dashed to pieces, and in truth it is only by the most skilful pilotage that such a consummation is avoided. The life or death of a party is often decided by a single touch of the helm, and it is occasionally necessary to pass even within a yard or two of a spot where keel never crossed without instant destruction.

On approaching any formidable rapid, all is silent on board. The conductor is at the helm, and each of the crew at his post. All eyes are steadfastly fixed on the countenance of th helmsman, whose commands seldom require to be expressed in words. Every look is understood and obeyed, with the promptitude of men who know their peril. Accidents rarely occur, and in truth the danger is just imminent enough to create a pleasant degree of excitement in the voyager. He knows that he is not safe, and that his chances of life depend on the skill and steadiness of the boatmen. The probability of safety, however, greatly preponderates; and the risk of being dashed to mummy on the rocks, though sufficiently strong to excite his imagination, wants power to perturb it.

A few hours after leaving Prescott, we entered the first rapid. It is called the Long Sault, and extends for about nine miles. We did the whole distance in little more than twenty minutes, and at some places our motion seemed rapid as that of a bird. One portion of the rapid, called the Big Pitch, is particularly formidable. The river is there divided by an island into two arms of nearly equal dimensions, and the descent must be very great, for the stream dashes through the rocks with fearful violence, and sends up pyramids of spray.

The chief point of danger, however, is where the branches, having passed the island, are again united. Men may talk of the charge of hostile armies, and no doubt a poet may spin very pretty, and even sublime verses out of such matter. But the charge of hostile torrents is altogether a more magnificent affair, and who shall describe the "dreadful revelry" of their conflict? At the Big Pitch, the two arms of the St Lawrence rush against each other with a thundering roar, and are shivered into spray by the violence of the concussion. The whole surface of the river boils like a cauldron, and the water on either side is driven back from the centre to the margin in a multitude of eddies and whirlpools. It is only by slow degrees that the commotion ceases, and the ordinary aspect of the river is restored.

In passing the scene of this alarming struggle, the boat for about a minute reeled and staggered very disagreeably, and two or three waves burst over us. Before we had time, however, to clear the water from our eyes, the Big Pitch was past, and we were borne forward on water comparatively smooth.

We slept at a poor village, the name of which I forget. Our boatmen, who had all day been pulling at the oars, like true Canadians, instead of going to bed, got up a dance with the village girls, and the ball was only stopped by the re-embarkation of the party on the following morning. The whole crew were drunk, with the exception of the conductor, but the appearance of the first rapid sobered them in an instant.

Our course now lay through Lake St Francis. There was not a breath of wind, and the assistance received from the current was very trifling. The lake is nearly thirty miles long, and about ten or twelve in breadth. At its lower extremity is the village of St Regis, where the boundary line of the United States leaving the St Lawrence, the river becomes exclusively Canadian.

We breakfasted at Coteau du Lac, and shot through another rapid with the speed of an arrow. In order to facilitate the communication between the provinces, canals have been made, by which these rapids may be avoided. The shores of the St Lawrence are chequered with patches of cultivation, but not so much so as materially to affect the general character of the scenery. Among rivers of first-rate magnitude, I imagine the palm of beauty must be yielded to the St Lawrence. In its aspect there is no dulness, no monotony. It is continually changing from the rapid to the lake, from excessive velocity of current to still and tranquil water, on which, but for sail and oar, the motion of the boat would be imperceptible.

Perhaps no two rivers afford a stronger contrast than the Mississippi and the St Lawrence. The scenery of the former is flat and unchanging; of the latter, infinitely diversified. The water of the Mississippi is ever dark and turbid; the St Lawrence is beautifully clear. The Mississippi traverses a continent, and enlarges gradually from a mountain rivulet into a mighty river. The St Lawrence is an Adam at its birth. It knows no childhood, and attains at once to maturity. The current of the Mississippi is smooth and equable; that of the St Lawrence rapid and impetuous. The volume of the Mississippi is continually influenced by the vicissitudes of season; it annually overflows its banks, and spreads a deluge over the surrounding region. The St Lawrence is the same at all seasons; rains neither augment its volume, nor do droughts perceptibly diminish it. The channel of the St Lawrence leads through a succession of lakes. There are no lakes connected with the Mississippi. The

St Lawrence, on approaching the termination of its course, gradually expands into a noble bay; and amid a region bounded by forest and mountain, mingles almost imperceptibly with the ocean. The Mississippi pours its flood into the Gulf of Mexico by a number of branches flowing through a delta formed by the diluvium of its own waters.*

Nor is their effect on the spectator less different. The one is grand and beautiful; the other awful and sublime. The St Lawrence delights the imagination; the Mississippi overwhelms it.

I shall not linger on the voyage. We passed the Cedar rapids and the Cascades, both of which are considered more dangerous than the Long Sault. But their character is the same, and I shall spare the reader the trouble of perusing certain long descriptions which I find in my journal. Suffice it to say, that at nightfall our voyage terminated at La Chine, a village nine miles from Montreal.

The inn was tolerable, but it must be confessed that

* Those who wish to see this parallel followed out with greater minuteness, I beg to refer to Mr Stuart's Travels in the United States, and those of Mr Hodgson.

the Canadian hotels are inferior to those of the United States, while the charges are considerably higher. There is no arrangement, no zeal to oblige, and the amount of civility at the disposal of a traveller is very limited. In the United States, an Englishman becomes accustomed to indifference, and has rarely to encounter insolence. In a country like Canada, subject to the British crown, he is apt to expect more, and the chances are that he will find less.

On the day following, I drove to Montreal, and was certainly agreeably surprised by the appearance of the city. It stands on an island, about thirty miles long, and at a short distance from the mountain whose name it bears. The houses are entirely constructed of stone; and the neatness of the buildings, and the general air of solidity and compactness, have a very pleasing effect to an eye accustomed to the trashy clap-board edifices of an American town. It is the fashion in Montreal to cover the roofs of the houses with tin, so that in looking down on it from the neighbouring heights, the city glitters with a mirror-like brightness. In the higher part of the town are some handsome streets, and the public buildings are in the best taste—plain, substantial, and without pretension of any sort. The suburbs are embellished by a number of tasteful residences, which are often surrounded by pleasure-grounds of considerable beauty. The inhabitants are hospitable; and the establishments of the more wealthy combine elegance with comfort.

The population of Montreal is about 30,000. The great majority of the mercantile class are English; but the lower orders, both in language and appearance, decidedly French. Their dress is at once primitive and peculiar. Like the Spaniards, they wear a sash of coloured worsted round the waist, a jacket, generally of blue or brown, and shoes fashioned after the Indian mocassin. The natives of the Montreal and Quebec districts are distinguished by the colour of their caps. The former wear the *bonnet bleu;* the latter, the *bonnet rouge.*

The prevailing religion is the Catholic; and the Cathedral does honour to the taste and spirit of the inhabitants. It is built of a bluish limestone, and of a fabric so substantial, that it bids fair to outlast every church now extant in the United States. The style of architecture is Gothic; and the only defects which struck me, are a bareness of ornament, —attributable, I imagine, to a deficiency of funds,— and a glare of light, which injures the effect of the interior.

There are several convents in Montreal, one of which I visited, in company with an eminent merchant of the city. The building is commodious and extensive, and the establishment consists of a *mère supérieure*, and twenty-four nuns. Its funds, which are considerable, are devoted to purposes of charity; and I saw a little troop of orphans, whom they support and educate. There is likewise an hospital for the insane and incurable, which I declined visiting. I saw several of the sisters,—pale, unearthly-looking beings,—who, accustomed to the ministrations of the sickbed, flit about with noiseless steps, and speak in a low and subdued tone. Their garb is peculiar. It consists of a gown of light drab, plain muslin cap, black hood, a sort of tippet of white linen, and the usual adjuncts of rosary and crucifix.

The interest excited by this pious and benevolent

institution was certainly not diminished by the communications of my companion. "It is impossible," he said, "that I can look on this establishment, without feelings of the deepest gratitude. Thirty-five years ago, I came to this city a penniless and friendless boy; and I had not one friend or connection in the colony from whom I might expect kindness. Shortly after my arrival, I fell sick. I could not work, and was utterly destitute of the means of subsistence. In this situation, these charitable nuns received me into this house, nursed me with tenderness, through a long and grievous illness, and supplied me with the means of support, until, by my own labour, I was enabled to rid them of the burden. By God's providence, I have prospered in the world. I am now rich, but never do I pass the gates of this institution without a silent blessing on its humble and pious inmates."

Lord and Lady Aylmer were in Montreal, and their presence rendered it at once the scene of gaiety and hospitality. I passed a week there, with great pleasure, and then embarked in one of those magnificent steamers which ply on the St Lawrence for

Quebec. The distance between the cities is a hundred and eighty miles, which is generally accomplished in about twenty hours.

As we approached Quebec, the scenery became more wild and mountainous. Cultivation rarely extends beyond a mile or two from the river, and agriculture appears to be conducted by the Canadians of the Lower Province on the worst principles. To me, they appeared a light-hearted and amiable people, who brave the chances of life, with apathy to its sufferings, and a keen sensation of its enjoyments. No contrast in human character can be greater than that exhibited by the inhabitants of Lower Canada and the United States. The one, averse from all innovation, content to live as his fathers have done before him, sluggish, inert, and animated by strong local attachment to the spot of his nativity. The other, active and speculating, never satisfied with his present condition, emigrating wherever interest may direct, and influenced in every circumstance by the great principle of turning the penny. The Canadian is undoubtedly the more interesting; but, on the standard of utility, I fear Jean Baptiste must yield the *pas* to Jonathan.

Quebec bears on its front the impress of nobility. By the most obtuse traveller, it cannot be mistaken for a mere commonplace and vulgar city. It towers with an air of pride and of menace—the menace not of a bully, but of an armed Paladin prepared for battle. No city in the world stands amid nobler scenery. The heights bristling with works; the splendid and impregnable citadel frowning on Cape Diamond; the river emerging in the distance from the dark pine forest, with its broad expanse covered with shipping; the Isle of Orleans reposing in tranquil beauty amid its waters; and the colossal ranges of mountains which close the prospect;—constitute an assemblage of splendid features, which may be equalled, but can scarcely be surpassed.

Till I landed from the steam-boat, Quebec was to me a mere abstraction, which it pleased my imagination to invest with attributes of grandeur. But the first aspect of the lower town contributed to dissipate the charm. It extends over a narrow ledge at the foot of the precipice. The streets are dirty and narrow—the *trottoirs* so much so, that two people can scarcely pass without jostling. It is in this quarter that merchants most do congregate; and here are the exchange, the custom-house, the banks, and all the filth and circumstance of inglorious commerce.

The pomp of war is displayed in a loftier region, which is approached by a very steep street leading upward through a natural cleft in the brow of the mountain. In the higher town are the court and the camp, the Castle of St Louis on its lofty pedestal of rock, with a formidable array of towering ramparts for their defence. In this quarter no sign of traffic is discernible, and the sound of military music, the number of soldiers in the streets, the sentinels in their solitary walk along the ramparts, and the vociferous revelry of young and idle officers, strike with pleasing novelty on the senses of a traveller from the United States.

The fortnight I passed at Quebec is associated with pleasant memories. By the officers of the 32d regiment I was admitted an honorary member of their mess; and I request these gentlemen to accept my thanks for the many agreeable hours spent in their society. I enjoyed the pleasure, too, of encountering an old military friend, with whom I had long served in the same corps. More recently, we had travelled together on the continent of Europe, and now, by one of those unanticipated chances which occasionally brighten life, we were again thrown together, with what feelings it is unnecessary to describe

At Montreal, Lord Aylmer had obligingly furnished me with a letter of introduction to Colonel Cockburn, the commandant of artillery; and the advantages I derived from it were very great. Colonel Cockburn is an accomplished artist, with a delicate perception, and fine feeling of the beauties of nature; and it was under his guidance, and generally in his company, that I visited the surrounding scenery.

My first excursion was to the falls of Montmorenci, about eight miles from the city. On emerging from the city gate, we crossed the St Charles, and then pursued our course through a pleasant and well-cultivated country, interspersed with villages. It was a holyday of some sort, and the inhabitants were all abroad clad in their best, and gay as the more fortunate inhabitants of less wintry regions. The heights of Montmorenci are interesting as having been the scene of Wolfe's first attack on Montcalm. It was unsuccessful. The French occupied an entrenched position on the summit, from which it was found impossible to dislodge them. About six hundred of Wolfe's army fell in the attempt.

The falls are very fine, but have unfortunately been disfigured by the erection of a mill on the very summit of the precipice; but the view from a platform adjoining this building is magnificent. The entire height of the fall is two hundred and forty feet, and though the body of water is—in summer, at least—of no great magnitude, it thunders down the steep with astonishing majesty, and makes glorious turmoil in a huge basin surrounded on three sides by precipitous cliffs. About a mile above is a geological curiosity called "the natural steps," which appear to have been worn in the rock by the attrition of the stream. These are so regular as to make it difficult to believe that art has had no share in their formation.

Close to the city are the Plains of Abraham. Traces of field works are yet visible, and an oval block of granite marks the spot on which Wolfe expired. About a mile higher is Wolfe's Cove, where he landed during the night, and the fearful cliff up which he led his followers to victory. A redoubt on the summit was carried by escalade, and by daydawn the army was formed in order of battle on the heights. Montcalm instantly quitted his entrenchments at Beaufort to meet him. By ten o'clock the armies were engaged, and in two hours the power of France on the American continent was annihilated.

Wolfe died young, and his name bears something of a melancholy charm to the ear of every Englishman. Yet there appear no grounds for attributing to him the qualities of a great general. His first attempt was a failure, and the second was successful only from the blunder of his opponent. In accepting battle, Montcalm gave up all his advantages. Had he retired into the city, Quebec never could have been taken. Winter was rapidly approaching, (the battle took place on the 12th of September,) and siege was impossible.

A monument has been erected to the memory of these brave men. It is an obelisk copied from some of those in Rome, and bears two Latin inscriptions, which to ninety-nine out of every hundred who look on it are unintelligible. There is nonsense and pedantry in this. The inscriptions should have been in French and English.

The citadel has been strengthened and rebuilt at an enormous expense. It perfectly commands both the city and the river, and is so strong, that in all human probability it will ever remain a virgin fortress. At all events, those who have skill, courage, and energy to wrest it from the grasp of British soldiers, will deserve to keep it. Assuredly their national annals will record no more brilliant achievement.

The chateau of St Louis is now converted into the residence of the Governor. It stands on the verge of a precipitous rock, down which it seems in danger of tumbling. In point of architecture it has nothing to boast. There is a total want of massiveness and grandeur.

The other public buildings are principally religious. The convents, which are numerous, I did not visit. The cathedral is a massive stone edifice, without ornament of any sort. The walls in the interior display a good many pictures, which I had not patience to examine The grand altar is as magnificent as waxen virgins and gilt angels can make it.

New York and the Canadas are the chosen regions of waterfalls. Their opulence in this noble feature is unrivalled. I had already seen many, but there were still many to be seen. I confess my appetite for cataracts had become rather squeamish, yet I walked nine miles under a burning sun to see that of the Chaudiere. It is still embosomed in the forest, whose echoes for many thousand years it has awakened. The wild commotion of the river contrasts finely with the deathlike quietude of all other objects. It was June, yet there were no birds pouring melody through these dismal woodlands. How different are the Canadian forests from the woods of Old England! *Living* nature was silent; *inanimate* spoke only in that voice

> ——— " which seemed to him
> Who dwelt in Patmos, for his Saviour's sake,
> The crowd of many waters."

The Chaudiere is about the size of the Tweed. The perpendicular height of the fall is upwards of a hundred feet. The finest view is from a ledge of rock projecting into the river about fifty yards below. The water in the basin, or, as it is called, the *Pot*, boils as water never did in pot before. It then dashes down a succession of rapids, and continues to fume, and toss, and tumble, until finally swallowed up by the St Lawrence. The sight is fine and impressive. No traveller should leave Quebec without visiting the Chaudiere.

The village of Loretto is a melancholy sight. It contains the last and only remains of the once powerful tribe of Huron Indians. Brandy and gunpowder have done their work, and about two hundred of this once noble people are all that survive. They have adopted the religion, and speak the language, of the Canadians. There is a church in the village, and a priest who mingles with his flock, and is beloved by them. Christianity is the only benefit for which the red man is indebted to the white. The latter cheats, robs, corrupts, and ruins him in this world, and then makes a merit of saving him in the next. The benefit is pure, but these poor Indians may reasonably distrust the gift, when there is blood on the hand by which it is bestowed.

The legislative bodies were not sitting, and I know nothing of Canadian politics. There is a Mr Papineau, however, who plays with great spirit the part of a colonial O'Connell. The field is not large, but he makes the most of it, and enjoys the dignity of being a thorn in the side of each successive governor. Mr Papineau and his party are continually grumbling at being subject to British dominion; but what would they have? They pay no taxes. John Bull spends his money pretty freely among them, as they may see by the works on Cape Diamond, and the Rideau Canal. The latter must be of immediate and great benefit to both provinces; but had the Canadians been left to their own resources, it could never have existed. What would they have? The Lower Province, at least, will not join the United

States; and it is too poor, and too helpless, to set up for itself. Withdraw British capital from the colony, and what would remain? Rags, poverty, and empty harbours.

With regard to the Upper Province, the time is fast approaching when it will join the United States. Every thing tends towards this consummation. The canals which connect the vast chain of lakes with the Ohio and the Hudson, must accelerate its advent. The Canadian farmer already has easier access to the markets of New York and New Orleans than he has to that of Quebec. The mass of the people are republicans in politics, and anarchists in morals. Let them go. The loss to England will be trifling. The eagle does not droop his wing for the loss of a feather.

It is well, however, that British statesmen should steadily contemplate this event, and direct their policy accordingly. Let them not hope to conciliate this people by concession. "The mighty stream of tendency" cannot be arrested in its progress. But it will become a matter of grave consideration whether a province so circumstanced should be enriched by any further expenditure of British revenue—whether England is still to lavish millions in building fortresses and constructing canals—and whether it be not, on the whole, more consonant to political wisdom, to leave the improvement of this vast region to individual enterprise, and the results of an unshackled industry.

The Canadians may rely on it, that whenever a considerable majority of the people become hostile to the continuance of British connexion, they will find little difficulty in achieving their independence. England could hold them in subjection by the bayonet; but she will not use it. She will bid them farewell; give them her blessing, and leave them to follow their own course. Whether they will be happier or more prosperous, is a question which another century must probably determine.

When Lower Canada first came into the possession of Great Britain, the latter committed a great error in not insisting that her language should be adopted in all public instruments. The consequence is, that eighty years have passed, and the people are still French. The tie of community of literature does not exist, and the only channel by which moral influence can be asserted or maintained has been wantonly closed. The people read—when they read any thing—French books; French authorities are quoted in the law courts; the French language is spoken in the streets; French habits, French feelings, French prejudices, abound everywhere. The lapse of three generations has witnessed no advancement, moral or intellectual, in the Canadians of the Lower Province. They are now precisely what they were at the period of the conquest.

Another decided blunder was the separation of Canada into two provinces. This has prevented any general amalgamation of the population. One province is decidedly French; the other no less exclusively English, or American. The latter enjoys a milder climate, and more fertile soil, and increases in wealth and population far more rapidly than its rival. It is to the Upper Province that the whole tide of emigration is directed. It is with the produce of the Upper Province that the ships navigating the St Lawrence are freighted; Lower Canada exports little but lumber.

The French Canadians, therefore, oppose every improvement by which the rival province may be benefited, and, with such feelings, collision on a thousand points is unavoidable. Internal improvement is impeded, for there could be no agreement as to the proportion of contribution to be furnished by each province. The breach instead of healing, is annually widened, and Upper Canada is thrown into an intercourse with the United States, the result of which I have already ventured to predict.

The government of Canada may in one sense be called a bed of roses, for it is full of thorns. Every governor must find it so. He has to deal with men of mean minds and selfish passions; to maintain the necessary privileges of the Crown; to prevent the rational freedom of a limited monarchy from degenerating into the unbridled license of democracy. He is beset by clamour, and assailed by faction, and must either become the leader of one party, or offend both. His difficulties and embarrassments increase. He appeals for support to his government, and receives a letter of thanks and his recall.

Such has been the story of many governors of these troublesome provinces, and will probably be that of many more. But if any man be calculated to conciliate all the passions and prejudices of the Canadians, it is Lord Aylmer. His amiable character, his kind yet dignified manners, his practical good sense, his experience of business, and extensive knowledge of the world, can scarcely fail to exert a salutary influence in soothing the asperities of party, and exposing the motives of turbulence, by depriving it of excuse. At the period of my visit to Canada, I rejoice to say it was so. In every society, I heard the new governor spoken of with respect, and even the "sweet voices" of the populace were in his favour.

The travels of the Schoolmaster have not yet led him to these wintry regions. Few of the lower order of Canadians can read, and the education even of the more wealthy is very defective. The ladies resemble those of the United States, and are subject to the same prematurity of decay. But they are pleasing and amiable, though given to commit sad slaughter among sensitive and romantic subalterns. The older stagers are generally charm-proof, and the marriage of a major is an event as remarkable in the colony as the appearance of a comet.

CHAPTER IX.

JOURNEY TO NEW YORK.

I LEFT Quebec with regret, for it was necessary to bid farewell to an agreeable circle, and an old friend. The voyage to Montreal presented nothing remarkable, and, after passing a few days in that city, I prepared to return to the United States.

After crossing the St Lawrence to Longueuil, it was discovered that a portmanteau had been left at Montreal. My servant accordingly returned in the steam-boat, while I was forced to wait several hours for his reappearance in a very miserable tavern. After all, this compulsory arrangement was not unfortunate. The heat was intense, and travelling, if not impossible, would have been very disagreeable. In order to pass the time, I bathed in the river, read all the old newspapers the house could afford, and, finally—discovering that the luxury of sofas was unknown at Longueuil—went to bed.

Why this dirty and paltry village should be more tormented by flies than other places, I know not. Every room in the tavern absolutely swarmed with them. Myriads of these detestable insects, duly officered by blue-bottles, kept hovering around, and perched in whole battalions at every favourable opportunity on the face and hands of the victim. Under these circumstances, a siesta was impossible, and, on descending to dinner, I could at first discern nothing but four dishes of flies. The sight was not calculated to increase appetite, and during the meal a woman with a large fan was obliged to defend the table from their approach. It was not till evening that my servant returned with the portmanteau, and having procured a carriage, I lost not a moment in escaping from a village which appeared to suffer under a plague, unparalleled since the days of Pharaoh.

The road to Chambly was execrable, and the journey both tedious and disagreeable. I passed the night there, and on the following morning proceeded to St John's. The road follows the course of the Sorell, which at St John's is somewhat more than a mile in breadth. A steam-boat, fortunately, was about to sail for Whitehall, at the southern extremity of Lake Champlain, and in ten minutes I was on board. From St John's, the river gradually widens, till it reaches Isle Aux Noix, a post of some strength, which is occupied by a British garrison. Here the traveller bids farewell to Canada, and enters the territory of the United States.

Lake Champlain is a beautiful sheet of water, about 140 miles long, with a mean breadth of about five or six. The surrounding country is undulating, and in most places yet unredeemed from a state of nature. It was the theatre of many interesting events in the early history of the colonies. Traces of the forts at Ticonderago and Crown Point are still visible.

We passed Plattsburg, the scene of the unfortunate naval action in 1814. I was then serving in the colonies, and had a good deal of correspondence with Commodore Sir James Yeo, relative to the charges he afterwards exhibited against Sir George Prevost.* The historian who would illustrate by facts the almost incredible amount of folly, ignorance, and imbecility, by which the arms of England may be tarnished, and her resources wasted with impunity, should bestow a careful examination on the details of the Plattsburg expedition. He will then precisely understand how war can be turned into child's play, and its operations regulated, as in the royal game of Goose, by the twirl of a teetotum.

On the following morning I quitted the steam-

* When the order for retreat was given, Sir Manly Power, who commanded a brigade, rode up to Sir George Prevost, and thus addressed him :—" What is it I hear, Sir George? Can it be possible that you have issued an order to retreat before this miserable body of undisciplined militia? With one battalion I pledge myself to drive them from the fort in ten minutes. For God's sake, spare the army this disgrace. For your own sake—for the sake of us all—I implore you not to tarnish the honour of the British arms, by persisting in this order." Sir George simply answered, " I have issued the order, and expect it to be obeyed."

In addition, it is only necessary to add, that the fort was of mud, that its garrison was only 3000 militia, while the retreating army consisted of 10,000 of the finest troops in the world. To heighten the disgrace, there was considerable sacrifice of stores and ammunition! It is deeply to be lamented, that the death of Sir George Prevost, shortly after his recall, prevented the investigation of his conduct before a court-martial.

boat, and, procuring a cart for the conveyance of my goods and chattels, walked across the mountains to Lake George. The scenery of this lake is celebrated, and though I visited it with high expectations, they were not disappointed. Lake George is thirty-six miles long, but rarely more than five broad. In form, it resembles Windermere, but its features are bolder and more decided. The country, in general, is yet unreclaimed, and the sides of the mountains are clothed with wood to the summit. Embosomed in the lake are many beautiful islands, only one of which appeared to be inhabited. Here and there the shore was diversified by cultivation, and occasionally, near some quiet and retired haven, stood a log cottage, with which the fancy delighted to connect a thousand pleasing associations.

The steam-boat which conveyed us through this beautiful region was somewhat old and rickety, and her progress slow. For the first time in my life I considered this an advantage. It was pleasant to linger in such a scene, to resign the spirit to its tranquil influence, to people the memory with fresh images of beauty, and at leisure to behold those objects on which the eye was destined to gaze but once.

The voyage terminated at Caldwell, a small village at the southern extremity of the lake. The inn was comfortable, and in the evening, having nothing better to do, I took a ramble in the neighbourhood. About half a mile distant are the remains of a British fort, called Fort William Henry. It was erected in 1755, by Sir William Johnson, and attacked in the same year by a French force under Baron Dieskau. The assailants were repulsed with great slaughter, and the loss of their general. In the following year, however, it was invested by Montcalm, at the head of 10,000 men. Colonel Munro, the governor, made a gallant defence, but was at length forced to capitulate. The whole garrison were afterwards treacherously attacked and massacred by the Indians attached to Montcalm's army. The fort was destroyed, and has never since been rebuilt.

On the following morning, I left Caldwell in the stage for Saratoga Springs, the Cheltenham of the United States. The road lay through a country of diversified features, and in a state of tolerable cultivation. It was only the end of June, yet the corn was yellow in the ear, and in many places the harvest had already commenced. The crops were luxuriant, and the wheat ears struck me as larger than any I had ever seen in England.

The Falls of the Hudson, which I stopped to examine, had not much to excite the admiration of a traveller fresh from Niagara and Lower Canada, yet they are fine in themselves; and if the imagination could abstract them from the numerous saw and corn mills they are employed to set in motion, and represent them as they were in the days when the bear and panther lorded it in the surrounding forest, and the wild-deer came to slake his thirst in their basin, doubtless the impression would be very striking. A fine waterfall is confessedly a noble feature in a landscape; but when the surrounding objects are found to be utterly inconsistent with grandeur and harmony of effect, the eye turns from the scene with disappointment, and a sentiment even allied to disgust. We feel that nature has been defaced, and that utility has been obtained at the expense of a thousand picturesque beauties and romantic associations.

There are people, no doubt, who are quite satisfied with seeing a certain mass of water precipitated from a given height, no matter by what process or in what situation. The cataract makes a grand splash, and they are satisfied. Their eye is offended by no inconsistencies, their ear by no discords. For them, there are no sublimities in nature, nor vulgarities in art. For minute and delicate beauty they have no eye, and estimate rock or mountain as they measure broadcloth, by the yard.

A blessing be on all such. They are honest men, no doubt, and useful. Their taste in dry goods may be unexceptionable, and they probably feel the whole beauty of a landscape—on a China basin. They will travel far to see a waterfall, or a lion, and if the former be made to turn a mill, or the latter a spit, their enjoyment will sustain prodigious augmentation.

Saratoga has all the appearance of a watering-place. There is a certain smartness about it; an air of pretension, like that assumed by a beau, who devours his shilling's worth of boiled beef, in the

Coal-Hole, or the Cheshire-Cheese. It may be called a village of hotels, for they abound in every street, and give a character to the place. These establishments are on a large scale; and that in which I took up my abode can accommodate two hundred visitors.

To this village, company flock in summer from all parts of the Union; and the Congress, annually assembled there, affords a fair representation of all the beauty and fashion of the Union. The truth is, that such is the unhealthiness of the climate in all the Atlantic cities, from New York to New Orleans, that their inhabitants are forced to migrate for several months, in order to lay in a stock of health for the consumption of spring and winter. All direct their course northward. Some visit the sea; others make a trip to Niagara, and Canada; but by far the greater number are to be found congregated at Saratoga.

When on the subject of climate, I may just mention, that there is no topic on which Americans are more jealously sensitive. It delights them to believe that theirs is in all respects a favoured land;

that between the St Lawrence and Mississippi the sky is brighter, the breezes more salubrious, and the soil more fertile, than in any other region of the earth. There is no harm in all this; nay, it is laudable, if they would only not insist that all strangers should view the matter in the same light, and express admiration as rapturous as their own.

Judging from my own experience, I should certainly pronounce the climate of the northern and central States to be only one degree better than that of Nova Scotia, which struck me—when there in 1814—as being the very worst in the world. On making the American coast, we had four days of denser fog than I ever saw in London. After my arrival at New York, in November, the weather for about a week was very fine. It then became cloudy and tempestuous, and during the whole period of my residence at Boston, I scarcely saw the sun. At Philadelphia, there came on a deluge of snow, by which the ground was covered from January till March. At Baltimore, there was no improvement. Snow lay deep on the ground during the whole period of my residence at Washington, and the roads were only passable with difficulty. On crossing the Alleghany Mountains, however, the weather became delightful, and continued so during the voyage to New Orleans. While I remained in that city, three days out of every four were oppressively close and sultry, and the atmosphere was damp and unpleasant to breathe. During my journey from Mobile to Charleston, though generally hotter than desirable, the weather was in the main bright and beautiful; but the very day of my arrival at the latter place, the thermometer fell twenty degrees; and in the 33d degree of latitude, in the month of May, the inmates of the hotel were crowding round a blazing fire. On my return to New York, I found the population still muffled in cloaks and greatcoats, and the weather bitterly cold. Not a vestige of spring was discernible, at a season when, in England, the whole country is covered with verdure. During the last week of May, however, the heat became very great. At Quebec, it was almost intolerable, the thermometer ranging daily between 84 and 92°. At New York, in July, the weather was all a salamander could desire; and I embarked for England, under a sun more burning than it is at all probable I shall ever suffer from again.

In the Northern and central States—for of the climate of the Southern States it is unnecessary to speak—the annual range of the thermometer exceeds a hundred degrees. The heat in summer is that of Jamaica; the cold in winter that of Russia. Such enormous vicissitudes must necessarily impair the vigour of the human frame; and when we take into calculation the vast portion of the United States in which the atmosphere is contaminated by marsh exhalations, it will not be difficult, with the auxiliary influences of dram-drinking and tobacco-chewing, to account for the squalid and sickly aspect of the population. Among the peasantry, I never saw one florid and robust man, nor any one distinguished by that fulness and rotundity of muscle, which everywhere meets the eye in England.

In many parts of the State of New York, the appearance of the inhabitants was such as to excite compassion. In the Maremma of Tuscany, and the Campagna of Rome, I had seen beings similar, but scarcely more wretched. In the "fall," as they call it, intermittent fevers come as regularly as the fruit season. During my journey, I made enquiries at many cottages, and found none of them had escaped the scourge. But enquiries were useless. The answer was generally too legible in the countenance of the withered mother, and in those of her emaciated offspring.

It seems ridiculous to compare such a climate with that of England, and yet there is nothing to which Americans are more addicted. It is a subject regularly tabled in every society. "How delightful our climate must appear to you," observed a lady, "after the rain and fogs of your own country!"—"Whether, on the whole, do you prefer our climate or that of Italy?" enquired a gentleman of New York, in a tone of the most profound gravity. My answer, I fear, gave offence, for it became the signal for a general meteorological attack. "I was three months in England," observed one, "and it rained every hour of the time."

Though attached to the soil of my country, I had really no inclination to vindicate its atmosphere. I therefore simply replied, that the gentleman had been unfortunate in the period of his visit. But I was not suffered to escape thus. Another traveller declared he had been nine months there, without better luck; and as the nine months, added to the three, precisely made up the whole year, of course I had nothing farther to say.

But this tone of triumph is not always tenable. During the days, weeks, and months when the weather is manifestly indefensible, the Io Pœans give place to apologies. A traveller is entreated, nay, sometimes even implored, not to judge of the climate by the specimen he has seen of it. Before his arrival, the sky was cloudless, and the atmosphere serene. He has just come in the nick of bad weather. Never, in the memory of the oldest inhabitant, was the snow so deep or so permanent. Never was spring so tardy in its approach, and never were vicissitudes of temperature so sudden and frequent. In short, he is desired to believe that the ordinary course of nature is suspended on his approach; that his presence in an American city deranges the whole action of the elements.

All this is simply a bore, and the annoyance merits record, only because it contributes to illustrate the American character, in one of its most remarkable features—a restless and insatiable appetite for praise, which defies all restraint of reason or common sense. It is far from enough that a traveller should express himself delighted with the country and its inhabitants—that he should laud the beauty and fertility of the former, and all that is wise, dignified and amiable in the latter: he is expected to extend his admiration even into the upper air; to feel hurricanes, and speak of zephyrs, to gaze on clouds, and behold the pure azure, and, while parching under the influence of a burning sun, to lower the thermometer of his words, and dilate on the genial and delightful warmth of the American summer!

At Saratoga, the whole company, as usual, dine in an enormous saloon, after which the gentlemen lounge about the balconies, smoking cigars, while the ladies within read, net purses, or endeavour to extract music from a jingling piano. At one or other of the hotels there is generally a ball, and gentlemen, who seem to have studied dancing at some Shaker seminary, caper gallantly through the mazes of the waltz or the quadrille.

In the morning, all are abroad to drink the waters. The springs are numerous, and vary both in the efficacy and nature of their effects. I made the tour of the most celebrated, and drank a tumbler of each. None of them are disagreeable to the taste, and all are slightly effervescent. The Congress spring is most in repute, and is supplied from a very neat fountain by boys, who dip the drinking-glasses into the well. This water is bottled, and sold all over the Union. Both in taste and appearance it resembles Seltzer.

Among invalids, the prevailing complaint was evidently dyspepsia, of which one hears a great deal more than is quite agreeable in the United States. Even ladies inflict their sufferings without compunction on the auditor. One—I confess she was married, and not young—assured me she had derived great benefit from employing an apothecary to manipulate her stomach every morning! At the end of a fortnight she was quite cured; and the practice of the apothecary became so extensive, that he was obliged to employ assistant manipulators.

After breakfast, the favourite place of resort was a lake about three miles distant, where the company drove in carriages to fish. There was a platform erected for the accommodation of the fishers, from which about fifty rods were simultaneously protruded. The scene was ludicrous enough. The rapture of a young lady or an elderly gentleman on securing a fish, apparently of the minnow species, would have made admirable matter for Matthews. There were two or three men whose sole occupation it was to bait hooks. During my stay none of the party had occasion for a landing net.

A few days of Saratoga were agreeable enough, but the scene was too monotonous to maintain its attraction long. I became tired of it, and moved on to Ballston Spa, about seven miles distant. The hotel at Ballston is excellent, but the waters are considered inferior to those of Saratoga, and the place has been of late years comparatively deserted. Near the hotel is the house inhabited by Moreau during his residence in the United States. He quitted it to join the allied army, and his fate is matter of history. With every allowance for his situation, one cannot but feel that his fame would have rested on a firmer foundation, had he declined to bear arms against his country.

If Saratoga was dull, Ballston was stupid. There was nothing to be seen, and nothing to be done, except loitering in the neighbouring woods, which, being intersected by a river called the Kayaderoseras, presented some pretty scenery. The party in the hotel was not numerous, and two days of Ballston were enough. On the third morning I departed for Albany.

Albany presents, I believe, the only instance of feudal tenure in the United States. At the first settlement of New York by the Dutch, a gentleman, named Von Ransellaer, received from the High and Mighty Lords a grant of the land on which Albany now stands, with the adjacent territory to the distance of twelve Dutch miles on every side. By far the greater portion of this princely domain has been disposed of on perpetual leases, with due reservation of all manorial privileges of tolls, quitrents, right of minerals, proprietorship of mills, &c. &c. The present possessor still retains the title of Patroon, and is one of the richest citizens of the Union. His family are treated with a sort of prescriptive respect, which it will probably require another half century to eradicate. They are likewise the objects of some jealousy. From every civic office in Albany they are rigidly excluded.

For the last time, I embarked on the beautiful Hudson. I had many friends in New York, and my pleasure in returning to it was tinged with melancholy at the thought that I was so soon to part with them for ever. During my absence a change had come over the appearance of the city. I now saw it under the influence of a burning sun. The gay and the wealthy had deserted it; the busy only remained. By day the temperature was oppressive, and there was no moving out before evening. The theatres were open, but who could enter them with the thermometer at ninety? There was a mimic Vauxhall, in the cool recesses of which one might eat ice in comfort, and an excellent French Café, which afforded all manner of refreshment to an overheated pedestrian. In spite of the season, many of my friends were in town, or at their villas in the neighbourhood. Hospitable doors were still open, as I had always found them. There was little gaiety, but abundance of society. The former I did not want, the latter I enjoyed.

It was at this period that I became acquainted with a young artist, who promises to occupy a high rank in his profession. His name is Weir. Like Harding, he is full of talent and enthusiasm, and if I do not mistake, his name is yet destined to become familiar to English ears. Mr Weir has enjoyed the advantage of passing several years in Italy, and has returned to his native city with a taste formed on the great masterpieces of ancient art, and a power of execution unusual in any country, to claim that patronage which genius too often demands in vain.

I was much gratified by many of his pictures. He displays a fine sense of beauty in them all; but I was particularly struck with one which represents a dying Greek. He has been wounded in the battle, and his limbs have with difficulty borne him to the presence of his mistress. His life-blood is fast ebbing, and his face is deadly pale. His head reclines on her arm, but the approach of death is indicated in the general relaxation of muscle, and we know not whether he be yet conscious of its pressure. The countenance which gazes downward with irrepressible agony on his, is animated by no gleam of hope. There is no convulsion of the features, because intense grief is uniformly calm. It is minor emotion alone which finds relief in tears.

The composition is harmonious. A tower surmounted by a flag, a few palm-trees, the battlements of a city in the second distance, and the setting sun, which sheds a melancholy radiance on the scene, complete this simple but impressive picture. The sketches of Mr Weir are perhaps even finer than the more elaborate productions of his pencil,—a circumstance which I am apt to consider as a test of power. I have the good fortune to possess one which I value very highly, and which has been admired by many first-rate judges of art.

Of the public press I have not yet spoken, and I have something to say on it, though not a great deal. Every Englishman must be struck with the great inferiority of American newspapers to those of his own country. In order to form a fair estimate of their merit, I read newspapers from all parts of the Union, and found them utterly contemptible in point of talent, and dealing in abuse so virulent, as to excite a feeling of disgust not only with the writers, but with the public which afforded them support. Tried by this standard—and I know not how it can be objected to—the moral feeling of this people must be estimated lower than in any deductions from other circumstances I have ventured to rate it. Public men would appear to be proof against all charges which are not naturally connected with the penitentiary or the gibbet. The war of politics seems not the contest of opinion supported by appeal to enlightened argument, and acknowledged principles, but the squabble of greedy and abusive partisans, appealing to the vilest passions of the populace, and utterly unscrupulous as to their instruments of attack.

I assert this deliberately, and with a full recollection of the unwarrantable lengths to which political hostility in England is too often carried. Our newspaper and periodical press is bad enough. Its sins against propriety cannot be justified, and ought not to be defended. But its violence is meekness, its liberty restraint, and even its atrocities are virtues, when compared with that system of brutal and ferocious outrage which distinguishes the press in America. In England, even an insinuation against personal honour is intolerable. A hint—a breath—the contemplation even of a possibility of tarnish—such things are sufficient to poison the tranquillity, and, unless met by prompt vindication, to ruin the character of a public man; but in America, it is thought necessary to have recourse to other weapons. The strongest epithets of a ruffian vocabulary are put in requisition. No villainy is too gross or improbable to be attributed to a statesman in this intelligent community. An editor knows the swallow of his readers, and of course deals out nothing which he considers likely to stick in their gullet. He knows the fineness of their moral feelings, and his own interest leads him to keep within the limits of democratic propriety.

The opponents of a candidate for office are generally not content with denouncing his principles, or deducing from the tenor of his political life, grounds for questioning the purity of his motives. They accuse him boldly of burglary or arson, or, at the very least, of petty larceny. Time, place, and circumstance, are all stated. The candidate for Congress or the Presidency is broadly asserted to have picked pockets or pocketed silver spoons, or to have been guilty of something equally mean and contemptible. Two instances of this occur at this moment to my memory. In one newspaper, a member of Congress was denounced as having feloniously broken open a scrutoire, and having thence stolen certain bills and bank-notes; another was charged with selling franks at twopence apiece, and thus coppering his pocket at the expense of the public.

It may be that such charges obtain little credit with the majority of the people, and I am willing to believe that in ninety nine cases out of a hundred they are exaggerated, or even absolutely false: yet they evidently obtain credit *somewhere,* or they would not be made. However unfounded, the paper loses no support from having advanced them; and where so much mud is thrown, the chances are, that some portion of it will stick. At all events, the tarnish left by the filthy and offensive missile cannot be obliterated. In such a case, innocence is no protection. The object of calumny feels in his inmost soul that he has suffered degradation. He cannot cherish the delusion that the purity of his character has placed him above suspicion; and those who have studied human nature most deeply, are aware how often "things outward do draw the inward quality after them," and the opinion of the world works its own accomplishment. In general, suspected integrity rests on a frail foundation. Public confidence is the corner-stone of public honour; and the man who is compelled to brave suspicion, is already half prepared to encounter disgrace.

The circumstances to which I have alluded admit of easy explanation. Newspapers are so cheap in the United States, that the generality even of the lowest order can afford to purchase them. They therefore depend for support on the most ignorant class of the people. Every thing they contain must be accommodated to the taste and apprehension of men who labour daily for their bread, and are of course indifferent to refinement either of language or reasoning. With such readers, whoever "peppers the highest is surest to please." Strong words take place of strong arguments, and every vulgar booby who can call names, and procure a set of types upon credit, may set up as an editor, with a fair prospect of success.

In England, it is fortunately still different. Newspapers being expensive, the great body of their supporters are to be found among people of comparative wealth and intelligence, though they practically circulate among the poorer classes in abundance sufficient for all purposes of information. The public, whose taste they are obliged to consult, is, therefore, of a higher order; and the consequence of this arrangement is apparent in the vast superiority of talent they display, and in the wider range of knowledge and argument which they bring to bear on all questions of public interest.

How long this may continue it is impossible to predict, but I trust the Chancellor of the Exchequer will weigh well the consequences, before he ventures to take off, or even materially to diminish, the tax on newspapers. He may rely on it, that, bad as the state of the public press may be, it cannot be improved by any legislative measure. Remove the stamp duty, and the consequence will inevitably be, that there will be two sets of newspapers, one for the rich and educated, the other for the poor and ignorant. England, like America, will be inundated by productions contemptible in point of talent, but not the less mischievous on that account. The check of enlightened opinion—the only efficient one—on the press will be annihilated. The standard of knowledge and morals will be lowered; and let it above all be remembered, that this tax, if removed, can never after be imposed. *Once abolished, be the consequences what they may, it is abolished for ever.* The duty on advertisements is undoubtedly impolitic, and should be given up so soon as the necessities of the revenue will admit of it; but I am confidently persuaded that the government which shall permit political journals to circulate in England without restraint, will inflict an evil on the country, the consequences of which will extend far beyond the present generation.

In America, the warfare of statesmen is no less virulent than that of journals, and is conducted with the same weapons. When discord lights her torch in the cabinet of Washington, it blazes with unexampled violence. It was about this period that the cabinet of General Jackson suddenly exploded like a rocket, and the country found itself without a ministry. This catastrophe was not produced by any external assault. All had gone smoothly in Congress, and never was any ministry apparently more firmly seated. Had the cabinet been composed of bachelors, there is no saying how long or how prosperously they might have conducted the affairs of the country. Unfortunately they were married men. One minister's lady did not choose to visit the lady of another; and General Jackson, finding his talent as a pacificator inadequate to the crisis, determined on making a clear deck, and organizing an administration whose policy might be less influenced by conjugal cabals.

The members of the dismissed cabinet had now

full liberty and leisure for crimination and abuse. A newspaper correspondence commenced between Major Eaton, the Secretary for the War Department, and Mr Ingham, the Secretary of the Treasury. The decent courtesies of life were thrown aside; the coarsest epithets were employed by both parties, the most atrocious charges were advanced, and even female character was not spared in this ferocious controversy. Nor is this a solitary instance. Nearly at the same period the newspapers contained letters of Mr Crawford, formerly a member of the Cabinet, assailing the character of Mr Calhoun, the Vice-President, in the same spirit, and with the same weapons.

The truth is, that in all controversies of public men, the only tribunal of appeal is the people, in the broadest acceptation of the term. An American statesman must secure the support of a numerical majority of the population, or his schemes of ambition at once fall to the ground. Give him the support of the vulgar, and he may despise the opinion of the enlightened, the honourable, and the high-minded. He can only profess motives palpable to the gross perceptions of the mean and ignorant. He adapts his language, therefore, not only to their understandings, but to their taste; in short, he must stoop to conquer, and having done so, can never resume the proud bearing and unbending attitude of independence.

In regard to religion, it is difficult, in a community presenting such diversity of character as the United States, to offer any observation which shall be universally or even generally true. A stranger is evidently debarred from that intimate and extensive knowledge of character and motive, which could alone warrant his entering very deeply into the subject. On the matter of religion, therefore, I have but little to say, and that little shall be said as briefly as possible.

Of these disgusting extravagances, recorded by other travellers, I was not witness, because I was not anxious to be so. But of the prevalence of such things as camp-meetings and revivals, and of the ignorant fanaticism in which they have their origin, there can be no doubt. It is easy to lavish ridicule on such exhibitions, and demonstrate how utterly inconsistent they are with rational and enlightened piety. Still, it should be remembered, that in a thinly-peopled country, any regular ministration of religion is frequently impossible; and if by *any* process religion can be made to exercise a strong and permanent influence on the character of those so situated, a great benefit has been conferred on society. Where the choice lies between fanaticism and profligacy, we cannot hesitate in preferring the former.

In a free community, the follies of the fanatic are harmless. The points on which he differs from those around him, are rarely of a nature to produce injurious effects on his conduct as a citizen. But the man without religion acknowledges no restraint but human laws; and the dungeon and the gibbet are necessary to secure the rights and interests of his fellow-citizens from violation. There can be no doubt, therefore, that in a newly settled country, the strong effect produced by these camp-meetings and revivals, is on the whole beneficial. The restraints of public opinion and penal legislation are little felt in the wilderness; and, in such circumstances, the higher principle of action, communicated by religion, is a new and additional security to society.

Throughout the whole Union, I am assured, that the Methodists have acquired a powerful influence. The preachers of that sect are generally well adapted, by character and training, for the duties they are appointed to discharge. They perfectly understand the habits, feelings, and prejudices of those whom they address. They mingle in the social circles of the people, and thus acquire knowledge of the secrets of families, which is found eminently available in increasing their influence. Through their means, religion becomes mingled with the pursuits, and even the innocent amusements of life. Young ladies chant hymns, instead of Irish melodies; and the profane chorus gives place to rhythmical doxologies. Grog parties commence with prayer, and terminate with benediction. Devout smokers say grace over a cigar, and chewers of the Nicotian weed insert a fresh quid with an expression of pious gratitude.

This may appear ludicrous in description; yet it ought not to be so. The sentiment of devotion, the love, the hope, the gratitude, the strong and ruling desire to conform our conduct to the Divine will, the continual recognition of God's mercy, even in our most trifling enjoyments, are among the most valuable fruits of true religion. If these are debased by irrational superstition, and the occasional ravings of a disturbed imagination, let us not reject the gold on account of the alloy, nor think only of the sediment, which defiles the waters by which a whole country is fertilized.

In the larger cities, there is no apparent deficiency of religion. The number of churches is as great as in England; the habits of the people are moral and decorous; the domestic sanctities are rarely violated; and vice pays at least the homage to virtue of assuming its deportment The clergy in those cities are men of respectable acquirements, and, I believe, not inferior to those of other countries in zeal and piety. If the amount of encouragement afforded to Sunday Schools, Missionary and Bible Societies, be assumed as the test of religious zeal, no deficiency will be discovered in the Northern States. These establishments flourish as luxuriantly as in England, when the differences of wealth and population are taken into account. Among the higher classes, I could detect no appearance of religious jealousies or antipathies. Those who, in the pursuits of politics or money, are vehement and intolerant of opposition, exhibit in matters of religion a spirit more tranquil and philosophical.

In the country, however, this is not the case. There differences of religious opinion rend society into shreds and patches, varying in every thing of colour, form, and texture. In a village, the population of which is barely sufficient to fill one church, and support one clergyman, the inhabitants are either forced to want religious ministration altogether, or the followers of different sects must agree on some compromise, by which each yields up some portion of his creed to satisfy the objections of his neighbour. This breeds argument, dispute, and bitterness of feeling. The Socinian will not object to an Arian clergyman, but declines having any thing to do with a supporter of the Trinity. The Calvinist will consent to tolerate the doctrine of free agency, if combined with that of absolute and irrespective decrees. The Baptist may give up the assertion of some favourite dogmas, but clings to adult baptism as a *sine qua non.* And thus with other sects. But who is to inculcate such a jumble of discrepant and irreconcilable doctrine? No one can shape his doctrine according to the anomalous and piebald creed prescribed by such a congregation, and the practical result is, that some one sect becomes victorious for a time; jealousies deepen into antipathies, and what is called *an opposition church* probably springs up in the village. Still harmony is not restored. The rival clergymen attack each other from the pulpit; newspapers are enlisted on either side; and religious warfare is waged with the bitterness, if not the learning which has distinguished the controversies of abler polemics.

In the New England, and many of the Western States, compliance with religious observances is classed among the moral proprieties demanded by public opinion. In the former, indeed, religion has been for ages hereditary, and, like an entailed estate, has descended, in unbroken succession, from the Pilgrim fathers to the present generation. But nowhere does it appear in a garb less attractive, and nowhere are its warm charities and milder graces less apparent to a stranger.

In the larger cities, I have already stated that the clergy are in general men competent, from talent and education, to impart religious instruction to their fellow-citizens. But in the country it is different. The clergymen with whom I had an opportunity of conversing during my different journeys, were unlettered, and ignorant of theology, in a degree often scarcely credible. Some of them seemed to have changed their tenets as they do their coats. One told me that he had commenced his clerical life as a Calvinist; he then became a Baptist; then a Universalist; and was, when I met him, a Unitarian!

There is one advantage of an established church, which only those, perhaps, who have visited the United States can duly appreciate. In England, a large body of highly educated gentlemen annually issue from the Universities to discharge the duties of the clerical office throughout the kingdom. By this means, a certain stability is given to religious opinion; and even those who dissent from the church, are led to judge of their pastors by a higher standard, and to demand a greater amount of qualification than is ever thought of in a country like the United States. This result is undoubtedly of the highest benefit to the community. The light of the established church penetrates to the chapel of the dissenter, and there is a moral check on religious extravagance, the operation of which is not the less efficacious, because it is silent and unperceived by those on whom its influence is exerted.

Religion is not one of those articles, the supply of which may be left to be regulated by the demand. The necessity for it is precisely greatest when the demand is least; and a government neglects its first and highest duty, which fails to provide for the spiritual as well as temporal wants of its subjects. But on the question of religious establishments, I cannot enter. I only wish to record my conviction, that those who adduce the state of religion in the United States as affording illustration of the inutility of an established church, are either bad reasoners, or ignorant men.